Counseling in Schools

Essential Services and Comprehensive Programs

JOHN J. SCHMIDT
East Carolina University

ALLYN AND BACON
Boston   London   Toronto   Sydney   Tokyo   Singapore

To counselors and colleagues who have taught me about helping, and in
the process have enriched my life

Senior Editor: Ray Short
Senior Editorial Assistant: Christine Shaw
Production Administrator: Marjorie Payne
Editorial-Production Service: Chestnut Hill Enterprises, Inc.
Cover Administrator: Linda Dickinson
Cover Designer: Suzanne Harbison
Manufacturing Buyer: Megan Cochran

Copyright © 1993 by Allyn and Bacon
A Division of Simon & Schuster, Inc.
160 Gould Street
Needham Heights, MA 02194

Library of Congress Cataloging-in-Publication Data

Schmidt, John J.,
   Counseling in schools : essential services and comprehensive
 programs / John J. Schmidt.
    p. cm.
   Includes bibliographical references and indexes.
   ISBN 0–205–14350–4
    1. Counseling in elementary education—United States.
    2. Counseling in middle school education—United States.
    3. Counseling in secondary education—United States. I. Title.
LB1027.5.S2585 1992
371.4—dc20
                                                            92–14011
                                                               CIP

Printed in the United States of America

10 9 8 7 6 5 4 3 2 1 98 97 96 95 94 93

— CONTENTS —————————

PREFACE

School counseling is one of several specialties that comprise the counseling profession. As a specialty area, school counseling consists of essential functions generally found in the counseling profession as well as services unique to school settings. In addition, school counselors practice at all levels of education, particularly elementary through high schools, and design their programs of services to reflect the different needs of divergent student populations.

Counseling in Schools: Essential Services and Comprehensive Programs traces the development of the school counseling profession, presents contemporary roles and functions of today's school counselors, and explores future possibilities for the profession. It is written for students preparing for a career in school counseling and for professionals seeking an overview of school counseling programs and services. As defined here, *school counseling* includes services designed to meet the needs of students, parents, and teachers during the elementary, middle, and high school years.

Twelve chapters illustrate the common goals and various functions found in the practice of school counseling at all three of these educational levels. The first three chapters describe the profession of school counseling, relate it to professional counseling in settings other than schools, and present the components and services of a comprehensive school counseling program.

Chapters 4 through 7 focus on the major functions of school counselors. These include counseling, consulting, coordinating, and appraising services for students, parents, and teachers. These are the essential services of the counseling profession, and the chapters in this section illustrate how each function is incorporated into the practice of school counseling.

Chapter 8 follows with an overview of educational planning and career development, two primary purposes of counselors working in schools. A major responsibility of school counselors is to help students with educational planning and career decisions. This process begins in the primary grades and expands in secondary schools with parents, teachers, and counselors guiding students toward adulthood, occupations, and higher education. A case study concludes this chapter, showing how all the essential services come together in a collaborative effort to assist students with their educational development.

Chapter 9 focuses on the professional school counselor and describes similarities and differences in the roles of elementary, middle, and high school counselors. A recap of the essential services shows how they are implemented at different levels of school practice. This chapter also presents the training and preparation expected of professional counselors and the credentialing processes by which school counselors are certified at state and national levels.

Chapters 10, 11, and 12 present professional issues related to the practice of school counseling. The first of these issues is the evaluation of school counseling programs. Chapter 10 highlights the importance of program evaluation and reviews methods of evaluating counseling services. School counselor performance appraisal and supervision are also addressed. Chapter 11 is an overview of legal and ethical issues related to school counseling. The ethical standards of the school counseling profession are reviewed and specific legal issues are discussed.

The last chapter of this book considers the future of school counseling. Schools of tomorrow are related to students of tomorrow, and both of these visions are examined within the context of school counseling programs and services. Technological advances and their impact on learning and counseling are explored, as are the continuous social changes expected in the years to come.

Practitioners and students who read this book will observe that the components of a comprehensive school counseling program, as advocated here, are the ideal elements and practices embraced by professional school counselors. In reality, the practice of school counseling often appears light years away from the roles and functions proposed in this text. The argument in favor of presenting an idealistic portrait is that traditional roles and functions have not always served the interests and needs of students, parents, and teachers, nor have they helped to clarify the professional identity of school counselors. Furthermore, traditional functions may no longer be relevant to meet the needs of future populations. This text embraces a futuristic, positive vision of what the school counseling profession should be today, and what it could become tomorrow.

This book is a reflection of over twenty-five years of training and experience as a school counselor, counseling supervisor, and counselor educator. As such, it is the product of countless relationships with educators and counselors who have taught me about counseling and encouraged me to write about this profession. I am indebted to many people, and wish to express particular gratitude to two colleagues who illustrate the support and encouragement I have received. I am grateful to Larry Osborne of the University of North Carolina at Greensboro for his guidance during my doctoral studies and his initial encouragement to write about my research and ideas. Likewise, I appreciate my association with William Purkey, also of UNC-G, who for many years has been my mentor, friend, and colleague.

Most of the important projects completed in one's life are the result of genuine support and guidance from others. This book is no different. I sincerely appreciate the direction given by the editorial staff of Allyn and Bacon, especially Jo Ellen Caffrey and Ray Short my editor, who guided this project, and the reviewers who gave clear feedback and helpful suggestions with the early drafts of this book. I also thank Joe Ciechalski and H. C. Hudgins, two colleagues at East Carolina University for their valued expertise and helpful suggestions in reviewing chapters and recommending resources. A special note of gratitude is extended to Charles Coble, Dean of the School of Education at ECU, for his commitment and support and to John Richards of ECU for his gentle exhortations in helping me see this project to its conclusion.

Finally, I thank my loving wife, Pat, who has encouraged and assisted me in this and other projects. Without her understanding and patience, this book could not have been written.

J. J. S.

1

The School Counseling Profession

Every year in schools across the United States of America, children and adolescents enroll in classes, acquire new skills, and learn information to expand their personal, social, and career development. This is true for students in elementary schools through universities. In all of these schools, students relate to various professionals, especially teachers, who assist them in pursuing and achieving their educational goals.

School counselors are among the professionals who assist students with these developmental tasks, particularly in elementary, middle, and high schools. Counselors also assist parents and teachers who are challenged by the countless needs of children and adolescents in today's society. These counselors offer services to students, parents, and teachers for the purpose of assuring that students have equal opportunity to reach their educational goals, choose appropriate career directions, and develop as fully functioning members of a democratic society.

School counselors are members of a helping profession that spans an array of services and includes practice in a variety of settings. Today, it is called the counseling profession (Baruth & Robinson, 1987; Gladding, 1992; Vacc & Loesch, 1987). In U.S. society, professional counselors are found in hospitals, mental-health centers, industries, family centers, schools and other work settings. Though they practice their professional relationships in different settings with dissimilar missions, these counselors are united by their understanding and command of basic communication and helping skills, a common knowledge base of psychological, sociological, and human development theories, and similar goals that identify them as colleagues in the counseling profession. While their work settings may differ, their professional practices are founded in a broad range of theories, an appreciation of

1

the developmental power of the human spirit, and a commitment to changing systems and relationships for the betterment of all concerned.

In this book, you will learn about the practice of professional counseling in schools. When compared with other notable professions such as medicine, law, and teaching, school counseling is a relatively young field, but its growth has been remarkable during the 20th century, particularly in the United States. To fully appreciate the role of school counselors in U.S. education during this period, and the role that they will continue to play into the 21st century, it is appropriate to begin with an understanding of the counseling profession as a whole. What is this field called counseling, and who are these professionals called counselors?

Counseling as a Profession

Throughout the history of humankind there have been many different people and professionals who have become confidants and helpers for persons who have sought assistance, who have been less fortunate than others, or who have simply needed the comfort of a friend. Literature and historical accounts are filled with references to philosophers, wizards, fortune tellers, medicine men, and others who in their unique and sometimes mythic ways created the advent of the helping professions. Gibson and Mitchell (1990) reported that the first counterparts of professional counselors were perhaps the elders of ancient tribes who advised the youth and guided them towards responsible decisions and behaviors. In ancient times, helping relationships between people probably focused on the development of fundamental skills for survival. As civilizations progressed, these relationships emerged into processes for encouraging youth to acquire proficiency in personal, social, as well as survival skills. History has taught us that a variety of helping relationships have been formed within cultures and between people. In all human encounters and relationships, people have sought out the wisdom and advice of other people and professionals they respected. This is basic human nature; to reach out to people for the purpose of being helped or for helping others. In most instances, those seeking guidance and assistance are concerned with issues that revolve around relationships with themselves and with others. Often these relationships involve questions of personal acceptance, social belonging, and future goals. People ask: "Who am I?", "Where do I belong?", "What should I being doing with my life?" In assisting with these and other questions, the helper creates a caring atmosphere where desired goals can be explored, and a plan for achieving these goals can be forged. This helping process of gathering information, becoming aware of oneself, exploring options and goals, and choosing a direction is, in essence, a description of counseling.

Professional counseling is the process of establishing a relationship to identify people's needs, design strategies and services to satisfy these needs, and actively assist in carrying out plans of action to help people make decisions, solve problems, develop self-awareness, and lead healthier lives. At times these relationships are formed to help people prevent negative events and harmful circumstances from impeding their growth and development. Other times, counseling relationships are formed to help people assess the progress they are making in life and plan strategies to assure continued development. A third type of counseling relationship is established when people experience difficulties and cannot remedy these problems without support and guidance from others. In summary, counseling relationships are established for the purpose of prevention, development, and remediation.

As one type of helping process, prevention can be understood in historical terms. Early civilizations worked to protect their camps and villages from natural disasters and human encroachment. Survival and expansion of the tribe was predicated on security measures that the members put in place. In a similar way, human survival and development are related to preventive plans that individuals and groups make and carry out for their own protection. Professional counselors, in schools and other settings, assist people and organizations in preventing losses, avoiding crises, and thwarting other calamities that impede progress in education and life.

Adequate prevention allows for optimal development. Comprehensive counseling programs in schools and other institutions provide services that encourage people to develop their fullest potential. In schools, these services include, as you will see in this book, a variety of counseling, instructional, and informational services. Students experience many of these developmental activities as part of a broad curriculum or in direct counseling relationships with school counselors.

While preventive and developmental services have the potential to enhance the lives of most people, including students in school, there are times when children, adolescents, and adults have difficulties that warrant direct intervention. As an example, today's students are challenged by an array of concerns that directly and indirectly affect their educational progress. School counselors assist students in meeting and resolving these challenges through individual counseling, group procedures, consultations with parents and teachers, and referrals to appropriate agencies and professionals in the community. As such, the services of counselors are aimed at preventing problems, focusing on developmental issues, and addressing critical concerns that pose an immediate threat to the individual's emotional, social, and psychological well-being.

The ancient Greeks are credited for creating a philosophy of living that focused on the nature of human development. The writings of Plato and Aristotle in particular contributed to our contemporary fields of education, psychology, and human development, three foundations of the counseling profession. Plato's wonderment about the nature of man and the influences on human development began the exploration of individual development and our journey into the science of human behavior. Later, Aristotle added to this learning process by studying environmental influence and discovering the importance of individual perception.

Following ancient Greek civilization, Hebrews and Christians of the post-Roman period proposed concepts regarding free will, self-determination, and human value, which have contributed to the development of democratic ideals cherished in most contemporary developed societies. In many ways, these democratic principles are the same beliefs as those that are central to effective counseling relationships. These beliefs are that people have the right to be free, can make choices to benefit their development, want to be accepted as equal members of the group, and can learn to be responsible members of society.

As western civilization continued through the Middle Ages, the spread of Christianity formalized educational opportunities as well as helping relationships through the work of priests, monks, and other clergy. For example, in the Catholic Church, the sacrament of penance, commonly called confession, created a type of helping relationship. While viewed as a process that places humans in a subservient relationship to God, this relationship also encourages the confession of sins, their absolution, the forgiveness of transgressions, and the act of assuming responsibility for one's misdeeds. The priest, acting as an agent of God, helps the individual through this process of confession and renewal of faith. Interestingly, the priest maintains a vow of silence on behalf of the person who confesses in much the same way that the counselor honors the confidential nature of relationships with clients.

During the Middle Ages, priests and other clergy were also among the few who were able to read and interpret scholarly works to the common person. As a result, they not only informed people about church doctrine, but also about developmental issues such as career choices. In a historical review of early occupational literature, Zytowski (1972) noted that most writings of this time probably placed priests in the role of counselors because what was written was intended for scholarly consumption not practical application.

Toward the end of the 16th and the beginning of the 17th century, books about vocational development and occupational choice were published. Zytowski (1972) reported that a major work of nearly 1,000 pages by an Italian, Tomasco Garzoni, provided detailed descriptions of a number of occupations and professions of the times. This work, translated as *The Universal Plaza of All the Professions of the World*, was published in 25 Italian editions and several other languages. In 1631, Powell published *Tom of All Trades; Or the Plain Pathways to Preferment*, a picture book of different occupations with information about how to enter these vocations and what education was necessary. Powell's was the first career information book published in English. In the 18th century, authors such as Joseph Collyer, Edmund Carter, Denis Diderot, and R. Campbell continued the focus on occupational choice and career development. Campbell's book, *The London Tradesman,* was promoted in 1747 as "a compendious view of all the trades, professions, arts, both liberal and mechanic, now practiced in the cities of London and Westminister . . . for the information of parents, and instruction of youth in their choice of business" (Zytowski, 1972, p. 446). These and other publications provided the first information services related to vocational development, and as such, were the precursors of what was to become career guidance and counseling.

Many other writers, philosophers, and leaders through the ages have added to the legacy that contributed to the development of the counseling profession. Rene Descartes's *Principles of Philosophy,* in which he explored the territory of human thought, Jean Jacques Rousseau's emphasis on the freedom of natural development, Immanual Kant's rational view of man, and later Paul Tillich and Martin Heidegger's existential teachings are among the many efforts that helped build the foundation for much of what we call counseling, psychology, and human development today.

The emergence of the field of psychology at the end of the 19th century began the systematic study and inquiry into human behavior and development. According to Gibson and Mitchell (1990), when Wilheim Wundt began his Psychological Institute at the University of Leipzig in 1879, psychology was begun "as a recognized discipline with its own distinct areas of specialization, inquiry, and training" (p. 5). A parallel event to the development of psychology as a scientific field of study was the psychiatric movement in the medical profession, which gave an organic focus to the treatment of seriously disturbed patients. In 1908, Clifford Beers published *A Mind That Found Itself,* an expose of the horrible conditions in mental institutions of the times. Beers himself was hospitalized as a schizophrenic patient on and off during his lifetime, and with this book aroused public attention and concern about the treatment of mental illnesses. With impetus from Beers' book and the efforts of a few psychologists, the mental-health movement began in the United States. This movement encouraged the establishment of local psychopathic hospitals, the forerunners of today's community mental-health programs and the mental-health counseling profession (Gibson & Mitchell, 1990).

A related movement in the development of the counseling profession was the establishment of child guidance clinics in Chicago by William Healy and his wife in 1909. The Healys were physicians and the clinic emerged from their work with physically ill children in the slums of Chicago. Their approach was to view the physical and psychological problems of children as related elements of a total picture. The clinic begun by the Healy's was the forerunner of over a hundred child guidance clinics established by 1914 in the United States. It was later administered by the state of Illinois and became the Institute of Juvenile Research (Miller, 1968).

These early movements led to the emergence of several professions that helped people with social, personal, and vocational concerns and difficulties. Social workers, psychologists, and counselors, who practice in mental health clinics, rehabilitation centers, and schools today, find their roots in these historical events. The theories of practice and helping skills of today's counseling profession are founded in many of the beliefs and discoveries presented by scholars and practitioners of these early times. As a result, the counseling profession relies on a broad knowledge of human development, psychology, sociology, and education. At the same time, it incorporates effective communication and leadership skills in combination with the essential human qualities of caring, genuineness, regard, and respect for others.

All counselors, regardless of their professional settings, have this broad knowledge base and use similar helping processes. What distinguishes them from one another and gives them a particular identity are the specific needs and developmental concerns of the clients who seek their help. For this reason, mental-health counselors practice their profession in slightly different ways than career counselors, family counselors, or school counselors do. While the breadth of their services and nature of their activities may differ, however, their essential goals and purposes are similar. The same comparison can be made among school counselors who serve different levels of educational practice—elementary, middle, and high school. The nature of specific activities at these levels may differ, but the broad goals and general processes used in comprehensive school counseling programs are the same across levels.

Because professional counselors are trained in a broad spectrum of theory and knowledge in the fields of psychology, education, and human development, and at the same time practice their professions in a range of settings, they often use titles that reflect their work environment. For example, mental health counselors are found in mental health centers, psychiatric hospitals, and employee assistance programs in business and industry. Their training generally takes place in counselor education or counseling psychology programs. In contrast, school counselors work in elementary, middle, or high schools, and are sometimes found in colleges and universities. They are trained in counselor education programs with an emphasis on human development, learning, and school environments. Nevertheless, a fundamental knowledge of human development and a command of helping processes and skills are essential for both mental-health and school counselors. This common background is what links them and other counselors as colleagues in the counseling profession.

While many different counseling professionals function in a variety of settings, other helping professionals also use counseling processes in their roles. Clinical social workers, psychiatric nurses, and counseling psychologists are among those who use counseling and consulting processes similar to the skills used by counselors in hospitals, mental-health centers, prisons, industries, and schools. In some instances, these individuals consider themselves members of both professions. For example, some members of the American Counseling Association (ACA) also belong to the American Psychological Association (APA). They consider themselves counselors and psychologists, which is not uncommon among professionals who are trained in both counseling and psychology. In fact, the APA has a division for counseling and development within its own organizational structure.

The proliferation of these overlapping professions has been particularly noticeable in the United States. Perhaps this is because, as this country developed in the 18th and 19th centuries and accelerated through the Industrial Revolution into the 20th century, personal, social, career, and educational issues became increasingly important. These factors, combined with the multicultural realities of the United States, have contributed to the complexity of living a productive, well-adjusted life in this country. Because the United States prides itself on democratic principles, equal opportunity, and human services, it is understandable how so many related helping professions could emerge. In particular, it is especially clear why counselors have played such an important role in our schools, which themselves incorporate principles of democracy, equity, and opportunity for all students. It is within this context that we now examine the development of the school counseling profession.

Development of School Counseling

The counseling profession entered the American schoolhouse in the early 20th century. Up to that time, classroom teachers provided whatever social, personal, or career assistance students needed. Perhaps the delay of the counseling profession's entry into U.S. schools occurred because the earliest schools were highly selective in admitting students. In fact, the earliest schools were exclusive academies, selecting only the wealthiest of students. The curricula of these schools were designed to prepare young men for professions, such as law or medicine, or for the religious ministry. As the country expanded and progressed, the selectivity of schools decreased and equal opportunity in education became a reality for men and women. At least this was true for Anglo-Saxon men and women. The beginning of publicly supported schools opened educational doors to women as well as men from all economic levels of society. Thus, an increasingly divergent population began entering schools, and teachers alone could no longer meet the broad spectrum of needs expressed by these students.

The school counseling profession began as a guidance movement that emerged from the Industrial Revolution at the beginning of the 20th century. At this time, social reform was advocated by proponents of the Progressive Movement, formed as a reaction to the negative effects of industrial growth and a corresponding neglect of human conditions. A by-product of the tremendous industrial growth of the late 19th and early 20th centuries was the emergence of city slums, ethnic ghettos, and the apparent neglect of individual rights and integrity. Miller (1968) recorded that George Merrill at the California School of Mechanical Arts in San Francisco began experimental efforts in vocational guidance in 1895. Merrill's program offered exploratory experiences for students in the occupational trades taught at the California school, and these experiences were accompanied by counseling, job placement, and follow-up services.

Generally, the guidance movement of this period instructed school children, adolescents, and young adults about their moral development, interpersonal relationships, and the world of work. Jesse B. Davis is thought to be the first person to implement a systematic guidance program in the public schools (Gladding, 1992). From 1898 to 1907, he was a class counselor at Central High School in Detroit, Michigan and was responsible for educational and vocational counseling with 11th grade boys and girls. Davis became principal of a high school in Grand Rapids, Michigan in 1907 and at that time began a schoolwide guidance program. He encouraged English teachers to include guidance lessons in their composition classes to help students develop character, avoid problem behaviors, and relate vocational interests to curriculum subjects.

The work of Jesse Davis was complemented by programs in other parts of the country. Frank Gooodwin organized a systemwide guidance program for the Cincinnati, Ohio schools in 1911, and in, 1980, Eli Weaver at the Boys High School of Brooklyn gained national recognition for his efforts in organizing guidance services in New York City (Miller, 1968). These and other early efforts in guidance established the beginnings of what was to become the school counseling profession.

Frank Parsons, often mentioned as the *Father of guidance,* is credited by most historians as the person who began the guidance movement in the United States (Beale, 1986). In 1908, he organized the Boston Vocational Bureau to provide assistance for young people. According to Gysbers and Henderson (1988), the bureau was established by philanthropist Mrs. Quincy Agassiz Shaw based on the ideas and plans developed by Frank Parsons. Parsons' plan for vocational guidance stressed a scientific approach to selecting a career. According to Parsons, "No step in life, unless it may be the choice of a husband or wife, is more important than the choice of a vocation" (1909, p. 3).

Parsons's attention to vocational development was framed by his concern about society's lack of focus on the need to develop resources and services for human growth and development. At the same time, he was concerned about helping young men make the transition from their school years into the world of work. In his book *Choosing a Vocation*, which was published after his death, Parsons (1909) highlighted three essential factors for choosing an appropriate vocation: (1) clear self-understanding of one's aptitudes, abilities, interests, resources, and limitations. (2) knowledge of the requirements, advantages, disadvantages, and compensation for different types of employment; and (3) an understanding of the relationship between these two groups of facts. This conceptualization of successful career development still holds credence today. Self-understanding and knowledge of one's career interests must go hand in hand for a person to be successful in life.

Parson's plan also included the training of counselors to help young students with the vocational development. Nine months after establishing the Vocational Bureau, he began a program designed to train young men to become vocational counselors and managers of vocational bureaus for YMCAs, schools, colleges, and businesses throughout the country (Miller, 1968). A few years later, the School Committee of Boston created the first counselor certification program. Requirements for this school counselor's certificate included: (1) study of education, and (2) experience in a vocational school or a vocational service. This certification program was eventually adopted by Harvard University as the first college-based counselor education program.

Frank Parsons's work had a significant impact on the vocational guidance movement. In Boston, for example, the superintendent of schools designated over a hundred elementary and secondary teachers to become vocational counselors (Nugent, 1981). As noted earlier, the guidance movement spread to many other parts of the country including New York City, Grand Rapids, and Cincinnati. Within a few short years, city school systems across the country had developed guidance programs.

Early developments in the guidance movement were complemented by the creation of the National Vocational Guidance Association in 1913 (NVGA). This organization began publishing the *National Vocational Guidance Bulletin* on a regular basis in 1921, and over the next several decades this publication would undergo several name changes, eventually becoming the *Career Development Quarterly*. In 1952, when NVGA joined with the American Personnel and Guidance Association (APGA), the *Personnel and Guidance Journal* became the major publication of this national association of counselors. Eventually this publication would be renamed the *Journal of Counseling and Development* of the American Association for Counseling and Development (AACD). The significance of the National Vocational Guidance Association is that it began the unification and identification of what has become the counseling profession of today. This is especially true for the school counseling profession.

Emergence of Guidance and Counseling in Schools

The work of Jesse Davis, Eli Weaver, Frank Parsons, and a host of other pioneers created the momentum for the development of a school counseling profession. During the 1920s, 1930s, and through the 1940s, many events would occur giving impetus, clarity, and direction to this emerging profession. Coincidentally, many of these developments, with their roots once founded in the vocational guidance movement, would raise questions about the profession's narrow focus on vocational development. According to Gladding (1992), some leaders of the counseling movement began encouraging a broader focus to include issues of personality and human development beyond vocational guidance. This broader view laid the groundwork for many of the counseling theories and approaches that were to be created in the years to come. Some of these were developed in the years prior to the second World War and helped to define school guidance and counseling of that period.

Before World War II   After the vocational guidance movement began in the 1900s, World War I was the next major event that had an impact on the developing counseling profession. During the first World War, the U. S. military began using group-training procedures to screen and classify draftees. Intelligence testing, developed in the beginning of the decade, was the catalyst for this movement. In particular, work begun by French psychologist, Alfred Binet, and later expanded by Lewis Terman and Arthur Otis was adapted by the military. According to Miller (1968), Arthur Otis developed a group intelligence test that "could be administered to large groups...by relatively unskilled examiners" (p. 28). Otis's test became the basis for the military's *Army Alpha Examination.* During this time and in the decade immediately following the war, a great number of tests were developed and marketed, but many were inadequately designed and inappropriately standardized. Nevertheless, the military's interest in using group measurement techniques was embraced by schools and the education profession when the war ended. As Gibson and Mitchell (1990) noted, "the possibility of applying these...techniques to pupil assessment resulted in the rapid development and expansion of standardized testing in education" (p. 8).

One by-product of this emphasis on data collection through group testing was the development of counseling approaches that stressed the measurement of student traits and characteristics. The 1930s saw the first theory of guidance and counseling, called Trait and Factor Theory, developed by E. G. Williamson at the University of Minnesota. Using Parsons's vocational program as a springboard, Williamson and his colleagues became leading advocates for what became known as the *directive* or *counselor-centered* approach to school counseling. In his book *How to Counsel Students,*

Williamson (1939) wrote that counselors should state their "point of view with definiteness, attempting through exposition to enlighten the student" (p. 136). In this direct approach, counselors were expected to dispense information and gather data to influence and motivate students.

In later development of this approach, Williamson and his followers softened this influential view to some degree. In 1958, he wrote that the counselor is responsible for helping "the student become more sophisticated, more matured in understanding the value option that he faces and to identify clearly those that he prefers. The search is the important educational experience—not a control of a behavior, a rigging in favor of one choice of the other, even though the counselor may have his personal preference . . . " (Dugan, 1958, p. 3). At the same time, the directive approach maintained that counselors cannot give complete freedom of choice to students who were not capable of making the best decisions for themselves. According to this approach, counselors were obliged to protect the interests of society, the school as an institution, and the student. Williamson believed that the development of individuality on the part of students must be balanced with concern with self-destructive and antisocial behaviors. He declared that people achieve individual freedom through effective group membership, interdependence, and adherence to high social ideals.

In his approach to counseling, Williamson (1950) developed six steps for assisting students:

1. *Analysis*—the gathering of data about the student and the student's environment
2. *Synthesis*—the selection of relevant data, the summary and organization of these data to understand the strengths and weaknesses of the student
3. *Diagnosis*—the development of a rationale regarding the nature and etiology of the student's problems
4. *Prognosis*—a prediction of outcomes based on the actions chosen by the student
5. *Treatment*—various approaches and techniques selected for the counseling relationship
6. *Follow-up*—an evaluation of the effectiveness of the counseling relationship and the student's plan of action

About the same time that Williamson and his colleagues were developing their clinical, directive counseling approach, others continued to question the narrow focus of the vocational guidance movement. Counselors and psychologists alike echoed this concern and stressed that vocational choice is simply one of many developmental issues with which counselors should assist students. These views began to broaden the goals of guidance and counseling in education.

World War II to the Space Age   The 1940s saw major changes in the counseling profession and these developments had significant impact on the practice of counseling in schools. Gladding (1992) identified three major events that shaped these developments: (1) the popularity of the client-centered approach to counseling developed by Rogers; (2) World War II; and (3) government involvement in the counseling and education professions following the war. In addition, organizational changes within the profession and emerging theoretical models of counseling were significant influences during this period. Each of these events had an impact on the developing identity and direction of the counseling profession.

The Rogerian influence   Carl Rogers probably had more influence on the counseling profession and the development of counseling approaches than any single person. Two of his books, *Counseling and Psychotherapy: Newer Concepts in Practice* (1942) and *Client-centered Therapy: Its Current Practice, Implications, and Theory* (1951), had a significant impact on counseling both in school and non-school settings. Most importantly, Rogers gave new direction to the profession by focusing on the helping relationship between counselors and their clients and recognizing the importance of personal development in these relationships. This focus moved the profession away from the counselor-centered perspectives of earlier times, and emphasized a growth-oriented counseling relationship as opposed to an informational and problem-solving one.

This new vision for the profession challenged both the trait-factor approaches that emerged from vocational guidance and the testing movement following World War I and the therapist-centered views embraced by Freudian psychoanalysts of the early 1990s. At the same time, Rogers's acceptance of self-concept theory as a foundation for effective therapeutic relationships disputed the strict behavioral views of the U.S. psychological movement, which was gaining prominence during this period. His works marked the beginning of a debate that continues today in contemporary discussions within the counseling and psychology professions. Ironically, both counseling and psychology identify Carl Rogers as a significant contributor to each profession's development (Gladding, 1992).

For nearly fifty years, Rogers's contributions to the development of counseling theory and practice helped strengthen and identify the emerging counseling profession. Most importantly, he encouraged counselors to focus on the person in the process. This view was highlighted by Rogers and his followers in the 1970s and 1980s as they gradually changed from a "client-centered" approach to a "person-centered" one (Purkey & Schmidt, 1987, p. 125).

Rogers not only developed a theory of counseling, he researched, tested, and revised it during his lifetime. He also encouraged other theorists and researchers to do likewise. The now classic works of Carkhuff and

Berenson (1967) and Truax and Carkhuff (1967) validated the variables of empathy, respect, and genuineness espoused by Rogers and his disciples as essential characteristics of all therapeutic relationships. In addition, early studies of client-centered counseling reported evidence of psychological adjustment, improved tolerance, accelerated learning, and other benefits of this approach (Axline, 1947; Grummon & John, 1954; Thetford, 1952).

World War II and government influence   Two other events that influenced the counseling profession at this time were World War II and increased government involvement in the counseling and psychology professions. As the United States was entering the war, the government was requesting assistance from counselors and psychologists to help in screening, selecting, and training of military and industrial specialists. This emphasis gave impetus to another area related to the counseling profession— personnel work in business and industry. After the war, the U.S. Veterans Administration (VA) provided funds for graduate students to become trained as counselors and psychologists. About this time, the term "counseling psychologist" emerged in VA specifications further distinguishing psychology from vocational guidance (Gladding, 1992).

Another example of governmental influence in the counseling profession was the George-Barden Act of 1946. This legislation provided funds to develop and support guidance and counseling activities in schools and other settings. For the first time in history, school counselors and state and local supervisors received resource, leadership, and financial support from the government. This action fueled the beginning of a period of rapid growth for guidance and counseling services in schools (Gysbers & Henderson, 1988).

One governmental change that occurred in the 1950s was the reorganization of the Guidance and Personnel Branch of the U.S. Office of Education (Gysbers & Henderson, 1988). In 1952, this office was disbanded under the Division of Vocational Education and from 1953 to 1954 a Pupil Personnel Services Section operated in the Division of State and Local School Systems. In 1955, a Guidance and Personnel Services Section was re-established. The development of this office during this period helped to move the school counseling profession further away from its original vocational emphasis to a broader student services' perspective. This trend would continue through the 1950s and into the 1960s.

In 1957, the Soviet Union lofted the world into the space age with its successful launching of Sputnik I, the first earth satellite. This single event rang a national alarm about the capability of the United States to stay ahead of the Russians in the space program, with industrial and technological advancements, and in military strength. Gibson and Mitchell (1990) indicated that an "indirect but nevertheless significant result of [Sputnik] was the 'lift-off' of the counseling and guidance movement into orbit in the

United States" (p. 12). The ensuing public outcry and criticism of educational institutions eventually led to the passage of Public Law 85–864, entitled the National Defense Education Act of 1958 (NDEA).

The NDEA was preceded by several national studies sponsored by the Office of Education, the National Science Foundation, and the Committee on Financing Higher Education during the early 1950s. These studies concluded that:

1. Schools needed to improve their testing of student aptitude, and design systems for identifying students' potential earlier in their educational careers.

2. Counselors were needed to encourage students to stay in school, concentrate on academic courses, and enter college.

3. Scholarships were needed to assist talented students who were financially unable to attend college after high school. These findings and conclusions set the stage for the immediate action that followed the launching of Soviet Sputnik I. As a result, public opinion was amenable to the swift passage of the National Defense Education Act to:

   a. Provide loans to students in colleges and universities
   b. Offer financial incentives to secondary schools to improve mathematics, science, and foreign language instruction
   c. Create National Defense Fellowships for graduate students interested in teaching at the college level
   d. Support the improvement of guidance and counseling programs in secondary schools
   e. Establish language institutes and research centers to improve the teaching of foreign languages
   f. Encourage research to develop the effective use of television and related media for improved instruction
   g. Establish vocational education programs
   h. Create a Science Information Services and a Science Information Council
   i. Improve statistical services for state educational agencies (Miller, 1968)

Title V of the NDEA focused specifically on school counseling and guidance services in two important ways. First, it provided funds to help states establish and maintain school counseling, testing, and other guidance related services. Second, it authorized the establishment of counseling institutes and training programs in colleges and universities to improve the quality of counselors who were working with students in secondary schools, or of persons who were training to become school counselors. These special institutes began during the summer of 1959 at fifty colleges and universities where over 2,200 counselors were trained (Miller, 1968). Title V, section A, of the NDEA provided fifteen million dollars a year to assist local school systems in developing and strengthening guidance and counseling services, and section B provided approximately seven million dollars a year for universities and colleges to establish training institutes to prepare school counselors (Shertzer & Stone, 1966).

As a result of the NDEA, Title V, all the states, the District of columbia, and three territories expanded school counseling services during the late 1950s and early 1960s. The Counseling and Guidance Branch of the U.S. Office of Education added consultants to its staff, thereby increasing its leadership role in the development of programs at the state level. According to Miller (1968), the following changes occurred in the years immediately following the passage of the NDEA (1958–1963):

1. The number of full-time counselors increased 126 percent from 12,000 to 27,180, and the ratio of counselors to students dropped from 1:960 to 1:530.
2. The number of state guidance consultants increased from 99 to 257.
3. Over 400 counseling institutes were funded by government with more than 13,000 counselors trained.
4. Local school district expenditures for guidance and counseling services rose from $5.6 million to over $127 million (Miller, 1968, p. 37).

Organizational changes and professional influences As a result of these national initiatives, the 1950s saw a continued acceleration of the developing counseling profession. This development was marked by particular events that altered the national counseling associations which were spearheading this professional movement. The first of these events was the establishment of the American Personnel and Guidance Association (APGA) in 1952. The APGA grew out of an alliance of organizations called the American Council of Guidance and Personnel Associations (ACGPA), which began in 1935. This group of organizations aligned with each other to share concerns about educational issues, vocational guidance, and other personnel matters (Harold, 1985). Initially, the four organizations who formed the American Personnel and Guidance Association were: the American College Personnel Association, the National Association of Guidance Supervisors, the National Vocational Guidance Association, and the Student Personnel Association for Teacher Education. Shortly afterward, APGA began a fifth association, the American School Counselor Association, which became Division 5 of APGA. In the years that followed, many more divisions emerged and joined with the larger parent association.

Another phenomenon that influenced the development of the counseling profession during this time was the introduction of several new theories of counseling (Gladding, 1992). As noted earlier, the influence of Rogers opened the debate between the directive and non-directive schools of thought in the 1940s. The 1950s continued this dialogue and witnessed the emergence of several new theories including behavioral approaches such as implosive therapy (Stampfl, 1961) and systematic desensitization (Wolpe, 1958). Cognitive and semantic theories such as Albert Ellis's Rational Emotive Therapy (1962), ego-psychology (Stefflre & Grant), 1972), and a host of other counseling and developmental theories began during this period. The humanistic and existential movements, illustrated in the writings of Combs (1962), May (1966), Jourard (1964), and Maslow (1957), and the emergence of group counseling also influenced the profession. While there was much overlapping among the concepts of some of these theories and approaches, there were enough differences in terminology and philosophy to create an array of counseling models, methods, and strategies. In 1976, Parloff identified more than 130 counseling theories and approaches, and, since that time, the number has continued to grow. Some approaches such as Reality Therapy (Glasser, 1965), multimodal counseling (Gerler, 1990), Adlerian counseling (Dinkmeyer, Dinkmeyer, & Sperry, 1987), and invitational counseling (Purkey & Schmidt, 1987, 1990) have been found to be useful in school counseling.

Post 1960s   The 1960s saw continued development and expansion of the counseling profession, further legislation to increase services and enhance existing programs, and refinement and clarification of the role of the school counselor. Expansion of the profession coincided with a shift in focus towards the developmental role of counselors. C. Gilbert's Wrenn's now classic book, *The Counselor in a Changing World* (1962), set the stage for a new, broader focus for counseling programs and services.

The United States and the rest of the world at this time were moving from the industrialization of the early part of the 20th century to the technological advances of a fast approaching 21st century. Among these technological changes would be a host of social, economic, educational, and career adjustments that would encourage people to seek the assistance of counselors in solving personal and social difficulties or in locating information to make career decisions. Automation in industry would impact on employment and career counseling for adults as well as students in schools. Changing roles of women would affect family structures and the accelerated pace of society would increase daily stress in most people's lives. A number of other developments, including altered sex roles and sexual preferences, a wider economic gap between lower and upper classes, an increased fear of nuclear war, and astonishing medical discoveries that promised to lengthen the life span, all contributed to human challenges and critical decisions for which counselors were needed.

Federal legislation during this period continued to have an impact on the counseling profession and the role of counselors, particularly school counselors. For example, the Elementary and Secondary Education Act of 1965 (Public Law 89–10) provided funds to help schools improve the educational opportunities of students from low-income families by supporting special programs. It also provided funds for services that would not normally be available in most schools.

The 1960s saw a new, expanded focus on the role of school counselors with movement away from an emphasis on guidance programs. The counseling literature of this time, particularly *The School Counselor* journal and a few major texts, began to delineate the role and functions of counselors in schools. Books such as C. H. Patterson's *Counseling and Guidance in Schools* (1962) and E. C. Roeber's *The School Counselor* (1963) gave impetus to the development of a clear professional role and defined specific functions of counselors in schools. These descriptions and definitions complemented the emerging roles of other student services workers such as school social workers, school psychologists, attendance officers, and health workers.

During this period, the term *guidance* was targeted by some authors as a vague and sometimes confusing label for counselors, teachers, and other people who attempted to define the role and functions of counselors in schools. In 1966, Shertzer and Stone wrote that "Guidance has been defined in many ways. An examination of the plethora of books and articles ... indicates that the word ... has been used to convey each author's opinions and biases. Indeed, a major criticism ... is that the word 'guidance' has been rendered relatively meaningless by the variety of ways ... it is used" (1966, p. 30). Almost thirty years later, the discussion about *guidance* and the choice of an appropriate language to identify the school counselor's role and functions continues to be an important professional issue (Schmidt, 1991).

The role and functions of school counselors emphasized in the literature of this time included programmatic and process functions. Programmatic functions focused on strategies to develop comprehensive programs of services, such as defining goals and objectives, assessing student needs, aligning services with the school's curriculum, coordinating student services, and evaluating results. In addition, educational and vocational planning, student placement, and referral systems frequently were included in this category. Process functions were described as specific activities by which counselors provided direct services to students, parents, and teachers. These functions included individual and group counseling, student assessment, parent assistance, and consultation with teachers and parents. In many respects, these components, as you will see in later chapters of this book, remain as essential functions of counselors in today's schools.

Clarification of the school counselor's role and functions during the 1960s led the way toward a broader professional perspective—a focus on programs of services offered by counselors in schools. Many writers at this time emphasized comprehensive guidance and counseling programs as essential aspects of the school curriculum. Within these comprehensive programs, school counselors and classroom teachers combine to play a vital, collaborative role.

In 1968, Miller wrote that an "effective guidance program requires the cooperative effort of every teacher in the school" (p. 75). Yet, this cooperative role for teachers remained unclear due to several factors. For one, guidance continued to be associated strictly with the role of the school counselor. To this day, this perception endures in many schools where the mere mention of the word *guidance* has teachers turning their heads towards the counselor's office. A second factor that made it difficult for teachers to embrace a guidance role was their narrow focus on the subject matter they were responsible for teaching. This is true today as well. Sometimes teachers, particularly in secondary schools, place so much emphasis on the instruction of English, mathematics, science and other subjects, they forget about broader, developmental concerns of students. A historic failing in American education has been the inability of our schools to infuse guidance, basically lessons of self-development and social skills, into the curriculum and daily instruction. The social ills of our society are only partly related to the lack of basic skills acquired by a large segment of U.S. school children. Another and perhaps more serious deficiency has been the failure of our educational, industrial, and governmental institutions to value human dignity at all levels, encourage equitable relationships, provide for the basic needs of all children, and teach social skills and character education in our schools.

The emerging emphasis on the role of teachers in guidance in the 1960s and 70s highlighted specific functions for establishing a foundation of collaboration between school counselors and teachers. This collaboration continues to be an essential ingredient of today's comprehensive school counseling programs (Gysbers & Henderson, 1988). Some of the functions mentioned for teachers in the late 1960s and early 1970s included the: (1) development of helpful cooperative classroom environments; (2) assessment of students; (3) orientation of students to classroom procedures; (4) establishment of helping relationships; (5) integration of educational and career information; (6) promotion of social and personal development; (7) encouragement of healthy study habits; (8) development of effective referral procedures; and (9) cooperation with schoolwide guidance activities (Miller, 1968; Shertzer & Stone, 1966, 1981). Many of these elements are found today in contemporary research on excellent teaching and effective schools (Purkey & Smith, 1983; Hoy, Tarter, & Kottkamp, 1991).

The re-examination of a focus for guidance and counseling occurred at a time when the expansion of counseling services into elementary schools began. While some elementary counselors were employed in the Boston schools in the early 1900s and elementary child consultants were found in other metropolitan areas during this time, educational and vocational development at the secondary level overwhelmed serious efforts in the primary and intermediate grades until the early 1960s. The introduction of the elementary counselor during this period was influential in the development of the school counseling profession and the expansion of services in our schools.

Expansion of School Counseling

During the initial five decades of school counseling's development and growth, little was written or designed to help elementary counselors define and describe their role in schools. For the most part, traditional secondary guidance views and approaches were borrowed by the few elementary counselors who were employed prior to 1950. According to Faust (1968a), the first signs of the contemporary elementary counselor appeared in the late 1950s and early 1960s. A national survey in 1963 reported that elementary counselors performed the following activities (McKeller, 1964):

- Counseling with individual children
- Conferring with teachers to assist them with understanding of children's needs and developmental characteristics
- Conferring with parents about student development and progress
- Referring children and families to agencies

One of the most influential events that helped elementary counselors identify their distinct role in the schools was the 1966 report by the Joint Committee on the Elementary School Counselor (ACES-ASCA), 1966). This report outlined the role and functions of elementary school counselors under the headings: Counseling, Consulting, and Coordinating. Subsequent writings in the 1960s and 1970s differentiated and expanded these three major functions (Hill & Luckey, 1969; Brown & Srebalus, 1972).

In 1967, Greene surveyed a large sample of elementary counselors with an inventory consisting of 104 counselor functions. Over 1100 counselors across the country responded with 65 percent of the sample being full-time certified counselors. Greene's study found a large difference in the functions performed at the upper elementary grades when compared with those at the lower grades. Counselors at the intermediate grades seemed to have more direct contact with children while primary counselors spent more time consulting with parents and teachers. The most common services in both intermediate and primary grades were referral services. Another study at this time surveyed the role and functions of elementary counselors as perceived by teachers, principals, counselors, and counselor educators (Foster, 1967). An *Elementary School Counselor Questionnaire*, consisting of 84 items, found that all five groups ranked counseling types of activities as most important to the role of the elementary counselor.

The proliferation of these types of studies gave visibility to elementary school counseling. As a result, more counselors were employed to work in elementary schools. In 1967, a national survey found almost 4,000 elementary counselors employed in 48 states (Van Hoose & Vafakas, 1968). Myrick and Moni (1976) reported that elementary counseling continued its growth with the total number of elementary school counselors reaching close to 8,000 by 1971. This growth was complemented by the publication of the *Elementary School Guidance and Counseling* journal by the American School Counselor Association beginning in the late 1960s.

Early studies of elementary school counselor's functions not only gave clarity to the emerging role of elementary school counselors, but also contributed in a larger sense to the direction of contemporary school counseling. In particular, the elementary movement gave a clearer identity to the school counseling profession as a developmental force in the education of children and adolescents (Gysbers & Henderson, 1988). The elementary counseling movement in combination with national legislative action broadened the scope of school counseling services. This broader perspective included a role for counselors to provide services to audiences beyond students in the school. In particular, it encouraged counselors to assist parents and teachers with the challenge of assuring optimal development of all children. This challenge was instrumental in moving school counselors into consulting roles: providing in-service help to teachers, offering parent counseling and education programs, and being team members with other student services' professionals (Faust, 1968b).

The Education Act for All Handicapped Children of 1975 was a catalyst in this consulting role becoming a reality. This bill, commonly referred to as Public Law 94–142, mandated that schools provide free public education for all children, and it established a formula for distributing financial aid from the federal government to the states and local school districts. While the role of school counselors was not specified, this law addressed special education and related support services. Humes (1978) outlined several of these related services and their relationship to the school counselor's role. Today, the school counselor's role with exceptional students generally consists of a range of services that include:

1. Participating in school-based meetings to determine appropriate services and programs for exceptional students
2. Assisting with the development of the Individual Education Plan (IEP) required for every student who has an identified exceptionality
3. Providing direct counseling services for students
4. Counseling and consulting with parents
5. Consulting with classroom and special education teachers

6. Planning, coordinating, and presenting in-service programs for teachers
7. Planning extracurricular involvement for special education students
8. Keeping appropriate records of services to students

The involvement of counselors in special education has been a mixed blessing in helping them decipher a clear role and appropriate functions. The inclusion of exceptional children in public education has expanded the role of school counselors by involving them in program planning, parent counseling and consulting, and curriculum monitoring. At the same time, this involvement has limited counselors' roles in some schools where they have been given primary responsibility for processing and monitoring the regulations and procedures of special education. In these instances, the clerical and administrative tasks needed to assure proper placement and protection of children's rights are cumbersome and time-consuming. A combination of federal, state, and local regulations has contributed to a maze of paper work, hearings, and meetings. Where counselors have been assigned primary responsibility for these procedures, they have found themselves removed from the expanded role of serving all students in comprehensive programs of services and relegated to the role of coordinator/administrators of special services. By contrast, in schools where counselors are not responsible for procedural aspects of special education, they are more likely to establish and implement counseling programs that offer a wide range of services to a larger portion of student populations. With regard to exceptional students, these counselors are able to provide direct counseling and consulting services, which is the intent of Public Law 94–142.

Other legislation of the 1960s and later years has influenced the changing and emerging role of school counselors. For example, various vocational education acts stimulated career guidance projects and refocused the school's role in vocational development. Also, the Family Educational Rights and Privacy Act of 1974, known as the Buckley Amendment, gave students access to records about themselves, requiring counselors to form closer relationships with students and parents. In 1979, a bill titled the Elementary School Guidance and Counseling Incentive Act, was intended to "assure the accessibility of developmental guidance and counseling to all children of elementary school age by providing funds for comprehensive elementary school guidance and counseling programs" (Gysbers & Henderson, 1988, p. 28). While this bill did not become law, it inspired a nationwide movement to address the need for services to elementary children.

Another national event that influenced school counseling was the publication of the *A Nation At Risk* report of 1983 by the National Commission of Excellence in Education. This report focused on the declining achievement of U.S. students and alarmed the country in much the same way that the launching of Soviet Sputnik I did in 1957. While no specific references to, or recommendations for, school counseling were found in this report, the emphasis on developing "effective schools" became synonymous with a call for accountability in the classroom and in special services such as school counseling programs.

This emphasis on accountability received attention somewhat earlier in the counseling literature of the 1970s and 1980s (Krumboltz, 1974; Wheeler & Loesch, 1981; Myrick, 1984). During this period, counselors were encouraged to design methods of assessing how they spent their time and whether the effects of their services made a difference in student development and performance. This focus was particularly sharp at the high-school level where Myrick (1987) noted that "counselors were receiving public criticism . . . were failing to provide a systematic and carefully organized response to the problems of adolescents . . . Consequently, many students kept their distance" (p. 20–21). In the 1980s, the attack on high-school counseling continued and positions were eliminated in some school districts (Herr, 1986).

At the same time, counselors were being placed in elementary schools without a clear definition, description, and focus on what their role should be at this level of education. In spite of the literature that attempted to describe a comprehensive role for these new counselors, local school systems and states seemed unable to create consistent expectations of their role and functions. On the one hand, elementary counselors attempted to create programs that replicated the one-to-one models of senior high-school counselors, and on the other, they adapted the role of guidance teachers, traveling from classroom to classroom presenting lessons in affective education. Neither of these models delivered a comprehensive program of related services.

The same dilemma existed in middle schools which evolved from junior high schools of the 1960s. Again, the counseling literature attempted to describe a comprehensive role for middle-school counselors (Stamm & Nissman, 1979; Thornburg, 1986), but in many instances these counselors struggled to find an identity and define their purpose. During the 1980s, the need for school counselors to develop a clear identity and describe their role and functions at the various levels of school practice became paramount. Today in the 1990s this need continues.

A Professional Identity

Many authors in recent years have stressed the importance of counselors creating a clear identity and purpose for their role in schools (Aubrey, 1982; Gladding, 1981; Gysbers & Henderson, 1988; Myrick, 1987; Schmidt, 1986, 1991). Nevertheless, uncertainty about the school counselor's role continues as a major professional issue and obstacle. In some respects, this is due to the continued confusion regarding the term *guidance* and its use in describing "guidance counselors," "guidance services," "guidance programs," and "guidance personnel." The failure of school counselors to choose and use a consistent language in describing *who* they are and *what* they do has contributed to a lack of consistent focus on the role and functions of counselors (Schmidt, 1991).

An historic example of how this issue clouded the development of the counseling profession, was the longstanding debate over the name of the national association. This debate was temporarily halted in 1983 when APGA changed its name to the American Association for Counseling and Development (AACD) and many of its divisions followed suit by removing *guidance* from their names and adopting the term *counseling* in its place. In 1992, the AACD Governing Council voted to change the name of the organization to the American Counseling Association (ACA) with the mission of the association "to enhance human development throughout the life span and to promote the counseling profession" (Sacks, 1992, p. 1.) Today the ACA has a membership of over 58,000 and consists of the following divisions*

American College Personnel Association (ACPA)

American College Counseling Association (ACCA)

American Mental Health Counselors Association (AMHCA)

American Rehabilitation Counseling Association (ARCA)

American School Counselor Association (ASCA)

Association for Adult Development and Aging (AADA)

Association for Counselor Education and Supervision (ACES)

Association for Humanistic Education and Development (AHEAD)

Association for Assessment in Counseling (AAC)

Association for Multicultural Counseling and Development (AMCD)

Association for Religious and Value Issues in Counseling (ARVIC)

Association for Specialists in Group Work (ASGW)

International Association of Marriage and Family Counselors (IAMFC)

National Career Development Association (NCDA)

National Employment Counselor Association (NECA)

---

* (Due to the association's name change and reorganization at the time this book went to press, some of these divisions' names may not be current. Also, the affiliations of some divisions may have changed).

In addition, two affiliate organizations belong to the AACD family:

Military Educators and Counselors Association (MECA)
American College Counseling Association (ACCA)

Each of these associations includes membership that represents a portion of the thousands of professional counselors practicing in this country. While they each practice in diverse professional settings, all these counselors adhere to the same ethical standards, come from similar training programs, and have common professional goals. What differentiates them, as noted earlier in this chapter, is the focus of their professional setting—the clients and counselees they serve. Among this group, the American School Counselor Association has one of the largest memberships of over 13,000 members. While impressive, this membership represents only a portion of the professional counselors who work in elementary, middle, and high schools across the United States.

The most recent name change of AACD to the American Counseling Association (ACA) illustrates once again how the identity of professional counselors is still emerging as the profession matures and establishes its role and place among other helping specialties. This will continue to be an evolving process among all professional counselors.

Another factor that has contributed to the identity dilemma of school counselors is a reluctance within the counseling profession itself to recognize school counselors as trained professionals on equal footing with counselors in other work settings. School counselors themselves often fail to acquire the self-perception that they are highly trained, capable, "real counselors." In some respects, the profession's national certification process, under the direction of the National Board of Certified Counselors (NBCC), while attempting to build a clear professional identity, may differentiate counselors to the point where a hierarchy of classifications is implicit if not explicit. Career counselors, gerontological counselors, and school counselors now have separate specialty certifications under the NBCC process. Added to these specialties are separate credentials in mental health, rehabilitation, and other counseling fields, which increases the complexity of this issue. While all these counselors belong to the same profession, the credentials that attempt to clarify their roles may in practice do some groups, and the profession as a whole, a disservice. This is particularly true if the credentialing process implies that some counselors have less training and expertise or are less valuable than counselors in other settings.

School counselors historically have been thought of as different from counselors in clinical settings such as mental-health and family counseling centers. In part, this is because the certification of school counselors varies from state to state. Admittedly, this lack of consistent criteria for professionals who call themselves school counselors does little to bring consensus to their role and functions.

Inconsistent perceptions by administrators and teachers add to the confusion about the school counselor's role. In some cases, administrators view counselors as "special" classroom teachers and require schedules and assignments that prevent them from establishing comprehensive counseling programs. For example, in some elementary schools counselors are required to spend a majority of their time presenting classroom guidance as a means of giving teachers breaks or planning periods. While classroom guidance is important and appropriate for both counselors and teachers to integrate in the school's curriculum, assigning counselors sole responsibility for this activity leaves little time for other equally important services in a comprehensive school counseling program. In other schools, counselors are viewed as therapists and "magicians" who have mystical powers, and therefore are kept apart from teachers and other school personnel. They are shielded from everyday responsibilities and functions of school life, and not asked to account for their role in the educational program. Because what they do is so mysterious, these counselors cannot be held accountable or be expected to measure the value of their services in the school. This myth and others like it must be destroyed if counselors are ever going to create beneficial programs with clear goals, realistic expectations, and measurable outcomes that enable these professionals to become integral members of school environments.

Neither view of counselors as "special teachers" or "magicians" facilitates the development of effective service for students, parents, and teachers in schools. What is needed is an understanding that school counselors are highly trained professionals who offer specific skills and services to help students with their educational development. This is the primary role of counselors in schools, and while they are different from counselors who practice in clinics, hospitals, and other settings, this difference is not due to their depth of training or level of expertise. Rather, it is a reflection of the educational and developmental focus of their programs and services. In this textbook, you will be introduced the scope and breadth of a comprehensive school counseling program and to the training and knowledge needed to become an effective school counselor. This text is an overview of the elements and ingredients that give an identity to the school counseling profession and enhance the credibility of practicing school counselors. The following suggestions offer a framework for counselors to create a clear identity and purpose for working in schools. I present them here as an overview of the professional themes and issues addressed in this text. To develop a clear professional identity, school counselors should:

1. Understand the history of school counseling and appreciate the significant events that led to its development and expansion. A knowledge of

one's professional roots and the events that contributed to the profession's growth gives clarity to future goals. Without knowing where we have been, it is difficult to know where we are going.

2. Establish consistent training standards that are on a par with professional counselors in other settings. If the nature and level of training is inconsistent between different types of counselors and among counselors in the same groups, misunderstanding and misinterpretations about these counselor's roles will persist, increasing public uncertainty and contributing to less than adequate programs of services.

3. Expect consistent certification standards. Current differences in certification requirements among the fifty states does little to enhance the professional identity of school counselors. Counseling is a profession that begins with study at the graduate level of training. Specific standards and guidelines developed by the Council for Accreditation of Counseling and Related Educational Programs (CACREP) have the potential to generate nationwide standards for school counselor training and certification. Certification standards should be associated with roles and functions stressed in the professional literature and research about effective counselor performance. Criteria that are unrelated to counselor performance should be discarded. For example, some states continue to require teaching experience for school counselor certification even though research has failed to show a relationship between school counselor effectiveness and teaching experience. Such guidelines detract from the uniqueness of the counselor's role and his or her potential contribution in the school.

4. Develop national guidelines for comprehensive school counseling programs at the high-school, middle-school, and elementary-school levels. School counseling continues to be an emerging field, and, as such, its overall purpose needs to be regularly assessed and adjusted accordingly. The American School Counselor Association has published many helpful resources for counselors to continue this evaluation process. What is needed, in addition to these resources, is an orchestrated effort to inform educational organizations of school administrators and teachers about the role and functions of school counselors.

The historical perspective in this chapter is presented to enhance your understanding and appreciation of contemporary school counseling practices and trends. School counseling, as with many aspects of life, is cyclical in its development. As such, some events and ideas that contributed to its early development are seen again in current professional literature. For example, in recent years Myrick (1987) and others have encouraged a developmental approach where counselors "move their work into places outside of the guidance offices—classrooms, playgrounds, cafeterias, and hallways—to have access to students and teachers" (p. 29). This theme is similar to an earlier view expressed by C. Gilbert Wrenn (1973) who wrote, "I believe that the counselor must accept the responsibility for helping teachers and other staff members as well as directly helping students . . . Counselors who appear indifferent to school improvement or incompetent to contribute to such improvement will be vulnerable" (p. 261). Today's counseling literature emphasizes strong teacher involvement in counseling programs similar to the position taken in 1955 by the Association for Supervision and Curriculum Development (ASCD) in its annual yearbook, *Guidance in the Curriculum*. That publication viewed guidance not as a separate, supplementary service in the school, but rather as an essential part of the curriculum, integrated everyday by teachers and counselors.

Gysbers and Henderson (1988) indicated that the 1970s were marked by action in many states that developed guidelines for comprehensive school counseling programs. Wisconsin, North Carolina, California, Missouri, and Oklahoma are among the many states that contributed to this movement. In the remaining chapters of this book you will learn about the nature of comprehensive school counseling programs, the necessary facilities and resources in school counseling centers at elementary, middle, and high school levels, the essential services offered by school counselors, the background and training of counselors, the importance of collaboration with teachers and student services personnel, and professional issues related to school counseling practices.

The future of school counseling as a profession depends on the ability of counselors to become an integral part of the school setting while maintaining their unique role and contribution to student welfare and development. To accomplish this goal, effective counselors identify their role, select appropriate functions, plan programs of services for students, parents, and teachers, strengthen their professional development, and evaluate their effectiveness in schools.

Selected Readings

Aubrey, R. (1977), "Historical Developments of Counseling and Guidance and Implications for the Future," *Personnel and Guidance Journal, 55*, 288–295. A comprehensive review of the history of the counseling profession in which the author addresses the "problems of identity and directionality" (p. 293). Aubrey looked beyond the 1970s and recommended that in planning for the future counselors "might do well to also look back." He contended that counselors need to find a system of counseling "to unify our members under common and mutually agreed upon purposes." (p. 294).

Aubrey, R. F. (1982), " A House Divided: Guidance and Counseling in the 20th Century America," *Personnel and Guidance Journal, 61*, 198–204. This article followed where Aubrey's 1977 article left off. In it, he warned that counselors were behind the times. In particular, he raised concern about how school counselors struggled in the 1950s and later to identify their role, and how in the 1980s "diversity and contradictions within the profession have seriously endangered any major sense of mission" (p. 203).

Wrenn, C. G. (1973). *The World of the Contemporary Counselor* (Boston: Houghton Mifflin). Written almost 20 years ago, this classic book withstands the test of time remarkably well. Wrenn's message to counselors then still holds true today.

Gladding, S. T. (1992). *Counseling: A Comprehensive Profession*, 2nd Ed. (New York: Macmillan). The first chapter of this book presents a readable overview of the counseling profession and highlights significant events, from the early 1900s to the present, that have affected the professions development in schools and other settings.

References

ACES-ASCA Joint Committee on the Elementary School Counselor. (1966), "The Elementary School Counselor: Preliminary Statement," *Personnel and Guidance Journal*, 44, 658–661.

Aubrey, R. F. (1982), "A House Divided: Guidance and Counseling in 20th Century America," *Personnel and Guidance Journal*, 61, 198–204.

Axline, V. M. (1947), "Nondirective Therapy for Poor Readers," *Journal of Consulting Psychology*, 11, 61–69.

Baruth, L. G., & Robinson, E. H. (1987). *An Introduction to the Counseling Profession* (Englewood Cliffs, NJ: Prentice Hall).

Beale, A. V. (1986), "Trivial Pursuit: The History of Guidance," *The School Counselor*, 34, 14–17.

Beers, C. (1908). *A Mind that Found Itself* (New York: Longmans Green; republished by Doubleday, 1953).

Brown, D., & Srebalus, D. (1972). *Contemporary Guidance Concepts and Practices* (Dubuque, IW: Wm. C. Brown Co).

Carkhuff, R. R., & Berenson, B. G. (1967). *Beyond Counseling and Psychotherapy* (New York: Holt, Rinehart & Winston).

Combs, A. W. (Ed.). (1962). *Perceiving, Behaving, Becoming* (Washington, D.C.: Yearbook of the Association for Supervision and Curriculum Development).

Dinkmeyer, D., Dinkmeyer, D., Jr., & Sperry, L. (1987). *Adlerian Counseling and Psychotherapy*, 2nd ed. (Columbus, OH: Merrill).

Dugan, W. E. (Ed.). (1958). *Counseling points of view.* Proceedings of the Minnesota Counselors Association Midwinter Conference, 1958 (Minneapolis: University of Minnesota Press).

Ellis, A. (1962). *Reason and Emotion in Psychotherapy* (New York: Lyle Stuart).

Faust, V. (1968a). *History of Elementary School Counseling: Overview and Critique* (Boston: Houghton Mifflin).

Faust, V. (1968b). *The Counselor-Consultant in the Elementary School* (Boston: Houghton Mifflin).

Foster, C. M. (1967), "The Elementary School Counselor: How Perceived?" *Counselor Education and Supervision*, 6, 102–107.

Gerler, E. R. (Ed.). (1990), "Special Issue on Multimodal Theory, Research, and Practice," *Elementary School Guidance and Counseling*, 24 (4), 242–317.

Gibson, R. L., & Mitchell, M. H. (1990). *Introduction to Guidance and Counseling*, 3rd ed. (New York: Macmillan).

Gladding, S. (1981), "Identity Crises," *Personnel and Guidance Journal, 60,* 132.

Gladding, S. T. (1992). *Counseling: A Comprehensive Profession,* 2nd Ed. (New York: Macmillan).

Glasser, W. (1965). *Reality Therapy: A New Approach to Psychiatry* (New York: Harper & Row).

Greene, K. (1967), "Functions Performed and Preferred by Elementary School Counselors in the United States" (Doctoral dissertation, Ohio University, 1967). *Dissertation Abstracts International, 28,* (University Microfilms No. 67–14 780)

Grummon, D. L., & John, E. S. (1954), "Changes over Client-Centered Therapy Evaluated on Psychoanalytically Based thematic Apperception Test Scales," in C. R. Rogers & R. F. Dymond (eds.), *Psychotherapy and Personality Change* (Chicago: University of Chicago Press).

Gysbers, N. C., & Henderson, P. (1988). *Developing and Managing your School Guidance Program* (Alexandria, VA: American Association for Counseling and Development).

Harold, M. (1985), "Council's History Examined after 50 Years," *Guidepost, 27* (10), 4.

Herr, E. L. (1986), "The Relevant Counselor," *The School Counselor, 34,* 7–13.

Hill, G., & Luckey, E. (1969). *Guidance for Children in Elementary Schools.* (New York: Appleton-Century-Crofts).

Hoy, W. K., Tarter, C. J., Kottkamp, R. B. (1991). *Open Schools/Healthy Schools* (Newbury, CA: Sage Publications).

Humes, C. W. (1978), "School Counselors and PL 94–142," *The School Counselor, 25,* 193–195.

Jourard, S. M. (1964). *The Transparent Self: Self-Disclosure and Well-Being* (Princeton, NJ: Van Nostrand).

Krumboltz, J. D. (1974), "An Accountability Model for Counselors," *Personnel and Guidance Journal, 52,* 639–646.

Maslow, A. H. (1957), "A Philosophy of Psychology: The Need for a Mature Science of Human Nature," *Main Currents in Modern Thought, 13,* 27–32.

May, R. (Ed.). (1966). *Existential Psychology* (New York: Random House).

McKellar, R. (1964), " A Study of Concepts, Functions, and Organizational Characteristics of Guidance in the Elementary School as Reported by Selected Elementary School Guidance Personnel" (Doctoral dissertation, Florida State University, 1963). *Dissertation Abstracts International, 24,* 4477 (University Microfilms No. 64–3601)

Miller, F. W. (1968). *Guidance: Principles and Services* (Columbus, OH: Merrill).

Myrick, R. D. (1984), "Beyond the Issues of School Counselor Accountability," *Measurement and Evaluation in Guidance, 16,* 218–222.

Myrick, R. D. (1987). *Development Guidance and Counseling: A Practical Approach* (Minneapolis, MN: Educational Media Corporation).

Myrick, R., & Moni, L. (1976), "A Status Report of Elementary School Counseling," *Elementary School Guidance and Counseling, 10,* 156–164.

Nugent, F. A. (1981) *Professional Counseling* (Monterey, CA: Brooks/Cole).

Parloff, M. B. (1976, February 21), "Shopping for the Right Therapy," *Saturday Review,* 14–16.

Parsons, F. (1909). *Choosing a vocation* (Boston: Houghton Mifflin).

Patterson, C. H. (1962). *Counseling and Guidance in Schools* New York: Harper and Brothers.

Purkey, S. C., & Smith, M. S. (1983), "Effective Schools: A Review," *The Elementary School Journal, 83,* 427–452.

Purkey, W. W., & Schmidt, J. J. (1987). *The Inviting Relationship: An Expanded Perspective for Profession Counseling* (Englewood Cliffs, NJ: Prentice-Hall).

Purkey, W. W., & Schmidt, J. J. (1990). *Invitational learning for counseling and development.* Ann Arbor, MI: ERIC/CAPS.

Roeber, E. C. (1963). *The School Counselor* (Washington, D.C.: The Center for Applied Research in Education).

Rogers, C. R. (1942). *Counseling and Psychotherapy: New Concepts in Practice* (Boston: Houghton Mifflin).

Rogers, C. R. (1951). *Client-Centered Therapy: Its Current Practice, Implications, and Theory* (Boston: Houghton Mifflin).

Sacks, J. I. (1992). AACD to become ACA. *Guidepost, 34* (12), 1;10.

Schmidt, J. J. (1986), "Becoming an "Able" Counselor," *Elementary School Guidance and Counseling, 21,* 16–22.

Schmidt, J. J. (1991). *A Survival Guide for the Elementary/Middle School Counselor* (West Nyack, NY: The Center for Applied Research in Education).

Shertzer, B., & Stone, S. C. (1966). *Fundamentals of Guidance* (Boston: Houghton Mifflin).

Shertzer, B., & Stone, S. C. (1981). *Fundamentals of Guidance* 4th ed. (Boston: Houghton Mifflin).

Stamm, M. L., & Nissman, B. S. (1979). *Improving Middle School Guidance* (Boston: Allyn and Bacon).

Stampfl, T. G. (1961), "Implosive Therapy: A Learning Theory Derived Psychodynamic Therapeutic Technique," in Lebarba & Dent (Eds.(, *Critical issues in clinical psychology* (New York: Academic Press).

Stefflre, B. & Grant, W. H. (1972). *Theories of Counseling,* 2nd ed. (New York: McGraw-Hill).

Thetford, W. N. (1952), "An Objective Measure of Frustration Toleration in Evaluating Psychotherapy," in W. Wolff (ed.), *Success in Psychotherapy* (New York: Grune & Stratton).

Thornburg, H. D. (1986), "The Counselor's Impact on Middle-Grade Students," *The School Counselor, 33,* 170–177.

Truax, C. B., & Carkhuff, R. R. (1967). *Towards Effective Counseling and Psychotherapy* (Chicago: Aldine).

Vacc, N. A., & Loesch, L. C. (1987). *Counseling as a Profession* (Muncie, IN: Accelerated Development).

Van Hoose, W. H., & Vafakas, C. M. (1968), "Status of Guidance and Counseling in the Elementary School," *Personnel and Guidance Journal, 46,* 536–539.

Wheeler, P. T., & Loesch, L. (1981), "Program Evaluation and Counseling: Yesterday, Today and Tomorrow," *Personnel and Guidance Journal, 59,* 573–578.

Williamson, E. G. (1939). *How to Counsel Students* (New York: McGraw-Hill).

Williamson, E. G. (1950). *Counseling Adolescents* (New York: McGraw-Hill).

Wolpe, J. (1958). *Psychotherapy and Reciprocal Inhibition* (Stanford, CA: Stanford University Press).

Wrenn, C. G. (1962). *The Counselor in a Changing World* (Washington, DC: American Personnel and Guidance Association).

Wrenn, C. G. (1973). *The World of the Contemporary Counselor* (Boston: Houghton Mifflin).

Zytowski, D. G. (1972), "Four Hundred Years before Parsons," *Personnel and Guidance Journal, 50,* 443–450.

2

A Comprehensive School Counseling Program

A school counseling program is a planned component of the larger school purpose and mission. The role of the school counselor is to design a comprehensive program of services that complements the goals and objectives of the school. By designing planned, purposeful programs of services, school counselors distinguish themselves from counselors in other professional settings who offer either a limited number of services, or services with a narrow focus, due to the specific populations they serve.

For example, marriage counselors serve couples who are experiencing difficulty in their marital relationships, or who are searching for meaningful ways to expand and nourish their relationships with each other. In providing beneficial services to these couples, marriage counselors use individual and group sessions and incorporate therapeutic, informational, and instructional strategies in these helping relationships. If no progress is made in these relationships and dysfunctional behaviors continue, marriage counselors refer their clients to other community agencies or professionals who can offer additional and more specific services. The primary mission of a marriage counselor is to enable couples to address and enhance communication processes in their marital relationships.

By contrast, school counselors who plan and implement comprehensive programs serve three populations that include students, parents, and teachers. The services provided for these three groups include individual and group counseling, consulting, testing and assessment, group instruction, and referrals. Most importantly, these services are delivered within the framework of an organized program, and the design of this counseling program is guided by the overall mission of the school and the goals of the local community and state (Gysbers & Henderson, 1988).

School counseling is a relatively young profession having emerged out of the vocational guidance movement of the early 1900s. In the decades since then, the counseling profession has searched for a clear identity and role for counselors in schools. Over fifty years ago, counselors struggled with their direction and purpose in schools, and today this struggle continues. Because of this uncertainty, school counselors are sometimes criticized for not fulfilling their obligations. Exactly what these obligations are is a basic question all school counselors must ascertain in developing appropriate goals and objectives for their programs. Without clear goals and objectives, a counselor's obligations can easily be misinterpreted and misunderstood by both the professional and the people who seek counseling services.

As indicated in Chapter 1, misunderstandings about the counselor's role are related in some measure to the confusion between the terms *guidance* and *counseling* and how these terms are used to describe what school counselors do. Aubrey (1982) wrote that "the terms *guidance* and *counseling* convey a variety of meanings and interpretations to lay persons and professionals alike. As a consequence, many criticisms aimed at guidance and counseling reflect disappointments of audiences vastly overrating the potential of school counselors" (p. 198). Successful counselors, whether in schools or other settings, are clear about the terms they use to describe and define their programs and services, and they use these terms in a consistent fashion.

To understand what you will do in schools as a professional counselor, you first need a consistent language to define and describe who you are and what you do. In this chapter, you will review the purpose, design, facilities, and resources of a comprehensive school counseling program. To fully understand these aspects, you must first know how the terms guidance and counseling are used in this book. The next section defines and describes the language of school counseling as used in this text.

A Definition of School Counseling

The challenge of offering a wide spectrum of services to several different audiences is what makes school counselors unique in their practice. While similar skills and expertise are required of counselors in other settings, school counselors, as noted throughout this text, apply their knowledge beyond the limited scope of a single service, and they do so in a comprehensive program of interrelated services and activities.

School counselors have training in many subject areas that contribute to their overall knowledge base and professional skills. Graduate courses in human development, sociology, psychology, career information and development, tests and measurement techniques, social and cultural foundations, educational research, and counseling processes and skills give school counselors a broad knowledge base and a variety of skills to practice in elementary-, middle-, and high-school settings. Courses in theory and practice provide counselors with a framework to formulate and clarify their professional role. In sum, this training enables school counselors to create a description of the variety of services offered to students, parents, and teachers.

To be consistent in developing program descriptions, counselors need a language that is clear and understandable to students, parents, teachers, and others who need to know why a counselor is in the school and what this counselor does. In this book, I use the term *school counseling* to describe both the profession and the program of services established by counselors in schools. The term *counseling*, as used here, is not limited to remedial relationships in which counselors help clients resolve problems, nor is it restricted to one-to-one relationships. As used in this text, *counseling* refers to a wide selection of services and activities that are chosen to help people prevent disabling events, focus on their overall development, and remedy existing concerns. The common ground for these three service areas is that, in each, the school counselor provides direct services to students, parents, and teachers. As such, the term *school counseling* accurately describes a broad program of services provided by professionally trained counselors in elementary, middle, and senior high schools.

The term *school counseling* is a more contemporary and definitive term than are *personnel services* or *guidance services*, which, as noted earlier, are vague descriptions encompassing conflicting roles and functions for school counselors (Schmidt, 1991). For example, personnel services imply record-keeping, class scheduling, attendance monitoring, and other functions that are administrative in nature and detract from direct counseling and consulting services with students, parents, and teachers. Meanwhile, the term guidance, while noted for its historical significance, is not the sole responsibility of school counselors, nor is it the domain of any single professional group.

Everything done in schools, whether by administrators, teachers, counselors, or others can be related in some way to the concept of "guiding students." For as long as schools have existed, teachers have guided children and adolescents in classroom behaviors and in their personal relationships. By the same token, school administrators have guided students with respect to policies, curriculum, discipline, and other aspects of the educational program. Student guidance is important, and everyone who works in schools and cares about children and adolescents has a role in this process. By accepting a broader application for the term "guidance," school administrators, teachers, and counselors recognize that the "entire educational program of the school...is guidance oriented (or should be). For this reason, it is inaccurate to confine guidance goals and objectives to a single program such as school counseling. Because guidance permeates every facet of the school, no one person or program has ownership" (Schmidt, 1991, p. 12).

The terms *school counselor* and *school counseling program* are compatible with the terminology used by the national professional associations, as seen in the name of the American School Counselor Association (ASCA) and its journal, *The School Counselor.* In addition, the National Board of Certified Counselors (NBCC) has created a specialty certification area for school counselors.

While the terms *school counseling program* and *school counselor* are the preferred descriptions used in this book, guidance and other terms have an important place in helping school counselors define and describe their programs of services. Herewith are some of these terms and their descriptions as used in this book. These descriptions briefly define some of the major terms used. In later chapters of this book, these terms are defined and described in greater detail.

Guidance—a term used to describe a curriculum area related to affective or psychological education (Sprinthall, 1971). The guidance curriculum generally consists of broad goals and objectives for each grade level, and ideally, is integrated into classroom instruction by teachers and counselors in a cooperative effort. Sometimes *guidance* is used to designate a particular instructional or informational service such as "classroom guidance" or "small group guidance."

Counseling—a primary service of school counselors. Its focus is to provide individual and small group counseling for students. Counseling relationships are defined as ongoing helping processes, confidential in nature, that assist people in focusing on concerns, planning strategies to address specific issues, and evaluating their success in carrying out these plans. Successful counseling relationships require a high level of knowledge about human development and behavior as well as effective and facilitative communication skills. Depending on circumstances, school counselors sometimes offer brief counseling services to parents and teachers. In these instances, their goal is to help a parent or teacher make a decision about future treatment in a community agency or service. By helping parents and teachers in short-term counseling, school counselors give indirect assistance to children and students.

Developmental Guidance and Counseling—activities and services designed to help students focus on the attainment of knowledge and skills for developing healthy life goals and acquiring the behaviors to reach those goals. Sometimes these activities are delivered in large or small group guidance sessions appropriate for all students, and other times they are designed specifically for targeted audiences of students in small group counseling sessions. In elementary, middle, and high schools, these developmental services are aimed at helping students focus on tasks and issues appropriate for their age and stage of life. For example, a middle grades' teacher might present the career implications of learning to speak fluently and write appropriately to help students see the connection between language arts in school and future vocational choices.

Consultation—relationships in which school counselors, as student development specialists, confer with parents, teachers, and other professionals to identify student needs and select appropriate services. Occasionally, counselors determine that the best way to help students is to provide information to parents or teachers. In these instances, consultation takes the form of parent education groups or teacher in-service workshops. Counselors also consult with students by providing brief individual and small group sessions to disseminate information or offer instruction about particular topics. For example, middle-grade students interested in a peer helper program might consult with a counselor to find out what peer helpers do in schools and how they can join this special group of students.

Schoolwide Guidance—planned activities to help all students focus on a particular issue or topic. Such schoolwide events might be planned jointly by school counselors, administrators, and teachers. Samples of these types of activities are: a "Career Day" for senior high school students; a "Develop a New Friendship Week" for middle graders; and a "Most Improved" bulletin board for elementary children.

Student Services Team—a team of professionals who specialize in providing counseling, consulting, assessment, and other related services to ensure the emotional, educational, social, and healthful development of all students. Typically, a student services team consists of a school counselor, social worker, psychologist, nurse, and other related professionals.

Counseling Center—the office and facilities of the school counselor. These facilities are located in the school and consist of office space, furnishings, equipment, and materials that are needed in implementing a comprehensive program. Depending on the level of the program and the size of the school and staff, the counseling center might include private offices for the counselors, a waiting or play area, a room for testing, and a conference room for group sessions.

Teacher-Advisee Program—a program designed to give every student adequate access to an adult advisor. While Teacher-Advisee programs (TAP) are relatively recent and found most commonly at the middle-school level (sometimes they are called advisor-advisee programs), they can be designed and implemented at all school levels (Myrick &

Myrick, 1990). Basically, these programs assign groups of students to teachers for advising about academic, social, and personal needs. Teacher-advisors also present special guidance sessions for their advisees during the year. In addition, Teacher-Advisee Programs are excellent networks by which teachers can refer students to counselors for additional services and attention.

Peer Helper Program—a program established to identify and train students who can assist classmates and other students. Often, school counselors work alone in isolation, particularly in elementary and middle schools where ratios of counselors to students are frequently quite high. Peer helpers can assist counselors and teachers in meeting the needs of a greater number of students. They can be trained as listeners to be first-line helpers in the school, as tutors to assist students who are experiencing learning problems, as guidance aides to help teachers present guidance activities in classes, and as office assistants to answer the counselor's phone, run errands, and do other helpful tasks. Training is essential for students who are selected as peer helpers to successfully address the identified needs and targeted goals of these programs.

Parent Education Program—a program designed to provide information to parents about child development issues, discipline strategies at home, school progress, and other related topics. Some counselors use packaged, commercially produced programs to assist parents (Dinkmeyer & McKay, 1976; Popkin, 1983), while others tailor and design their own programs and activities in schools. Occasionally, these programs are a single session, such as a presentation to a meeting of the PTA, and other times they are ongoing sessions, such as a support group of single parents lead by an elementary counselor.

Advisory Committee—a volunteer group established to guide the planning and development of a comprehensive program. The scope and breadth of comprehensive school counseling programs requires input from administrators, teachers, parents, and students (Duncan, 1989). An advisory committee (sometimes called a Guidance and Counseling Committee) is one way that counselors enlist the assistance of these groups to determine the needs of school populations, advise the counselor about essential services to meet these needs, and plan schoolwide activities to enhance student learning, improve relationships, and create a beneficial school climate.

Many other terms are used in describing comprehensive school counseling programs and most of them are included in this chapter. By having a clear understanding of the language and terms used to describe who they are and what they do, school counselors are in a stronger position to outline the purposes of their programs. Every school has an educational mission and within that mission there lies a purpose for special programs such as school counseling.

The Purpose of School Counseling Programs

To some extent the struggle of the school counseling profession to develop a clear identity has contributed to the confusion about why counselors are employed in school settings. Unfortunately, the inability to identify a clear purpose has placed some counselors in clerical, administrative, and instructional roles, diminishing their value in the school. In contrast, by developing a clear understanding of their purpose, other school counselors establish a philosophical basis on which to build a credible program. To begin, they first ask themselves the question, "Why am I here?"

In a previous work, I hypothesized that the essential reason counselors are employed by schools is to help people become "more able" (Schmidt, 1986, 1991). As such, school counselors assist students in becoming "able" learners, they support parents in their supervising and nurturing roles, and they help teachers to provide effective instruction and create healthy classroom climates for all students. This hypothesis of the role and purpose of school counselors is summarized here as a mission to provide services that ensure an opportunity for all students to learn and develop to their fullest potential. While this premise seems simple enough, the task of reaching this goal may appear overwhelming in light of today's challenges brought by children, adolescents, and their families to the school. For this reason, it is imperative that school counselors view their role, not as a series of unrelated crisis-oriented services, but rather as an orchestrated program of essential services and activities that complement the instructional program of the school.

In the past, school counselors have been viewed as "support" personnel. As such, it was believed that school counselors provided ancillary services to the instruction offered by teachers and the administration required of principals. This emphasis on supporting teachers and administrators, while illustrating caring and helpful aspects of a counselor's role, tended to lessen the importance and value of school counseling services. At the same time, supportive services were more vulnerable to economic, political, and institutional changes that occur in society. Because school counselors have historically accepted a role that is "supportive" as opposed to "essential," they have occasionally let other create their role and functions, dictate their mission, and design their programs.

A key element in describing a comprehensive counseling program is the notion that the services are *essential* to the school. In this book, the services of a school counseling program are presented as *essential* aspects at all school levels, elementary through high school. The purpose of school counseling programs is to provide a array of services that facilitate the development of all students. As Meeks wrote in 1968, "If the purpose of counseling is to facilitate development, then the counseling process must be a part of the educational process from kindergarten through the secondary school" (p. 101). Children and adolescents in contemporary U.S. society face challenges that will continue to evolve in complexity and importance for generations to come. For this reason, schools and other institutions need to address the total development of all children. As such, educational goals can not be separated from personal, social, physical, and other developmental processes. In this way, school counseling services are and will remain essential to the total education of our youth.

School counselors who see an essential role in the overall school mission are able to convince administrators and teachers about how counseling, consulting, and other services in a comprehensive school counseling program contribute to the effectiveness of the school. To do this, they design programs and services that address the development of students in three essential areas: educational development, career development, and personal and social development.

Educational Development

A fundamental belief of effective schools is that "all children can learn" (Edmonds, 1979). The challenge in U.S. society today and in the future is to see this belief become reality in all schools for all children, and to do so schools must create climates that give every student an equal opportunity to succeed academically. Counselors contribute to this goal by assessing students' abilities, guiding teachers in placing students in the instructional program, providing services for parents to learn about their children's development and progress in school, and counseling students about their goals and plans in life.

School counselors use many different services to focus on the educational development of students. For example, counselors and teachers use classroom guidance activities to encourage positive self-concept development and alter behaviors for improving school success (Downing, 1977; Gerler, 1985; Wilson, 1986). These classroom activities are integrated with daily lessons or designed as specially planned presentations. Individual and small group counseling with students who need additional or more intense services are also part of a comprehensive program (Hutchins & Cole, 1977; Matthews, 1986; Warren, Smith, & Velten, 1984). In addition, school counselors consult with teachers, parents, and other professionals to assure that all available services are considered in planning a student's educational program.

Educational development is not the sole responsibility of classroom teachers. In today's society, optimal educational achievement is realized when teachers are assisted by school counselors who provide direct services to students, offer support to parents and guardians, and form collaborative relationships with teachers and other school personnel. Through this type of team effort, students' progress is adequately monitored and appropriate services are designed and implemented. In this way, counselors identify and address student learning as a main goal and purpose of comprehensive school counseling programs.

One aspect of educational development that counselors include in their counseling programs is a focus on lifelong learning. In elementary through secondary schools, the educational focus for all students should be on learning throughout one's life rather than simply moving to the next grade level or merely "finishing school." Unfortunately, the design of American schools emphasizes movement through the grades and graduation from one level to the next, and this structure inhibits a broader lifelong self-development focus. School counselors have a responsibility to see that their schools encourage lifelong learning as an essential objective for all students. This process of learning throughout life is closely related to the second purpose of school counseling programs, one that focuses on career development.

Career Development

The school counseling profession, as noted in the first chapter, has its roots in vocational guidance. Over its brief history, the profession has changed and expanded its role, but career development remains a vital part of comprehensive school counseling programs. Today, and in the future students will face difficult decisions regarding career choices in a changing complex world (Gysbers, 1984). Having the knowledge and ability to make informed choices about career direction is essential for self-development and fulfillment in life. School counselors have a responsibility to assist students in this endeavor.

An essential part of every person's development includes his or her success in planning, choosing, and following a satisfying career. The success people have in pursuing this goal influences many other aspects of their lives. Alfred Adler, a noted theorist and therapist, wrote that three main tasks in life include contributions through work, successful sharing with others, and satisfying love relationships (Dinkmeyer, Dinkmeyer, & Sperry, 1987). Each of these three tasks is related to the other two, but of the three, the success people achieve in their careers most strongly influences their social achievements and loving relationships.

The social strata to which people belong, the personal relationships they establish, the economic success they achieve are among many factors related to the career choices made over a lifetime. For this reason, schools have a responsibility to help students take their knowledge and skills and develop realistic and self-satisfying career goals. School counselors help with this process by: (1) providing students with accurate information about the world of work and existing career opportunities; (2) assessing students' interests and abilities and sharing these findings to enable students to make appropriate career choices; and (3) encouraging students to broaden their options as a precaution to future changes in career opportunities and the job market.

As a lifelong process, career development is an important component of all school counseling programs, elementary through secondary schools. To some people, career information and development seems out of context with the elementary curriculum. This is particularly so considering the current focus of U.S. schools on learning basic skills and nurturing personal development. In elementary schools, career development may get only "a cursory glance with a unit on career exploration taught in some grades, or a Career Week planned for students to learn about occupations in their community" (Schmidt, 1991, p. 110). While children at early ages should not be exposed to occupational information or formal presentations about career choices, they are nevertheless influenced by family, media, and other events that lead them toward career decisions at this early age. Counselors and teachers can help with this decision-making process by infusing career information, self-interest activities, and illustrations of the relationship between work and education into daily instruction. At the same time, the school curriculum should guard against gender stereotyping in materials, information, and activities it presents to these young impressionable minds.

At the secondary-school level, counselors and teachers continue this integration of career guidance into the curriculum, and also provide direct services to help students narrow their career interests and choices. In middle and junior high schools, students are exposed to activities and services that enable them to explore current trends and developments in different careers. This exploration process helps these pre-teens and young adolescents to view career choices more realistically. In senior high schools, counselors offer an array of services including career interest inventories, aptitude testing, and up-to-date occupational information to assist students in deciding about their careers. During high school years, students' decisions about career choices are tied to their future educational plans about entering the job market, enrolling in vocational schools for technical training, or attending college after graduation. In sum, all these services, in elementary through high school, are aimed at helping students link their educational development with career goals.

Personal and Social Development

A third purpose of comprehensive school counseling programs is to facilitate the personal and social development of all students. Achieving academically and choosing a successful career are incomplete goals unless students understand and accept themselves personally, and use this understanding to successfully relate with others.

Many students achieve academic success in school only to fail in their personal and social development. These failures often lead to dissatisfying lives of social isolation, broken relationships, substance abuse, depressions, and most tragically, suicide. Comprehensive school counseling programs help students to learn social skills and identify personal strengths and weaknesses to lead more satisfying lives.

In elementary schools, counselors and teachers develop programs and services that help students learn who they are, explore the similarities they share with others, and examine the differences that make them unique and special as individuals. Classroom guidance, individual counseling, and small group activities are used to reach these goals. The elementary child's world is quite egocentric. As a result, the role of the elementary teacher and counselor is to help children emerge from their self-centered view of the world and move towards a view that is more accepting of others. Activities that encourage sharing, helping, and cooperation allow children to begin this transformation process.

In the middle grades, students become more interested in social groups and members of the opposite sex. Developmentally, boys lag behind girls in many respects, and this gap is noticeable to teachers and counselors who plan activities and services for these students. Middle-grade services in comprehensive counseling programs continue the self-development processes begun in the elementary school, and in addition, place stronger emphasis on physical changes, sexual development, and the importance of social belonging. In many respects, the pre-adolescent's adjustment to physical changes—growth spurts, body hair, sexual development—has a tremendous influence on all other aspects of student development. At the same time, a student's social acceptance and rejection has significant implications for future educational, career, and social choices.

Personal and social development in high school is frequently a continuation of patterns that emerge in the middle grades. Students who make smooth transitions from middle school to high school usually are successful in achieving a degree of social acceptance. On the other hand, students who are unable to resolve critical developmental issues in their middle-school years usually need a counselor's assistance in high school.

Even students who have had few difficulties in elementary and middle school, occasionally find challenges and obstacles in the high-school years that prove overwhelming. For example, relationships between boys and girls become more serious during this stage and the success or failure of these relationships can have a significant effect on future social encounters, educational plans, and career aspirations. Failed relationships can relate to dropping out of school, depression, and tragic suicides, all of which are concerns of high school counselors (Hitchner, & Tifft-Hitchner, 1987). In addition, sexual disease, teen pregnancy, substance abuse, violence, and other social ailments jeopardize a student's social and personal development. High-school counselors and teachers plan classroom and schoolwide events, individual and small group counseling, parent education programs, and referral processes to assist students with normal, healthy development, prevent obstacles from interfering with this developmental process, and remedy existing concerns that are blocking student progress.

The processes used at elementary, middle, and high-school levels to help students with their educational, career, and personal and social development are similar. What distinguishes the practice of school counselors at these different levels are the developmental stages and needs indicated by the students in these schools. Because the career-development needs of elementary children are different from seniors in high school, the specific activities and services provided for these two populations by counselors in their respective schools will also be different. Nevertheless, there are some common processes and services used by school counselors across all the educational levels. These processes and services help define and describe the nature and scope of comprehensive school counseling programs.

A Comprehensive Program

Comprehensive school counseling programs consist of counseling, consulting, coordinating, and appraisal services offered in response to the identified needs, goals, and objectives of the school and community. In a comprehensive program, goals and objectives are identified and given priority as the result of adequate assessment and analysis of students, parents, and teachers' needs. A school counselor's decisions, therefore, to focus on particular issues and to select specific activities in the program do not happen randomly or accidentally. Rather, they occur in a series of processes that include planning, organizing, implementing, and evaluating procedures. The first two of these, planning, and organizing, go hand in hand to define and describe a school counseling program.

Planning consists of procedures and decisions that help counselors evaluate schoolwide goals, assess students, parents, and teachers' needs, and select goals and objectives for their counseling programs. Planning processes are most noticeable at the beginning of the school year when an accurate assessment of school populations is likely to occur. At the start of a school year, decisions about district lines, reorganizations, and other major events have been made by local boards of education, and schools in these districts are fairly certain about the students who will enroll and the communities to be served for the year. Having this knowledge enables school counselors to assess the general needs of the school and community and make appropriate decisions about preventive, developmental, and remedial services. While most planning occurs at the beginning of each school year, it remains a continuous process as counselors, teachers, and administrators evaluate ongoing services.

Organizing is part of the planning process and includes the selection of major goals and objectives and a determination of which services can best address and meet these goals. Program organization also entails assignments and timelines for carrying out specific activities. These assignments and schedules help the school identify *who* is responsible for *which* services and *when* they will be implemented. With adequate organization, school counseling programs clearly identify annual goals and objectives, make specific assignments for counselors, teachers, administrators, and other personnel, and develop a schedule of major functions and events that will take place during the year. In this way, program organization includes all professionals, and establishes each of their roles in a school counseling program.

Implementing is the action phase of a comprehensive school counseling program. In this phase, counselors, teachers, and others deliver the services that comprise a comprehensive program. Included in these services are individual and small group counseling, teacher and parent consultation, classroom and small group guidance, testing, crisis interventions, and referrals. In school counseling programs where counselors fail to do adequate planning and organizing, implementation may be the only phase that is readily observed. These programs illustrate counselors who are busy performing activities but their services are not orchestrated or aligned to address the major needs of students, parents, and teachers in the school. In these cases, counselors are busy "getting the job done," but the job they have identified is not one that is essential in helping students reach their educational goals.

Implementing a program that is void of clear goals and objectives is like piloting a plane without a flight plan. The plane is airborne, all instruments are working, but the pilot has no idea where the plane is heading or why it is going in that direction. School counselors who set sail without clear direction tend to implement services that haphazardly "hit and miss" the real issues and needs of students, parents, and teachers. Without adequate planning and organizing, the "hits" of these counselors are mostly fortuitous and not likely to be repeated. Conversely, repetition of successful services is more likely to occur when counselors complement their plans and activities with accurate evaluations.

Evaluating consists of procedures that enable counselors to determine the success of their services, identify apparent weaknesses, and recommend program changes for the future. This phase of a comprehensive school counseling program is essential to the counselor's identity and credibility.

Excellent and effective school counseling programs are guided by planned involvement of all school personnel, adequate organization, appropriate assignment of responsibilities, competent delivery of services, and accurate measurement of outcomes. A truly effective school counseling program is one that makes a difference in the lives of students, parents, and teachers. By making a difference, school counselors create a clear identity and enhance their value in elementary-, middle-, and high-school settings.

Adequate and accurate program evaluation also enables counselors to return to the initial goals and objectives of the program and assess what changes, if any, are needed. In this way, a comprehensive school counseling program is cyclical in nature. Figure 2–1 illustrates this cycle of planning, organizing, implementing, and evaluating a counseling program. Each of these phases of a comprehensive program consists of specific elements which we will now examine.

Assessing Needs

In determining which goals and objectives should be part of a comprehensive school counseling program, counselors first investigate and assess the

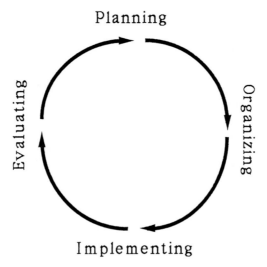

FIGURE 2–1   Phases of a Comprehensive Program

needs of the populations to be served. As you learned earlier, these populations consist of students, parents, and teachers, whose needs will vary from school to school and from community to community. This variability will depend on the size of the school, the socio-economic status of the community, the concentration of learning problems found in the school, the educational backgrounds of parents, the community's attitudes toward the school and education in general, and the leadership of the school and district.

Because each of these factors influences schools in unique and different ways, the needs of students, parents, and teachers have a similarly unique influence on the design and implementation of a school counseling program. For example, students and families who come from impoverished backgrounds will express quite different needs than students and families of affluence. These differences will be reflected in the school as a whole and in the services provided in a comprehensive counseling program. This is true in elementary, middle, or senior high schools. As an illustration, elementary counselors in schools with students who require substantial attention to meet their basic needs for food and shelter often find themselves playing the dual role of crisis counselor and social worker. In these situations, the scope and breadth of the counseling program may not span the full spectrum of preventive, developmental, and remedial services advocated in this text. By nature of its school population, this counseling program will have more of a remedial focus. Of course, even in this type of school a futuristic counselor will find ways to include prevention and development in the goals and objectives of the program and teachers in the classroom will be agents who carry out this plan. The rationale for such an approach is founded in the belief that to remedy existing concerns without helping students learn about themselves and make sound educational choices is merely a Band-Aid solution to a larger social problem.

To create programs that maintain a realistic vision, counselors assess school needs and interpret these data accurately. Usually, counselors assess students, parents, and teachers' needs in the beginning of the school year, and then develop year-long goals and objectives around these established needs. In most instances, counselors will identify a few annual goals that remain consistent from year to year regardless of how the student population changes over time. These goals become an ongoing part of the program. For example, in most secondary schools, counselors are concerned with helping seniors make plans for after graduation. These plans might include employment, marriage, child rearing, military service, technical school, trade school, or college. While student populations might change over the years, and subsequently their needs after high school, the process of assisting all students with their plans for the future will continue as an essential service in every school counseling program.

One way that counselors collect needs' assessment data is through surveys with students, parents, and teachers. In large schools, counselors might take a random sample of students in each grade level to cut down on time, and paper costs, and to streamline the analysis process. They may do the same with samples of parents. Usually, counselors will seek needs assessment input from all teachers in the school. Forms 2–1, 2–2, and 2–3 illustrate sample assessment surveys for students, parents, and teachers. The survey form for students is designed for middle graders (2–1), the parent form is for elementary schools (2–2), and the teacher form for high schools (2–3).

Data from these surveys are summarized by the counselor and presented to the School Counseling Advisory Committee. At that presentation, the counselor interprets the results, solicits input from committee members, and determines major goals and objectives for the annual program. These goals and objectives are discussed by the committee and strategies and activities for the year are planned. As an example, assume that a middle school survey has found that eighth grade students express anxiety about moving to the ninth grade, housed in the senior high school. The goals, objectives and strategies planned by the Advisory Committee of this middle school might look like this:

Goal: Students will be successful in high school.
Objectives: Students will:

1. *Learn about senior high-school courses, credit requirements, schedules, and ninth-grade regulations*
2. *Know their way around the senior high school and become familiar with different services that are available to them*

Strategies	Assignment	Time-line
1. Each eighth grade student will be given a orientation brochure to be discussed in Advisor-Advisee sessions.	Teacher-Advisors	By January 1st
2. Each eighth grader will write an essay about his or her expectations of high school.	Language Arts Teachers	By April 1st
3. Each eighth grader will have a group session with a counselor to discuss special concerns regarding high school.	Counselors	By April 30th
4. Eighth graders will visit the high school for a half-day program to met with ninth-grade teachers and counselors, and to tour the school's facilities.	Principals & Counselors	By May 1st

FORM 2–1   Middle School Students Needs' Assesment

Instructions: Please read the following statements and circle Yes, No, or Sometimes, showing how each one applies to you.

1. I usually do well in school.	YES	NO	SOMETIMES
2. My teachers think I can do better school work.	YES	NO	SOMETIMES
3. I like coming to school.	YES	NO	SOMETIMES
4. I do not have any close friends.	YES	NO	SOMETIMES
5. I want to learn how to study better.	YES	NO	SOMETIMES
6. I am happy about my family life.	YES	NO	SOMETIMES
7. My parents (or guardians) listen to me when I have a problem.	YES	NO	SOMETIMES
8. I would like to talk with someone about a problem I have.	YES	NO	SOMETIMES
9. Most people like me the way I am.	YES	NO	SOMETIMES
10. I am lonely much of the time.	YES	NO	SOMETIMES
11. I want to learn more about jobs and careers.	YES	NO	SOMETIMES
12. I would like to join a group of other students to help them with problems.	YES	NO	SOMETIMES

The above plan to help students address their anxiety about moving to high school includes services and activities provided by a number of people. Teachers who are advisors are actively involved; language arts teachers incorporate learning strategies into their instruction; counselors use group sessions to consult and counsel with students; and the principal and counselors coordinate a orientation trip to the high school.

The above example illustrates how needs' assessments are analyzed and summarized into plans for a counseling program. It also shows that the school counseling program involves the services of many professionals in the school and, as such, is more than individual counseling or classroom guidance provided solely by the school counselor. Rather, it is a myriad of services and activities planned to meet specific goals and objectives and delivered by designated personnel in the school.

Needs' assessments can be done by using methods of data collection other than surveys. For example, counselors might interview students, parents, and teachers, or they might simply observe in the school and community and draw conclusions from these observations. Also, student records can be reviewed as another method of assessment. In comprehensive school

FORM 2–2 Elementary School Parents Needs' Assessment

Instructions: Please help us plan this year's school counseling program by completing the following questions. Return this form with your child who will give it to the teacher. Thank you for your assistance.

Circle your responses:

1. My child likes going to school most of the time.	YES	NO	UNSURE
2. My child has many friends at school.	YES	NO	UNSURE
3. The school is a warm and caring place to be.	YES	NO	UNSURE
4. My child needs special attention for learning.	YES	NO	UNSURE
5. My child is responsible at home and usually does what he/she is told.	YES	NO	UNSURE
6. I would like my child to be in a group with other children to learn about getting along together.	YES	NO	UNSURE
7. I am worried about my child's progress in school and would like to talk with someone about it.	YES	NO	UNSURE
8. I would like to join other parents in a group to talk about children and parenting skills.	YES	NO	UNSURE
9. My child has physical problems that the school should know about.	YES	NO	UNSURE
10. I want my child to see the school counselor.			
11. I have some concerns I would like to share with the school counselor.	YES	NO	UNSURE
12. I am available to volunteer at school if needed.	YES	NO	UNSURE

counseling programs, counselors use a variety of methods and alter these approaches year after year to assure an accurate assessment of their schools' needs. In some instances, counselors might use the results of their annual program evaluation as an assessment procedure. Program evaluation is presented in a later section of this chapter.

Once the needs' assessment is complete, the school counselor determines available resources in order to suggest appropriate services for meeting selected goals. Determining available resources is another aspect of planning and organizing comprehensive counseling programs.

FORM 2–3   High School Teachers Needs' Assessment

Instructions: Please help us plan the School Counseling Program this year by completing this needs' assessment form. Circle your responses and return the form in the school counselor's mail box in the office. Thank your for your input.

1. I want my student's to have access to group counseling this year.	YES	NO	UNSURE
2. I want students to receive more career guidance.	YES	NO	UNSURE
3. Students need to learn better study skills.	YES	NO	UNSURE
4. Many of my students have concerns about substance and alcohol abuse.	YES	NO	UNSURE
5. We need to do more about pregnancy prevention this year.	YES	NO	UNSURE
6. I want to help integrate guidance into my lessons.	YES	NO	UNSURE
7. I want to join a teacher support group this year.	YES	NO	UNSURE
8. I have students who seem quite depressed.	YES	NO	UNSURE
9. Some students need help handling problems without resorting to violence.	YES	NO	UNSURE
10. I have difficulty getting support from parents.	YES	NO	UNSURE
11. I need better communication skills with students.	YES	NO	UNSURE
12. I need help with class management skills.	YES	NO	UNSURE

Determining Resources

Comprehensive school programs cannot operate in isolation. For this reason, school counselors learn about the various resources and support services available in their schools, districts, and communities. When speaking of resources for a school counseling program, we usually refer to people as the primary resource. A comprehensive program also benefits from the materials, equipment, and space available to the counselor, but without adequate human support all these other elements will make little difference.

School counselors who have successful comprehensive programs are adept at learning about the talents of their teaching colleagues and are creative in soliciting support from other personnel. They recruit capable volunteers for the school, generate support from businesses and industries who donate money and materials to the program, use student helpers to network with their peers, and cooperate with other student services team members, such as school nurses, social workers, and school psychologists. In addition, counselors learn about the services and resources of the communities and states in which their schools reside. By knowing about health services, psychiatric treatment centers, family counseling clinics, recreational programs, and other resources, counselors create professional alliances that benefit students and families of the school. Without this knowledge, counselors run the risk of working in a vacuum and becoming frustrated and overwhelmed by the level of need expressed by students, parents, and teachers.

Comprehensive programs also consist of adequate materials, equipment, and space to do the job. In counseling, adequate and appropriate materials are determined by the developmental needs of students in the school. Games, educational kits, films, recordings, catalogues, books, and a variety of other items are used by elementary, middle, and senior high counselors depending on the focuses of their programs. By the same token, equipment demands run the gamut of typewriters, computers, recorders, telephones, and other machinery to enable counselors and their support staff to provide efficient and effective services. Adequate space for private counseling, individually and in groups, is desirous. Later in this chapter you will learn more about the location, design, materials, and equipment of a school counseling center.

As with developing a comprehensive program, designing an adequate counseling center and choosing appropriate materials for school counseling programs requires input from administrators and teachers. School counselors recognize the importance of collaboration and cooperation in developing successful programs and services and readily seek suggestions from their colleagues.

Seeking Input

The advisory committee of a school counseling program is a vehicle counselors use to obtain input from teachers, administrators, parents, and students about appropriate services and activities (Duncan, 1989). An advisory committee might be appointed by the principal, selected by the counselor, or established by soliciting volunteers. In some schools, the advisory committee could be combined with other teacher committees, such as a child study committee or a student assistance team. Whatever its organization, the advisory committee assists the school counselor in designing needs assessments, selecting annual goals and objectives, planning major school events to focus on student development, and developing program evaluation activities.

Another reason school counselors seek input from teachers is to supplement the findings of the yearly assessment process. Typically, surveys of students, parents, and teachers will discover some critical concerns and needs of students in the school. While these crisis-oriented goals are imperative to address, they do not begin to satisfy the developmental needs of a majority of the students. Preventive and developmental goals broaden the vision of a school counseling program. In this way, counselors do more than repair wounds, mend fences, and solve mysteries. Instead, they do all these things and at the same time, create healthy school climates, enhance human relationships, and develop systems for students to strengthen their self-awareness, motivation, and responsibility.

Counselors use a number of processes and systems for gathering input about their programs. The advisory committee is supplemented by suggestions from school volunteers, ongoing evaluations by administrators and counseling supervisors, informal conversations with students, input from the school nurse, social worker, and psychologist, and ideas learned through professional associations. These avenues for receiving suggestions about how to develop a comprehensive program enable school counselors to focus on the major services they are expected to provide for students, parents, and teachers.

Providing Services

The third phase of a comprehensive program is implementing services, and there are some essential services for which school counselors are uniquely trained. These include counseling, consulting, coordinating, and appraising.

Counseling As noted earlier, counseling services include individual and small group relationships in which counselors help students, parents, or teachers focus on specific concerns, make plans to address these issues, and act on these plans. Counseling in schools covers a wide range of issues and concerns, from peer relationships to suicidal thoughts. Counseling services can address academic areas, personal adjustment, career decisions, and a host of other topics. Generally speaking, school counselors usually offer short-term counseling relationships when dealing with serious and critical concerns. If progress is not noted in these brief relationships, counselors refer students to other professionals such as mental-health counselors, counseling psychologists, or psychiatrists in the community. In many cases, students with normal, developmental concerns will establish relationships with school counselors and continue these helping relationships throughout their school years. In these long-term relationships, different topics and issues are addressed and significant growth and development is observed.

Group counseling is a relatively recent development in the school counseling profession with the literature emphasizing these relationships beginning in the 1960s (Gazda, 1989; Gladding, 1991). In schools, group counseling is an essential service, yet it is often difficult to incorporate due to scheduling problems, lack of suitable space, and misunderstandings about what it is. Group counseling and other group processes will be examined in greater detail in Chapters 3 and 5.

Consulting School counselors assist parents and teachers with many aspects of child development and behavior. In most instances, counselors take the role of a consultant, bringing to the relationship a level of knowledge about human growth and development, needs of children and adolescents, and approaches for assisting people, such as students, in making behavioral changes. Many of the communication skills used in counseling relationships are similar to those found in consulting processes. In fact, some research indicates that the difference between counseling and consulting relationships may lie more in their design and structure than in actual process differences (Schmidt & Osborne, 1981).

Parent education programs and teacher in-service activities are forms of group consultation. School counselors who design comprehensive programs offer these types of services as indirect methods of assisting students with their development. For example, parents who learn behavior management skills or how to structure homework time are better able to support and guide their children in beneficial ways. By the same token, teachers who hear about different learning styles will be better prepared to create appropriate instructional activities for students in their classes.

Consulting services are also used in working with professionals outside the school. Counselors frequently consult with health officials, social services, and other agencies in seeking the most appropriate services for students and families. In forming these consulting relationships, school counselors share their expertise, including student information when it is appropriate to do so, and they learn about the programs and services of the agency from which assistance is sought. Gathering information from agencies, making initial referral contacts, and seeing that the referrals are followed through are processes that relate to another primary service of a school counseling program—coordinating.

Coordinating Because a comprehensive school counseling program consists of several components and activities, to be effective, it must be coordinated efficiently. Some research has shown that school counselors spend a significant portion of their time coordinating events and activities (Kameen, Robinson, & Rotter, 1985). Functions and skills that relate to program coordination include scheduling services, providing clear communication, setting timelines, delegating responsibilities, following up on services and commitments, and time management to name a few. Given this expansive list of functions and skills, it seems appropriate to say that almost every service provided by a school counselor, every activity performed, in some way relates to program coordination.

As seen above, coordinating consists of many skills and processes, which gives it a rather general, perhaps undefineable connotation. While it may have this broad, apparently all-encompassing meaning, coordination is essential to successful programs. If comprehensive school counseling programs include a variety of related services, all these services must be organized to be in harmony with the school's educational program. A counselor who provides effective individual counseling but fails to follow up referrals from teachers and parents will find that his or her services are requested less and less frequently. In contrast, a counselor who accepts referrals, makes prompt contact with students, and provides appropriate feedback to parents and teachers will be appreciated and valued.

Appraising   In offering effective services, school counselors begin by gathering the necessary information to make appropriate and accurate decisions. When students are referred to counselors, a process of assessing the situation, appraising the student, and choosing appropriate services is required. In comprehensive programs, counselors know that all students do not need, and will not necessarily benefit from individual or group counseling. Other services, such as small group guidance, parent education, and teacher in-service programs may be more appropriate in addressing some concerns raised by students, parents, and teachers.

School counselors use many different appraisal methods including observation, interviews, review of records, tests, and inventories. Gathering data from these sources, analyzing it, drawing accurate conclusions, and making recommendations to address the concerns of students and others is an important aspect of effective school counseling. When counselors fail to appraise situations fully and resort to using the same mode of operation regardless of the case at hand, they limit their power as collaborators and restrict the services of their counseling programs. Counselors who perform adequate appraisal, make accurate diagnoses, and select appropriate services win the respect of their colleagues and the people who seek their assistance. This is a hallmark of professional counselors regardless of the settings in which they work.

Scheduling Services

To provide the major services of a comprehensive program, school counselors must gain control of their time, and schedule activities to satisfy the goals and objectives of the program as well as the critical needs of students, parents, and teachers. Having a schedule helps counselors plan and allot time for selected services and at the same time illustrates for everyone in the school the comprehensive nature of the school counseling program.

As specialists who focus on broad areas of student development, school counselors have a unique role. This role distinguishes them in many ways from their teaching colleagues, and one way this difference is illustrated is by how counselors structure their time and establish their schedules. Classroom teachers have schedules set by administrators or by committees of teachers who design curricula, schedule courses, and assign students to classes. A teacher's schedule is therefore consistent from day to day. This may vary from elementary schools where teachers are responsible for the same students all day long, to high schools where teachers maintain identical schedules every day. In elementary and middle schools, for example, teachers have flexibility and control over their schedules because they decide when particular subjects or certain activities will take place. At the senior high level, however, schedules usually tend to be more rigid. In all these settings, school counselors have control of their daily schedules. The degree of control may vary from school to school, depending on administrative policy, but most counselors are able to design programs and establish schedules that reflect desired services and activities. The schedule of a comprehensive school counseling program illustrates its focus on a wide range of preventive, developmental, and remedial issues.

School counselors seek input from teachers and administrators in establishing their schedules so that the counseling services complement rather than interfere with the instruction of students. By collaborating with teachers, counselors are better able to determine when are the best times to schedule individual counseling, group sessions, classroom presentations, parent education programs, and other activities of their programs. Many counselors post their schedules, weekly or monthly as the case may be, to announce services and let people see how they are spending their time.

By seeking input from others, establishing schedules that fit the instructional program, and posting their schedules for others to see, school counselors accomplish several important goals. First, they demonstrate that the most important function of the school is to educate children and adolescents, and programs such as school counseling should enhance this process. When school counseling services and activities detract from student-teacher relationships or impede student learning, they contradict the purpose of a comprehensive counseling program. Second, collaboration and cooperation with teachers place counselors in the visible role of letting people know what services are offered and when they are being implemented. Such visibility eliminates doubt and confusion about the role of a school counselor. And lastly, by seeking input and establishing visible schedules, school counselors demonstrate that the services they offer are essential to the development of all students and are an integral part of the school.

Input from teachers and administrators in designing and scheduling a school counselor program also contributes to the annual evaluation of the services offered. In comprehensive school counseling programs, evaluation is a final element that helps define the program, establish its credibility, and demonstrate the important role that counselors play in the school.

Evaluating Results

Accurate assessment, as seen earlier, is important to establishing desirous school counseling services. By the same token, adequate evaluation is essential in determining the value of the services counselors have rendered. School counselors who design and follow through with reasonable evaluation processes are considered valuable members of their school staffs. Chapter 10 of this text describes evaluation procedures in detail, so here we outline only a few important elements of evaluation.

A successful school counseling program is one that demonstrates results. By this I mean that students who seek and receive counseling services are able to improve school performance, increase social skills, make sound educational and career decisions, or realize other identified goals. At the same time, all students in the school benefit form the counselor's presence by information received or through instruction about developmental needs. Teachers and parents benefit from consulting services as demonstrated by their increased knowledge of child and adolescent behavior and higher level communication skills for improving listening and teaching processes.

Evaluation in school counseling is both an ongoing process of collecting data from students, parents, and teachers to assess services and activities and an annual process of gathering reactions and opinions regarding the counseling program as a whole. Counselors who design ongoing and annual evaluation processes demonstrate their effectiveness, alter services that are not achieving desired results, and continuously assess the direction of their programs. In addition to the input from students, parents, and teachers, school counselors also use self-assessment procedures, such as those designed by the American School Counselor Association (1986, 1990a, 1990b), and work with their principal or other school system evaluators to design appropriate and accurate annual performance appraisal systems (Schmidt, 1990).

Through evaluation procedures, school counselors select appropriate and effective services to meet the needs of students, parents, and teachers. This is what is meant by counselor accountability; the ability to show what services are being offered and the difference these services make in lives of people. Counselor accountability has long been an important professional issue (Crabbs & Crabbs, 1977; Krumboltz, 1974; Schmidt, 1986; Wheeler & Loesch, 1981). Without demonstrating positive results, counselors are unable to substantiate their essential role and value in the school. Simply "being there" is not sufficient to warrant the cost of developing and staffing a school counseling program. Today's counselors must show that the services they provide help the school reach its educational mission.

As indicated earlier, adequate evaluation enables the counselor and school to return to the assessed needs of students, parents, and teachers and the overall goals of the school counseling program. In this cyclical process, renewed planning, organizing, and implementing of services continues. Gibson and Mitchell (1990) outlined four procedures of evaluation to facilitate this ongoing cycle. They included: (1) identifying the goals to be evaluated; (2) developing a clear evaluation plan; (3) implementing the evaluation plan; and (4) using the findings of the evaluation process. In a comprehensive school counseling program, these procedures are coordinated by the counselor in cooperation with the school principal, the advisory committee, and the supervisor of counseling services.

All the preceding components and aspects of a comprehensive program contribute to the development and implementation of successful services. Each will be described in greater detail in later chapters of this book. In addition to these aspects, a comprehensive program has adequate facilities and resources to carry out the services that are planned. In the next section, we will examine some of these physical aspects of a school counseling program.

Facilities and Resources

As with other institutions, schools consist of more than philosophies, programs, and services. They are also buildings, materials, equipment, finances, personnel, and other vital items that enable them to perform their educational function. As part of this function, school counseling programs also have physical needs of their own. One such need is to have sufficient physical space to provide individual and small group counseling.

The Counseling Center

To adequately provide confidential counseling and consulting services for students, parents, and teachers, counselors need appropriate space within the school setting. A counseling center usually reflects the level and nature of the school counseling program. Centers in elementary schools, middle schools, and high schools vary due to the development needs of students, the size of the schools, and the types of activities selected for programs in those schools. All these factors influence the design of a counseling center.

Design   Many elementary schools were built before elementary counseling existed. As a result, elementary counselors often work in facilities that were once classrooms, health offices, administrative offices, or used for other purposes. Some elementary counselors serve more than one school, and in these situations they share space with other itinerant personnel such as speech therapists, school nurses, or special education teachers. These are not the best arrangements in which to develop comprehensive programs, but many counselors are able to create exceptional programs even in the most difficult circumstances.

Ideally, an elementary school counseling center includes a private office for confidential sessions with students, parents, teachers, and others, with an adjoining, larger room for group sessions, play activities, and other services. This larger room might include tables and chairs, shelves for storing games, books, and other materials, a sink for cleaning up after playing with paint, clay or similar media, and a computer center for self-awareness inventories and problem-solving questionnaires.

In middle schools, counseling centers consist of one or more counselor's offices and a larger outer space for students to use books, computers, games, and other materials for self-instruction. In some instances, middle schools have a secretary assigned to the counseling program and a reception area in the center. Also, counselors have access to a conference room for holding small group sessions with students, parents, and teachers. Because space in schools is usually at a premium, conference rooms are generally shared with administrators and teachers and scheduling their use must be carefully coordinated.

Senior high-school counseling centers are similar to middle-school designs except that in large high schools there are more offices for counselors, and space may be designated for career materials and equipment. Senior high counseling centers usually store and display career and college materials in an area where students can have ready access to this information. In some centers, computer terminals are available to students who want to search for career and college information. Senior high counselors also have access to one or more conference rooms that are used for small groups, testing, departmental meetings, and other activities.

Student records should be accessible to all teachers and counselors in a school. In past years, cumulative student records were frequently filed in the counseling center. While this seems a logical procedure, it also has negative aspects. For one, teachers may not have easy access to student records when folders are locked in a counselor's office and the counselor is in conference or in a classroom doing a presentation. Furthermore, having student records in the counseling center perpetuates the "guidance image" of the 1940s and 1950s; the image of being a keeper of the vault and manager of all records. In elementary and middle schools, student records should be filed in the administrative offices where all appropriate school personnel can have adequate access. In high schools, where counselors may need more frequent access to student folders, a separate file room near the counseling center is recommended so that teachers can obtain student information without interrupting the services of the counseling program.

Figures 2–2, 2–3, and 2–4 illustrate counseling centers at the elementary,- middle-, and high-school levels respectively. These illustrations are samples of what school counseling centers might look like, and by no means are intended as ideal designs.

Location   Equally important to the design of a school counseling center is its location. In elementary schools, for example, if the center is located at one end of a sprawling complex away from very young children, the counselor will not be readily available to these students. Counseling centers should be located so that everyone in the school has equal access. Generally speaking this means being in a central location. Historically, the counseling office was located near the school's administration suite. While this had some advantage in terms of communication between counselors and administrators, it was sometimes a handicap because students and teachers tended to associate counselors with the administration. This association did not always enhance the image of school counselors as advocates for all students.

The location of a counseling center should enhance its visibility, facilitate communication between all groups in the school, and invite people to enter and use its facilities (Purkey & Schmidt, 1987). A location that accomplishes these goals places the school counselor in an optimal position to create and deliver beneficial services to a wide audience. In this way, everyone in the school is included in the counseling program.

Materials and Equipment   A well-designed and optimally located counseling center is complete when it includes appropriate and adequate materials and equipment to deliver intended services. In elementary centers, these materials include games and toys to use in play therapy and for establishing rapport with children. Art media, computer assisted programs, games, developmental learning kits, filmstrips, puppets, and a variety of other items are used to help children express themselves, experience success, and learn social skills in a safe, non-threatening setting.

Middle-school centers have similar materials, only they are geared for pre-adolescents. In addition, career exploration materials, self-development resources, and high-school information are included. For example, books in a middle-school counseling center are available to help students address developmental needs such as adjusting to their physical changes, handling peer pressure, and preventing substance abuse.

High-school centers typically have a stronger focus on career choice materials, college catalogues, test-taking skills packages, assessment inven-

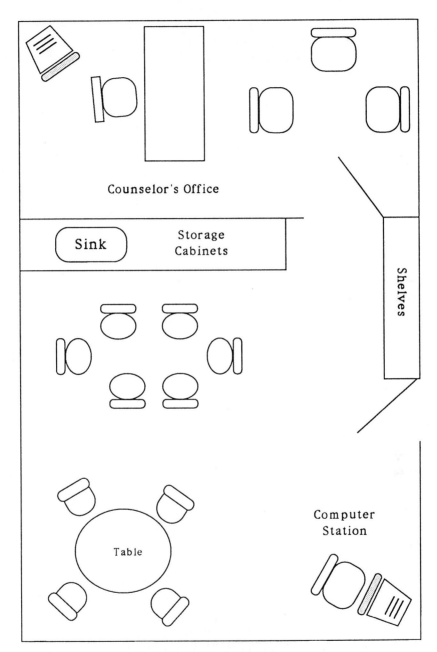

Counselor's Office

Sink

Storage Cabinets

Shelves

Table

Computer Station

FIGURE 2–2   Elementary School Counseling Center

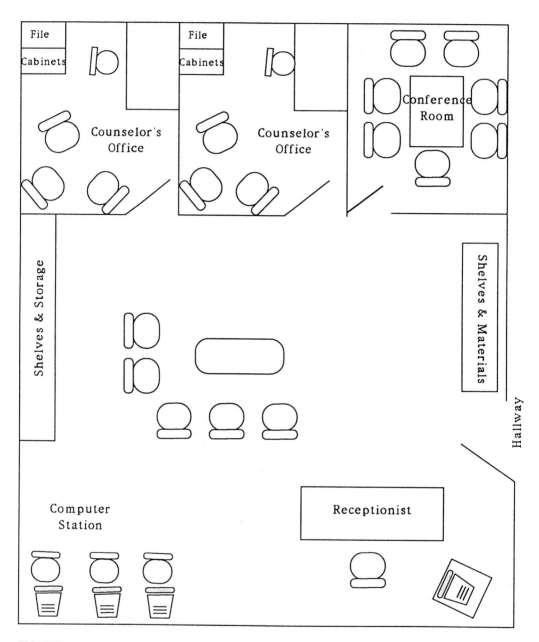

FIGURE 2–3 Middle School Counseling Center

tories, as well as substance abuse, pregnancy, and similar materials that address critical health and social issues. As with materials in elementary- and middle-school centers, information in high-school programs is up-to-date and developmentally appropriate for students.

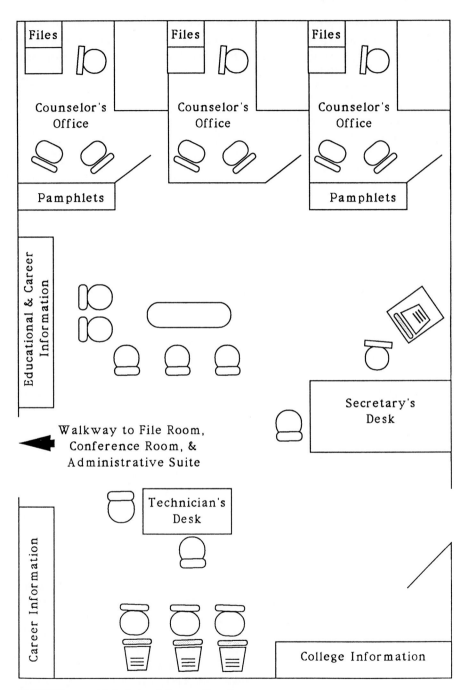

FIGURE 2–4   High School Counseling Center

In addition to counseling and guidance materials, a school counseling center is adequately furnished with appropriate-size tables and chairs and equipment to use with selected filmstrips, videos, computer programs, and other media. All this equipment might not be stored in the counseling center, but school counselors and teachers have access to these supplies and apparatus through the media centers in their schools. Elementary counseling centers should have tables and chairs for both young children and adults because these are the populations served. All counselors should have a telephone with a private line for consultations and referrals. Other equipment might include file cabinets, projectors, audio and video players, computers, and typewriters. In sum, school counseling centers typically have:

- Appropriate and sufficient furnishings for students and adults
- Audio and visual privacy for counselors' offices
- Tables for group activities and conferences
- A telephone for each counselor
- A storage area for materials and equipment
- Computers for self-instruction and guidance related programs
- Access to a conference room
- A waiting area or activity area outside the counselor's office(s)
- A secure room where student records can be stored away from the counseling center so appropriate personnel can have adequate access

Budget   Materials and equipment need to be assessed annually as do other aspects of the counseling program. As items become worn or out-dated, they are replaced. To do so, counselors control a budget or have input into a budgeting process.

Table 2–1 illustrates items found in a budget for a school counseling program. Usually, individual school counselors will not have much input regarding personnel positions and costs, but they should be involved in decisions about other budget categories such as materials, equipment, and professional development.

Most school counselors will not have substantial budgets with which to operate their programs. Typically, counselors are allotted a small budget to purchase disposable materials during the year. In some school systems, counselors are supervised by a central office coordinator who is trained in counseling and this person is allotted a systemwide budget to help counselors purchase new materials and equipment. Innovative and creative counselors find ways to develop materials and locate resources to supplement funds provided by the school and system. As with their teaching colleagues, many school counselors discover that homemade materials and their own personal funds are needed to sustain the program due to limited local, state, and federal revenues.

TABLE 2–1   Budget Items for a School Counseling Program

I. Personnel
    1. School Counselors
    2. Clerical Assistants
    3. Technical Assistants
II. Furnishings and Equipment
    1. Desks/Chairs
    2. Tables/Chairs
    3. Cabinets and Other Office Furnishings
    4. Media Euipment
    5. Maintenance Contracts
III. Materials
    1. Books and Reference Materials
    2. Subscriptions
    3. Games, Toys, Puppets, etc.
    4. Media Equipment
    5. Test and Inventories
    6. Educational Kits
    7. Computer Programs
    8. Career Decision-Making and Educational Materials
IV. Center Supplies
    1. Paper, Pencils, Tape, etc.
    2. Crayons, Paint, Markers, etc.
    3. Computer Disks
    4. Miscellaneous
V. Communications and Travel
    1. Telephone
    2. Postage
    3. Travel (School to School and Professional Meetings)
VI. Professional Development
    1. Conferences, Meetings, Seminars, Course Work
    2. Research

Commercially produced kits, tests, inventories, films, games, and other products are available for counselors to use in delivering appropriate services. Because of the expense of these items, new counselors find it is best to contact experienced counselors to find out what has been tried and what has been successful before making major purchases. In some school systems, counselors share materials to avoid duplicating unnecessary purchases. These and other ideas can help stretch limited budgets. Gysbers and Henderson (1988) encouraged counselors to tap federal and state resources outside their school systems. Where counselors are supervised by central office coordinators of counseling services, they can request that these supervisors be their contacts with state and federal agencies and seek funds through grants and special projects. Most states continue to have counseling and guidance consultants in their departments of education who are available to assist school systems in applying for federal and states monies.

Generally, these funds are intended to focus on special topics or issues such as career development, substance abuse, teen pregnancy, and other concerns addressed by school counseling services.

Personnel

While facilities, materials, equipment, and finances provide the physical structure and set fiscal limits for school counseling programs, it is the people in the program who determine its true value and potential. Comprehensive counseling programs include roles for administrators, teachers, other student services specialists, student helpers, volunteers, and, of course, counselors. In addition, these programs use support staff, especially secretaries and other clerical assistants. Some high schools hire technical assistants who specialize in information management, computer scheduling, and similar services. These assistants allow counselors and teachers more time to perform the professional functions for which they were trained and hired. All these personnel contribute to the comprehensive nature of a counseling program, beginning with school counselors.

Counselors The number of counselors hired in a school counseling program makes a difference in the quantity and quality of services offered. Usually schools hire enough counselors to meet counselor to student ratios recommended by professional associations and accrediting organizations. While these groups do not always have consistent guidelines for schools to follow, recommended ratios generally suggest one counselor for every 300–500 students enrolled, depending on the level of the school. Professional associations, such as the American School Counselor Association, tend to recommend lower ratios than do regional and state accreditation bodies.

While it is helpful to have sufficient numbers of trained counselors, the numbers themselves do not supplant the need for a well-planned program of comprehensive services. Regardless of the number of counselors employed or the ratio of students to counselors, the success of a school counseling program is dependent on the overall design of the program, the goals and objectives selected, and the way counselors spend their time serving students, parents, and teachers. Some schools are blessed with an ample number of qualified counselors, yet they fail to meet the needs of students because little effort is made to do an adequate assessment, seek input from teachers, schedule appropriate services, and evaluate their results. At the same time, some comprehensive programs are designed with limited resources and few personnel. Counselors in these poorly funded programs plan, implement, and evaluate to the best of their ability, and usually are successful in meeting the needs of many students.

Clerical Assistants Schools receive and generate a large amount of paperwork. Sending communications to homes and other agencies, updating student records, filing report cards, preparing local, state, and federal reports, and doing a host of other paper processes contribute to a school's clerical demands. School counselors are not exempt from this burden. To help counselors, teachers, and other education professionals perform their designated duties in a timely fashion, schools need adequate clerical staff. Excellent secretaries and technical assistants are indispensable in today's schools, and this is true for school counseling centers as well.

In elementary and middle schools, counselors do not typically have the amount of paperwork found in secondary schools. But *any* significant clerical tasks that remove elementary- and middle-school counselors from the essential functions of providing direct services to students, parents, and teachers should be eliminated or reassigned. To assign counselors these types of activities is not cost effective and is a misuse of school personnel.

In high schools, counselors usually work more closely with student records, transcripts, and similar items. A secretary placed in the counseling center is essential, and, in large schools, a technical assistant to do data input and analysis is equally important. These professionals are an integral part of a secondary school's counseling center, advising counselors on efficient ways to handle data, handling the flow of communication, scheduling appointments, ordering materials, entering schedule changes, and managing the budget. In some instances these services might be handled by paraprofessionals or volunteers who assist in the counseling program.

Paraprofessionals and Volunteers Paraprofessionals and persons who have some training in human services and can assist counselors with academic advising, career information, and other initial relationships. These assistants can also perform clerical tasks as the need arises, as can volunteers in the school.

Volunteers offer valuable assistance and time to support many services including those of a school counseling program. Parents, grandparents, guardians, retired citizens, and other people offer a large pool of available volunteers. Some ways that school counselors use volunteers are as tutors to help students receive additional individual help, guidance assistants to assist with information in the counseling center, and clerical assistants to help secretaries keep up with communications, filing, and other responsibilities.

In all cases where schools and school counselors elect to use paraprofessionals and volunteers, adequate training and orientation to the counseling program is necessary. School counselors who accept the services of these people must take time to train them in the nature and purpose of the counseling program. In addition, counselors ensure that these paraprofessionals and volunteers have basic communication and helping skills that complement the services of the counseling program, accept the limits of their role, and understand the roles of counselors and other staff members in the school.

A comprehensive school counseling program, as defined and described in this chapter, includes a broad focus on student development goals and objectives, which are selected through a process of needs assessments and input from administrators, teachers and other school personnel. In addition, a comprehensive program is complemented by physical facilities, materials, personnel, and funds to carry out its overall purpose. Within a comprehensive program there are essential services that define and describe the role and functions of a professional school counselor. The next chapter introduces and examines these essential services in greater detail.

Selected Readings

Gysbers, N. C., & Henderson, P (1988). *Developing and Managing your School Guidance Program* (Alexandria, VA: American Association for Counseling and Development). This is a comprehensive, clearly written book that charts the history of the school counseling profession and guides the reader through practical ideas and suggestions for developing a contemporary school counseling program. It contains many useful strategies for establishing comprehensive programs and services.

Myrick, R. D. (1987). *Developmental Guidance and Counseling: A Practical Approach* (Minneapolis, MN: Educational Media Corporation). Myrick's popular book offers a developmental perspective on comprehensive counseling programs. The book has a practical tone with each chapter containing a section on "Helpful Hints."

Hitchner, K. W., Tifft-Hitchner, A. (1987). *A Survival Guide for the Secondary School Counselor* (West Nyack, NY: The Center for Applied Research in Education, Inc). This book is a practical guide for secondary counselors to design a comprehensive program of services. It provides a structure for developing an identity as a junior or senior high-school counselor, and offers useable ideas and strategies to address a range of issues with students, parents, and teachers.

Schmidt, J. J. (1991). *A Survival Guide for the Elementary/Middle School Counselor.* Englewood Cliffs, NJ: Prentice Hall. This book is a guide for elementary- and middle-school counselors to help them establish comprehensive programs, develop effective services, and evaluate their performance. It encourages counselors to look beyond their immediate survival and design programs in which they can flourish as professional helpers.

References

American School Counselor Association. (1986). *Professional Development Guidelines for Secondary School Counselors: A Self-Audit* (Alexandria, VA: Author).

American School Counselor Association. (1990a). *Professional Development Guidelines for Middle/Junior High School Counselors: A Self-Audit* (Alexandria, VA: Author).

American School Counselor Association. (1990b). *Professional Development Guidelines for Elementary School Counselors: A Self-Audit* (Alexandria, VA: Author).

Aubrey, R. F. (1982), "A House Divided: Guidance and Counseling in 20th century America," *Personnel and Guidance Journal, 61*, 198–204.

Crabbs, S. K., & Crabbs, M. A. (1977), "Accountability: Who Does What to Whom, When, Where, and How?" *The School Counselor, 25*, 104–109.

Dinkmeyer, D., Dinkmeyer, D., Jr., & Sperry, L. (1987). *Adlerian Counseling and Psychotherapy*, 2nd ed. (Columbus, Oh: Merrill).

Dinkmeyer, D. C., & McKay, G. D. (1976). *Systematic Training for Effective Parenting* (Circle Pines, MN: American Guidance Services).

Downing, C. J. (1977), "Teaching Children Behavior Change Techniques," *Elementary School Guidance & Counseling, 11*, 277–283.

Duncan, J. A. (1989), "The School Guidance Committee: The Counselor's Support Group," *The School Counselor, 36*, 192–197.

Edmonds, R. R. (1979), "Effective Schools for the Urban Poor," *Educational Leadership, 37*, 15–24.

Gazda, G. M. (1989). *Group Counseling: A Developmental Approach*, 4th ed. (Boston: Allyn and Bacon).

Gerler, E. R. (1985), "Elementary School Counseling Research and the Classroom Learning Environment," *Elementary School Guidance and Counseling, 20*, 39–48.

Gibson, R. L., & Mitchell, M. H. (1990). *Introduction to Guidance and Counseling*, 3rd ed. (New York: Macmillan).

Gladding, S. T. (1991). *Group Work: A Counseling Specialty* (New York: Macmillan).

Gysbers, N. C. (1984). *Designing Careers: Counseling to Enhance Education, Work, and Leisure* (San Francisco: Jossey-Bass).

Gysbers, N. C., & Henderson, P. (1988). *Developing and Managing your School Guidance Program* (Alexandria, VA: American Association for Counseling and Development).

Hitchner, K. W., & Tifft-Hitchner, A. (1987). *A Survival Guide for the Secondary School Counselor* (West Nyack, NY: The Center for Applied Research in Education).

Hutchins, D. E., & Cole, C. G. (1977), "A Model for Improving Middle School Students' Interpersonal Relationships," *The School Counselor, 25*, 134–136.

Kameen, M. C., Robinson, E. H., & Rotter, J. C. (1985), "Coordination Activities: A Study of Perceptions of Elementary and Middle School Counselors," *Elementary School Guidance and Counseling, 20*, 97–104.

Krumboltz, J. D. (1974), "An Accountability Model for Counselors," *Personnel and Guidance Journal, 52*, 639–646.

Matthews, D. B. (1986), "Discipline: Can It Be Improved with Relaxation Training?" *Elementary School Guidance & Counseling, 18*, 194–199.

Meeks, A. R. (1968). *Guidance in Elementary Education* (New York: The Ronald Press).

Myrick, R. D., & Myrick, L. S. (1990). *The Teacher Advisor Program: An Innovative Approach to School Guidance* (Ann Arbor, MI: ERIC/CAPS).

Popkin, M. H. (1983). *Active Parenting Videorecording* (Atlanta: Active Parenting, Inc).

Purkey, W. W., & Schmidt, J. J. (1987). *The Inviting Relationship: A Expanded Perspective for Professional Counseling* (Englewood Cliffs, NJ: Prentice Hall).

Schmidt, J. J. (1986), "Becoming an "Able" Counselor," *Elementary School Guidance and Counseling, 21*, 16–22.

Schmidt, J. J. (1990), "Critical Issues for Counselor Performance Appraisal and Supervision," *The School Counselor, 38*, 86–94.

Schmidt, J. J. (1991). *A Survival Guide for the Elementary/Middle School Counselor* (West Nyack, NY: The Center for Applied Research in Education).

Schmidt, J. J., & Osborne, W. L. (1981), "Counseling and Consulting: Separate Processes or the Same?" *Personnel and Guidance Journal, 60,* 168–171.

Sprinthall, N. A. (1971), *Guidance for Human Growth* (New York: Van Nostrand Reinhold).

Warren, R., Smith, G., & Velten, E. (1984), "Rational-Emotive Therapy and the Reduction of Interpersonal Anxiety in Junior High School Students," *Adolescence, 19,* 893–902.

Wheeler, P. T., & Loesch, L. (1981), "Program Evaluation and Counseling: Yesterday, Today and Tomorrow," *Personnel and Guidance Journal, 59,* 573–578.

Wilson, N. S. (1986), "Effects of a Classroom Guidance Unit on Sixth Graders' Examination Performance," *Journal of Humanistic Education and Development, 25,* 70–79.

3

Essential Program Services

Originally, school counseling programs focused primarily on individual student development and offered services that typically emphasized one-to-one relationships. These traditional programs were established by counselors without much input from teachers, administrators, or other professionals. Since many were begun at the senior high-school level, these programs also were heavily weighted with administrative and clerical tasks, such as scheduling students in classes, managing cumulative files, and recording grades on transcripts. With the expansion of school counseling into middle and elementary schools, and the call for counselors to be accountable for services provided to students, parents, and teachers, contemporary school counseling began to accept a wider focus for program development (Gysbers & Henderson, 1988).

In Chapter 1, you learned that a comprehensive school counseling program consists of a wide range of services to address students, parents, and teachers' needs. The position taken here is that contemporary school counseling services are essential to a school's educational mission. In this chapter, you will see how these essential services, individually and in combination with one another, create the structure of a comprehensive school counseling program. In doing so, they illustrate how today's school counselors have moved from an emphasis on one-to-one services for students to programs that advocate group processes as well as individual counseling to serve a wider audience of clients. Today's school counselor embraces a role that requires direct services to students, parents, and teachers as opposed to one comprised mostly of administrative and clerical tasks.

As noted in Chapter 2, a school counseling program consists of four major areas of service including counseling, consulting, coordinating, and appraising, and they are defined and described by specific activities that compose each of these areas. In this chapter, we will explore each of these services and their unique contributions to school counseling programs. This is a broad overview of how counselors integrate these essential services into a comprehensive program. Later in Chapters 4 through 7, these essential services will be described individually in greater detail. To begin, let us describe the area and activities known as counseling.

Counseling

In helping students, parents, and teachers collect information, explore options, and make appropriate decisions, school counselors use processes and skills commonly referred to as counseling. As a helping process, counseling has been described and defined in numerous texts, articles, and other sources. Over the years, many definitions of counseling have been written with as many differences as there are similarities among them. In addition, counselors have tried to distinguish counseling processes from other therapeutic relationships, such as psychotherapy (Shilling, 1984). Some theorists and practitioners believe that these efforts are fruitless because the two processes are the same, while others insist that psychotherapy is much more intense, in-depth, and long-term than counseling. As George and Cristiani (1981) stated, "Indeed, efforts to distinguish between the two have not met with universal approval" (p. 3).

Our purpose here is not to continue this debate. Instead, it is to focus on what counseling is as a helping process and how this process is used in schools by elementary, middle, and senior high counselors with students, parents, and teachers. Chapters 4 and 5 of this text explain the processes of individual and group counseling more thoroughly. For now, we will begin with a brief description of individual counseling.

Individual Counseling

School counselors spend a significant amount of time working with individuals to help them focus on particular concerns and make decisions about their future goals, current relationships, and self-directions. In many instances, these helping relationships are defined as counseling because they are confidential, ongoing processes that consist of specific stages or phases. These relationships are founded on particular theoretical models of counseling, and they require a high level of helping skills. Not all individual contacts are categorized as counseling. Some are informational meetings where counselors share data, materials, and other information to help people make educational, career, and other types of decisions. These relationships, as we will see later, are more accurately defined as consultations.

Usually, individual counseling relies on verbal interactions between counselors and counselees (also called clients). In these relationships, the counselee raises a concern or question that is bothersome or problematic. While individual counseling can have a developmental focus by looking toward future plans and goals, it most often has a remedial purpose. The counselee seeks assistance with clarifying a particular concern, exploring options to resolve this issue, deciding on a plan or strategy, and being successful in remedying the situation. Because these relationships rely to a great extent on verbal skills and abilities of both the counselee and the counselor, they are not an appropriate service for everyone in every situation. For example, young elementary school children with limited verbal skills probably would not benefit solely from talking relationships as used in individual counseling.

In cases where children have limited verbal ability, counselors may use individual relationships, but the goals of these sessions are primarily to build rapport with the child and gather information through observation and play. Such information helps counselors make decisions about appropriate services to assist children, parents, and teachers with identified concerns. Sometimes, individual counseling relationships that rely heavily on nonverbal interactions, play therapy, and modeling techniques with young children can be successful and elementary school counselors find that their time is well spent in these instances. More often, however, a child who lacks the verbal skills to interact successfully in individual counseling also lacks other developmental abilities that will contribute to a successful counseling relationship.

Behavioral and cognitive development are two other areas that complement a counselee's verbal skills to make individual counseling successful (Thompson & Rudolph, 1988). Clients, who are unable to attend for any length of time or cannot focus on one issue at a time, usually need to acquire these behavioral skills before individual counseling can be successful. At the same time, if clients do not understand the relationship between their behaviors and successful development, or cannot comprehend concepts such as responsibility, self-determination, and acceptance, it is unlikely they will benefit from individual counseling as defined here.

In schools where counselors are responsible for a large number of students, the decision of whether or not to use individual counseling is also related to the time they have available. Typically, individual counseling sessions last from twenty minutes to an hour, depending on the age and developmental level of the counselee. If a large percentage of students in the school receive individual services, this would be a substantial investment of time and would reduce the time available to provide other services for students, and parents and teachers. For this reason, school counselors supplement individual counseling services by forming groups to meet the needs of more students.

Group Counseling

Gazda (1989) and other authorities have pointed out that the origins of group counseling are uncertain. Most likely its earliest beginnings in schools were in the form of *group guidance,* instructional and informational services to assist with student development. Allen (1931) is credited for the earliest use of the term *group counseling,* but his description of the process was closer to what today we know as group guidance (Gazda, 1989). In the late 1950s and early 1960s, descriptions of group counseling were more frequent in the counseling literature and during this time, group guidance seemed to lose status, particularly in the schools. In the late 1960s, the popularity of group counseling continued to grow with the publication of several major textbooks fully devoted to this helping process. Today, as we will see in Chapter 5, group procedures used in schools include both counseling and guidance, and each has a particular focus and purpose in comprehensive school counseling programs.

Group counseling is typically formed by having a few students meet on a regular basis in confidential sessions to help them handle specific concerns or support each other with particular developmental goals. In these sessions, the counselor is the leader who facilitates discussions, supports all group members, and gives direction to the process. Group counseling can take different forms and requires careful planning so it complements other services in a comprehensive program.

Groups are used by school counselors to address a wide array of preventive, developmental, and remedial issues. There are also many ways that counselors form groups, choose group members, and structure group processes. Sometimes counselors form groups because certain students have similar needs, and they believe that, by asking students in groups to share these mutual concerns with each other, they will benefit more from groups than through individual sessions. For instance, a middle-school counselor might have several students referred by their parents because of family divorces. After interviewing each of the students, the counselor invites them to join together and form a group to work through their feelings and support each other during this crisis in their lives. By forming groups in this way, counselors use common concerns as a basis for counseling, solicit the support and assistance of each group member, ask members to focus on their major concerns, and thereby use time more efficiently to reach a greater number of students.

While group counseling remains prominent in counseling literature, many counselors resist using this service in their schools. In part this resistance is due to the difficulty of scheduling group sessions, especially in secondary schools designed with tight class schedules. Teachers are often protective of their instructional time with students, and counselors struggle to create workable group schedules that interfere minimally with class time. In comprehensive school counseling programs, group counseling is an essential service, and to include it counselors seek input from teachers and administrators to design reasonable schedules so group sessions can be held without significant disruption to the instructional program. In Chapter 5, you will review some practical scheduling strategies used by school counselors.

Student Counseling

Of the three populations served in the school counseling program, students are the primary target group. Because students are challenged by critical issues affecting their personal, social, educational, and career development, it is essential that counselors schedule time for individual and group counseling relationships. With the ever-changing structure of the American family and the need for parents to be out of the home to increase family incomes, many children and adolescents need someone with whom they can share concerns and receive accurate information to make appropriate decisions. To be most effective, these critical helping relationships, should be private and individual in nature. Other times, students may be comfortable sharing concerns with a few other students, but they still will want these discussions to remain private, and this is why group counseling is appropriate in school settings.

Because comprehensive school counseling programs have a broad focus and attempt to serve a wide range of student needs, counselors try to keep their counseling relationships brief. For this reason, school counselors rely on other mental health professionals, public service agencies, and private practitioners who serve as referral resources for students and families in need. The decision of when to refer a student is guided by asking questions such as:

1. Is sufficient progress being made with the student in the current helping relationship?
2. Does the school counselor have adequate training and knowledge in the area of concern to assist this student?
3. Is there a more appropriate source to whom this student could be referred?

4. Are other services in the counseling program being neglected due to time being devoted to this relationship?

These and other questions guide counselors in all educational and clinical settings in making decisions about whom to counsel and for how long? Similar questions also guide counselors when they receive requests from parents and teachers to participate in counseling for themselves.

Parent and Teacher Counseling

Sometimes school counselors are approached by parents and teachers who begin by sharing concerns about students and end up disclosing personal concerns of their own. At these times, counselors face difficult decisions about how to handle these requests for assistance. The first question counselors ask themselves in situations such as this is: Should I be providing this service in the school counseling program? As noted earlier, students are the primary clients of a school counseling program, so counselors must determine what place, if any, parent or teacher counseling has in the school.

There is not clear consensus among professional school counselors regarding this question. Each situation and each request is unique and, therefore, is difficult to judge according to any single guideline. As a result, school counselors take each situation as it develops and use their best ethical and professional judgment to seek appropriate services for whomever is in need. Again, a series of questions to help counselors make the best decisions includes:

1. Am I qualified to offer the assistance requested by this person?
2. Do any ethical standards guide me in making this decision?
3. Is there another professional or service to whom I should refer this person?
4. Will students benefit if I assist this person?
5. How much time will be invested in helping this person?

Every school counselor at some time or other is approached by a parent or teacher with a request for services. Generally, counselors listen fully to the request, decide what short-term assistance could be provided, and offer to list referral services from which the person can choose to address his or her concerns. In offering service options, counselors usually list more than one choice so that the person has responsibility for selecting one that is most appealing and comfortable. To some extent, this type of helping relationship is a combination of counseling and consulting processes. Consulting is second major function of school counselors that we will now introduce.

Consulting

School counselors frequently receive requests or perceive a need for services that do not require direct counseling, either individually or in a group. At times, counselors are asked to provide information, present instruction, give suggestions for handling situations, and facilitate planning processes. When requests such as these are received, the helping relationship established by counselors is called a consultation.

Consulting is a relatively new function for school counselors, but one that has received considerable attention in recent years (Brown, Pryzwansky, & Schulte, 1991; Ritchie, 1982; Schmidt & Medl, 1983; Umansky & Holloway, 1984). Faust (1968) was one of the first authors to emphasize this role for school counselors. He recommended several types of consultations that could be used in individual and group settings. According to Faust, consulting could take place with students, parents, teachers, student services specialists, administrators, and community agency professionals.

Most commonly, consulting is viewed as a relationship in which two or more people identify a purpose, establish a goal, plan strategies to meet that goal, and assign responsibilities to carry out these strategies. In consulting relationships, one person is the consultant who leads the process and the other person (or persons) is called the consultee(s). In school counseling, the counselor is the consultant and students, teachers, and parents are usually the consultees. The focus of a consultation is a need or situation for which information, instruction, or facilitation is requested by a student, parent, or teacher. For example, a mother may ask a school counselor about her child's progress in school. In the consulting relationship that follows this request, the counselor becomes the consultant, the parent is the consultee, the child's school progress is the situation, and the purpose of the relationship is to receive information. In this case, the consulting relationship is called an informational conference or consultation.

In many respects, the communication skills used in consulting relationships are similar to those found in counseling. Effective listening, facilitating, and decision-making skills are required by both counselors and consultants to help people identify purposes, make plans, and implement strategies. What makes consulting different from counseling are two criteria: (1) Consulting establishes a triangular relationship including the consultant, consultee, and an external situation usually involving a third individual or a group of people; and (2) Consulting services often use indirect helping processes to address an identified situation. In contrast to this second criteria, counseling is a direct service to assist people in achieving self-awareness, focusing on their self-development, or learning new coping behaviors. A more detailed description of consulting skills and processes is given in Chapter 6 of this text.

Another way of understanding how school counselors use consulting functions is to observe the different types of consultations they establish with students, parents, teachers, and others. By using a variety of consulting services, counselors are able to disseminate information, instruct groups, lead teacher-parent conferences, and plan other services to help a large number of students in schools. One of the most frequent types of consulting used by school counselors is information services.

Information Services

School counselors often act as resources of information for students, parents, and teachers. They locate and dispense information to help students make choices about educational, career, and personnel goals. As examples, high school students seek information from counselors to help them select appropriate courses of study in satisfying their educational goals, middle graders ask for information to help them with peer relationships and friendships, and elementary students need to know about the school, its facilities, and its programs. Parents and teachers consult with school counselors about special services to help students, summer programs for learning and development, scholarships and other financial aid for college, and many other reasons. Informational consultations usually address the need students and parents have for community and school resources, career and educational materials, and financial assistance.

Community and School Resources   While schools are primarily responsible for educating children, this developmental process does not take place in isolation. Many factors influence a student's ability to take advantage of a school's instructional program. Physical and medical problems, family concerns, and learning disabilities are among the many issues that influence a child's progress throughout his or her school life.

As a resource in the school, the counselor is available to help parents and teachers find information in the school system and community to assist with children's total development. For this reason, counselors find out about special programs and services in the school systems where they work, and they make every effort to learn about community resources and programs that can benefit students in their school. Special education programs, tutoring services, child nutrition information, and other school services can be the resources to help students move smoothly through their school years. By the same token, mental health services, recreational programs, church-sponsored support groups, social services, and youth clubs are among the resources organized and funded by local communities to assist with human development.

Career Opportunities School counselors are trained in career theory and development and are concerned with linking career decisions to educational progress. At the senior high-school level, counselors consult with students to help them find information in making appropriate career selections. Information about career opportunities is found in local news resources, employment offices, and federal guides such as the *Dictionary of Occupational Titles* and the *Occupational Outlook Handbook.* In addition, school counselors use computer-based systems to help students gather information about careers of interest to them.

In elementary and middle schools, counselors provide information to students and teachers about the world of work and career opportunities to help with early career exploration. Usually this information is used by counselors and teachers to design career guidance experiences that are integrated with classroom instruction. As such, a middle-school teacher who plans to introduce chemicals into a classroom science lesson might search for information about chemical production and careers that exist in the local community and surrounding area. In this way, career goals and objectives are linked with science objectives in the curriculum. The school counselor assists the teacher in planning this integration of science and career guidance.

Counselors also cooperate with the school's media coordinator to suggest materials for review and purchase. At all school levels, elementary through high school, the media center is a vital resource center for a wide range of materials including career information. By cooperating with their media coordinators, school counselors ensure that career information is the most current and accurate that is available to students and teachers.

Educational Opportunities Another type of informational consultation by school counselors is when they locate educational services, programs, and opportunities that complement and support students' overall development. Facts and details about talent searches for gifted students, summer camps for enrichment activities, college and university programs for elementary, middle grade, and high-school ages, and business-supported ventures in the community are a few example of information counselors can obtain concerning learning opportunities for students.

At the senior high-school level, educational consultation becomes more visible as an essential service of the school counseling program. Students in these years are narrowing their choices of career and post-secondary educational opportunities, and senior high-school counselors are a primary source of information about jobs, technical schools, and colleges. Ideally, this information is also part of the teachers' role in academic advising. When this is so, information about educational opportunities is widely disseminated through the counseling program, homeroom classes, and teacher-advisee activities. Teacher-advisee services are commonly thought of as middle-school programs, but high schools can also establish them to strengthen school counseling and provide more efficient services and information to students (Myrick, 1987).

Consulting with parents and students about educational opportunities raises another concern for which counselors can be a resource. Extracurricular programs and educational endeavors beyond high school cost money, and counselors frequently consult with students and parents about financial resources. The cost of sending a child to summer camp or the tuition for college may be an awesome barrier for many families. Helping them find information to address these and other financial concerns is another way that school counselors act as consultants. Elementary and middle school counselors work with social service agencies, health departments, churches, and other community services to find assistance for family needs. High-school counselors do likewise and also cooperate with colleges and universities to locate grants, loans, and scholarships for students' tuition.

Financial Assistance   Parents want the best for their children, but often the best is economically out of reach. In schools, children and adolescents come from a wide spectrum of economic deprivation and affluence to study and learn side by side, and frequently this diversity separates groups of students rather than unites them. Schools attempt to provide equitable programs, services, and opportunities to disparate groups of students and the wider this difference is, the greater the challenge of providing equal education for all. Sometimes simple procedures, such as eating lunch together in the cafeteria, become striking illustrations of the differences that exist among students in the same school. One child whose family does not qualify for federal assistance opens a meager lunch and sits between another student with a full plate of "free lunch," and a third student whose affluence is measured not only by the luxurious fare, but also by the space-age container in which it is carried to school.

School counselors are frequent providers of information regarding financial resources for families and their children. In schools fortunate enough to have social workers, counselors are happy to share this responsibility. For some students in elementary and middle schools, financial assistance can make the difference in meeting basic clothing and nourishment needs for children to adequately learn in school. Consulting with parents and guardians about where to seek financial assistance is essential for optimal student learning to take place.

In high schools, counselors are concerned about helping adolescents with the resources to meet their basic needs, and as mentioned above, are also concerned about helping families find the funds to send students to appropriate post-secondary educational institutions. Technical schools and colleges are expensive ventures and most of today's families need assistance in helping their children reach this goal. School counselors alone do not own this responsibility, but because of their role in academic advising, many senior high counselors assume financial assistance as one of their primary responsibilities. This role was assumed by secondary counselors during the early years of school guidance and counseling, and for many high-school counselors it has continued and is even a major function for some. Other secondary counselors use volunteers, such as parents, to assist students with college information and financial aid forms. In this way, counselors provide accurate financial information without allowing this function to consume an inordinate amount of time and replace other essential services of the counseling program. Parent volunteers receive training in current financial aid information and schedule time in the counseling center to answer questions for students and parents. They also help counselors with classroom presentations to distribute materials to students at appropriate times during the year.

As seen above, informational consultation takes many forms. School counselors use individual consultations, large group sessions, computer-based self-assessment, interest inventories, and printed media to disseminate accurate and current information. When presenting information in large group sessions, counselors adopt another type of consulting mode; they instruct students, parents, and teachers.

Instructional Services

As integral members of school programs, contemporary school counselors include large group instruction as part of their consulting services for students, parents, and teachers. These instructional relationships are similar to classroom instruction in that they impart information or teach new skills, but they also are different because they are free of evaluative appearances. As such, students who receive instruction from a counselor are typically not evaluated by their participation in these activities; students do not receive a grade. Without this element of evaluation, these instructional sessions are less inhibitive and more facilitative in encouraging students to ask questions and share opinions about important issues. These kinds of instructional consultations are usually structured as classroom guidance with students, educational programs for parents, and in-service workshops for teachers.

Classroom Guidance   As noted in Chapter 1, the school counseling profession began in the early 1900s with a focus on classroom guidance and eventually moved toward a one-on-one counseling focus in the 1960s. Contemporary school counseling programs include large group services as well as individual counseling to meet the unique needs of students. In these programs, *guidance* is an essential area of the curriculum, and teachers and counselors collaborate to plan effective educational goals and objectives and create guidance activities for daily instruction (Schmidt, 1991).

Counselors sometimes present guidance lessons as part of their consulting role in schools. These presentations usually are the result of requests from teachers who want students to receive specific information or skills about particular concerns. At times, teachers may be uncomfortable about sensitive issues, such as sexual development in adolescence, and want counselors to assist in planning and presenting guidance lessons to address these concerns. Other times, teachers may feel that an "objective" presenter would be more effective in achieving desired results, such as having the counselor lead classroom guidance discussions to focus on student behaviors in class.

In comprehensive programs, guidance instruction is also used by counselors in small group sessions. These small group guidance sessions are either one-time meetings or ongoing sessions to share information or teach coping skills to students who have a particular need. In these groups, counselors use some type of media or other instructional material to help students understand and achieve identified goals. Sometimes, the difference between ongoing small group guidance and group counseling becomes blurred. This is particularly true when working with young children for whom group counseling can be quite structured due to their maturational levels. The major difference between guidance and counseling in these instances may simply be the aspect of confidentiality and privacy which are essential in all counseling relationships. Instructional relationships, such as small group guidance, do not necessarily include the element of privacy or the parameter of confidentiality.

Parent Education   Another type of instructional consultation used by school counselors is found in parent education programs. As with classroom guidance, parent education can take place in a single session, such as a counselor's presentation to a parent-teacher association meeting, or can be scheduled as several meetings to focus on parental and family needs. In all these presentations, school counselors assume different roles depending on the nature of the programs they have designed. For example, in presenting information about child development to a group of elementary school parents, a counselor may take the role of an "expert consultant," sharing research and other factual data. In contrast, another counselor may lead a parent discussion group about child discipline and takes a "facilitator" role to keep the discussion on target and give all participants an opportunity to share their opinions. In this second case, the counselor facilitates learning by having parents share their own "expertise" as family leaders.

By using their consulting skills and instructing parents in various aspects of child development, adolescent behavior, and communication skills, school counselors provide indirect services to a larger number of students. As parents become more knowledgeable and skilled, they create beneficial relationships with their children and optimal home environments for learning. For this reason, these types of functions for school counselors are essential in comprehensive programs. When counselors are unable to provide these services directly to parents, they rely on community resources, such as private counselors, mental practitioners, or social workers, who are willing and able to organize and lead parent education groups.

Teacher In-service Workshops A third type of instructional format used by school counselors is teacher in-service workshops. Because teachers are the first-line helpers in schools, they need information and instruction to provide initial services to students who request assistance or are identified as having a need. School counselors assist teachers by planning and presenting workshops on particular topics or skill development. As with parent education groups, when counselors are unable or unqualified to lead such training, they seek appropriate instructors or consultants to present these seminars. In many cases, teachers in schools are well qualified to present in-service for their colleagues. Perceptive school counselors survey teachers at the beginning of each year to assess their needs and establish a list of potential presenters. Form 3–1 is a sample of this kind of survey instrument.

By planning and organizing various instructional services, school counselors illustrate how they contribute to the overall school mission. They also strengthen their relationships with parents, teachers, administrators, and other school personnel, enabling themselves to establish ties to enhance

FORM 3–1

Teachers: Please check below the topics of interest about which you would like in-service presentations this year. If you want to hear about topics not listed, please indicate so on the bottom of the form. Also, if you have expertise in a particular area and are willing to present a workshop or at a faculty meeting, please indicate so at the bottom of this form.

Topics for in-service this year:

___ Learning Disabilities	___ Suicide Prevention
___ Classroom Management	___ Conferring with Parents
___ Instructional Techniques	___ CPR Training
___ Special Education Regulations	___ Communication Skills
___ Computers in the Classroom	___ Handling Crises
___ New Instructional Material	___ Using the Media Center

Other Topics: _____

_____

I am willing to present on: _____

Name: _____

---

their role in problem-solving and mediating situations, another area of consultations.

Problem-Solving Services

As with any large organization consisting of diverse groups, schools are sometimes challenged by threats and hazards posed by students, parents, and teachers. Students sometimes feel school rules are unfair, parents become dissatisfied with instructional procedures, and teachers want support from home and family in educating children. These and other conflicts can disable schools if they are not addressed openly and with regard for all parties. Counselors use consulting skills and processes to assist people in resolving these conflicts, accepting the views of others, and selecting agreeable goals to move forward. In these consulting relationships, counselors use effective communication skills, support all sides involved in the conflict, and attempt to negotiate reasonable solutions.

Parent-Teacher Conferences

One way that school counselors assume a consulting role to resolve problems is by facilitating parent-teacher conferences. These meetings are scheduled either at regular times during the year to report student progress, test results, and other educational information to parents, or when teachers and parents become concerned about student development and behavior. The role of the school counselor in these conferences varies depending on the issues at hand and who has initiated the conference. When a teacher calls the conference and invites the counselor to attend, the purpose of the conference and role of the counselor is defined by the teacher. Sometimes counselors and teachers need to negotiate this role, particularly if the counselor feels the role defined by the teacher conflicts with professional or ethical guidelines. Occasionally, counselors will arrange a parent-teacher conference and will assume a leadership role.

In parent-teachers conferences held for informational purposes, a counselor's involvement may simply be to share and interpret data, such as a child's test results. When conferences are scheduled to resolve differences between parents and teachers, or to solicit parental support about children's behaviors, a teacher may ask the counselor to lead the conference, mediate differences, and facilitate decision-making to assist parents and teachers in reaching an agreeable solution.

Parent-teacher conferences, particularly those that rely on the counselor's ability to mediate and facilitate solutions, can test a counselor's leadership skills as well as his or her professional relationships with parents and teachers. Counselors want to establish helpful relationships with both parents and teachers, but sometimes the support they give to one side in a conference causes them to lose favor with the other party. Ideally, counselors remain neutral in these consulting roles, and draw on the expertise of parents as leaders of the family and the knowledge of teachers as instructional leaders in the school. The goal in these conferences is to have all these "experts" share their views, select common goals for the good of the child, and agree on reasonable strategies to reach these goals. A school counselor's training in communication and helping skills are tested in these types of consultations. It is often difficult trying to satisfy all parties, particularly when clear alternatives are not easily agreed on.

Administrative Conferences   Another situation in which school counselors use their consulting skills is when principals and other administrators seek information about problems they are having with particular students or difficulties they observe in the school as a whole. School principals are charged with managing all aspects of the educational and extracurricular programs. This is an awesome responsibility and most principals rely on specialists, such as school counselors, to provide accurate information and use their specialized training to assist with problem situations.

Effective school counselors meet with their principals on a regular basis to report on the progress of the school counseling program and on significant events affecting the school. In these conferences, counselors keep administrators up to date about counseling services and critical issues they are handling in the program. While confidentiality that is promised to students, parents, and teachers cannot be broken in these conferences with principals, counselors can share general information about major concerns and situations occurring in the school. For example, a senior high counselor who has seen a sudden rise in substance abuse referrals may not be able to give the names of students receiving counseling, but could alert the principal about the increased use of drugs and alcohol by students in general. In this way, administrators, teachers, and counselors place themselves in position to plan preventive services in the school, solicit community support, and involve parents as necessary in assisting students in need.

Communication between administrators and counselors is essential in providing appropriate and comprehensive services in schools. Such cooperation allows for respect and acceptance of professional roles and builds a level of trust with which the judgment of counselors and the leadership of principals can be balanced to meet the needs of students. When school counselors fail to achieve this level of cooperation and trust, they become limited in the services they can offer to students, parents, and teachers.

Student Services Team Conferences   Many authors of articles and books on counseling advocate a team approach to coordinating student services in schools (Gibson & Mitchell, 1990; Humes & Hohenshil, 1987; Hummel &

Humes, 1984; Kameen, Robinson, & Rotter, 1985; Schmidt, 1991). These team approaches are identified by various titles that include student services team, pupil personnel team, and child study team. While these names may differ, their purposes and goals are similar. Generally, these teams include the school counselor, a psychologist, a social worker, a nurse, an administrator, and teachers, with special education teachers usually represented. Occasionally, these teams include professionals from agencies outside of the school, such as mental-health counselors, case workers from social services, and pediatricians from diagnostic centers. Involvement of these professionals widens the range of expertise on the team, opening more options and alternatives to help with student development.

The main purpose of student services teams is to follow cases of children and adolescents who are experiencing particular learning and behavioral difficulties. The teams coordinate services and see that each student receives adequate attention to meet his or her needs. Sometimes, teams include agency representatives who help to coordinate services between the school and community. In the most difficult cases, coordination of this nature is essential if students are to receive beneficial, comprehensive services.

Because school counselors usually serve individual schools with responsibility in designated schools, they are a logical choice to lead student services teams. As such, they apply consulting skills to coordinate the services of these professional groups, resolve differences of opinion, and assure that students' needs are being met by the school and community. Making sure that services are provided in a timely fashion and smoothing differences among professionals whose areas of expertise often overlap is indeed a challenge. For this reason, mediation, negotiation, and facilitation are among the consulting skills required by school counselors in these leadership roles.

Planning Services

In addition to establishing consulting relationships to disseminate information, present instruction, and facilitate conferences, school counselors assist schools in planning schoolwide activities for the benefit students, parents, and teachers. These activities help schools maintain a focus on the development of all students and foster awareness of the factors that influence student welfare. The ability to maintain a wide-angle focus on student development is the hallmark of an effective school counseling program, and correspondingly, a successful school.

Many factors contribute to successful schools. As Purkey and Schmidt (1990) noted, *everything counts;* every program planned, every policy drafted, every process implemented makes some difference, positive or negative, to someone in the school. To ensure that school programs, policies, and processes contribute in positive ways to the development of people, counselors help plan appropriate services and activities. This begins with the guidance curriculum

Guidance Curriculum   As indicated earlier, guidance is the responsibility of everyone and is best implemented when it is integrated as an essential part of the school curriculum. Guidance does not occur at a single moment or as a solitary event with a teacher saying "Students put your books away; it is time for guidance!" Rather, it is infused with all subjects, and in all daily instruction. For this infusion to happen successfully, teachers and counselors plan appropriate activities for classroom instruction.

In elementary and middle schools where teachers team by grade levels or subject areas to plan instructional programs, counselors consult with these groups to share guidance objectives and offer suggestions of activities to use in classroom instruction. In high schools, counselors meet with departments to achieve a similar purpose. This process of planning together allows teachers to use counselors as resources while maintaining their leadership role in the instructional program. These consultations also allow counselors and teachers to share information about particular students who are struggling and in need of additional services beyond classroom guidance.

Individual Student Planning   Adequate and appropriate services for students do not occur by accident. They require conscious and careful planning. By the same token, students do not achieve educational career goals without finding a direction and choosing methods to reach these objectives. School counselors are involved in planning services to meet individual student needs and in assisting all students in selecting goals and strategies to satisfy their aspirations.

A guidance curriculum provides developmental and preventive activities for all students in the school (Dagley, 1987). This is the primary reason why counselors and teachers integrate guidance into classroom lessons. However, some students struggle with serious concerns that demand attention beyond participation in affective education programs. These students need more intense preventive and remedial services. To select and schedule these types of services for students, counselors consult with teachers and parents so that appropriate plans are made.

In special education programs, schools develop individual education plans (IEPs) for all exceptional students. Planning and consulting by counselors, teachers, and parents to develop these IEPs for individual students is the same preparation needed for students who do not qualify for special education services, but who nonetheless are failing in school.

Students who do not have exceptional needs and do not require intensive interventions also consult with counselors to review their educational and career goals. Many contacts made by students, particularly in middle and high schools, are for the purpose of gathering information and making plans for the future. Sometimes these consultations between counselors and students are brief, single sessions, and other times they may last for several meetings. These sessions are defined as consulting rather than counseling relationships because of their emphasis on sharing information and making plans for the future. In addition, they usually do not reveal any underlying emotional or personal problems that need to be addressed by the student and counselor.

School Climate Another area of school life in which counselors use their consulting and planning skills is in advocating for healthy school climates. Over the years, the counseling literature has emphasized an important role for counselors as agents of change in schools and society (Wrenn, 1973). To help schools realize the impact of environmental factors on student learning, counselors consult with administrators, teachers, parents, and others to examine aspects of the school that enhance or detract from educational processes. Schools that intentionally create beneficial environments, and counselors who actively assess school processes, programs, and policies to assure healthy climates, combine to develop effective educational opportunities for all students (Purkey & Schmidt, 1987, 1990).

In planning healthy school climates, counselors help administrators and teachers evaluate programs that are designed to enhance learning and they determine whether these programs accomplish what is intended. Sometimes schools create programs to benefit all students, but in practice they end up excluding rather than including students who need services. An example of this is the senior high school that designed an extensive after-school program of extracurricular activities to benefit students, particularly disadvantaged students. Unfortunately, the school neglected to plan after-school bus transportation and, as a result, many students did not attend because they had no way home. Once this oversight was corrected, more students were able to participate and the program was successful in reaching its goal.

Counselors also ask administrators to assess physical aspects of schools, such as lighting, floor coverings, painted walls, and building cleanliness. These and other features influence students' morale and attitudes about school and learning. In a similar way, school policies relate to a positive climate. Counselors review school policies to determine if they are necessary and whether they contribute to healthy environments. Sometimes policies are passed for the convenience of a few staff members rather than for the benefit of students as a whole. When this happens, resentment towards the school is inevitable.

School counselors have a responsibility for seeing that schools are designed, organized, and governed with the welfare of students foremost in mind. Their ability to consult effectively with administrators and teachers and make suggestions for altering programs, changing policies, renovating places, and adjusting processes affects the success of their school counseling program and services for students, parents, and teachers. One way that counselors directly enhance school climate is by the special events and projects they plan during the year.

Special Events and Projects   Many events in elementary, middle, and high schools supplement instructional programs during the year. Counselors become involved in planning some of these events so that they are available to all students, and the programs incorporate objectives that parallel broader school goals. Counselors who plan events such as "substance abuse awareness week," "Good Citizen of the Month Award," and "Special Olympics" illustrate their commitment to the school and student development.

Other special events and projects that require planning and consulting on the part of school counselors include teacher-advisee programs, testing services, peer helper programs, and many others included in the school counseling program. These programs and services require a high degree of coordination for counselors to be successful in schools. Coordinating is another essential service of a comprehensive school counseling program, and one we will now explore.

Coordinating

By this point, it is probably clear that a comprehensive school counseling program consists of a variety of services and activities, some of which counselors provide directly to students, parents, and teachers, and others that indirectly affect the welfare of students. Counselors deliver many of these direct services and also have responsibility for coordinating a number of other activities that benefit students and schools. In this section, we examine some essential coordinating activities used by most school counselors. These activities are not the only ones counselors use, but they offer a sample of the kinds of responsibilities assumed and directed by counselors to help schools use appropriate and accurate data, follow through on essential services, and plan a schoolwide focus for student development.

Data Collection and Sharing

Education begins with the process of determining what is already known so that schools can design appropriate curricula and instruction to enhance and build upon existing knowledge. In addition, the design of appropriate curricula and instruction depends on many student characteristics including their abilities and learning styles. Throughout students' educational careers, schools gather data and other information to help teachers make accurate decisions about programs and processes related to learning. School counselors are professionals who are trained in testing and measurement and are available to assist teachers in collecting accurate data to make these important decisions.

One major area of data collection in which schools have become involved in recent years is testing. Most schools, elementary though high school, use standardized tests to assess students' abilities and evaluate students' achievement at the end of the school year. School counselors traditionally have had responsibility for organizing, scheduling, and monitoring the administration of these types of group tests. These responsibilities constitute in part the essential function known as student appraisal, which we will examine at the end of this chapter and in more detail in Chapter 7. For now, we will consider how the use of tests, inventories, and other measurement procedures are coordinated in comprehensive school counseling programs.

Test Administration   Depending of the level of the school, there are several types of tests and assessments used with students. Tests are generally used to determine students' aptitude and achievement in school. Schools administer aptitude tests at different times during the year, depending on how the results are to be used. For example, if test data will help teachers place children into appropriate instructional programs for the coming school year, the tests will be administered during the prior spring semester so that scores will be available at the start of the next school year. Typically, schools administer achievement tests towards the end of the year, so that teachers can evaluate the progress of students and share these results with both students and parents.

Counselors also administer individual tests and other assessments to students depending on the need. For example, a new student to a school may need an achievement test if recent data are not received from the transferring school. Such assessment would help teachers place the student in an appropriate course of study so that valuable instructional time would not be wasted.

In most schools, counselors have responsibility for seeing that tests are administered properly and according to standardized instructions. With individual tests, it is the counselor's responsibility to choose appropriate instruments for which he or she is adequately trained, and to administer these assessments according to proper procedures. With group testing programs, counselors assist their schools in coordinating materials, training teachers and test monitors, and scheduling administration of the examinations. In large schools that test students frequently, this coordination is a tremendous responsibility. Sometimes it interferes with other functions of the counseling program. When this happens, counselors need to rely on teachers' assistance, clerical aides, and parent volunteers to help coordinate materials, monitor test administrations, and schedule make-up examinations.

Test results are useful only if obtained under the proper circumstances. This means that tests materials must be secured before and after the administration, students should be properly prepared and ready for the test that is selected, teachers must be familiar with instructions for administering the test, and proper environments should be created to give students the opportunity to achieve optimal results. When these conditions are satisfied and valid tests are used, schools can be comfortable with the reliability of students' results. To achieve this aim, school counselors and other personnel assume coordinating responsibilities for the testing program. In schools where coordination of the testing program is a major administrative and clerical task, teachers and counselors might form a testing committee to assign different responsibilities for various tasks. In this way, coordination is accomplished without interfering with other essential counseling services.

Test Results   After tests have been administered and scored, the data need to be used for the purposes intended. Appropriate distribution and utilization of test data require adequate coordination. Again, counselors trained in testing and measurement have the background to help students, parents, and teachers interpret and understand test data, and to use these results in making educational and career decisions. In addition, counselors assist administrators in understanding the schoolwide results and accurately reporting these outcomes to the school system and local media.

Tests can be useful in diagnosing and assessing student progress, or they can become diabolical tools of the misinformed. School counselors who coordinate the use of test results have an obligation to help schools convey an accurate picture of their instructional programs' strengths and weaknesses. At the same time, they must protect individuals from interpretations that lump all students into a single category based on norm-referenced data. For example, when test summaries indicate the average student's score is below the normative mean, public reports should also show the range of scores including the percentage of students above and below the mean. By reporting results in this manner, schools present a clear picture of how the total student population performed on the test. Mean scores, on the other hand only show one dimension.

The most important role counselors have in coordinating test reports is the use of these data with students, parents, and teachers. Students in elementary, middle, and high schools can gain insightful understanding of themselves by learning about their performance on tests and interest inventories. Of course, the explanations they receive must be developmentally appropriate to their comprehension level, and counselors at all school levels should be able to develop and convey these explanations accurately. Parents also need to know how their children perform on educational tests. With accurate knowledge, they can help children learn about areas of strengths and weaknesses, and they can better guide children in educational and career choices.

Teachers are equally important in the processes of using an interpreting standardized tests and inventories. Tests and other measurement techniques play a vital role in helping teachers plan effective instruction and choose appropriate materials for students (Gronlund & Linn, 1990). The school reform movement of recent years in the United States has placed additional emphasis on student assessment and the relationship between teaching effectiveness and student performance. School counselors have the knowledge and training to assist teachers in selecting appropriate evaluative processes and instruments, and in using data collected from these assessments to improve instruction and student learning.

Chapter 7 presents specific examples of how school counselors help teachers select tests and utilize results to improve instructional programs. The major point to be made here is that counselors are trained in testing and measurement techniques and this training is used, not only to administer tests and inventories, but also in coordinating the appropriate use of data collected from these assessment instruments. Such coordination includes planning ways to disseminate accurate information and following up to assure that the information has been used appropriately. As examples, school counselors discuss test results with individual teachers in conferences about specific students and entire classes. They also present in-service workshops to teachers to help them use test data in identifying instructional strengths and weaknesses, and in planning adjustments to the curriculum.

Data collected on students usually are filed in cumulative folders. These folders are stored in a central file room in the school where appropriate personnel can have access. Decisions about the use of these student records relate to another area of program coordination for which counselors often have responsibility.

Students' Records   In most school systems, students' records begin when children enter kindergarten and follow each child through his or her school career. Decisions about what information should be placed in students' cumulative folders are guided by local policies, state regulations, and federal laws. A major guide for schools and counselors is the Family Educational Rights and Privacy Act passed by Congress in 1974. This bill, commonly called the Buckley Amendment, gives parent of minor students the right to review all school records about their children. After this law was passed, school counselors were encouraged to examine all students' records and avoid misinterpretations by including only information that could be clearly understood by laypersons. Further, recommendations were made to remove material from students' records that potentially violated a student's right to privacy (Getson & Schweid, 1976).

Since the passage of this act, schools have become more careful and sensitive about the types of information placed in students' folders. They have also implemented clear procedures for students, parents, school personnel, and officials outside the school to follow when requesting and using information about students. These procedures include policies about who has legal access to students' folders, waivers regarding letters of recommendations written on behalf of students, and permissions required for officials outside the school to obtain access to students' records.

Because of their involvement with testing and confidential information, school counselors historically have had a role in coordinating and managing students' records. The Buckley Amendment focused attention on the need to have clear guidelines and careful coordination of record-keeping procedures. As a result, while all school counselors may not have primary responsibility for managing and recording data in students' folders, they help the school staff, especially secretaries and clerical assistants, to know about appropriate procedures and legal guidelines. Counselors also advise administrators and teachers about the proper use of students' records. In this way, school counselors act as gatekeepers, coordinating the data that go in and out of students' files and thereby assuring the rights and privacy of students and parents. To assist counselors in this task, it is preferable that schools assign secretarial staff to the counseling program. Having responsible staff to handle school records ensures their proper use.

Information gathered by schools is also helpful to other agencies that provide services to students and families. Sometimes school counselors and teachers share information about students with community agencies or physicians, psychologists, and counselors in private practice. This process of sharing information brings us to another area of coordination, specifically referrals and follow-up of students who benefit from additional services beyond the school counseling program.

Referrals and Follow-up

Occasionally, a social, psychological, financial, or other factor that hinders a student's progress in school cannot be adequately addressed by the school alone. In such cases, counselors and teachers search for appropriate services in the community to assist students and their families. School counselors are the logical choice among school staff members to coordinate these referrals, and to follow up cases of students and families being served by outside agencies and private practitioners. Counselors are familiar with the breadth of community services, they design assessment techniques to gather initial data for referrals, and, as members of a helping profession, they establish effective communication with service providers outside the school.

By having their counselors coordinate referrals and follow-up activities, school avoid duplication of effort when seeking services for students and their families. This kind of coordination results in more efficient referral processes and subsequently more cooperative relationships with agency personnel in the community. Mental-health counselors, social workers, clinical psychologists, pediatricians, and other professionals appreciate it when they communicate with one referral source rather than dealing with a large number of teachers from the same school. Counselors who coordinate referrals for their schools are able to establish consistent procedures that conform to the needs and requirements of particular agencies. At the same time, feedback from these resources can be channeled through the school counselor, who in turn gives accurate reports to teachers and other appropriate personnel.

In coordinating referrals, school counselors typically deal with two primary resources—community agencies and private practitioners. The following sections offer brief descriptions of the typical referrals made to public agencies and private institutions and practitioners.

Community Agencies   In most communities in the United States, several public and private agencies offer services to children, adolescents, and families. School counselors, as coordinators of referrals for their schools, attempt to gather current information about these resources so that students, parents, and teachers can make the best decisions about services outside the school. Usually, the number and level of various services in a given community are related to the size of the population, the tax base to support these services, and the demand of the citizenry to have these services available. In poor rural communities, the desire and need for these services is sadly outweighed by a lack of financial resources. In these cases, school counselors may be the only human service available (Sutton & Southworth, 1990).

Typically, schools look for community health services, social services, mental-health and substance-abuse services, residential treatment centers for severe emotional or behavioral problems, recreational programs, and centers that offer educational opportunities to students and parents. In most instances, health programs, social services, and mental-health clinics are provided through county and state departments established and financed with public funds. Because of their public affiliation, these agencies have interagency relationships that, when coordinated properly, facilitate the location and delivery of services to people in the community. School counselors frequently refer students and families to these agencies for evaluation purposes and for more intense counseling and treatment than what schools are able to provide.

Recreational programs such as boys and girls clubs, scouts, and camps are also sought by schools to provide additional creative and social outlets for students. School counselors coordinate referrals to these types of organizations by having current literature and applications available to students and parents. Students benefit from involvement in a wide range of recreational and civic activities, and school counselors are one source of information concerning these opportunities.

Churches, synagogues, colleges, universities, and similar institutions offer other resources for referrals. Students and parents sometimes seek additional educational opportunities to support and enrich the learning process. School counselors invite these institutions to send materials for distribution to students and parents. Usually, this kind of information is offered to students and parents without endorsement from the school. Nevertheless, counselors and other school personnel who distribute this information to students and parents for consideration should be familiar with the programs and services being advertised. This is especially true when counselors give information about private organizations and professionals in the community.

Private Practitioners In addition to public agencies and programs, most communities have private practitioners and institutions that offer educational, psychological, recreational, and other services for children and families. School counselors coordinate referrals to private resources in the same way that they work with public agencies. Examples of these resources include private residential treatment centers and hospitals; psychiatrists, counselors, clinical social workers, and psychologists in private practice; and educational centers that assist students who have learning problems, want to improve their test-taking skills, or desire enrichment activities.

The role of the counselor in coordinating referrals and following up with public and private agencies and practitioners in the community is to assist the school and the family in locating resources and providing services to enhance student learning and development. Comprehensive school counseling programs, as seen so far in this text, offer a wide range of services toward meeting this goal. By coordinating referrals for additional services beyond their own school program, counselors increase the probability that all students will reach their educational goals. At the same time, counselors work with administrators and teachers to develop programs and services within the school to include all students and encourage development for everyone.

Schoolwide Events

Coordinating the activities of a school counseling program includes planning, organizing, implementing, and evaluating schoolwide events that focus on developmental guidance issues. These activities are either part of ongoing programs in the school, or they are special events planned to address particular developmental needs of students. While school counselors take an active role in coordinating these events, teachers and other school personnel usually share responsibilities for planning and implementing schoolwide activities. The advisory committee of a school counseling program is often the group that plans and orchestrates these special events.

Countless examples of schoolwide events and programs are found in today's schools. In some instances these are created and planned by teachers, such as a field day, or by organizations, such as a beautification project planned by the parent-teachers association (PTA). The following ideas are a few schoolwide events and programs for which counselors might assume some coordinating responsibility. these events and programs offer examples of how counselors coordinate activities that target developmental goals of students in the schools.

Student Recognition Activities   Schools are made up of diverse student populations with every child and adolescent choosing from an array of educational, social, and career goals. Schools are active places with many students achieving and moving toward higher levels of performance. With all this activity, it is sometimes possible to forget about particular students who may not excel and therefore not receive recognition for their accomplishments. Because school counselors and teachers are sensitive to the needs of all students, they try to create atmospheres where everyone can succeed and be recognized for their achievements.

Student recognition activities include a variety of schoolwide events, from award ceremonies to bulletin boards, that give students multiple opportunities to let their peers know who they are and ways in which they are successful. Counselors assist with these recognition processes by helping teachers design events and activities that focus on a broad range of student developmental issues and objectives. In this way, a wide spectrum of students in academic, athletic, drama, art, music, and other ventures receive appropriate recognition for their accomplishments and contributions to the school and community. Through these activities, individual pupils are invited to be an integral part of the school and the student body. By coordinating these kinds of events and programs, counselors assist teachers in encouraging student participation in the school and also in creating healthy environments for optimal learning.

Career Awareness Programs   Career development is an essential goal of education and begins formally when students enter school for the first time. Excellent instruction includes a philosophy about how learning connects with career development and vocational choices in life. In elementary schools through senior highs, counselors assist with this goal through the counseling and consulting services they provide to students and parents, and by coordinating schoolwide events.

Career awareness is achieved as a result of many learning activities, cooperatively planned by teachers and counselors. Classroom guidance lessons, integrated with daily instruction to highlight special types of careers, are an example. As an illustration, let us imagine that a middle school wants its science classes to focus on health occupations and how the study of science relates to these career choices. To assist in this effort, counselors in this middle school help teachers plan and implement this guidance approach by locating appropriate resources, scheduling health professionals as guest lecturers, and presenting lessons with teachers in the science classes.

In secondary schools, counselors coordinate job fairs, college days, and similar events to help students survey the range of occupational opportunities available and review the educational requirements of various tracks. The time required to plan these types of events is usually substantial, so counselors seek assistance from student organizations, teacher committees, parent volunteers, and the advisory committee of the school counseling program. The success of these types of programs has positive effects on student development as well as on school-community relationships. Therefore, planning and coordination is essential. Businesses, colleges, and universities that participate in well-planned schoolwide events form positive perceptions about both the school and the counseling program, and they carry these perceptions into the community. This evaluation process is invaluable in helping the school create an accurate image and in enabling the school counseling program to gain support for its services.

Teacher-Advisee Programs   In most schools, student-counselor ratios are quite high, particularly in elementary and middle schools where counselors are frequently responsible for services to as many as 1,000 students or more. To assist with advising of students, counselors train teachers in basic communication skills and assign them students as advisees (Michael, 1986; Myrick & Myrick, 1990). In teacher-advisee programs, teachers are assigned students whom they advise about educational planning and assist with school progress. In some programs, teachers advise the same students as these pupils progress through all the grades. For example, a high-school teacher might be assigned the same group of students to advise each year as they move through the ninth, tenth, eleventh, and twelfth grades. By designing programs in this way, teachers develop stronger relationships with the students assigned to them.

In teacher-advisee programs, teachers schedule time to confer with individual advisees and also to meet with their entire group of advisees on a regular basis. Individual conferences allow students and teachers the opportunity to review academic progress and discuss concerns that may impede growth and development. When teachers reach the point where they believe students need additional help, they refer to the school counselor. This is also true when teachers present guidance activities to groups of advisees and determine that particular students need direct counseling services.

Coordinating teacher-advisee programs requires a process for assigning students, designing a schedule for teachers and students to meet, and training teachers in skills to facilitate relationships with their advisees. In addition, school counselors offer resources and topics to help teachers choose guidance activities for their advisee groups. In this way, teacher-advisee programs become avenues by which developmental guidance is integrated with instructional goals and objectives.

Training is a key ingredient of successful advising programs. Teachers, who are equipped with adequate communication and facilitation skills and understand the essential characteristics of effective helpers, have the potential to provide excellent assistance to students. They also form an important referral network with school counselors to ensure that all students receive appropriate services in the school and from community agencies.

Peer Helper Programs   Another service that school counselors organize and coordinate to reach a wide audience of students is called a Peer Helper Program (Bowman, 1986; Myrick & Bowman, 1981). In this program, students are selected and trained to perform various helping functions, such as assisting teachers with classroom guidance activities, tutoring students who need assistance, showing new students around the school, and listening to peers who have concerns. By offering these activities through peer helpers, counselors expand their programs, bringing services directly to students and thereby reaching a wider audience. In addition, peer helpers, like teacher-advisors, form a communication network to help counselors receive referrals of students who have serious concerns or have difficulty overcoming barriers to learning.

Coordinating peer helper programs takes time. It is necessary to train participating students in communication skills and referral procedures. It also requires a clear description and understanding of the role each peer helper will play in the program. Some counselors schedule regular sessions with the peer helpers for supervision and skill building. In high schools, peer helper training and selection is sometimes integrated into the curriculum through a psychology of other human services course. In these instances, school counselors team-teach courses with classroom teachers, and students receive high-school credit for their training and participation in these programs.

The preceding examples illustrate activities that are designed to help counselors and teachers reach a higher percentage of students. Through special events, such as "career night" and other student awareness programs, information can be distributed widely. By the same token, student advising by teachers and peer helper programs allow school counseling services to extend beyond the counseling center, using teachers and students as additional resources to assist a greater number of students in the school.

To determine which students need what services, counselors evaluate the needs, characteristics, and factors that affect student development. Assessment of these elements includes evaluation processes that encompass the fourth essential service of comprehensive school counseling programs—appraising.

Appraising

Since the beginning of the school counseling profession, counselors have used appraisal instruments and assessment processes to measure students' needs, interests, intellectual functions, and academic performance. Today's school counselors continue to coordinate the assessment of students' characteristics and school progress in a variety of ways. In addition, counselors and other student services professionals are concerned with the influence of environmental factors on students' development. Later, in Chapter 7, we will examine specific methods and instruments used in student appraisal. By way of introduction, the following sections briefly describe student assessment and environmental evaluation processes used by counselors in schools.

Student Evaluation

School counselors use many assessment processes to help students, parents, and teachers gather accurate data and make sound decisions about educational programs, instructional placements, career directions, and a host of other issues. These evaluations include the use of standardized tests, interests inventories, behavior rating scales, and non-standardized procedures that include observations and interviews. Test are among the most common instruments used by school counselors.

Tests   Evaluation through standardized testing has been and will continue to be an important service of school counseling programs. In part, this is due to the mobility of U.S. society and the transfer of students from school to school during their educational careers. Sometimes new students arrive at schools with little information and few records about their educational progress. At these times, counselors can help teachers plan appropriate instructional placement by administering individual achievement and aptitude tests. A current measurement of students' abilities and academic achievement will assist teachers in placing students at the proper instructional levels and in designing beneficial learning experiences. Without this assessment, teachers can only estimate students' levels and risk misplacing them in a proper instructional program. One caveat is necessary here. The selection of appropriate assessment instruments to avoid cultural biases and other factors leading to inaccurate results is imperative.

Expanded special education services for students, aided by Public Law 94–142, have also increased the need for individual assessment of students to identify strengths and weaknesses in their learning styles and intellectual functions. Sometimes, school counselors begin this assessment process by assisting special education teachers with screening procedures. These procedures include the use of behavior rating scales, short-form ability tests, and achievement batteries. Results of these screening procedures help teachers decide if a more complete educational and psychological profile is required to determine appropriate services and placement. If so, a referral to the school psychologist or other evaluator is then initiated.

Inventories   School counselors use a variety of questionnaires and inventories to assist students in making educational and career decisions. In addition, some inventories are designed to help students learn about personal and social characteristics that enhance or inhibit their relationships with others. Interest inventories have many potential applications in schools, including helping students learn about interests they did not know they had and contrasting their expressed interests with their assessed abilities (Gibson & Mitchell, 1990).

Selection of inventories depends on the purpose of the assessment and the training of the counselor for using and interpreting these instruments. Since some of these inventories are founded on particular psychological theories, a counselor's theoretical training is an additional factor to consider when selecting these types of inventories.

Student assessment does not always require standardized tests or inventories. School counselors and teachers often gather valuable information through observations and interviews. These procedures are an important part of the overall assessment process.

Observations and Interviews   School counselors frequently receive referrals from teachers and parents about particular concerns or behaviors exhibited by students at home or in school. The first step after receiving a referral is to gather data for deciding who needs what? In determining what services best address identified concerns and behaviors, counselors use direct observations and interviews to gather relevant data. For example, when a teacher refers a student because of inattentive classroom behaviors, a first step the counselors takes is to observe the student during class while instruction is taking place. Occasionally, counselors will recommend behavioral rating scales for the teacher or parent to complete. These rating scales might be developed by the counselor or selected from published sources. In either instance, the findings from these rating scales supplement the observations made by counselors, teachers, and parents. By using these processes, the counselor in the example above is better able to recommend appropriate services, which could include direct counseling with the student, classroom management techniques for the teacher, or home strategies for the parents to use in encouraging appropriate behavior at school.

In addition to rating scales and observations, counselors interview teachers, parents, and students as part of the evaluation process. Structured interviews ask specific questions and focus on particular information. Through these interviews, counselors are able to compare the perceptions of teachers, parents, and students regarding problem situations. These perceptual differences must be sorted out and explicated if progress in these situations is to be realized.

Students' records provide an added source of information about past events and academic progress that assist in evaluation and decision-making processes. These records also contain information collected in group assessment procedures that enable counselors and teachers to learn more about individual students and how they compare to other students in the school.

Group Assessment   Schools use group standardized tests to measure the academic ability and progress of students. There are two major types of group tests used measuring student achievement: criterion-referenced and norm-referenced instruments. Criterion-referenced tests measure students' performance in relationship to an identified criteria or dimension, such as vocabulary skills. By contrast, norm-referenced exams generate scores that compare students and rank them against one another by using scores derived form sample reference groups. These reference groups are called "normed populations." In schools, the norms are usually established by grade levels or age levels. In other words, students assessed by norm-referenced tests are compared with other students in the same grade level or age range. Further description of these types of standardized tests is presented in Chapter 7.

Both criterion-referenced and norm-referenced instruments have value in helping counselors and teachers make decisions on behalf of students. At times, decisions need to be made based on performance of a particular skill and other times schools need to know how students compare with others in their age or grade level. Knowing what kind of information is needed guides the counselor in deciding which type of assessment to use.

School counselors and teachers also apply sociometric techniques in assessing students' roles and relationships in groups (Gibson & Mitchell, 1990). Basically, these techniques are used to evaluate the acceptance of students in the social structure of their peer groups, such as in classrooms.

There are different ways of designing sociometric assessments and schools are full of everyday examples of these processes. One of the simplest methods is to ask students who they want to work or play with in a particular activity. By identifying the students who are most often and least often chosen by their classmates, counselors and teachers can construct a sociogram of these relationships. By drawing a diagram of these relationships, they can identify the most popular students as well as the social isolates in particular groups or classes. This information may be helpful in designing work and play activities to strengthen student relationships and enhance the self-esteem of those who are social isolates. Additional information about sociometric techniques is presented late in Chapter 7.

Environmental Evaluation

A third area of appraising that is coordinated by school counselors focuses on environmental factors that influence students' development and learning. These factors include the school atmosphere, classroom environment, peer groups, and home environments. Gathering data to help students, parents, and teachers make appropriate plans and decisions is incomplete without an evaluation of the environments and social groups that interact with student development. An examination of school climate is a logical place to begin this area of assessment.

School Assessment   As noted earlier, many problems can be avoided in schools if adequate assessment of places, policies, programs, and processes is initiated, and schools use this information to create beneficial conditions for optimal learning (Purkey & Schmidt, 1990). In determining what services to provide for students, parents, and teachers, counselors save precious time when they first look at the physical environment of the school, the policies that govern the school, procedures and processes for administering school regulations, and programs established for student learning and development. Part of a counselor's role in the appraisal process is to help the school assess itself.

By creating appraisal processes to help teachers and administrators assess school environments, counselors gather data with which to plan efficient and effective services. Form 3–2 illustrates a sample questionnaire used with middle graders to help teachers evaluate classroom climate. Re-

FORM 3–2   School Climate Assessment

Students: Please check your responses to the following statements and return this form to the counselor's mailbox in the school office. Your answers will help us in evaluating our school. Thank you.

1. Is the school building neat and clean?	YES	NO	SOMETIMES
2. Is the cafeteria food good?	YES	NO	SOMETIMES
3. Do you enjoy being in your classroom?	YES	NO	SOMETIMES
4. Are the restrooms clean and supplied with soap, paper towels, and tissues?	YES	NO	SOMETIMES
5. Is the playground safe and with enough to do?	YES	NO	SOMETIMES
6. Does the air smell fresh inside and outside?	YES	NO	SOMETIMES
7. Are windows and doors in good working order?	YES	NO	SOMETIMES
8. Are people friendly in your school?	YES	NO	SOMETIMES
9. Do your teachers listen to you?	YES	NO	SOMETIMES
10. Are the school rules fair to everyone?	YES	NO	SOMETIMES
11. Do the teachers have enough supplies for all students in your class?	YES	NO	SOMETIMES
12. Is the equipment working in your school?	YES	NO	SOMETIMES
13. Do volunteers help in your school?	YES	NO	SOMETIMES
14. Is the counselor a good person to ask for help?	YES	NO	SOMETIMES
15. Are you learning in your classroom?	YES	NO	SOMETIMES
16. Are boys and girls treated the same?	YES	NO	SOMETIMES
17. Is the media center in your school a good place to find things?	YES	NO	SOMETIMES
18. Do students usually follow the rules in school?	YES	NO	SOMETIMES

sults of surveys like this one give teachers a way of assessing students' perceptions about the school and its programs. Altering negative aspects of a school and its programs is the first step in creating healthy environments and helping students to learn.

Family Assessment   The best of school environments may not help students who struggle because of deprivation, neglect, or abuse at home. By assessing home environments and family functioning, counselors determine the level of support a chid or adolescent is receiving from his or her family structure and use this information to seek appropriate community services.

The processes used to assess home environments and family functioning include interviews, observations, and students' records. For example, home visits enable counselors and teachers to examine the physical and social surroundings in which students live. Golden's (1988), "Quick Assessment of Family Functioning," uses a structured interview approach to assess five criteria: parental resources, chronicity of the problem, family communication, parental authority, and rapport with professional helpers. Assessment of these criteria permit counselors to distinguish between functional and dysfunctional families, and thereby make appropriate decisions about school services and referrals to outside agencies.

Peer Group Assessment   A final aspect of environmental evaluation that contributes to the overall appraisal of students is the assessment of social peer groups. Again, many of the methods already discussed are useful for assessing peer relationships. In particular, structured interviews and observations are viable assessment techniques.

Having students take stock of their friendships and peer associations adds to their overall self-awareness and contributes to their total profile. When students assess the behaviors, goals, and attitudes of their peers, they also examine and question their own traits, objectives, and beliefs. Part of the helping process is confronting the discrepancy that appears between how a person *is*, and how the person *wants to be*. Students who want to be successful in their school performance and social relationships can benefit by examining the peer associations that are most important to them and by determining the contradictions between the way they want to be and the way their peer groups are. A first step in making changes in one's life is to give up traditions and associations that keep a person locked to, or engaged in, non-productive and destructive behavior patterns.

The appraisal procedures and methods chosen by school counselors create a diagnostic process by which to choose appropriate services for students, parents, and teachers. In this way, appraisal procedures interact with the other essential services of a comprehensive school counseling program. By using appropriate and accurate assessment instruments and procedures, counselors are able to determine which services are most likely to generate successful outcomes.

In this chapter, we have examined the four essential services of a school counseling program: counseling, consulting, coordinating, and appraising. These four services form distinct categories that together establish and identify a broad role for professional counselors in schools. In the next four chapters, we will focus on specific knowledge, skills, and practices related to these four functions. In particular, we will examine the theoretical foundations and practical applications of individual counseling, group procedures, collaborative consultation, and student appraisal processes.

Selected Readings

Gibson, R. L., & Mitchell, M. H. (1990). *Introduction to Counseling and Guidance,* 3rd ed. (New York: Macmillan). This work is one of the most extensive texts written about the counseling profession. It covers all the major services provided by counselors in comprehensive programs, and pays particular attention to the role of school counselors.

Faust, V. (1968). *The Counselor-Consultant in the Elementary School* (Boston: Houghton-Mifflin). This classic text was one of the first major presentations of the consulting function for school counselors. Although written more than twenty years ago, it still has useful information about consulting with students, parents, and teachers.

Kameen, M. C., Robinson, E. H., & Rotter, J. C. (1985), "Coordination Activities: A Study of Perceptions of Elementary and Middle School Counselors," *Elementary School Guidance and Counseling, 20,* 97–103. This article reports the findings of a study that examined the coordination function of elementary and middle school counselors in the southeastern United States. The results showed that counselors are greatly involved in disseminating information, managing records, testing, and other coordinating activities.

Myrick, R. D., & Myrick, L. S. (1990). *The Teacher Advisor Program: An Innovative Approach to School Guidance* (Ann Arbor, MI: ERIC/CAPS). This monograph, published as one of a series on guidance and counseling programs, offers an excellent resource for planning and implementing teacher-advisee programs. It consists of articles by contributing authors who have established successful teacher-advisor programs in their schools.

References

Allen, R. D. (1931), "A Group Guidance Curriculum in the Senior High School," *Education, 52,* 189–194.

Bowman, R. P. (1986), "Peer Facilitator Programs for Middle Graders: Students Helping Each Other Grow," *The School Counselor, 33,* 221–229.

Brown, D., Pryzwansky, W. B., & Schulte, A. C. (1991). *Psychological Consultation: Introduction to Theory and Practice* 2nd Ed. (Boston: Allyn and Bacon).

Dagley, J. C. (1987), "A New Look at Developmental Guidance: The Hearthstone of School Counseling," *The School Counselor, 35,* 102–109.

Faust, V. (1968) *The Counselor-Consultant in the Elementary School* (Boston: Houghton-Mifflin).

Gazda, G. M. (1989). *Group Counseling: A Developmental Approach,* 4th ed. (Boston: Allyn and Bacon).

George, R. L., & Cristiani, T. S. (1981). *Counseling: Theory and Practice* (Englewood Cliffs, NJ: Prentice-Hall).

Getson, R., & Schweid, R. (1976), "School Counselors and the Buckley Amendment—Ethical Standards Squeeze," *The School Counselor, 24,* 56–58.

Gibson, R. L., & Mitchell, M. H. (1990). *Introduction to Guidance and Counseling,* 3rd ed. (New York: Macmillan).

Golden, L. B. (1988), "Quick Assessment of Family Functioning," *The School Counselor, 35,* 179–184.

Gronlund, N. E., & Linn, R. L. (1990). *Measurement and Evaluation in Teaching,* 6th ed. (New York: Macmillan).

Gysbers, N. C., & Henderson, P. (1988). *Developing and Managing Your School Guidance Program* (Alexandria, VA: American Association for Counseling and Development).

Humes, C. W., & Hohenshill, T. H. (1987), "Elementary Counselors, School Psychologists, School Social Workers: Who Does What?" *Elementary School Guidance and Counseling, 22,* 37–45.

Hummel, D. L., & Humes, C. W. (1984). *Pupil Services: Development, Coordination, Administration* (New York: Macmillan).

Kameen, M. C., Robinson, E. H., & Rotter, J. C. (1985), "Coordination Activities: A Study of Perceptions of Elementary and Middle School Counselors," *Elementary School Guidance and Counseling, 20,* 97–103.

Michael, J. (1986). *Advisor-Advisee Programs* (Columbus, OH: National Middle School Association).

Myrick, R. D. (1987). *Developmental Guidance and Counseling: A Practical Approach* (Minneapolis, MN: Educational Media Corporation).

Myrick, R. D., & Bowman, R. P. (1981). *Children Helping Children: Teaching Students to Become Friendly Helpers* (Minneapolis, MN: Educational Media Corporation).

Myrick, R. D., & Myrick, L. S. (1990). *The Teacher Advisor Program: An Innovative Approach to School Guidance* (Ann Arbor, MI: ERIC/CAPS).

Purkey, W. W., & Schmidt, J. J. (1987). *The Inviting Relationship: An Expanded Perspective for Professional Counseling* (Englewood Cliffs, NJ: Prentice-Hall).

Purkey, W. W., & Schmidt, J. J. (1990). *Invitational Learning for Counseling and Development* (Ann Arbor, MI: ERIC/CAPS).

Ritchie, M. H. (1982),"Parental Consultation: Practical Considerations," *The School Counselor, 29,* 402–410.

Schmidt, J. J. (1991). *A Survival Guide for the Elementary/Middle School Counselor* (West Nyack, NY: The Center for Applied Research in Education).

Schmidt, J. J., & Medl, W. A. (1983), "Six Magic Steps of Consulting," *The School Counselor, 30,* 212–216.

Shilling, L. E. (1984). *Perspectives on Counseling Theories* (Englewood Cliffs, NJ: Prentice-Hall).

Sutton, J. M., Jr., & Southworth, R. S. (1990), "The Effect of the Rural Setting on School Counselors," *The School Counselor, 37,* 173–178.

Thompson, C. L., & Randolph, L. B. (1988). *Counseling Children,* 2nd ed. (Pacific Groves, CA: Brooks/Cole).

Umansky, D. L., & Holloway, E. L. (1984), "The Counselor as Consultant: From Model to Practice," *The School Counselor, 31,* 392–338.

Wrenn, C. G. (1973). *The World of the Contemporary Counselor* (Boston: Houghton-Mifflin).

4

Individual Counseling

The counseling profession, including school counseling, takes its name from the essential function that defines and describes the primary role of its members. As noted in Chapter 1, counseling emerged as a major function of the profession due in large part to the work of Carl Rogers in the 1950s and 1960s. Throughout the development of the profession, the counseling function has continued as the mainspring for all other practices and services. This is true in all professional settings in which counselors work, whether they are mental-health centers, family clinics, prisons, hospitals, or schools. The basis for most services provided by professional counselors is a knowledge of counseling theories and the effective use of helping skills.

Counseling theories provide a framework in which counselors construct their personalized view of human development and behavior. Accordingly, counselors choose behaviors that are consistent with their theoretical beliefs to give their counseling relationships and other related services a dependable direction. Without this clear philosophical and theoretical focus, counselors would haphazardly choose from an array of counseling theories and models. Such random selection of professional practices would hardly result in effective or efficient services for their clients.

Effective and efficient helping skills encompass a wide range of behaviors, techniques, and practices that are compatible with the counselor's theoretical perspectives. Successful counselors are adept at choosing and developing skills and strategies that bring their theoretical beliefs to life for themselves and their clients. The hallmark of an effective counselor is the ability to take a particular theoretical stance, mold it to fit one's unique perspectives and beliefs, and acquire the communication and facilitation skills necessary to use these views and assumptions in helping oneself and others achieve optimal development.

In this chapter, we examine aspects and skills associated with the counseling process, particularly individual counseling. In addition, some counseling approaches are briefly presented with particular attention to theories and models suitable for counseling in school settings. Before exploring the processes, skills, and theories associated with the practice of counseling, we address some fundamental questions: What is counseling? For whom is it intended? And, what is its purpose?

What Is Counseling?

The counseling profession has discussed, presented, debated, and labored over this question since its beginning. The term counseling has been defined extensively in the professional literature, but this effort has not always resulted in consistent definitions. In part, this inconsistency is due to the varied settings in which counselors have come to practice and the abundant theories upon which these definitions have been based. *Webster's New International Dictionary* (1976) defined counseling as a "practice of professional service designed to guide an individual to a better understanding of...problems and potentialities by utilizing modern psychological principles and methods" (p. 518). Perhaps this may be the most accurate definition because it is free of theoretical influences. For historical reasons, however, it is helpful to review other sources in answering the question, "What is counseling?"

Early writings attempted to establish a clear meaning of counseling by distinguishing the practice of counseling from psychotherapy (Shertzer & Stone, 1966; Stefflre & Grant, 1972). Today this tradition continues in much of the counseling literature (George & Cristianai, 1990; Gladding, 1992). Shilling (1984) wrote that attempts "to distinguish counseling from psychotherapy have been less than totally successful. Some think that no distinction is necessary; others think it is essential" (p. 1). Gladding (1992) claimed that *"Psychotherapy (therapy* for short) differs significantly from counseling" (p. 6). Gladding noted that traditional psychotherapies:

1. Handle serious problems of mental illness
2. Focus on the past more than the present
3. Are concerned more with client insight than behavior change
4. Expect therapists to withhold rather than reveal their values and feelings
5. Require therapists to assume the role of an expert as opposed to an equal collaborator with the client (adapted from Pietrofesa, Hoffman, & Splete, 1984, pp. 6–7).

Twenty years earlier, Blocher (1966) listed five parallel conditions that defined counseling and the relationship between counselors and counselees accordingly:

1. Counselees are not "mentally ill," but rather capable of setting goals, making decisions, and being responsible for their behaviors.
2. Counseling is concerned with the present and the future.
3. Counselors are essentially partners and teachers and counselees are collaborators as they move toward mutually defined goals.
4. Counselors do not impose values on their counselees, nor do they attempt to hide their own values, feelings, and moral beliefs.
5. The goal of counseling is to change behavior, not simply to gain personal insight (adapted from George & Cristiani, 1990, p. 3).

In a humorous vein, Eysenck (1961) described psychotherapy as "an unidentified technique applied to unspecified problems with unpredictable outcomes. For this technique we recommend rigorous training" (p. 698). Many more authorities have delineated the differences between counseling and psychotherapy. Generally, these efforts have examined the goals of each process, the types of clients served, the training of counselors and therapists, and the work settings in which the helping relationship occurs.

George and Cristiani (1990) advocated a position that is closest to the view held by this author. They stated that "both counseling and psychotherapy utilize a common base of knowledge and a common set of techniques. Both involve a therapeutic process but they differ in terms of severity of the client's situation, in terms of the client's level of problem and/or functioning" (p. 5). For the purpose of this text, there is no need to make further distinctions or to point out additional similarities between counseling and psychotherapy. Overall, the processes of both are similar, with many overlapping elements and skills. In this book, we are more concerned about *what* counseling is, than about what it is *not*.

In 1945, Good's educational dictionary defined counseling as "individualized and personalized assistance with personal, educational, vocational problems" (Good, 1945, p. 104). Since that time, authors have provided a broad range of descriptions and definitions for the counseling process and relationship. As mentioned, many of these definitions incorporate the theoretical stance of their creators. For example, Carl Rogers's client-centered perspective defined counseling "as the process by which the basic nature of the self is relaxed in the safety of the relationship with the counselor, and where previously denied experiences are perceived, accepted, and integrated into an altered self" (Purkey & Schmidt, 1987, p. 142). In contrast to this self-oriented definition, behavioral theorists define counseling as a learning process that allows counselees to acquire new skills to change and control their behaviors (George & Cristiani, 1990; Shilling, 1984).

Psychodynamic definitions of the counseling process offer yet another perspective. Counselors who embrace psychodynamic theories view human development and behavior as an organization of related mental processes consisting of rational and irrational components. These components are characterized by constructs such as the *id,* the *ego,* the *self,* and others. One psychodynamic view defines counseling as a process of reducing "the anxiety of the client to manageable limits in order for the go to function in a more discriminating and effective manner"' (King & Bennington, 1972, p. 187). Harry Stack Sullivan, who based his theory of counseling on psychoanalysis, "viewed the therapeutic process as a unique interpersonal relationship, differing from other intimate relationships in its basic purpose...In short, the ultimate goal...is that clients leave with a greater degree of clarity about themselves and how they are living with others" (Corey, 1986, p. 30). The Adlerian school defines counseling as "enabling someone to modify self-defeating behaviors, make effective decisions, and solve problems efficiently," in a helping relationship that views people as "social, creative, active, decision-making beings moving toward unique goals and influenced by unique beliefs and perceptions" (Dinkmeyer, Dinkmeyer, & Sperry, 1987, p. 63).

Counseling has also been defined according to the specific focus and content of the helping relationship process. For example, one definition described counseling as a goal-oriented "process in which the counselor assists the counselee to make interpretations of facts related to choice, plan or adjustment which he needs to make" (Smith, 1955, p. 156). Similarly, Cottle and Downie (1970) proposed that the counseling process assists people in accepting and understanding information about themselves, so they are better able to make appropriate life decisions.

In addition to myriad theoretical orientations and varied views on process and content, the diverse locations and settings in which counselors practice compound the difficulty of arriving at a single precise definition of the counseling practice. Purkey and Schmidt (1987) noted that "In addition to working in a variety of settings, counselors confront such an array of human concerns that finding a common specific definition of their professional service is extremely difficult" (p. 144). Perhaps Orr (1965) said it best:

> *The breadth and diversity of counseling may be suggested by such characterizations as the following: It is the* art *of helping people to help themselves. It is the applied* science *of psycho-socio-biological pathology. It is the* process *of solving human problems in a professional setting. It is a* relationship *between a trained helping-person and other persons with problems from which the latter draw strength, confidence, and insight in the process of working out their own solutions to the difficulties. (p. 3)*

More recent definitions of the counseling process illustrate the profession's focus on a wide range of human needs, including preventive, developmental, and remedial relationships. Pietrofesa, Hoffman, and Splete (1984) presented counseling as a process facilitated by trained professionals with persons "seeking help in gaining greater self-understanding and improved decision-making and behavior-change skills for problem resolution and/or developmental growth" (p. 6). By constructing a broader purpose for their helping relationships, counselors offer services for an array of people who are basically healthy functioning individuals. Among this group, some people have psychological and social concerns, and others seek information and support for developmental aspects of their lives and to make decisions for their future. Gladding (1992) summarized these elements by defining counseling as a "short-term, interpersonal, theory-based, professional activity guided by ethical and legal standards that focuses on helping persons who are basically psychologically healthy to resolve developmental and situational problems" (p. 9).

Schools are specific settings in which the counseling process is practiced. As with other professional settings, the primary mission of schools colors the practice of counseling with a focus on the educational needs of students, parents, and teachers. As such, counseling in schools is a process of helping students, parents, or teachers learn about themselves, understand how their personal characteristics, human potential, and behaviors influence their relationships with others, and make choices to solve current problems while planning strategies for optimal development. By using a broad definition, school counselors assess which students, parents, and teachers will benefit from counseling relationships, and determine whether or not they are the best professionals to provide this service to these groups.

Who Needs Counseling?

In elementary, middle, and senior high schools, counselors provide counseling services for a multitude of reasons. As seen so far in this text, school counselors offer a wide range of related and interrelated services to help people resolve problems and make decisions. Unfortunately, because counseling has retained a mystical aura in much the same way that psychology and psychiatry have, some people believe that counseling is the answer to all problems. In short, counseling should "fix people" who are not behaving the way others want them to be. For example, sometimes teachers bring students to school counselors with a combined plea and command that a "student is not doing work in class, and needs counseling." While such a student may benefit from helping relationship with counselors, it may be equally beneficial in these situations for teachers to learn about the student's academic needs, learning styles, or other characteristics that impede progress in school. In this case, a consulting relationship with the teacher may be as beneficial as counseling with the student.

When receiving referrals from students, parents, and teachers, school counselors first ask the question: "Who needs what?" In deciding whether or not counseling is an appropriate service to provide in a given referral, counselors investigate a number of criteria and ask several questions. The information they collect and the answers they generate from this investigation enable counselors to make appropriate decisions about counseling services. Some of the criteria they review and the questions they ask are:

1. Does the counselee see the situation in ways similar to those who made the referral? There is little reason to counsel someone about a problem identified by others, when the individual does not see, or admit, that any problem exists. At the very least, the individual who is referred must know that a conflict exists with the person who made the referral.

2. Does the counselee perceive a need for assistance and accept counseling as one method of addressing this concern? Not all individuals enter counseling relationships with a strong desire to change. Gladding (1992) observed that a majority of counselees are reluctant or unmotivated to change. In such cases, success is possible if counselors and counselees establish genuine working relationships. As counseling research has repeatedly documented, genuineness on the part of counselors is fundamental in developing effective helping relationships (George & Cristiani, 1990). In instances of reluctance and discouragement on the part of counselees, counselors use persuasion and confrontation (Ivey, 1991; Kerr, Claiborn, & Dixon, 1982; Olson, & Claiborn, 1990) to encourage counselees to take initiative and pursue helping relationships.

3. How much control does the prospective counselee have in bringing about necessary change? One criteria that enables counselees to be successful is their ability to gain control of the situation in question. Students in schools rarely have total control over situations in their lives. This is particularly true with younger children in the intermediate and primary grades. Family relations, parental substance abuse, socio-economic status, and a host of mitigating factors are beyond the control of individual students. In deciding whether or not counseling is appropriate, counselors identify the behavior or situation needing to change and determine the degree to which the counselee will be able to affect that change. If students have the capability to control situations, make necessary adjustments, and choose new behaviors to cope in the future, counseling may be appropriate. At the very least, individual counseling might offer support for students who are trapped in circumstances beyond their control, and might suggest coping skills to survive what appears to be an unbearable situation. By surviving initially, students gain time to make long- term plans, develop new skills, and strengthen positive self-perceptions.

4. Is the counselee committed to making changes, learning new behaviors, or seeking alternatives to the present situation? Counseling that begins and continues without eliciting commitment is a one-sided and often frustrating process for both the counselor and the counselee. Commitment may not exist at the start of the counseling process, but if the counselor estab-

lishes a genuine relationship, it eventually will emerge. Without commitment there is no counseling relationship.

The preceding questions and answers help counselors assess their clients' readiness for counseling and willingness to enter beneficial helping relationships. In the examples above, these questions and answers focus on problem-solving and crisis-oriented counseling. But counseling, particularly school counseling, serve other purposes as well, including developmental goals and objectives. In developmental counseling relationships, the need is established by a referring agent (such as a parent or teacher) or a client (student) who has the desire to explore opportunities, assess potential, and energize interactions with other people. By helping students cultivate opportunities for development and growth, school counselors move from problem-oriented perspectives to "wide-lens" views of their helping relationships (Purkey & Schmidt, 1987). As such, the answer to the question, "Who needs counseling?" depends on the goals and objectives of these helping relationships. Effective counseling is achieved by establishing appropriate and clear goals.

Goals of Counseling

What are the goals of counseling? On the surface, this appears to be a simple enough question, but it is not easy to answer. As Shilling (1984) illustrated, determining the goals of counseling relationships depends on whose goals we are talking about—the counselor's or the counselee's. Sometimes the goals of counselors and their counselees differ. For example, a high-school student may seek ways of "getting my parents off my back about college," while the counselor's goal is to assist the student in self- assessment, career planning, and educational decision-making. In many instances, people who ask counselors for assistance are searching for answers and ways to solve problems without taking any risks themselves. They wish to avoid the issue of changing their own behaviors or of making important decisions, and instead want others to change or make decisions for them.

George and Cristiani (1990) presented five major goals that are emphasized in most counseling theories and models. An adaptation of these goals includes objectives to:

1. facilitate changes in one's behavior
2. improve social and personal relationships
3. increase social effectiveness and one's ability to cope
4. learn decision-making processes
5. enhance human potential and enrich self-development (pp. 6–8)

Setting goals in counseling relationships is particularly important in school settings where finding solutions and alleviating difficulties in a timely manner are essential. Remembering that the primary purpose of school counseling is to enhance educational planning, expand opportunities for learning, and strengthen students' achievement, school counselors should consider the following guidelines when selecting goals for individual counseling:

1. Relate goals to some aspect of learning. When counseling students in schools, the ultimate objective is to enhance learning and development. Therefore, the goals of counseling should relate in some way to this outcome. Whether the main concern is social, such as peer relationships; personal, such as the loss of a loved one; or psychological, such as dealing with fears and anxieties, the counseling relationship needs to address these issues in the context of their impact on educational development.

2. Generalize the achievement of educational goals to other relationships. Because time is precious in schools, it is helpful for students to take the knowledge and understanding achieved in counseling and apply it towards other relationships and situations in school and at home.

3. Share learning experiences and skill development with others. The assistance that individual students receive in counseling can be magnified and expanded if they share experiences with others. Group counseling, classroom guidance, and peer helper programs are a few of the vehicles school counselors and students use to accomplish this goal.

4. Involve parents whenever possible. Students of all ages, children through adolescents, benefit from the support and nurturing of caring parents. In their counseling relationships, school counselors are wise to win the cooperation of their counselees and persuade students of the importance of parental involvement. In some counseling relationships, such as in child-abuse cases, parental involvement may not be feasible, but in the majority of school counseling relationships this goal is not only possible, it is desirable.

Knowing what counseling is, determining who needs what kind of counseling service, and establishing appropriate goals for counseling relationships enables counselors and other services of a school counseling program, is a process. It has a beginning, it is characterized by a series of sequential steps or stages, and it ends when identified goals are achieved. Just as there is an abundance of counseling theories (Parloff, 1976), there is also a wide selection of helping models from which to choose (Brammer, 1988; Egan, 1986; Ivey, 1991; Pietrofesa, Hoffman, & Splete, 1984). Having effective models on which to base their counseling relationships permits counselors to structure and direct effective helping processes. In schools with young students, structure and direction are appropriate, even in counseling relationships.

The Helping Process

Models of counseling include anywhere from three to a multitude of stages. The following sections illustrate a four-stage approach to the counseling process. Specific stages, such as those that follow, offer a blueprint for counselors to build effective relationships. By mentally processing the different stages of their helping relationships, counselors stay on course and consistently encourage counselees to move closer to their identified goals.

Establishing a Relationship

Counseling is the process of disclosing personal hopes, desires, concerns, fears, and failures in a attempt to change behaviors, alter external factors, and set future goals. This kind of intimate sharing and communicating is only possible in relationships founded on acceptance, understanding, and positive regard. As seen in Chapter 1 this foundation is believed to consist of "core conditions" that include empathy, respect, and genuineness on the part of the counselor (Carkhuff & Berenson, 1967; Rogers, 1951; Truax & Carkhuff, 1967). Counselors demonstrate empathic understanding when they perceive the world (or situation) the way that their clients do, and accurately communicate this perceptual comprehension back to their clients. Two levels of empathy, primary and advanced empathy, have been described to illustrate different behaviors and skills counselors use to reflect understanding with their clients (Carkhuff, 1969; Gladding, 1992). Primary empathy is the process of understanding and communicating the essential feelings and beliefs expressed by the client and acknowledging the "experiences and behaviors underlying these feelings" (Gladding, 1992, p. 205). Advanced empathic responses move the relationship beyond initial understanding toward increased "self-exploration by adding deeper feeling and meaning to the client's expression" (George & Cristiani, 1990, p. 158).

For training purposes, Carkhuff (1969) identified five levels of empathic responses to illustrate how counselors and other helpers use verbal and behavioral expressions to add to or detract from the messages conveyed by clients and helpers. The lowest levels of this training model depict responses that demonstrate little or no empathic understanding, and, in fact, they may damage the helping relationship. In contrast, upper levels are highly facilitative by relating to the surface feelings expressed and accurately stating underlying feelings and dynamics that the client does not openly convey in the process.

Respect is another essential condition of the first phase of counseling relationships. Sometimes referred to as "unconditional positive regard," respect includes the ingredients of equality, equity, and shared responsibility. In counseling, nothing is more important "than the people in the process, and so it embraces a special 'being with' attitude with oneself and others. Central to this 'being with' attitude is a respect for the rich complexity and unique value of each human being" (Purkey & Schmidt, 1987, p. 8). In schools, this condition of respecting the person's value is vital to the successful outcome of helping relationships with students. Sometimes schools are designed, built, and programmed without regard or concern for the primary clients they intend to serve. This is illustrated by the tragic refrain spoken by the burned-out teacher: "I love teaching, it's students I can't stand!"

School counselors have an obligation to actively and visibly demonstrate regard for students, showing that they have value, can be responsible, and are deserving of respectful treatment. This respect is not easily achieved. Counselors who practice honorably, with care, and at the highest level of professional performance are able to win the respect of students, parents, and teachers. Counselors who neglect their obligations, divulge confidences, behave in non-accepting ways, use ridicule, and defame the education and counseling professions demonstrate disrespect toward themselves and others, and invariably are avoided by students, parents, and teachers.

Genuineness is related to respect because counselors who are accepting of others are in a better position to disclose their true feelings and reactions to the concerns expressed by their clients. At the same time, genuine counselors demonstrate consistent behaviors without discrepancy between what they say and do. Genuineness, sometimes called congruence, is a characteristic that allows counselors to be who they are without playing a role or hiding behind a facade. This congruence emerges from respectful relationships to gently, yet accurately, let clients know how they appear and come across to others.

One caveat is appropriate here. Genuinely facilitative responses are not blunt, frank reactions and reflections to "let students know what life is *really* all about." Quite the contrary, a genuine counselor balances empathy and respect with honest opinions and feelings in quest of a mutually beneficial relationship. Through the process of sharing feelings and perceptions, counselors and counselees establish beneficial interactions in the helping process and move from this introductory phase to a deeper and more meaningful exploration of concerns.

Exploring Concerns

Counseling is more than simply forming a relationship. It is the process of using a helping relationship to focus on concerns, either developmental or problem-oriented, and make decisions to remedy a situation, acquire new skills, or enhance one's awareness of self. Relationships that fail to move to this next stage cannot be viewed as counseling. They may be friendships, conversations, or other types of interaction, but they are not professional helping.

Many counselors in schools and other settings seem unable to move their counseling relationships beyond the phase of building rapport toward a deeper exploration of issues and concerns. In part, this may be due to their lack of understanding of specific counseling theories and practices. All counseling approaches use similar skills and behaviors in the initial phase to establish a viable working relationship. Beyond this first stage, however, the language, assumptions, and beliefs of these various counseling theories and models begin to distinguish themselves from one another. Counselors who do not have clear understanding and command of specific approaches struggle to assist their clients in further exploration to take action to address their concerns adequately.

The exploration phase is characterized by constructs, language, techniques, and strategies created and endorsed by particular models and approaches selected by counselors. For example, Adlerian counselors focus on birth order, family constellation, goals of behavior, and feelings of inferiority, and they use life-style assessment techniques to help clients understand their private logic and its relationship to success in life (Dinkmeyer, DInkmeyer, & Sperry, 1987). In contrast, behavioral counselors identify specific problem behaviors, collect baseline data, examine stimuli and antecedents of behaviors, and develop behavioral techniques, such as skills training, relaxation training, systematic desensitization, and other methods to correct or change behaviors during the next phase of the counseling process.

Counselors who do not have clear understanding and knowledge of specific models and techniques are unable to explore clients' concerns and move toward resolution, awareness, and learning. In short, these counselors do not help their clients fully understand the concerns that have been raised and the factors that make these concerns barriers to future development. Therefore, such counselors are lost as to what means can best assist their clients in moving forward from a point of uncertainty, indecision, or destructive behavior towards a more productive direction in life.

Counselors who know their theoretical foundations, and have command of basic skills and techniques compatible with their assumptions about human development, behavior, and helping relationships, are in a position to be a beneficial presence in the lives of others. They are able to guide their clients through adequate exploration of pertinent issues to the selection of alternatives for resolving conflicts, gaining greater awareness, and making life-enriching decisions. This process moves the relationship towards the next stage, sometimes called the action phase of counseling.

Taking Action

A helping relationship that does not include definitive action to address the client's concerns is not counseling. Earlier, you learned the importance of goal setting in the initial phase of the counseling process. The action phase of counseling relationships enables clients and counselors to realize the goals they have chosen. Similar to the exploration phase of counseling, the action phase is influenced by the theoretical beliefs and helping models embraced by practicing counselors. Adlerian and other psychodynamic approaches, for example, usually feature development of insight, reorientation of attitudes and beliefs, redefining goals, and choosing alternative behaviors. In contrast, behavioral strategies tend to include social modeling techniques, behavioral contracts, skills training, self-monitoring, decision-making models, and similar approaches.

In the action stage, the counselor and client agree on a particular plan and strategy, monitor the implementation of that plan, and evaluate the outcome of the strategy used. When evaluation indicates that the problem has been resolved, the counselor and client have the opportunity to examine other issues of concern or other areas for developmental growth. If their decision is to continue in a helping relationship, they return to the exploration phase once again. When no other concerns or issues to address are identified, the counseling relationship is ended.

Ending the Relationship

All relationships come to an end, either naturally or circumstantially. Counseling relationships are no different. They too complete a final stage which is called closure or termination. In this stage, the counselor and counselee arrive at a point where the purpose and goals of their relationship have been successfully achieved, and now it is time to move on to other goals and other relationships.

Gladding (1992) emphasized that this phase of counseling is the least understood and most neglected of all the stages. Perhaps this is because in many successful helping relationships, both the counselor and counselee find it difficult to sever the ties that bind them. In some ways, the concept of ending a helping relationship is contradictory. By definition, a helping relationship is continuous. On the other hand, however, counseling that sets no time frame or goal for closure may continue indefinitely without adequate attention to the exploration of concerns, commitment for change, and decisions about appropriate plans of action. This is a poor use of counselors' time and passive deceit of counselees who believe they are being helped.

Some theorists believe that each individual counseling session should have a specific time limit (Pietrofesa, Hoffman, & Splete, 1984). In schools, sessions may range from about twenty to fifty minutes depending on the age and development of the student and the school schedule. Other authorities maintain that the duration of the counseling relationship should be established early in the process so that time can be used efficiently and effectively (Gladding, 1992). According to this view, the counselor and counselee should make tentative agreement on the number of sessions they will have in the counseling process.

In school counseling, the process of ending or terminating a helping relationship deserves extra care and consideration (Henderson, 1987). Because students remain in school with the counselor, the closing of specific helping relationships takes on a different meaning than when counselors terminate relationships with clients in clinical and agency settings. Students who see counselors for individual sessions also interact with them in other ways during the school day. They may talk with counselors about career information, participate in classroom guidance, or be supervised by a counselor in after-school extracurricular activities. Because these interactions are ongoing, closure of an individual counseling relationship must be planned and done gradually.

In some cases, the decision to end counseling with a student may be made jointly with the child, parents, and teachers giving input to the process. Ending counseling relationships with students is also facilitated by preparing them gradually for termination during the latter phases of counseling. By reinforcing the progress students have made, emphasizing the skills they have attained, encouraging them to express their feelings about ending the counseling relationship, and helping them learn about other avenues for continued support, school counselors bring appropriate closure to successful helping relationships.

As with all communication processes and relationships, counseling requires a high level of leadership and facilitative skills to help clients reach their goals. Generally, the skills used in counseling cut across different theoretical and practical perspectives adopted by counselors. In most instances, these skills are also applied in other helping relationships, such as consulting. In the following section, we explore some general skills found in most counseling approaches.

Counseling Skills

The ultimate purpose of any individual counseling relationship is for the counselee to adapt and develop effective self-help skills. To reach this goal, school counselors select reliable models and approaches to counseling, and they practice with skills appropriate for and compatible to these models and approaches. For an in-depth review of counseling skills, the reader is encouraged to examine Egan's *The Skilled Helper* (1986), Brammer's *The Helping*

Relationship: Process and Skills (1988), and Ivey's *Intentional Interviewing and Counseling* (1988) among other resources.

Brammer (1988) listed a wide range of helping skills that counselors select depending on the focus and intent of their relationships. Some of these skills enhance and facilitate understanding, others offer support and assistance in crisis situations, and a few focus on positive action in counseling relationships. Table 4–1 illustrates the many communicating, facilitating, problem-solving, and behavior changing skills available to counselors and their clients.

Skills that facilitate understanding begin with basic listening and attending behaviors by the counselor to let counselees know they are being heard and understood. Similarly, reflection of feeling and content tell coun-

TABLE 4–1   Counseling Skills

FOR UNDERSTANDING	FOR SUPPORT AND CRISIS INTERVENTION	FOR POSITIVE INTERACTION

1. Listening
   1.1 Attending
   1.2 Paraphrasing
   1.3 Clarifying
   1.4 Perception checking
2. Leading
   2.1 Indirect leading
   2.2 Direct leading
   2.3 Focusing
   2.4 Questioning
3. Reflecting
   3.1 Feeling
   3.2 Content
   3.3 Experience
4. Summarizing
   4.1 Feeling
   4.2 Content
   4.3 Process
5. Confronting
   5.1 Describing feelings
   5.2 Expressing feelings
   5.3 Feeding back
   5.4 Meditating
   5.5 Repeating
   5.6 Associating
6. Interpreting
   6.1 Explaining
   6.2 Questioning
   6.3 Fantasizing
7. Informing
   7.1 Giving information
   7.2 Suggesting
	1. Supporting
	   1.1 Contacting
	   1.2 Reassuring
	   1.3 Relaxing
	2. Crisis intervention
	   2.1 Building hope
	   2.2 Consoling
	   2.3 Controlling
	   2.4 Developing Alternatives
	3. Centering
	   3.1 Identifying strengths
	   3.2 Reviewing growth
	      experiences
	   3.3 Recalling peak
	      experiences
	4. Referring
		1. Problem solving and
		   decision making
		   1.1 Identifying problems
		   1.2 Changing problems to goals
		   1.3 Analyzing problems
		   1.4 Exploring alternatives and
		      implications
		   1.5 Planning a course of action
		   1.6 Generalizing to new
		      problems
		2. Behavior changing
		   2.1 Modeling
		   2.2 Rewarding
		   2.3 Extinguishing
		   2.4 Desensitizing
		   2.5 Shaping

Source: Brammer, L.M. (1988). *The Helping Relationship: Process and Skills*, (4th Edition). Englewood Cliffs, NJ: Prentice Hall. Reproduced with permission.

selees that their messages are heard, their feelings are accepted, and their concerns are understood. Other skills, such as helping students focus on pertinent issues and set specific direction in the counseling relationships, also contribute to better understanding. Summarizing skills help counselees remain focused and become goal-oriented in the helping relationship process.

Returning to the four phases of the helping process referred to earlier, we might assume that listening, facilitating, and other skills for understanding are particularly important in the first phase—establishing a relationship. Of course, these skills are beneficial, if not essential, throughout the entire helping process, but they are of critical value early in a counseling relationship.

Some additional skills for understanding, such as confronting, questioning, interpreting, and informing tend to move the helping relationship toward the second phase—exploring concerns—by enabling the client to express issues and problems clearly. In schools, counselors use these skills as a means of checking student commitment to change, explaining school rationale, and offering information to help students make accurate choices.

The skills Brammer (1988) identified for positive action in the counseling relationship include identifying and analyzing problems, planning action, generalizing skills learned to solve new problems, and turning problems into challenges and goals. His behavior-changing skills, such as modeling, rewarding, and extinguishing are commonly practiced in school environments by teachers and counselors. These skills are particularly identified with behavioral approaches to counseling, and can be helpful in enabling students to modify behaviors through individual counseling relationships.

School counselors also enter crisis-oriented relationships with students, and in doing so, establish initial processes that proceed referrals to other professionals and agencies in the community. In addition to the skills listed by Brammer (1988) and others, which include supporting, implementing crisis intervention skills, and centering, school counselors have knowledge of assessment procedures to determine the degree of risk and the level of crises students face. These assessment procedures include interviews with students, parents, teachers, and others, observations of students' behaviors, medical records, questionnaires, and other methods.

Crisis counseling, by nature, tends to be directive and action- oriented. When students are in crisis, counselors do not have the luxury to allow time for client self-reflection and in-depth exploration of perceptions and concerns. "Typically, students in crises want direction, and it is only after they are stabilized and secure that they are able to assume some decision-making responsibilities. This responsibility comes gradually, after an initial plan of action has been established and the student has experienced preliminary success" (Schmidt, 1991, p. 176).

A final aspect of crisis counseling, as with all other forms of helping relationships, is the follow-up and evaluation of outcomes. When students have made changes, adjusted behaviors, chosen direction, or made other significant decisions that parallel the goals and objectives of the counseling relationship, school counselors assess the results of their helping skills. Even though students may make progress in the helping relationship, counselors sometimes decide that they have gone far enough within the scope of their competencies and program guidelines. In these instances, counselors refer to other services in the school system or community.

Whatever skills counselors use in their helping relationships, the overall process is influenced by the theoretical models and approaches they select. School counselors are trained in many different theories and approaches to helping. While there appear to be countless theories and models from which to choose, a few approaches have gained prominence in school counseling. Four of these approaches are reviewed in the next section as examples of counseling methods used by school counselors.

Counseling Approaches and Models

In practice, most school counselors, like counselors and psychologists in clinical settings, embrace an *eclectic* philosophy (Corey, 1986). Eclectic counseling is the integration of a number of related theories, approaches, and techniques into a personalized and systematic process. Over the years, eclectic practice has been both encouraged and condemned in the counseling literature (Rychlak, 1985). When counselors select approaches systematically, with purpose and understanding, their integrative styles allow them to appropriately expand options for their clients. On the other hand, when this selection process is haphazard without any rationale, the counseling process may appear unfocused, without clear direction. As Corey described it: "In this brand of 'sloppy' eclecticism the pragmatic practitioner grabs for anything that seems to work, often making no attempt to determine whether the therapeutic procedures are indeed working" (Corey, 1986, p. 289).

As noted earlier, there are numerous counseling theories and approaches from which counselors must make rational, logical choices. Simultaneously, school counselors face the challenge of helping students, parents, and teachers evaluate their situations, explore concerns, examine alternatives, and make expeditious decisions within a reasonable period of time. These two conditions, make it palatable for school counselors to adopt an eclectic posture, choosing from a range of approaches found to be successful in school settings. In doing so, they search for common elements among compatible theories and approaches and recognize the important differences that exist when integrating various philosophies and practices (Purkey & Schmidt, 1987). Counselors who borrow from different perspectives to establish an *eclectic practice* are successful when they choose intentionally, with adequate knowledge of the approaches selected, awareness of related research findings, and a clear understanding of their therapeutic purposes and goals.

In this section, we consider four counseling theories and approaches that have had wide acclaim in school counseling literature, research, and practice. They are offered here as a sample of the theories and models from which school counselors select in establishing counseling relationships with students, parents, and teachers. By necessity, the following descriptions are brief. The reader is encouraged to review the references at the end of the chapter for additional information about these and other approaches, and to gain understanding of compatible counseling theories and models.

Adlerian Counseling

One approach used in schools is Adlerian counseling, founded on the theories of individual psychology and developed by Alfred Adler. A collaborator of Sigmund Freud, Adler split with Freud in 1911 because he opposed the emphasis of psychoanalytic theory on the sexual etiology of most human difficulties. In contrast, Adler framed his theory of human development around the belief that "individuals were motivated by social responsibility and need achievement, not driven by the inborn instincts" (George & Cristiani, 1990, p. 48).

Adler theorized that people are basically social beings who consistently search to find their position in life. The process of striving for a successful position in life is fundamental to the theory of individual psychology, and gives Adlerian counseling a positive, optimistic posture upon which to build beneficial helping relationships. This positive, developmental view of human behavior is much more compatible with educational environments than is the deterministic, pessimistic outlook of traditional psychoanalysis.

In addition to the emphasis on an individual's social responsibility and power to control life and make conscious decisions, the Adlerian approach focuses on the role of family relationships and interactions between parents and children. One of Alfred Adler's major accomplishments was his founding of child guidance clinics throughout the Vienna public schools where he began teaching social workers and school teachers the theory and practice of individual psychology. These clinics pioneered early attempts at teaching psychological principles and interaction skills through live demonstrations. They also added another dimension, one of instruction, to the Adlerian approach that contributes to its compatibility with school settings.

The principles of Adlerian psychology adapt well to the practice of counseling in schools. In individual and group counseling, students explore their positions in families, examine perceptions of self and others, attack detrimental actions, and establish goals for becoming responsible in their personal and social lives. A variety of techniques suggested by Adlerian theorists are appropriate for school counseling relationships, including play therapy, exploration of life tasks, use of imagery, and completion of life-style questionnaires (Dinkmeyer, Dinkmeyer, & Sperry, 1987). The practical application of Adler's theory is largely the result of methods developed by his disciples, such as Dreikurs (1964, 1968), Dinkmeyer (1987), Corsini (1979, and others.

Adlerian approaches have potential for wide application in comprehensive school counseling programs. In addition to individual counseling relationships, Adlerian principles are applied in small group counseling, guidance activities, family counseling, teacher in-service, and parent education programs (Dinkmeyer & Dinkmeyer, 1982; Dinkmeyer & McKay, 1976; Dinkmeyer, McKay, & Dinkmeyer, 1980). While many of these programs and techniques are applicable in school counseling programs, research has been mixed on their effectiveness (Jackson & Brown, 1986; Morse, Bockoven, & Bettesworth, 1988). One criticism of Adlerian approaches is the lack of rigorous research to document its effectiveness. Nevertheless, its educational focus makes it appealing to school counselors who attempt to establish comprehensive programs of services for students, parents, and teachers.

Reality Therapy

Glasser first presented the tenets of reality therapy in his book, *Mental Health or Mental Illness?* (1961) and followed with *Reality Therapy: A New Approach to Psychiatry* in 1965. In 1969, his book *Schools Without Failure* popularized this approach with school counselors. More recent writings by Glasser, including *Stations of the Mind* (1981) and *Take Effective Control of Your Life* (1984), have further developed and expanded his theory of counseling and human behavior.

Today, reality therapy adheres to the belief that the human brain operates as a control system acting as kind of a gyrocompass that guides peoples' behaviors. This internal system allows people to screen their options through a type of perceptual filter, and select behaviors that satisfy their needs. In this respect, Glasser's approach "does not rest on a deterministic philosophy . . . but is built on the assumption that people are ultimately self-determining and in charge of their life" (Corey, 1986, p. 245). Therefore, the individual is responsible for decisions made and behaviors chosen.

This focus on personal responsibility and the power of the individual to make choices to gain control of life is appealing in school settings which emphasize learning and instruction. According to Gibson and Mitchell (1990), "From a reality therapy standpoint, counseling is simply a special kind of teaching or training that attempts to teach an individual what he should have learned during normal growth in a rather short period of time" (p. 134). Glasser's theory has been widely applied in school settings for counseling, behavior management, and classroom guidance discussions. Its effectiveness has been suggested and documented in a number of areas including work with special student populations, student self-concept, and self-directed behavior (Borgers, 1980; Heuchert, 1989; Omizo & Cubberly, 1983).

Another appeal of Glasser's approach is that, like Adlerian counseling, it is directive, positive, and practical in its approach. Unlike Adlerian counseling, which emphasizes personal insight and reorientation of fictional goals (Dinkmeyer, Dinkmeyer, & Sperry, 1987), reality therapy focuses on behavior change through the use of behavioral plans and contracts. Reality therapy is not as interested in past dynamics as much as it is concerned with the present perceptions and behaviors that are problematic. Glasser described eight steps to the reality therapy process (1965, 1969). In these steps, the counselor is encouraged to:

1. Become involved with the counselee and develop a caring genuine relationship. Thompson and Rudolph (1988) noted that involvement may imply complex relationships, but its use in reality therapy is a straightforward encouragement of honesty, openness, and empathy for the counselee.

2. Focus on current behaviors. Many counseling approaches ask counselors to emphasize feelings with their clients. In reality therapy, counselors attend to the counselee's behaviors, which contribute to various feeling states.

3. Emphasize the present rather than the past. In this approach the counselor and counselee are more concerned about what *is* than what *was*. Past events are only significant in terms of their relationship to present behavioral choices for which the counselee is responsible. These past events do not, however, cause the present behaviors; for, as we have noted, behaviors are chosen by the individual.

4. Encourage counselees to make judgments about their behavior. Since individuals are responsible for choosing their own behaviors, it is logical that they can assess the value these behaviors have regarding their development and the development of others. With students in schools, this process takes the form of questioning whether of not students' behaviors are the best way of reaching their goals.

5. Make a plan. When a counselee decides that present behaviors are unproductive or destructive, the next step is to design a plan for changing to more productive, constructive behaviors. At the same time, commitment is sought to assure that the counselee will work toward this goal.

6. Get commitment. A plan is useless unless the parties involved have the desire to see it through. Counselees who struggle with commitment tend to have a history of failure in other aspects of their lives. This cycle of failure is often seen with students in schools, and that is why commitment is essential in applying reality therapy concepts in school counseling.

7. Eliminate punishment. Reality therapy endorses the use of logical consequences and "maintains that punishment aimed at changing behavior is ineffective and . . . results both in reinforcing the client's failure identity and in damaging the client/therapist relationship" (Corey, 1986, p. 253). Glasser's strong stance against punishment as a behavioral strategy has been instrumental and influential in creating effective positive approaches to school discipline.

8. Never give up. Many of the problems school counselors and students confront seem insurmountable. Reality therapy encourages counselors to "keep the faith." Sometimes school counselors need to search for other resources to effectively help children and adolescents. This is not a sign of failure or of giving up. Rather, it is good professional judgment when counseling relationships have not resulted in noticeable progress or desired outcomes.

While reality therapy has been criticized because it is seemingly simplistic, ignores past events, and de-emphasizes the role of the unconscious, it remains a popular approach in counseling, and particularly with school counselors. Its strength is derived from a positive focus on human capability and the individual's power to control life's goals and one's own behaviors. As an educative process, reality therapy is a viable approach for counseling in schools. This is particularly true given the evidence of its success with discipline problems, student achievement, and special populations (Shilling, 1984).

Cognitive-Behavioral Counseling

Several approaches to counseling emphasize the individual's ability to receive information and analyze messages through cognitive processes that give them psychological, emotional, and behavioral meaning. Cognitive theorists attempt to bridge the gap between behaviorists, who attend strictly to observable,measurable actions, and advocates of perceptual principles who believe people are thinking, reasoning brings who choose behaviors through a process of internally receiving, reviewing, accepting, and rejecting messages from themselves and others. According to George and Cristiani (1990), "The synthesis of cognitive and behavioral approaches has occurred as theorists and practitioners have recognized that both approaches were dealing with inner cognitive processes such as thoughts, perceptions, and covert speech as a means of guiding actions that would lead to a more satisfying emotional state" (p. 81). Although there are differences among the approaches that can be categorized within the cognitive-behavioral school, we summarize their common concepts here, particularly as applied in school counseling.

Ellis is credited as one of the pioneers of cognitive approaches to counseling with his rational-emotive therapy (Ellis, 1962). Ellis's theory presents a number of assumptions about human nature and development that, in sum, describe people as having the capacity to be either rational or irrational in their thinking. When they are rational, people tend to function in effective and satisfying ways. In contrast, when people think irrationally, they behave in a disturbing, illogical manner.

Emotional and psychological well-being relates to people's rational and logical thoughts. As a result, cognitive processes, emotional feelings, and selected behaviors are interrelated. For the counselor and client to address any one of these concepts, it is necessary to consider the other two. For example, a counselor cannot help students alleviate ill feelings about being rejected by others without examining students' thoughts about peer relationships and their behaviors towards themselves and others. A student who is sad because "nobody likes me,"needs to explore the events (perceptions) and subsequent thoughts that have led to this conclusion. Through this process, the student can accurately and logically assess relevant events, determine how he or she would like to be accepted by others, and design behaviors with which to pursue reasonable goals toward acceptance.

Rational-emotive therapy (RET) uses an approach to counseling that has been described as the A, B, C, D, and E method. In this model, A is the event that triggers the though. Returning to the example above, the student is excluded from an activity by other students (A) and concludes "nobody likes me." This concluding thought is B, the rational or irrational thought that the student creates. When the student thinks, "nobody likes me," the feelings experienced may be sadness, rejection, anger, or other negative emotion. Consequential feelings are the third component, C, of the RET paradigm.

By using rational-emotive therapy, counselors help their counselees examine the activating events and dispute the irrational thoughts they have about them. The approach designates D as the process of attacking and debunking irrational beliefs, such as negative thoughts to put oneself down or choose hopeless directions. In counseling, this process includes questioning the validity and accuracy of these destructive thoughts. The logical and rational answers to these questions become the last part of the process, E, to help counselees learn positive self-messages and choose healthy behaviors.

Meichenbaum (1977) developed another cognitive-behavioral approach that attempts to identify and alter people's negative self-messages rather than interpret their irrational beliefs. His approach, called cognitive behavior modification, teaches specific problem-solving and coping skills to assist with behavior problems. In this approach, a fundamental concept for describing and understanding human behavior is the *internal dialogue,* also referred to as *self-talk.* An internal dialogue is, as the term indicates, a combined process of listening and talking to oneself. Meichenbaum (1977) has noted research to document the importance of internal dialogue in three ways: (1) interpersonal actions and self-instructions; (2) cognition and stress; and (3) physiological effects. Interpersonal instructions are shown to be interactions with oneself that provide a governing principle by which an individual mediates his or her own behavior. Studies of stress have indicated that people tend to personalize stressful events to varying degrees depending on their overall self-instructions. People who self-deprecate, for example, handle stressful situations less effectively, than those who are more positive with their self-message and tend to be less worrisome in difficult circumstances.

Meichenbaum (1977) also demonstrated a relationship between physiological effects and cognitive processes. His research indicated that cognitive behavior modification helped clients identify physiological cues to assist them in learning coping behaviors. While physiological responses may remain the same in stressful situations, the counselee's ability to recognize the response and identify it as a signal to implement coping skills can make significant behavior change toward positive self-development.

Meichenbaum (1977) described his model of counseling as a process of cognitive restructuring. This process helps clients attack their debilitating thoughts by re-examining the basic assumptions and attitudes that support these self-messages. Through cognitive restructuring, the counselor helps the counselee to examine perceptions and beliefs and take responsibility for altering destructive thought patterns and related behaviors. In this respect, cognitive behavior modification consists of elements similar to the perceptual basis of Adlerian counseling and the focus on self-responsibility found in reality therapy.

Cognitive approaches, such as rational-emotive therapy and cognitive behavior modification, have been successful with school-age clients. Research and literature indicate success with a compulsive behaviors, anxiety, shyness, class work, homework, disruptive behaviors, and self-concept development (Cangelosi, Gressard, & Mines, 1980; Genshaft, 1982; Harris & Brown, 1982; Ownby, 1983; Patton, 1985; Zelie, Stone, & Lehr, 1980). In addition, these approaches have been used to teach self-counseling skills to students (Maultsby, 1986). An advantage of using cognitive approaches in school settings is their emphasis on instruction and teaching as methods of helping students learn responsibility, coping skills, and healthier ways of sending self-messages.

Multimodal Counseling

Developed by Lazarus in the 1970s, multimodal counseling has become a popular approach with school counselors. The research and application of this approach has been extensive considering the two short decades since its inception (Lazarus, 1990). In part, its popularity is due to the eclectic orientation of the model, which is anchored in behavioral theory while at the same time embracing a holistic philosophy of assessing a broad spectrum of aspects affecting human relationships, development, and learning. This assessment process is aimed at designing specific counseling and treatment interventions to meet the individual needs of clients. As Lazarus explained it, "The multimodal approach is predicated on the assumption that counseling and therapy need to be tailored to the individual needs of each person and situation" (1978, p.7).

In tailoring the counseling relationship to meet the needs of clients, multimodal counselors focus on seven factors: behavior, affect, sensation, imagery, cognition, interpersonal relationships, and biological functioning. The multimodal approach assesses these aspects of personality development and functioning in a comprehensive treatment program. As such, a basic premise of the model is that people are complex beings who behave, feel, sense, imagine, think, and relate to themselves and others (Corey, 1986).

In multimodal counseling, each of these modes is evaluated systematically. By using the first letter of each factor, and changing the last from "B" for biology to "D" for drugs, Lazarus formed the acronym BASIC ID, which is the assessment format used in the multimodal approach. The BASIC ID offers a framework with which the counselor asks the counselee questions and gathers data through other assessment processes to evaluate each of the modalities. The following overview of this assessment process illustrates how each mode is reviewed to create a profile of the client (Corey, 1986; Lazarus, 1978, 1982; Stickel, 1990).

Behavior: What are the observable actions, reactions, habits, and other behaviors that are contributing to the individual's present situation? What behaviors need to be increased and decreased, and are there strengths and weaknesses that can be used in helping the client achieve what he or she wants?

Affect: What emotions seem to be contributors in the individual's development and relationships with others? What makes the client laugh, cry, shiver, cringe, or explode?

Sensation: What senses give the client special pleasures or significant displeasures? What does the client enjoy hearing, seeing, smelling, tasting, and touching? In contrast, what sensations are annoying and discomforting?

Imagery: How does the person perceive himself or herself? What are essential aspects of the self that are favored or disfavored by the individual? How would the client like to be seen differently?

Cognition: What values, beliefs, and attitudes interact with decision-making and problem-solving processes in helping the individual choose particular behaviors? How do these thoughts and beliefs affect the person's emotions and subsequently relate to behaviors? "What are the main *shoulds, oughts,* and *musts*" in the client's life (Corey, 1986, p. 194)?

Interpersonal Relationships: In what significant relationships is the person presently involved? What does the individual expect from these relationships, and what do others expect of this person? What relationships, if any, would the client like to change and how?

Drugs/Biology: What is the overall physical well-being of the individual? Is there any inappropriate use of drugs or alcohol? Is the client health-conscious, or physically destructive? Does the individual take prescribed drugs, exercise regularly, have medical problems, eat a proper diet on a regular schedule, have a good hygiene, and get sufficient rest and sleep?

Keat (1978, 1990) adapted the BASIC ID format to use multimodal counseling with children. In the process he developed another acronym, HELPING, which stands for *H*ealth, *E*motions, *L*earning, *P*ersonal, *I*magination, *N*eed to know, and *G*uidance of behaviors. Keat's adaptation of the BASIC ID compensates for the differences that exist between helping children alter their behaviors and counseling adults about behaviors they want to change. According to Keat (1990), "with children the issues are different, because usually an adult (e.g., parent, teacher) is the one who wants the child to change" (p. 249). As such, the motivation for change is external to the child. By contrast, counseling adults relies primarily on internal motivation to change behaviors. In the HELPING paradigm all the factors of multimodal therapy and the BASIC ID are included. Health includes drugs, diet, and other biological factors. Emotions encompass the affective domain. Learning consists of sensations from the environment, both at home and in school. Personal relationships are the same as interpersonal relations. Imagination includes interests as other aspects of the self-image. Need to know involves thinking skills and other cognitive processes, and Guidance focuses on relationships among actions, reactions, and consequences of the child's behaviors.

When the assessment of these different modes is complete, the counselor examines the relationship and interactions among them. Based on this evaluation and analysis of information, the counselor is prepared to choose a multitude of strategies, if needed, to assist the counselee. In this process of selecting different treatment interventions, multimodal counselors use techniques and approaches from a variety of counseling and therapy models. In addition, multimodal counseling encourages collaboration between the school counselor and other professional helpers, such as the school nurse, health educator, and physician (Drugs/Biology; Health), the school psychologist (Cognition; Need to know), and classroom teachers (Sensation; Learning).

The application of multimodal counseling is found in many counseling settings, and its use in schools has been extensive (Gerler, 1984; Keat, 1990; Lazarus, 1990). School counselors in elementary and middle schools particularly have reported positive results in assisting students with phobias, behavioral disorders, family divorce, academic achievement, peer relationships, attitudes toward school, and physical fitness. The multimodal model has also been applied in educational programs for parent training and teacher in-service (Gerler, 1980; Judah, 1978).

The eclectic orientation of multimodal counseling, combined with its emphasis on assessment and systematic selection of intervention strategies, is compatible with school environments. School counselors do not have the luxury of establishing long-term helping relationships with time devoted to building rapport and allowing counselees to emerge as a fully functioning, integrated and independent persons. While this is an admirable and ultimate goal for all helping relationships, it is not always practical in schools where students' self-concepts, behaviors, physical ailments, social relationships, and coping skills are among numerous factors to be addressed if they are to be successful. By focusing on these issues initially, counselors help students with immediate concerns thereby establishing a posture to explore opportunities for becoming successful, growth-oriented, healthy individuals. As such, multimodal counseling provides the structure within which school counselors can perform adequate assessment, choose appropriate intervention strategies, and establish genuine relationships with students.

The four approaches to counseling presented in this chapter offer a limited selection of theories of professional practice available to school counselors. These approaches offer a sample of models used in school counseling programs to illustrate methods with potential for broad application with students, parents, and teachers. Other counseling approaches, including transactional analysis (Woollams & Brown, 1979), Gestalt Therapy (Passons, 1975), and Behavior Therapy (Rimm & Masters, 1974), are also used by school counselors in providing comprehensive services.

Person-centered counseling, which evolved from the writings and research of Rogers (1951), offers all counselors and therapists a humanistic philosophy and foundation for basic helping skills that are essential for all effective counseling relationships. The four approaches highlighted here, Adlerian counseling, cognitive-behavioral counseling, reality therapy, and multimodal counseling, each rely to a great extent on the therapeutic principles put forth in the person-centered approach. Regardless of which approach or approaches counselors select in delivering individual counseling services, they want to know what the research says about their effectiveness

Research on Counseling

Much of the research on counseling has focused on the "core conditions" first proposed by Rogers (1951). Although he developed the person-centered approach, and subsequently these conditions have been closely associated with this perspective, research of other counseling models has indicated that these qualities are universally important to all helping relationships. The research efforts of Rogers, Carkhuff, Truax, Berenson, and many others have extensively examined the contribution of genuineness, empathy, positive regard, and concreteness to the establishment of beneficial relationships and the attainment of successful outcomes in counseling (Carkhuff & Berenson, 1967; Rogers, Gendlin, Kiessler, & Truax, 1867; Truax & Carkhuff, 1967). In addition, investigations by these and other researchers have expanded this list of essential conditions to include other dimensions of effective counseling.

Beyond knowing what the research says about fundamental characteristics of effective counselors and about basic skills essential to positive outcomes, school counselors must stay current in their knowledge of prevailing practices. This means reading professional literature and reports about approaches and techniques that demonstrate success with students in school. It also means learning how to research the value and effectiveness of counseling approaches selected in one's own school program.

Examples of research studies can be found in numerous scholarly journals, including *The School Counselor* and *Elementary School Guidance and Counseling*, two national journals of the American School Counselor Association. A few examples were mentioned in previous sections about common approaches to counseling found in school settings. Typically, research studies reported in the counseling journals use group procedures to investigate effective approaches to counseling. By using group procedures, researchers measure differences among and between clients using statistical methods. These procedures, however, may negate actual differences between competent and incompetent counselors because "such group research may cancel itself out and yield no significant difference" among the counselors in the study (Corey, 1986, p. 315). Nevertheless, school counselors should be aware of research that examines different approaches to use with students, and adapt available research to select viable strategies and approaches for their individual counseling.

Because school counselors have responsibility for a wide spectrum of student needs, and they provide such an array of different services for students, parents, and teachers, they usually find that more than one view and approach to counseling is required to satisfy all their program goals and objectives. They also know that individual helping relationships have limitations, and absorb a considerable amount of time. For this reason, group processes need to be an integral part of a comprehensive school counseling program. Group procedures are the topic of the next chapter.

Selected Readings

Corey, G. (1986). *Theory and Practice of Counseling and Psychotherapy*, 3rd Ed. (Belmont, CA: Brooks/Cole). Gerald Corey's popular text offers a comprehensive overview of the major theories of counseling. A readable guide, it gives clear description of the philosophical and psychological foundations for each approach as well as their application and process.

Ivey, A. E. (1991). *Developmental Strategies for Helpers* (Pacific Grove, CA: Brooks/Cole). This text illustrates in practical terminology and with clear examples how counselors integrate their knowledge of human development with counseling skills and techniques. Different developmental models are presented to show how counselors move from theory to practice.

Thompson, C. L., & Rudolph, L. B. (1988). *Counseling Children*, 2nd Ed (Pacific Grove, CA: Brooks/Cole). An excellent guide for counseling children, this book offers a wealth of ideas and practices for counselors of elementary and middle grade students. Specific problems and issues are presented and counseling approaches suggested.

Purkey, W. W., & Schmidt, J. J. (1987). *The Inviting Relationship: An Expanded Perspective for Professional Counseling* (Englewood Cliffs, NJ: Prentice Hall). This book adopts the humanistic and existential philosophies of Rogers, Jourard, Combs and others to combine the perceptual tradition and self-concept theory into an educative approach to helping. Springing from the *invitational theory* of Purkey and others, this model encourage counselors to look beyond their individual helping relationships toward strategies that impact on school environments, regulations, and programs for the benefit of all students.

References

Blocher, D. H. (1966). *Developmental Counseling* (New York: Ronald Press).

Borgers, S. B. (1980), "Using Reality Therapy in the Classroom with Gifted Individuals," *Gifted Child Quarterly*, 24, 167–168.

Brammer, L. M. (1988). *The Helping Relationship: A Process and Skills*, 4th Ed. (Englewood Cliffs, NJ: Prentice Hall).

Cangelosi, A., Gressard, C. F., & Mines, R. A. (1980), "The Effects of a Rational Thinking Group on Self-Concepts in Adolescents," *The School Counselor, 27,* 357–361.

Carkhuff, R. R. (1969). *Helping and Human Relations: Selection and Training,* Volume 1 (New York: Holt, Rinehart & Winston).

Carkhuff, R. R., & Berenson, B. G. (1967). *Beyond Counseling and Psychotherapy* (New York: Holt, Rinehart & Winston).

Corey, G. (1986). *Theory and Practice of Counseling and Psychotherapy,* 3rd Ed (Pacific Grove, CA: Brooks/Cole).

Corsini, R. J. (Ed.). (1979). *Current Psychotherapies,* 2nd Ed. (Itasca, IL: Peacock).

Cottle, W. C., & Downie, N. M (1970). *Preparation for Counseling,* 2nd Ed (Englewood Cliffs, NJ: Prentice Hall).

Dinkmeyer, D., & Dinkmeyer, D., Jr. (1982). *Developing Understanding of Self and Others, D-1 & D-2,* Rev. Ed. (Circle Pines, MN: American Guidance Service).

Dinkmeyer, D. C., Dinkmeyer, D. C., Jr., Sperry, L. (1987). *Adlerian Counseling and Psychotherapy,* 2nd Ed. (Columbus, OH: Merrill).

Dinkmeyer, D., & Mckay, G. (1976). *Systematic Training for Effective Parenting* (Circle Pines, MN: American Guidance Service).

Dinkmeyer, D., McKay, G., & Dinkmeyer, D., Jr. (1980). *Systematic Training for Effective Teaching* (Circle Pines, MN: American Guidance Service).

Dreikurs. R. (1968). *Psychology in the Classroom,* 2nd Ed. (New York: Harper & Row).

Dreikurs, R., & Soltz, V. (1964). *Children the Challenge* (New York: Meredith Press).

Egan, G. (1986). *The Skilled Helper,* 3rd Ed. (Pacific Grove, CA: Brooks/Cole).

Ellis, A. (1962). *Reason and Emotion in Psychotherapy* (New York: Lyle Stuart).

Eysenck, H. J. (1961), "The Effects of Psychotherapy," In H. J. Eysenck (Ed.), *Handbook of Abnormal Psychology* (New York: Basic Books).

Genshaft, J. (1982), "The Use of Cognitive Behavior Therapy for Reducing Math Anxiety," *School Psychology Review, 11* (1), 32–34.

George, R. L., & Cristiani, T. S. (1990). *Counseling: Theory and Practice,* 3rd Ed. (Englewood Cliffs, NJ: Prentice Hall).

Gerler, E. R. (1980), "The Interpersonal Domain in Multimodal Teacher Groups," *Journal of Specialists in Group Work, 5,* 107–112.

Gerler, E. R. (1984), "The Imagery in BASIC ID: A Factor in Education," *The Journal of Humanistic Education and Development, 22,* 115–122.

Gibson, R. L., & Mitchell, M. H. (1990). *Introduction to Counseling and Guidance,* 3rd Ed. (New York: Macmillan).

Gladding, S. T. (1992). *Counseling: A Comprehensive Profession,* 2nd Ed. (New York: Macmillan).

Glasser, W. (1961). *Mental Health or Mental Illness?* (New York: Harper & Row).

Glasser, W. (1965). *Reality Therapy: A New Approach to Psychiatry* (New York: Harper & Row).

Glasser, W. (1969). *Schools without Failure* (New York: Harper & Row).

Glasser, W. (1981). *Stations of the Mind* (New York: Harper & Row).

Glasser, W. (1984). *Take Effective Control of your Life* (New York: Harper & Row).

Good, C. V. (Ed.). (1945). *Dictionary of Education* (New York: McGraw-Hill).

Harris, D. R., & Brown, R. D. (1982), "Cognitive Behavior Modification and Informed Teacher Treatments for Shy Children," *Journal of Experimental Education, 50* (3), 137–143.

Henderson, P. A. (1987), "Terminating the Counseling Relationship with Children," *Elementary School Guidance and Counseling, 22,* 143–148.

Heuchert, C. M. (1989), "Enhancing Self-Directed Behavior in the Classroom," *Academic Therapy, 24,* 295–303.

Ivey, A. E. (1988). *Intentional Interviewing and Counseling: Facilitating Client Development* (Pacific Grove, CA: Brooks/Cole).

Ivey, A. E. (1991). *Developmental Strategies for Helpers.* (Pacific Grove, CA: Brooks/Cole).

Jackson, M. D., & Brown, D. (1986), "Use of Systematic Training for Effective Parenting (STEP) with Elementary School Parents," *The School Counselors, 34,* 100–104.

Judah, R. D. (1978), "Multimodal Parent Training," *Elementary School Guidance and Counseling, 13,* 46–54.

Keat, D. B. (Ed.). (1978), "Multimodal Approaches [Special Issue]," *Elementary School Guidance and Counseling, 13,* 1–80.

Keat, D. B. (1990), "Change in Child Multimodal Counseling," *Elementary School Guidance and Counseling, 24,* 248–262.

Kerr, B. A., Claiborn, C. D., & Dixon, D. N. (1982), "Training Counselors in Persuasion," *Counselor Education and Supervision, 22,* 138–140.

King, P. T., & Bennington, K. F. (1972), "Psychoanalysis and Counseling," in B. Stefflre & W. H. Grant (eds.), *Theories of Counseling,* 2nd ed. (New York: McGraw-Hill).

Lazarus, A. A. (1978), "What is Multimodal Therapy? A Brief Overview," *Elementary School Guidance and Counseling, 13,* 6–11.

Lazarus, A. A. (1981). *The Practice of Multimodal Therapy* (New York: McGraw-Hill).

Lazarus, A. A. (1990), "Multimodal Applications and Research: A Brief Overview and Update," *Elementary School Guidance & Counseling, 24,* 243–247.

Maultsby, M. C. (1986), "Teaching Rational Self-Counseling to Middle Graders," *The School Counselor, 33,* 207–219.

Meichenbaum, D. (1977). *Cognitive Behavior Modification: An Integrative Approach* (New York: Plenum Press).

Morse, C. L., Bockoven, J., & Bettesworth, A. (1988), "Effects of DUSO-2 and DUSO-2-Revised on Children's Social Skills and Self-esteem," *Elementary School Guidance and Counseling, 22,* 199–205.

Olson, D. H., & Claiborn, C. D. (1990), "Interpretation and Arousal in the Counseling Process," *Journal of Counseling Psychology, 37,* 131–137.

Omizo, M. M., & Cubberly, W. E. (1983), "The Effects of Reality Therapy Classroom Meetings on Self-Concept and Locus of Control Among Learning Disabled Children" *Exceptional child, 30,* 201–209.

Orr, D. W. (1965). *Professional Counseling on Human Behavior: Its Principles and Practices* (New York: Franklin Watts).

Ownby, R. L. (1983), "A Cognitive Behavioral Intervention for Compulsive Handwashing with a Thirteen-Year-Old Boy," *Psychology in the Schools, 20,* (2), 219–222.

Parloff, M. B. (February 21, 1976), "Shopping for the Right Therapy," *Saturday Review,* 14–16.

Passons, W. R. (1975). *Gestalt Approaches in Counseling* (New York: Holt, Rinehart, & Winston).

Patton, P. L. (1985), "A Model for Teaching Rationale Behavior Skills to Emotionally Disturbed Youth in a Public School Setting," *The School Counselor, 32,* 381–387.

Pietrofesa, J. J., Hoffman, A., & Splete, H. H. (1984). *Counseling: An Introduction* (Boston: Houghton Mifflin).

Purkey, W. W., & Schmidt, J. J. (1987). *The Inviting Relationship: An Expanded Perspective for Professional Counseling* (Englewood Cliffs, NJ: Prentice Hall).

Rimm, D. C., & Masters, J. C. (1974). *Behavior Therapy: Techniques and Empirical Findings* (New York: Academic Press).

Rogers, C. R. (1951). *Client-Centered Therapy: Its Current Practice, Implications, and Theory* (Boston: Houghton Mifflin).

Rogers, C. R., Gendlin, E. T., Kiessler, D., & Truax, C. B. (1967). *The Therapeutic Relationship and Its Impact: A Study of Psychotherapy and Schizophrenics* (Madison: University of Wisconsin Press).

Rychlak, J. F. (1985), "Eclecticism in Psychological Theorizing: Good and Bad," *Journal of Counseling and Development, 63,* 351–353.

Schmidt, J. J. (1991). *A Survival Guide for the Elementary/Middle School Counselor* (West Nyack, NY: The Center for Applied Research in Education).

Shertzer, B., & Stone, S. C. (1966). *Fundamentals of Guidance* (Boston: Houghton Mifflin).

Shilling, L. E. (1984). *Perspective on Counseling Theories* (Englewood Cliffs, NJ: Prentice Hall).

Smith, G. F. (1955). *Counseling in the Secondary School* (New York: Macmillan).

Stefflre, B., & Grant, W. H. (1972). *Theories of Counseling,* 2nd Ed. (New York: McGraw Hill).

Stickle, S. A. (1990), "Using Multimodal Social-Skills Groups with Kindergarten Children," *Elementary School Guidance and Counseling, 24,* 281–288.

Thompson, C. L., & Rudolph, L. B. (1988). *Counseling Children,* 2nd Ed. (Pacific Grove, CA: Brooks/Cole).

Truax, C. B., & Carkhuff, R. R. (1967). *Towards Effective Counseling and Psychotherapy* (Chicago: Aldine).

Webster's Third New International Dictionary. (1976) (Springfield, MA: G. C. Merriam Co.).

Woollams, S., & Brown, M. (1979). *TA: The Total Handbook of Transactional Analysis* (Englewood Cliffs, NJ: Prentice Hall).

Zelie, K., Stone, C. I., & Lehr, E. (1980), "Cognitive-Behavioral Intervention in School Discipline: A Preliminary Study," *Personnel and Guidance Journal, 59,* 80–83.

5
Group Procedures

School counselors search for methods of intervention that enable all students to develop their fullest potential. While individual counseling relationships are effective in helping certain students, one-to-one processes are not always the most efficient use of a counselor's time and resources. More importantly, individual relationships do not capitalize on the human resources available to counselors through the expertise of students, parents, and teachers. Group methods are essential services that allow counselors to reach out to more people.

Chapter 3 introduced two main types of group processes used by school counselors: group counseling and group consultation. Group counseling is a confidential helping relationship in which the counselor encourages members to focus on developmental, preventive, or remedial issues with which they are concerned. Group consultation encompasses a range of experiences and activities that utilize instructional, informational, and problem-solving processes. Examples of group consultation include: teacher inservice activities, classroom guidance for students, and parent education programs.

In this chapter, we focus on two types of group processes used by school counselors specifically with students: group counseling and group guidance. This chapter presents the purposes of these two types of groups, their advantages and limitations, and how they are implemented by counselors in schools. We begin by defining and differentiating group counseling and group guidance.

Group Counseling and Group Guidance

Group counseling and group guidance are two processes used by school counselors to handle a wide range of student concerns and interests. Many students in schools have concerns that are similar in nature. Sometimes these are normal, developmental issues such as making friends, becoming comfortable with physical changes, making educational decisions, and learning problem-solving skills. Other times, students confront major problems, often of crisis magnitude, that must be dealt with expeditiously. Group procedures offer efficient and effective formats for assisting students with many different issues, from educational planning to grieving over the loss of a loved one. Groups allow diverse activities with dissimilar audiences who have various goals and objectives. Part of the school counselor's role is to select appropriate group processes to meet these expanded needs.

Numerous texts and articles have described group processes and procedures in detail (Corey, 1990, Gazda, 1989; Gladding, 1991), and school counseling literature has encouraged the use of group guidance and counseling since the late 1950s, beginning with Driver's now classic book, *Counseling and Learning through Small Group Discussion* (1958). Today, the American School Counselor Association (1981, 1984) identifies group counseling and guidance as primary services of elementary, middle, and secondary school counselors.

According to Myrick (1987), group counseling "in schools is a valid counselor intervention that can meet the needs of many students" through "a unique educational experience in which students can work together to explore their ideas, attitudes, feelings, and behaviors, especially as related to personal development and progress in school" (p. 233). By using group counseling in school programs, counselors encourage interaction among students, thereby facilitating their willingness and ability to help each other. Under the leadership of a trained counselor, students share concerns, self-disclose in a safe environment, listen to the ideas and opinions of other group members, and give one another support and feedback about the concerns they have raised.

Purpose and Nature of Groups

An essential difference between group counseling and group guidance is that counseling creates a confidential and personal relationship, and group guidance is more instructional and informational in nature. Gladding (1991) described the purpose of group guidance as "the prevention of personal or societal disorders through the conveying of information and/or the examining of values. Group guidance stresses growth through knowledge" (p. 14). Myrick (1987) encouraged counselors to differentiate large group guidance from small group counseling by observing "the focus of the group and the way in which it functions" (p. 276).

The purpose of group counseling is for members to explore concerns and issues affecting their development and to form intimate relationships in which they accept and support one another in the process of resolving and coping with their concerns. As noted above, group guidance is more instructional in nature, and differs from counseling in the depth of personal interactions and the level of sharing among group members. While many of the leadership skills used in group counseling and group guidance are similar, group guidance activities tend to be more didactic than group counseling sessions. Typically, guidance groups focus on specific learning objectives or information needed by students for some aspect of their development. In sum, the differences between group counseling and group guidance are found in the purposes of the groups, the level of dynamic and personal interactions among group members, the leadership behaviors of the counselor, and the size of the groups.

Size of Groups   Determining the size of groups depends on the purpose of the group, age of the group members, the number of sessions scheduled, and the nature and severity of problems and concerns of group members. With young, elementary children, Gazda (1989) recommended limiting group counseling to no more than five students. With adolescents and adults the group may be slightly larger, but as the size of the group expands, cohesiveness among the members is diminished (Jacobs, Harvill, & Masson, 1988). Regarding group size in general, "the group should have enough people to afford ample interaction so that it doesn't drag and yet be small enough to give everyone a chance to participate frequently without, however, losing the sense of 'group' " (Corey, 1990, p. 91).

Myrick (1987) defined large group guidance as processes that include more than ten students. He observed that if the size of a counseling group "goes beyond 10 members, the counseling process is diffused and the dynamics of multiple relationships and interaction change the group's character" (Myrick, 1987, p. 275). When this happens, the group process becomes different than counseling; it becomes more instructional and informational, and personally less intense for the group members.

Group Procedures and Comprehensive Programs   Both group guidance and group counseling are essential functions in comprehensive school counseling programs. Yet, literature indicates that some school counselors have become disenchanted and "discouraged with implementing small groups because of seemingly insurmountable resistance from teachers, administrators, or parents" (Bowman, 1987, p. 256). At the same time, other counselors resist the use of group processes due to feelings of inadequacy regarding their leadership skills and abilities. In a national survey of elementary, middle, and senior high school counselors, Bowman (1987) summarized counselors' views regarding group procedures, and found that:

1. Counselors at all levels agreed that small group guidance and counseling are important functions to include in their programs.

2. Counselors used groups to focus on a variety of topics depending on the developmental age and needs of students.

3. Counselors agreed that their school counseling programs would be more effective if they increased the number of groups they scheduled, but at the same time, they noted the difficulty of restructuring the time available to do this, and the challenge of obtaining teacher support.

4. Senior high counselors indicated that scheduling and leading groups in their schools is more difficult and less practical than at the elementary and middle grades.

5. Opinions were mixed among the counselors regarding their training to effectively run small group guidance and counseling as part of their programs. A total of 22 percent of the counselors indicated they needed additional training to implement effective groups.

The important role of group processes in comprehensive school counseling programs continues to be sustained in the literature, in counselor training programs, and among practicing counselors. Counselors who examine this issue and choose to establish group counseling and group guidance services in their school programs begin by choosing the types of group structures most conducive to their setting.

Group Structures

In small group guidance and group counseling, there are essentially two types of structures—open and closed. Open groups allow students to enter and leave the group as needed, and the group sessions are scheduled for an indefinite period of time. By contrast, a closed group begins with identified members, who continue with the group until it ends. In closed groups, there is a specific number of members who are selected through a screening process. These participants are expected to attend all sessions and remain in the group until the last session. Corey (1990) commented that this "practice offers a stability of membership that makes continuity possible and fosters cohesion" (p. 90). One problem with closed groups occurs when too many members stop attending and the support network is diminished. Open groups replace members who leave with new members who rejuvenate the group by bringing fresh perspectives and ideas. While this open structure may afford new stimulation, adding new members to a group risks discomfort and could adversely effect the cohesiveness established earlier in the group.

Schmidt (1991) recommended that school counselors choose closed groups because schools "are typically rigid organizations with precise schedules and traditional routines to follow" (p. 78). Closed groups, by definition, are structured and tightly scheduled, which may be more appealing to teachers and administrators. Too, open groups may be confusing and difficult for students who have to remember which group they are in, and when their groups meet. Furthermore, students in closed groups have the advantage of knowing when their group sessions will end. In practice, this helps students focus on their concerns, bring up issues more readily, and attempt new alternatives and behaviors to address their problems. By knowing when groups will end, students and counselors set a time line of sorts, which can be used to influence and facilitate desired changes. In contrast, open groups may unintentionally encourage members to procrastinate and put off disclosing their concerns or making the necessary decisions to effect change.

One aspect related to group structure and success is member participation. In particular, each member's voluntary participation in a group, as opposed to involuntary assignment, can make a significant difference in how the group functions. In schools, students are sometimes asked to participate in groups to address their behaviors, academic progress, alcohol and drug use, or other problematic aspects of their development. In these cases, students may be assigned to groups as a condition of their continued progress and attendance in school. Such students may be reluctant participants at best.

Even though some students' assignment to particular groups may be involuntary, it is essential that their actual participation—sharing, self-disclosing, and supporting others—remain voluntary. While counselors may initiate the group relationship as a result of referrals from parents, teachers, and administrators, "each person must voluntarily participate" (Myrick, 1987, p. 244). As such, students in groups may choose *not* to actively contribute in the group sessions to which they are assigned without their consent. Effective counselors, who are highly skilled in group relationships, call upon all their leadership abilities to encourage these students and invite them to participate for their benefit and the good of other group members.

By determining the types of groups to include in their programs and carefully choosing the processes for establishing particular groups, school counselors clearly identify their professional role in developing and leading groups. Because teachers and parents sometimes oppose services that remove students from classes, counselors want to have a clear process for establishing groups by informing people about the program, carefully selecting and including students, scheduling sessions, and obtaining permissions when required.

Establishing Groups

When organizing and scheduling group counseling sessions and group guidance activities, school counselors develop a clear plan that informs the administration, educates the faculty, introduces groups to students, develops an acceptable schedule, and involves parents when possible. The first step in this process is for counselors to determine what needs of students will best be met through group processes, and which group procedures are most appropriate. Next, counselors must convince the school administration and their teaching colleagues of the value of these group services.

Informing the Administration

Because group guidance and counseling services require special consideration to schedule students for sessions that remove them from normal class schedules and instruction, counselors need to inform their principals about the nature and value of these activities. To do so effectively, counselors must be knowledgeable about group procedures, clear about their goals, and up-to-date about current research and literature regarding group procedures in schools. School principals want effective services for students, but instructional time and teacher satisfaction are two sacred tenets that cannot be disturbed by new approaches started on a whim. To convince their principals, school counselors readily demonstrate that group guidance and group counseling complement classroom instruction by helping students examine behaviors, attitudes, and perceptions that inhibit learning and restrict their development.

Once school administrators are persuaded that group sessions are worth implementing in the counseling program, the next step is to sell the idea to teachers. Teachers are important allies of counselors who want to make program changes and develop new services. Without teachers' support and confidence, new services, such as group counseling, are not likely to be approved, or to succeed.

Persuading the Faculty

One of the most effective ways school counselors convince teachers of the importance of new services is by demonstrating positive results in the services they already provide. Competent, reliable school counselors are respected by their colleagues, and have a decided edge over counselors who are uncertain and inconsistent with their practices. Beyond their overall capabilities, effective counselors also illustrate to teachers the relationship between student self-development and school achievement. Research on students' self-concepts and beliefs about themselves as learners demonstrates a connection with school achievement (Purkey, 1970; Purkey & Novak, 1984). Group processes, particularly group counseling, facilitate the process of self-exploration, self-learning, and self-acceptance because:

1. As with all people, students are social beings, and by belonging to a group they interact with one another, reflect and evaluate perceptions of who they are, and practice new behaviors in a safe, unthreatened environment.

2. Group members help each other, often more effectively than an individual counselor can one-to-one with a client. In groups, students relate to what other members are saying, they compare similarities and differences in the concerns shared among group members, and they pool their ideas to offer a range of suggestions and alternatives to assist each other.

3. Groups offer a sense of belonging and camaraderie to students who feel isolated, rejected, and alone. Through group counseling and small group guidance, students are encouraged to bond with other members, form friendships and alliances, and recognize the value of caring, helpful relationships.

4. Groups allow participation without demanding that students be active. Some students are not very verbal, or are not as outgoing as other students. In groups, these students still benefit from the helping process by listening and watching other members. In time, with the appropriate encouragement and support, they may become more active, but even if not, they can learn about themselves and others by observing the proceedings of the group.

5. Groups are an efficient use of counselors' time. By establishing helping relationships with more than one student at a time, counselors are able to reach a broader population, offering more services to a greater number of students.

In sum, persuading teachers of the value and importance of group processes in a school counseling program is grounded in the assumption that students who work together learn essential skills and strengthen their self perceptions. For example, Rose (1987) described skills training groups with elementary students that demonstrated positive results in helping students develop social competence. Similarly, Marianne Corey (Corey & Corey, 1992) reported favorable comments from teachers after students participated in group sessions. According to teachers, children improved their self understanding, altered aggressive behaviors, and demonstrated increased willingness to belong and get along with others (pp. 289–290). These results translate into responsible behaviors and academic progress in the classroom, two strong selling points with teachers.

Introducing Groups and Selecting Students

School counselors introduce their groups to students in a variety of ways. In elementary schools and middle schools, counselors present classroom guidance activities with teachers and use these opportunities to introduce other topics suitable for small group sessions. Through this introductory process, counselors assess students' interest in participating in these groups. At the same time, counselors observe students during classroom guidance lessons and identify those who will benefit from either individual or group counseling.

Teachers, parents, and students are the referral sources who bring group ideas and suggestions to counselors. One senior high counselor reported that he approached a female student who was overweight and seemed withdrawn and isolated in the school. The student discussed her feelings and perceptions about her weight and relationships she had with her peers. During this exchange, the counselor asked the young lady if she thought other students might have similar concerns and would want to share them in a group. The next day the student returned with seven overweight classmates who wanted to establish a support group to work on their self-concepts.

When students are selected to participate in small groups, counselors take precautions to assure compatibility of group members. This is not to say there can be no differences among participants, but a wide divergence does not lend itself to the cohesiveness that is so important to group success. While group cohesion is difficult to define and evaluate, common descriptions include: "a climate of support, bonding, attractiveness, sharing of experiences, mutuality within a group, the togetherness that unites members, a sense of belonging, warmth and closeness, and caring and acceptance" (Corey & Corey, 1992 p. 216). In selecting students for small groups, school counselors consider age differences, language development, types of concerns, degree of concerns, and social class. A wide disparity within any one or more of these factors may inhibit sharing, supporting, and relating among group members. For example, an elementary counselor who places five-year- olds in the same group with ten-year-olds may find that the age spread is too great and the students have little in common to share adequately in group sessions. By the same token, students who are in groups because of acting out behaviors may not relate well with students who are shy, withdrawn, and overly anxious about school. Sometimes, however, divergence is helpful in groups. For example, by including students of different cultures to share their feelings and observations, counselors create an excellent forum for learning sensitivity and acceptance among students.

Selection processes are essential in creating successful groups. Gazda (1989) suggested individual interviews with each potential member. In these interviews, the counselor introduces the group idea to the student, explains the purpose of the group, listens to the student's reactions, and assesses whether or not the student would make a good group member. At the same time, the counselor hears what the student's expectations of the group might be, if he or she were to join. Corey (1990) surmised this screening process as "an opportunity for the leader to evaluate the candidates and determine what they want from the group experience . . . [and] . . . a chance for the prospective members to get to know the leader and develop a feeling of confidence" (p. 89). In this interviewing process, the counselor explains the group rules and seeks commitment from students to abide by the rules and work on issues of concern to them if they join the group.

By using a clear selection process, school counselors retain control over group membership. This is critical to their success as leaders of small group guidance and counseling. At times, school administrators and teachers recommend students for counseling, either individual sessions or group counseling, and they insist that the students receive counseling services. When counselors relinquish their professional role and responsibility to assess students' needs and determine the suitability of particular interventions and helping processes, they diminish their control of and thereby jeopardize their overall effectiveness in the school counseling program. Counselors want to accept referrals from others, assess situations properly, and make informed, responsible decisions about what services to provide for whom. Sometimes students who are referred for counseling may benefit more from other services such as a medical examination and consultation, assistance from social services, or participation in a youth program. Other times, it may be that teachers or parents may benefit from instructional or informational services that indirectly help students. On the occasions when counselors decide that group services will be beneficial to students, their next step is to schedule the sessions.

Scheduling Groups

In designing group schedules, counselors determine the frequency of meetings, the length of each session, the place where the sessions will be held, the number of sessions if they plan a closed group. Input from teachers is essential in helping counselors design reasonable and efficient group schedules. The counselor's advisory committee, consisting of teachers, administrators, parents, and students (at the middle-and high-school level) can assist with the task of designing an appropriate schedule that satisfies the faculty, is reasonable to the counselor, and meets the expectations of the groups.

Scheduling large group guidance is not difficult if teachers and counselors integrate these lessons into daily instruction. As emphasized throughout this book, the most effective large group guidance occurs in the classroom as a result of a collaborative relationship between the teachers and counselor. When integrated as part of the ongoing curriculum, classroom guidance poses few logistical problems in setting a schedule. By having teachers and counselors co-lead classroom guidance, the schedule allows for flexibility. For example, if a crisis occurs and the counselor is needed elsewhere in the school, the teacher is able to continue the guidance lesson without interruption.

Small group guidance and small group counseling are more difficult to schedule, particularly if a counselor leads many groups involving a large number of students. In elementary and middle schools where individual teachers or teams of teachers instruct the same students during the day, scheduling should be coordinated between the counselors and teachers. To prevent students from missing the same subject matter every time their group meets, one solution is to stagger the times of the group meetings. For example, the first group session might begin on Monday at 10:00 A.M. The second session would meet the next week on Tuesday at 2:00 P.M., and so forth. This method of changing the day and time is also reasonable to use with groups at all levels—elementary, middle, and high school. By scheduling group sessions in this manner, counselors avoid taking students from the same teacher and out of the same course for the entire duration of the group. Instead, students miss only one or two classes from a given subject area.

Involving Parents

Because group counseling and group guidance complement and supplement the instructional program of the school, counselors want to inform and involve parents in the process of selecting children to participate in these services. In most instances, parental permission is not required for student participation in these programs, unless there is a local or state or other policy that stipulates the need for parental approval (Schmidt, 1987). Nevertheless, counselors are wise to inform parents of group opportunities through their presentations to parents at school functions such as parent teacher association (PTA) meetings and by publishing and distributing brochures about their school counseling program.

When students are selected for groups, parents should be informed about their children's participation. This is not necessarily a request for permission, but rather a courtesy extended to parents to include them in the helping process. One counselor uses the following announcement to parents:

> *Your child has asked to be in a group led by the school counselor. The group*
> *will meet once a week for eight weeks and will focus on school achievement,*

student relationships, and other aspects of school life and concerns of students. I encourage you to talk with your son or daughter about his or her participation and contribution in the group. Please call me if you have questions about the group or your child's participation.

In some instances, students may want to join groups without their parents' knowledge. Whenever possible, this request should be honored and protected. For example, students who have been physically or sexually abused have the right to receive support and treatment without fear of retribution at home or elsewhere. Such relationships must remain confidential as should all counseling relationships. By informing administrators, persuading faculty, involving parents, and implementing the other steps mentioned above, counselors take a strong position to be successful in establishing group procedures as part of their programs. Their ultimate success depends on each counselor's leadership abilities, knowledge of counseling theories and approaches, and communication skills.

Leading Groups

Small group counseling requires the same knowledge of theory and approaches that is needed in individual counseling. The process of group counseling is similar to individual counseling in that the group members start by forming relationships, continue by exploring concerns and issues of importance to them, examine alternatives and options, and create individual action plans. When all issues have been adequately addressed and action plans implemented, the group reaches closure. The counseling and consulting skills described in Chapters 4 and 6 of this book apply to group counseling and group guidance processes as well. Active listening, appropriate questioning, adequate structuring, and other communication and leadership skills are required in group work with students.

Small group guidance involves communication skills similar to those used in counseling and presentation skills used in classroom guidance. Because small group guidance takes the form of instructing or informing, counselors tend to use more didactic skills and approaches in these sessions with students. Sometimes group guidance consists of a single session to focus on a particular learning objective. In these instances, the counselor's use of time, preparation of materials, group management skills, and use of feedback from students to evaluate the lesson are vital processes to assure that the session's goal is reached with most, if not all, the students.

In both group counseling and small group guidance, it is important for counselors to retain their leadership role. To achieve this, counselors set ground rules with each group member during the screening interview and they reiterate these rules at the start of the group and during subsequent sessions as needed. Sample ground rules used with students in group counseling and small group guidance are:

1. Set your goals early in the group, and stick to your commitment to address these learning objectives and behavioral goals
2. Present your concerns clearly to the group and discuss them honestly
3. Listen to the opinions and concerns of other group members, and respect their point of view.
4. Keep information discussed in the group confidential. You may discuss what *you* say with your parents, but you must not discuss what other members reveal in the group sessions.
5. Be on time for the group and remain for the entire session.
6. Accept and respect the counselor's role to lead the group.
7. Agree that group decisions will be made by consensus.

Ground rules set the foundation for cooperative relationships in the group process. Combined with effective counseling skills, ground rules and other structural aspects of establishing groups increase the likelihood that group counseling and small group guidance sessions will be successful. To ensure the appropriate use of group services, counselors understand all the advantages as well as the limitations of these helping relationships.

Advantages of Group Counseling

1. Group counseling offers a social setting in which students can share concerns, practice new behaviors, and support one another in a safe, non-threatening setting. In groups, students have the opportunity to exchange ideas, test out assumptions about themselves and others, and compare and contrast their views with others. Individual counseling does not offer the opportunity for such broad experiences and exchanges.
2. By sharing their concerns in groups, students learn about and identify with common issues and perceptions held by others. This process of identifying with others increases cohesiveness and enhances understanding about students' concerns.
3. Group counseling encourages listening and facilitates learning. For group members to reach an acceptable level of understanding, empathy, and helpfulness with their peers in the group, they must develop effective listening skills. Any services that help students improve their listening skills should be beneficial to the learning process.
4. Controlled "peer pressure" can be used in groups to encourage and confront students about their behaviors, goals, and attitudes that inhibit their development and progress in school. Under the direction of a competent group counselor, students gently persuade and cajole their peers to

accept the group's consensus about changes they need to make, and to choose appropriate plans of action.

5. Group counseling is action-oriented. The purpose of placing students in groups for counseling is to help them select goals, identify changes they want to make in their lives, formulate plans of action, and implement steps to realize their objectives. The decision-making processes and skills are valuable to students in all areas of learning and development.

6. Group counseling can be less intense and threatening than individual counseling. In one-to-one relationships, students are sometimes overwhelmed by the presence of the counselor and feel inhibited to share personal concerns without support from others.

7. Group counseling is economically more efficient than individual counseling because more students can receive services in the same time span. While this is an advantage, it is not so important that individual counseling should be relegated to a lower priority in school counseling programs. Both individual and group counseling are important services and each should be considered based on the needs of students, objectives of the helping relationships, and preference of the clients seeking services.

Limitations of Group Counseling

1. Effective group work takes a high degree of leadership skill. Group counseling is more complex than individual counseling because the factors to consider and input into the process are multiplied. According to Myrick (1987), counselors who attempt groups "may feel less in control since there are persons who need special attention and there are more interactions to observe and manage" (p. 273).

2. Group counseling requires a high energy level from the counselor to keep track of the group direction, address members equally, and establish effective relationships. Fatigue can occur when counselors attempt to lead too many groups in a give period of time. Keeping track of the dynamics in the group and relating to each group member effectively can be emotionally draining as well as physically exhausting.

3. Scheduling groups, as noted earlier, can be difficult. It is much easier for school counselors to call in one student at a time, than it is to schedule groups of students out of classes. Counselors who work closely with their teaching colleagues in designing group schedules are likely to be successful with their group counseling services.

4. Group counseling may not be suitable or effective with some students. Students who have severe behavioral disorders or other dysfunctions may not be suitable for group processes. Disruptive behaviors, limited cognitive abilities, and severe emotional disabilities, for example, may make the likelihood of success in groups limited.

Advantages of Group Guidance

1. In group guidance, counselors and teachers can impart information or instruction to larger numbers of students. Group guidance reaches more students than individual consultations, and opens avenues for discussion and sharing that may not occur with individual students.

2. Group guidance does not require any special training in counseling theories and techniques since it uses instructional processes. Effective teachers who have strong facilitative skills can be quite successful in leading group guidance.

3. Guidance is best implemented as an interdisciplinary approach. Group guidance activities can be integrated with other subjects in the school curriculum, such as language arts, social studies, mathematics, physical education, and others.

4. Group guidance has the potential to enhance the total environment of the classroom or school by emphasizing positive aspects of human development and relationships. Information learned and behavioral skills achieved through classroom guidance can be generalized by students to address personal, education, and career goals in their lives.

Limitations of Group Guidance

1. Because guidance groups are more educational and informational than they are therapeutic or personally enhancing, they may not result in significant changes with students who have critical conflicts or serious difficulties in their lives and in school. However, group guidance activities often help to identify such students, so they can be referred to the school counselor for more intense interventions.

2. Depending on the size of the group, guidance activities do not allow as much interaction among group members, as do group counseling sessions. Therefore, personal support, caring, and the development of trust are not as in-depth as they are in group counseling.

3. Group guidance does not necessarily offer consistent assistance toward specific personal, educational, or career goals for all group members. When group guidance is designed to present a series of topics, it is possible that attention to individual needs of students may be overlooked in attempting to reach the instructional objectives of the guidance lessons. In contrast, group counseling focuses directly on the individual needs and expectations of each group member.

4. Because group guidance uses instructional processes and techniques, and the size of groups is sometimes 25 or more students, counselors need to be more structured and directive in these activities. This leadership style

may seem contradictory to counselors who prefer helping relationships with more freedom of expression for students.

In determining whether to use group counseling or group guidance approaches in school programs, counselors consider all the advantages and limitations, the primary goals and objectives for groups, their own group skills, and the acceptance of the school and community for such services. In addition, counselors become familiar with the research about the effectiveness of group services with students.

Research on Groups

Gazda (1989) noted that research studies of group processes have increased in the counseling literature in the past two decades. He analyzed 641 research studies published between 1938 and 1987 according to the following variables: type of controls, treatment period, type of group, assessment instruments, statistics used, type of study, experimental designs, size of samples, and the nature of outcomes. Based on his analysis of these studies, Gazda (1989) concluded that generally the research on group counseling has made considerable progress in identifying variables related to group effectiveness. While the research methodology has improved in recent years, Gazda noted that some areas of group counseling knowledge need additional study, and some existing problems with research methods are still to be corrected.

The remainder of this chapter presents research studies of group counseling and group guidance. The studies presented form a sample of research to give a broad view of the types of groups used by school counselors, and some results reported in the counseling literature. We begin with group guidance research.

Group Guidance Research

Although the school counseling literature has advocated the use of small and large group guidance for several years, research on the effectiveness of guidance activities has been limited in comparison to studies on individual and group counseling. In some instances, reports of research studies do not clearly indicate whether the groups were guidance oriented or group counseling sessions. The following summaries are of studies that appear to be instructional or informational in nature, and therefore are classified here as group guidance.

Stickel (1990) reported on a multimodal group project with kindergarten students to improve social skills, develop problem-solving skills, increase cooperation in small groups, and enhance their expression of feelings.

Four groups of five children each made up the study, and each group met for seven sessions, 20 minutes every other day. The sessions consisted of three segments including a leader-directed activity, a student-involvement activity, and a sharing time among group members. Each session focused on one of the modalities described in the BASIC ID paradigm of the multimodal model (see Chapter 4). While research statistics were not reported in the results of this study, the kindergarten teacher "noted increased cooperation and interaction among certain children following the groups and thought it allowed the counselor to get to know the children better as individuals and give them some needed individual attention" (p. 286).

A Florida study demonstrated that classroom guidance units can generate positive results in altering student attitudes and behaviors (Myrick, Merhill, & Swanson, 1986). Fourth grade students in 67 elementary schools were randomly assigned to either treatment or control groups. A pre-treatment assessment by teachers rated each student's attitude. Counselors presented six guidance lessons to the treatment groups with sessions focused on: (1) understanding feelings and behaviors; (2) learning about perceptions and attitudes; (3) helping someone new to the school; (4) making positive changes; (5) experiencing the "I am lovable and capable" activity; and (6) looking for personal strengths. Results from 37 schools were complete enough to use in the analysis. Data were collected using teacher and student inventories of their perspectives on a number of behaviors and attitudes. The results indicated that students who participated in classroom guidance "were significantly different from those in the control group in terms of finishing class assignments on time . . . and saying kind things to others" (p. 247).

In this study, teachers' perceptions of the control groups and treatment groups also demonstrated significant differences. Teachers viewed treatment groups more positively than control groups on a number of factors including: (1) getting along with others; (2) working hard on assignments; (3) following directions; (4) liking their teachers; (5) being liked by their teachers; and (6) believing they were important and special persons. These positive results were noted across student populations, from those in pre-assessment who were identified with poor attitudes to students who were rated highly on the attitude scale. All students seemed to benefit from the classroom guidance sessions. The Florida study was replicated in Indiana with 731 fourth graders and similar results were found.

A study using affective education to improve reading performance of second grade students indicated positive results in a 12-week program (Hadley, 1988). Three treatment groups and four control groups of second graders were included. A program consisting of self-esteem activities to diminish negative attitudes, improve patience, and enable students to handle anxieties was presented to the three treatment classes. Results indicated a significant impact on academic growth as measured by reading scores on the Stanford Achievement Test for students who participated in the classroom guidance program.

Gerler and Anderson (1986) investigated the effects of classroom guidance on students' attitude toward school, achievement in language arts and mathematics, and classroom behavior. In this study, 896 fourth- and fifth-grade students from 18 different schools were presented a classroom guidance unit entitled "Succeeding in School." The unit consisted of 10 classroom guidance lessons presented by the 18 counselors in the participating schools. Results of the study indicated that the program had a positive effect on students' classroom behaviors. In a comparison with a control group, the treatment groups improved behaviors while the control groups remained the same or became worse. Attitudes about school and academic achievement were additional variables indicating favorable results for the treatment groups.

These and other research studies demonstrate that classroom guidance, also referred to as affective education, developmental guidance, and psychological education, can have positive effects on students' attitudes and behaviors. While changes in attitudes and behaviors have been realized in many studies of guidance groups, significant change in self-concept views as a result of classroom guidance has not been consistently found. This is not surprising since self-concept theory postulates that self-perceptions create a certain stability in the human personality (Purkey & Schmidt, 1987). As such, change in the self-concept can be expected to occur gradually after intense treatment over a period of time. Classroom guidance does not allow for this type of intense, long-term intervention. Group counseling, on the other hand, is more conducive to establishing this type of helping relationship.

Group Counseling Research

Research on group counseling covers a broad area of treatment topics, student behaviors, and models of counseling. The following are examples of recent studies using group counseling with student populations.

Omizo, Hershberger, and Omizo (1988) researched the use of group counseling with elementary-grade students who were identified as aggressive and hostile by their teachers. Students in the study were assigned to either experimental or control groups. Students in the experimental groups received group counseling using cognitive-behavioral techniques, modeling, role-playing, and positive reinforcement. Results indicated that students who participated in the group counseling tended to decrease their aggressive and hostile behaviors to a greater degree than students assigned to control groups.

Divorce has been a popular topic for group counseling in recent years. Tedder, Scherman, and Wantz (1987) used group counseling with fourth and fifth graders whose parents had divorced and who were referred by teachers or parents because divorce adjustment was a concern. Two groups of students participated in eleven sessions of groups counseling and guidance. Parents and teachers completed two instruments, the Walker Problem Behavior Identification Checklist (Walker, 1962) and the Child Behavior Rating Scale (Cassel, 1970), in pretest and posttest assessments for all the children. Results showed that while teacher ratings of students' behaviors did not change, parents noted that children were less distractible and exhibited fewer behavior problems at home.

Omizo and Omizo (1987) also investigated the use of group counseling with children of divorce. With a sample of 60 elementary students from divorced families randomly assigned to an experimental or a control group, this study examined differences in student aspiration, anxiety, academic interest and satisfaction, leadership initiative, identification and alienation, and locus of control. The experimental group met for ten sessions, which specifically addressed divorce using bibliotherapy, role-play, and discussion. Findings indicated significant differences between students in the group counseling and those assigned to the control group in aspiration, anxiety, identification versus alienation, and locus of control. Group counseling was found to be "beneficial for enhancing some areas of self-concept and an internal locus on control among elementary school children experiencing divorce" in this study (p. 51).

Myrick and Dixon (1985) identified 24 students in two middle schools who demonstrated poor attitudes about school. Six students in each school were randomly assigned to group counseling and the other six were placed in a comparison group to receive counseling later. Group counseling consisted of six sessions that focused on topics related to feelings about school, how feelings relate to behaviors, consequences of behaviors, giving and receiving feedback, taking the first step toward improvement, and being positive. Data collected on the two groups indicated that teachers rated students in group counseling significantly higher in improved classroom behavior. This was true for both boys and girls in the groups. Students who participated in the groups reported positive feelings about themselves and greater understanding of others.

Schmidt and Biles (1985) investigated the use of puppetry in group counseling with exceptional students in seventh and eighth grade. The students were identified as either educably handicapped or learning disabled. Five dependent variables were compared to determine differences between the puppet group and a control group. These variables were: student self-attitudes, school attendance, school suspensions, and achievement in language arts and mathematics. Nine group counseling sessions were held. The study found no differences in student attitudes or academic achievement between the treatment and control groups, but students who participated in the puppet groups "tended to improve their school attendance and to reduce significantly their school suspensions to a greater degree than did the students in the control group" (p. 71). Although limitations existed in this study, the authors suggested that the use of puppets with this age student "may help to facilitate group processes, particularly in role-play activities with special students" (p. 71).

Many research studies of group counseling and group guidance offer similar results to those listed above. School counselors who want to persuade their principals and teachers of the efficacy of group work need to be familiar with research findings to make a strong case. In addition, counselors develop a rationale for using group processes to help students learn from one another, instruct them in social skills, and enable them to become caring, cooperative members of society.

A Rationale for Group Process

In the history of education, many philosophers and scholars have encouraged a proactive role for schools to instill values and develop students' character. Kohn (1991) proposed that this process of character education should include aspects of learning to care about others. He surmised, "If we had to pick a logical setting in which to guide children toward caring about, empathizing with, and helping other people, it would be a place where they would regularly come into contact with their peers and where some sort of learning is already taking place" (p. 499). Schools offer this ideal setting, and school counseling programs, in the context of group guidance and group counseling, provide the structure to help students learn empathic behaviors, problem-solving skills, and a host of other cooperative, prosocial attributes.

An essential role for school counselors implied in the major functions addressed in this test is one of an agent for change. Today's schools are under fire from all directions and all segments of society to overhaul their services to students, improve instruction, and increase learning. School counselors should be part of this movement, and in fact, should be leaders for change. By advocating more group processes in the instructional and counseling programs of the school, counselors lend their expertise to the process of restructuring education and enhancing student development and learning.

Through their leadership in group counseling and group guidance, school counselors contribute to the broad effort and mission of educating the whole student. Group guidance in particular, especially when integrated into the curriculum by teachers and counselors, uses the classroom as a social setting to explore issues and values essential to students' character development. This is not a new concept. Good teachers have applied these ideas in their relationships with students since schools began. Therefore, group guidance and group counseling are vehicles with which counselors can assist teachers in continuing beneficial traditions in education.

Selected Readings

American School Counselor Association. (1984). *The School Counselor and Developmental Guidance* (ASCA position statement). Alexandria, VA: Author. This position statement gives an overview of developmental guidance and encourages school counselors to take an active, leadership role in its development and implementation.

Kohn, A. (1991). "Caring Kids: The Role of Schools," *Kappan, 72* (7), 496–506. In this article Kohn makes a clear case for schools becoming more concerned about and involved in helping children learn cooperative skills. At the same time, he contrasts the current popular school approached of punishing and bribing students to the more effective method of encouraging students' commitment to values. The concepts presented by Kohn have implication for group work by teachers and counselors in schools.

Corey, M. S., & Corey G. (1992). *Groups: Process and Practice,* 4th Ed. (Pacific Grove, CA: Brooks/Cole). This book by Marianne and Gerald Corey is a readable overview of issues and concepts related to group work. The section on school counseling is particularly helpful in seeing how one counselor overcame obstacles to develop a strong component in the counseling program.

References

American School Counselor Association. (1981). ASCA role statement: "The Practice of Guidance and Counseling by School Counselors," *The School Counselor, 29,* 7–12.

American School Counselor Association. (1984). *The School Counselor and Developmental Guidance* (ASCA position statement). Alexandria, VA: Author.

Bowman, R. P. (1987), "Small-Group Guidance and Counseling in Schools: A National Survey of School Counselors," *The School Counselor, 34,* 256–262.

Cassel, R. N. (1970). *Child Behavior Rating Scale* (Los Angeles: Western Psychological Services).

Corey, G. (1990). *Theory and Practice of Group Counseling,* 3rd Ed. (Pacific Grove, CA: Brooks/Cole).

Corey, M. S., & Corey, G. (1992). *Groups: Process and Practice,* 4th Ed. (Pacific Grove, CA: Brooks/Cole).

Driver, H. I. (1958). *Counseling and Learning through Small Group Discussion.* (Madison, WI: Monona Publications).

Gazda, G. M. (1989). *Group Counseling,* 4th Ed. (Boston: Allyn and Bacon).

Gerler, E. R., & Anderson, R. F. (1986). "The Effects of Classroom Guidance on Children's Success in School," *Journal of Counseling and Development, 65,* 78–81.

Gladding, S. T. (1991). *Group Work: A Counseling Specialty* (New York: Macmillan).

Hadley, H. R. (1988). "Improving Reading Scores through a Self-Esteem Intervention Program," *Elementary School Guidance and Counseling, 22,* 248–252.

Jacobs, E. E., Harvill, R. L., & Masson, R. L. (1988). *Group Counseling: Strategies and Skills* (Pacific Grove, CA: Brooks/Cole).

Kohn, A. (1991). "Caring Kids: The Role of the Schools," *Kappan, 72* (7), 496–506.

Myrick, R. D. (1987). *Developmental Guidance and Counseling: A Practical Approach* Minneapolis, MN: Educational Media Corporation).

Myrick, R. D., & Dixon, R. W. (1985), "Changing Student Attitudes and Behavior through Group Counseling," *The School Counselor, 32,* 325–330.

Myrick, R. D., Merhill, H., & Swanson, L. (1986). Changing Student Attitudes through Classroom Guidance," *The School Counselor, 33,* 244–252.

Omizo, M. M., & Omizo, S. A. (1987), "Group Counseling with Children of Divorce: New Findings," *Elementary School Guidance and Counseling, 22,* 46–52.

Omizo, M. M., Hershberger, J. M., & Omizo, S. A. (1988). "Teaching Children to Cope with Anger," *Elementary School Guidance and Counseling, 22,* 241–146.

Purkey, W. W. (1970). *Self-Concept and School Achievement* (Englewood Cliffs, NJ: Prentice Hall).

Purkey, W. W., & Novak, J. (1984). *Inviting School Success: A Self-Concept Approach to Teaching and Learning* (Belmont, CA: Wadsworth).

Purkey, W. W., & Schmidt, J. J. (1987). *The Inviting Relationship: An Expanded Perspective for Professional Counseling* (Englewood Cliffs, NJ: Prentice Hall).

Rose, S. R. (1987), "Social Skill Training in Middle Childhood: A Structured Group Research," *Journal for Specialists in Group Work, 12,* 144–149.

Schmidt, J. J. (1987), "Parental Objections to Counseling Services: An Analysis," *The School Counselor, 34,* 387–391.

Schmidt, J. J. (1991). *A Survival Guide for the Elementary/Middle School Counselor* (West Nyack, NY: The Center for Applied Research in Education).

Schmidt, J. J., & Biles, J. W., "Puppetry as a group Counseling Technique with Middle School Students," *Elementary School Guidance and Counseling, 20,* 67–73.

Stickel, S. A. (1990), "Using Multimodal Social-Skills Groups with Kindergarten Children," *Elementary School Guidance and Counseling, 24,* 281–288.

Tedder, S. L., Scherman, A., & Wantz, R. A. (1987). "Effectiveness of a Support Group for Children of Divorce," *Elementary School Guidance and Counseling, 22,* 102–109.

Walker, H. M. (1962). *Walker Problem Behavior Identification Checklist* (Los Angeles: Western Psychological Services).

6

Collaboration with School and Agency Professionals

As indicated in the first three chapters of this book, school counselors have responsibility for planning, implementing, and evaluating a number of services for students, parents, and teachers. Although school counselors have primary responsibility for developing comprehensive programs, this challenge cannot be fully met without assistance and support from other professionals in the school system and the community. For this reason, school counselors carefully and systematically initiate collegial relationships with a variety of educational, medical, and other professionals who provide auxiliary services to school populations. These alliances formed by school counselors and other helping professionals are essential for delivering the broad spectrum of services expected in a comprehensive school counseling program. In sum, they ensure the availability of appropriate services for students, parents, and teachers who seek the assistance of school counselors.

Forming successful alliances of this kind requires a clear understanding of the services needed, and knowledge of the types of services offered in the community. At the same time, professionals who work in community agencies, health departments, families centers, and other services need to know about the role and training of school counselors. By achieving mutual understanding of their professional roles and functions, school counselors and community practitioners are able to establish beneficial helping relationships with clients, as well as cooperative consulting relationships with each other.

These collaborative relationships are not limited to professionals in the school and community. Rather, they include and perhaps begin with the cooperation school counselors create in their interactions with parents. Throughout this text, parental involvement is identified as a vital ingredient of successful counseling programs at all levels of school practice. Because this is so, school counselors make every effort to establish lines of communication with the home, invite parents to join in planning educational goals for their children, advertise services of the school counseling program, and when appropriate, include parents to learn about the critical concerns of children and adolescents.

Collaboration is an important aspect of all relationships formed by school counselors. In this chapter, you will learn about the many individuals, professionals, and agencies with whom school counselors create and maintain working relationships on behalf of students, parents, and teachers. In addition, this chapter presents an overview of the consulting skills and processes that enable counselors to establish and facilitate collaborative relationships with these different participants. Counselors who develop effective consulting skills are in an excellent position to create superior programs of expanded services for their schools. They learn about the various agencies and services offered in their communities, develop effective communication networks, and use this knowledge and skill in establishing strong alliances to benefit students and their families.

In the next two sections, we examine many groups and professionals with whom school counselors consult and collaborate to establish effective services for students. For clarity, these groups are classified into two categories: the school and community agencies.

The School

Today's schools and school systems consist of a multitude of professionals and volunteers who provide countless services to students, parents, and teachers. In comprehensive programs, school counselors interact, directly and indirectly, with all these groups. This is not an easy accomplishment. The demands on their time often prevent counselors from seeking supportive services beyond their own counseling program.

Because their primary role is to give direct services to students in the school, counselors occasionally create a narrow focus for their programs by overemphasizing their own counseling and consulting services with students. As a result, they neglect to collaborate and consult with agencies and individuals who could supplement these counseling services. In some cases, the tendency to overlook beneficial school or community programs becomes an oversight that misses a vital service which counselors could use to assist students more directly and effectively than they are able to do by themselves.

The first step in ensuring that this does not happen is to take time to learn about all school-based services and the professionals who perform these functions. At the same time, counselors take time to learn about parents and other guardians of students in the school. As mentioned before, collaboration with parents and guardians has significant impact on direct counseling services with students.

Although the U.S. family follows countless organizational structures, in most instances we find that one or two adults in a given family play significant leadership and guardian roles. In traditional two-parent families, these adults would be the mother and father, but in other structures we would discover that a single parent, stepparent, grandparent, aunt or uncle, foster parent, or friend of a parent assumes the leadership role. In all these cases, whether the child is relating with a parent or other guardian, the school counselor has responsibility for establishing collaborative working relationships.

Parents and Guardians

Later in Chapter 9, we will see that parental involvement may be strong in the elementary years and then taper off as students move through the secondary school level. (Note: The terms *parent* and *parental involvement* refer to all forms of parental and guardian relationships.) As such, we might expect that collaborative relationships are more apparent in the primary and intermediate grades than in secondary schools. While this may be true, parental involvement continues to be an important factor during the early adolescent years, and in contemporary U.S. culture, seems to be retaining its importance well into early adulthood. This extended role for parents is due in part to the higher percentage of people attending college and pursuing advanced degrees in professional and graduate school. Economically, parental involvement appears to be an essential ingredient that enables young people to continue their formal education well into their twenties. At the same time, employment trends and the cost of living have encouraged continued parental support in providing housing for children who are beginning careers, and offering financial assistance for young couples who are just starting out.

This apparent trend toward longer parental involvement in children's developmental and decision-making processes has an effect on the overall involvement that parents expect to have in their children's education. The result is that schools, and particularly school counselors, must form cooperative working relationships with parents and guardians in designing educational programs for students, selecting helping processes and strategies, and making plans for future educational and career directions. The first step in this process is for counselors to learn about the families served by their schools, and determine the needs of parents by assessing the role they expect to play in the schooling of their children.

Through needs' assessment procedures, counselors determine what services to offer parents, the types of programs parents will participate in and respond to, and the services for which parents will volunteer to assist in the school. A comprehensive school counseling program touches all these areas because counselors counsel and consult with parents and guardians; they design informational and instructional programs for parents; and they invite parents to assist with functions such as student tutoring, test monitoring, career guidance, and educational information (House & Brown, 1980).

Perhaps the relationships counselors establish with parents and guardians of students are the most important ancillary functions to individual and small group counseling with students. This may be particularly so for elementary counselors who serve students with little control over the environments and situations influencing their lives. Parents of young students and middle graders have a tremendous impact on the choices their children make regarding school performance, career direction, friendships, and other elements of their development. By consulting with parents, school counselors design support networks and channels of communication to complement their goals and objectives of counseling with students. Parents and guardians who want children to benefit from these helping relationships welcome the opportunity to meet with school counselors, gain understanding about their children's needs, and develop strategies to nurture positive parent-child relationships at home.

When collaborating with parents and guardians, school counselors create many avenues through which to provide direct services or offer indirect assistance. For example, counselors frequently contact parents about students' progress in school and consult about ways to support childrens' educational development at home. Relationships such as these illustrate a cooperative stance that says, "We are together in this effort to help children learn and develop their fullest potential." Such a stance is much more facilitative than one that views parents as the opposition, a "them against us" mentality. Counselors who believe facilitative relationships are essential for improving home-school communications work to establish mutual respect between parents and teachers.

Another direct service counselors provide for parents is through educational programs. Parenting is a challenging role for which few of us are prepared in any formal sense. The parenting skills most of us have learned were adapted by modeling what we saw our parents and guardians do when we were children. Unfortunately, these behaviors are not always conducive to the development of healthy affirmative relationships. To assist in the parenting process, school counselors facilitate parent meetings, establish support groups, and lead parent education programs. Sometimes these events are informal get-togethers where parents exchange ideas about what works with children in their families. Such exchanges are beneficial as ways of brainstorming limitless strategies to assist parents in communicating effectively with their children and adolescents. By facilitating these exchanges and designing educational activities for parents, counselors demonstrate the school's willingness to cooperate and work with parents in creating optimal learning opportunities for all students.

As indicated in Chapter 2, some educational programs for parents are packaged and marketed commercially. Typically, these programs have a trainer's manual for the counselor to follow and participants' handbooks for parents to read about the approaches advocated in each of the lessons. Parent education programs can be organized in a single session or in a series of meetings to present specific information about child behavior, leadership strategies, and other issues of interest to parents. Some programs continue for several sessions covering a wide range of issues and topics about child development and parenting skills.

When school counselors plan parent education programs, they arrange their work schedules to accommodate this service. Most often, parent groups meet at night to fit work schedules, but occasionally, counselors lead parent groups during the day when students are in school. When counselors schedule groups during the daytime, they seek input from their principals and advisory committees to examine the ramifications of using school time to assist parents. If positive parenting skills equate to increased learning and participation of students in schools, counselors will be able to convince principals and teachers of the importance of these daytime activities.

Support groups for parents are usually centered around a particular concern or issue, such as being a single parent, and counselors lead these groups in discussing common concerns and exploring actions to handle everyday problems. Parent support groups endorse each member as an "expert" on his or her child. The assumption is that no one knows the child better than the parent. This expertise is "pooled" in group discussions, and counselors utilize this collective knowledge to assist individual parents in choosing appropriate alternatives to their current situations. Support groups such as this allow parents to see that they are not alone in their struggles, and at the same time, enable them to feel supported by the collective wisdom of the group. During this process the counselor is simply the facilitator of discussion, the keeper of time, and the coordinator of the group activity.

Few students develop at optimal levels without support and encouragement from their parents and guardians. Through services such as the ones mentioned above, school counselors let parents know about available resources to help students. One way of informing parents is to make direct contact with them. By consulting directly with parents, counselors provide current information, needed instruction,and essential problem-solving services.

Counselors who address the informational and educational needs of parents make certain that schools and parents move in the same direction and have similar goals for students. To verify this parallel movement, counselors also consult and collaborate with teachers in their schools.

Teachers

No school counseling program is successful without the support and acceptance of the teachers in the school. As you have already seen in this text, teachers are a vital link in the integration of affective education into the curriculum; they are the first-line helpers in the school counseling program; and they are referral sources for students in need of additional assistance. For these reasons, school counselors at all levels of educational practice wisely cultivate helpful, working relationships with all the teachers in their schools.

One of the first signs of collaboration between counselors and teachers is the input counselors request about the nature, scope, and focus of their school counseling programs. Counselors who send these requests are well-received and respected because they demonstrate mutual regard for teachers and the teaching profession. This partnership is not merely a mutual admiration society, but rather a genuine respect for what it takes to be an excellent teacher, balanced by an acceptance of the unique role that counselors play in school programs.

Counselors collaborate with teachers in many other ways, some of which are similar to the individual and group processes for parents described earlier. For example, teachers and counselors consult with each other to identify the needs of individual students, gather data to assess these needs, make decisions about practical strategies to assist students, and evaluate outcomes of these strategies. Counselors also consult and collaborate with teachers in group sessions, such as team meetings in middle schools and departmental meetings in senior high schools. Counselors who are sought out by individual teachers and invited to team meetings are respected for their collaborative skills and empathic understanding of the teacher's role. By the same token, these counselors seek teachers out for their guidance and suggestions, thereby demonstrating respect for teachers' knowledge of curriculum and command of effective instructional methods.

Teacher support groups are another medium by which school counselors collaborate with their colleagues. As with parent support groups, teachers' groups rely on the expertise of group members to explore concerns, identify pertinent issues, suggest alternatives, and plan reasonable action. The emergence and application of this kind of "teachers' expertise" is made possible through the facilitative skills of the counselor as group leader. By relying on the observations and suggestions of other teachers in the support group, counselors lead these groups in discussions while avoiding the role of "master advisor." This is another way that counselors learn to appreciate the difficult role of teachers in elementary, middle, and high schools, while at the same time, teachers in a support group have an opportunity to watch the communication and facilitation skills of their counseling colleagues.

Collaboration between counselors and teachers also occurs when they cooperate to plan and present in-service activities for staff development. Sometimes these in-service presentations are given by the counselor as a result of input from teachers. Other times, counselors recruit teachers who are skilled in particular areas of instruction or child development. Experienced teachers who are skilled facilitators are often the best people to present faculty in-service in their schools. Whatever the case, instructional and informational programs for school faculties are successful when teachers and counselors cooperate in setting staff development goals, planning appropriate activities, and following through on these action plans.

Teachers of Exceptional Children

Other teachers who are especially important collaborators with school counselors are the teachers of exceptional children. These professionals are highly trained to identify and provide instruction for children and adolescents who require special education services.

Since 1977, when the Education for All Handicapped Children Act took effect, students with a wide range of physical, emotional, and educational needs have attended elementary, middle, and senior high schools. Special education programs designed and implemented to address exceptional needs, from educably handicapped to gifted and talented students, have ensured the "least restrictive" mandate for educating all our citizens. The least restrictive environment means that, as much as possible, handicapped students must be instructed in classes with students who are not handicapped. As such, the school's educational "philosophy is to move as close to the normal setting (regular classroom) as feasible for each child" (Kirk & Gallagher, 1989, p. 51).

With the development of special education programs has emerged a professional specialty for teachers of exceptional students (sometimes called special education teachers). These teachers are trained in the expected pedagogical theories and methods of curriculum and instruction, and they have specialized knowledge and skills to address the needs of students identified with specific exceptionalities. Educably handicapped, learning disabled, emotionally handicapped, academically gifted, physically impaired, and multi-handicapped children and adolescents are among those served by special education teachers.

Because school counselors are committed to provide services for all students in schools, they especially want to collaborate with special education teachers in assessing students' needs, locating school and community resources, planning counseling services, and examining school policies that have positive or negative effects on the educational progress of exceptional children and adolescents (Schmidt, 1991). Special education teachers assist counselors in all these functions and, in addition, collaborate to keep counselors up-to-date about current regulations and research findings regarding various areas of exceptionality. At the same time, counselors offer these special teachers support and understanding as they create and deliver appropriate instruction for the school's most challenging, and challenged, students.

Teachers of exceptional students and school counselors also cooperate by helping the parents and guardians adjust to the challenges of nurturing, guiding, and caring for these precious children and adolescents. Parents of exceptional children face obstacles unknown to most mothers and fathers. This is particularly so when students have a debilitating mental, emotional, or physical handicap. The guilt associated with having borne a child with any type of disability, combined with the challenges of daily care, supervision, and parenting, often seems insurmountable. Teachers of exceptional students and counselors who offer parent support and guidance can help immeasurably.

School counselors who form close alliances with teachers of exceptional students are better able to create effective helping relationships with these students and their parents. They are informed about the exceptionalities and handicaps with which the family and child are dealing, and, therefore, are in a better position to design and implement successful interventions and services. Counseling exceptional students and consulting with their parents have special features that require particular knowledge and skills of counselors. By collaborating with teachers of exceptional students, counselors are able to acquire this knowledge and skill.

Principals

Schools are managed by principals trained in educational administration, curriculum, law, and other aspects of school governance. These administrators are ultimately responsible for everything that goes on in school buildings and in educational programs. As such, every service and activity scheduled and provided by school counselors is directly or indirectly supervised by a school principal. This awesome responsibility makes it essential for principals and counselors to collaborate about the design of the counseling program, selection of major goals and objectives, identification of essential functions, implementation of evaluation processes, and countless other details related to comprehensive school counseling programs. This collaboration between principals and counselors is an ongoing process that enables counselors to include their principals in program planning processes, and at the same time, to inform school administrators of issues and concerns affecting students' educational development.

Many activities planned by counselors have a schoolwide focus to meet the needs of a broad spectrum of students, parents, and teachers. In determining goals and strategies for these schoolwide events, counselors collaborate with school principals to check on the feasibility and appropriateness of their implementation. Principals have knowledge of local policies, financial limitations, and other restrictions that will guide the selection and implementation of activities and events planned by the school. By establishing working relationships with their principals, school counselors are better informed about the parameters within which their programs of services need to function. Similarly, effective communication with administrators allows counselors the opportunity to convey their assessment of students' needs and school climate, and how these two elements interact in the school.

When sharing information with principals, counselors are careful to follow ethical standards and legal guidelines regarding confidential material and privileged communications. Counselors frequently receive confidential information in helping relationships with students, and this information must remain private unless there is imminent danger to students or others. Consequently, school counselors cannot reveal confidential information to principals or other people without the consent of their clients. However, because counselors are privy to information that reflects on the overall condition and climate of the school, they have no obligation to inform principals about these conditions. For example, if a senior high counselor has learned from students that a number of girls are pregnant, the counselor needs to inform the school administrator of this situation. Of course, the counselor cannot reveal the identities of the young women, but he or she can tell the principal that the condition exists. By having this information, the school administrator is in position to plan the educational services these students will need, and to consult with the school nurse about appropriate health services to provide. In addition, the principal might confer with the counselors and teachers about preventive services the school should develop for the future.

By collaborating with their principals, school counselors take charge of their counseling programs. They inform the administration about their annual plans, they focus on essential services for students, parents, and teachers, and they keep lines of communication open to receive input from their school administrators. In addition, counselors become the coordinators for all student services, including those provided by school nurses, psychologists, and social workers.

Nurses, Psychologists, and Social Workers

Some schools and school systems are blessed with student services beyond the essential elements of a school counseling program. These additional components of comprehensive programs include nursing and health, psychological, and social services, and they are provided by highly trained professionals in the respective areas. These student services overlap to some degree in that they each focus on the physical, emotional, and social health and welfare of students and families. Because their functions overlap, student services professionals realize it is imperative for them to collaborate with each other and coordinate activities. In schools where counselors work full-time, it is logical for them to coordinate student services. This is especially true, when the nurse, psychologist, and social worker are only at the school part-time. Being full-time, the school counselor coordinates referrals, follows cases, schedules team meetings, and performs other functions to make certain students receive appropriate services.

One form of collaboration is a team approach where student services staff members meet on a regular basis. Through these regular meetings, the counselor, nurse, psychologist, and social worker share information, update cases, assign responsibilities, and avoid duplication of services. They also focus on specific cases to ensure that students are receiving appropriate services from the school and that referrals to community resources are adequately pursued and monitored.

Effective collaboration among these student services professionals begins with a mutual understanding and respect for their unique roles in schools and regard for their individual areas of expertise. In situations where this respect and regard are not achieved, student services are not well-coordinated and as a result, students' needs are inadequately addressed. In today's schools, students, parents, and teachers are faced with sufficient challenges to require services from all these professionals. Adequate coordination and timely collaboration provide appropriate and effective service for all concerned.

Collaboration within the school and school system helps counselors stay abreast of students' needs and select appropriate services to meet these demands. Sometimes, schools seek assistance from agencies and resources within the local community and from country and state organizations. By collaborating and consulting with available agencies, counselors give their schools an edge in initiating referral procedures and receiving timely services for students and families. In the next section, a few of the agencies that are typically used by schools to locate social, health, psychological, and family services for their students are presented.

Community Agencies

Schools themselves are a major agency in the community, but schools alone cannot offer all the human services necessary to help a town, city, or county educate its citizens, provide health care, and offer basic services to improve the human condition. The primary mission of schools, and, tangentially, the primary mission of school counseling programs, is to ensure the educational development of all students. In their attempt to reach this goal, school personnel offer an array of related services such as counseling, psychological evaluation, health care consultation, and social services. These services are offered to assist the school in its primary mission of education. The assumption is that as students' personal needs, health concerns, and learning difficulties are identified and addressed, their educational progress is improved and their opportunity for success in life is enhanced.

When services offered by schools are insufficient to remedy the concerns of students an families, counselors and teachers turn to community resources. Not all communities have ample services, so school counselors locate those that exist and establish collaborative professional relationships to benefit students, parents, and teachers. Successful collaboration rests, in part, on the school's ability to convey its role and mission to these community resources while learning about agency roles. Public agencies and private practitioners in the community have as their primary mission to assist in one or more of the human service areas. For example, most communities have access to a county health department that offers a wide range of medical services and health eduction programs.

Health Departments

School counselors and other student services professionals collaborate with health departments in a variety of ways. Elementary- and middle-school counselors rely on community health services to assist families with medical check-ups and offer recommendations to the school about health and medically related issues affecting the educational development of students. In some communities, health consultants work closely with the school to develop appropriate guidance activities on physical growth, sexuality, and health care needs of students. Similar services are available to senior high schools and in addition, health services are provided for pregnancy, sexually transmitted diseases, substance abuse, and other critical problems.

As you can see, a strong cooperative relationship between the school and health professionals is vital to student welfare. When schools and health professionals collaborate in active ways, adequate services and accurate information become accessible and available to students and their families. When health concerns appear to be other than physical, schools turn to community mental health services.

Mental Health Centers

At times, the emotional and personal concerns raised by students with counselors, nurses, psychologists, and social workers require in-depth, intensive interventions. While student services professionals may be competent to offer these interventions, time, schedules, and other factors associated with comprehensive school- based programs make it more practical and appropriate to refer students and families to mental health centers.

Mental health counselors, social workers, and psychologists spend a majority of their time in one-to-one and small group counseling and therapy to help clients remedy exiting social, emotional, and behavioral problems that interfere with human development and learning. Collaboration between school counselors and mental health practitioners is essential because while students are receiving treatment at the centers, they usually remain in school and continue their contacts with school counselors regarding classroom work, academic progress, and school behavior. By collaborating about services for students, the mental health counselor and the school counselor are careful not to confuse students in these respective helping relationships. In most instances, the agency counselor has primary responsibility for focusing on immediate social, emotional, or behavioral concerns. The school counselor supports this intervention by encouraging the student at school, locating support systems such as tutoring, and implementing strategies suggested by the mental health professional and agreed on by the school and classroom teachers.

Social Services

Among the challenges faced by American families in today's society is the real prospect of economic disadvantage, unemployment, and financial ruin. The gap between the lower and upper classes of our society continues to widen, and frequently, students and their families are confronted by loss of jobs, homelessness, lack of heating fuel, need for food, or other critical concerns. School counselors and teachers are usually the first to learn about severe economic losses and limitations of families, and therefore, they are frequently in touch with departments of social services in their communities.

In addition to severe economic needs, children and adolescents in many families are increasingly at physical and emotional risk due to parental neglect and abuse. In part, economic stress contributes to this social illness, but alcohol and substance abuse are often found to be significant factors. School personnel are required by law to report instances of suspected child abuse to the appropriate authorities (Morrow, 1987), and in most communities this would be the protective services of the department of social services (DDS), or a similar agency.

Because the issue of child abuse and neglect is potentially so sensitive and explosive, counselors normally collaborate with DSS to ascertain the proper reporting procedures, the respective responsibilities of each agency, and the role of the school in handling these cases. Without this type of communication and cooperation, reporting procedures may be misunderstood, responsibilities blurred, and the safety of children unattended.

Family Services

When children and adolescents struggle in their educational development, contributing factors often emanate from familial disturbance and dysfunction. In other cases, students' educational problems contribute or add to family stress and hardship. It is often impossible to separate students' educational, behavioral, or other disorders and limitations from their interactions with family members. For this reason, school counselors establish collaborative relationships with clinics and professionals who specialize in family counseling services.

Frequently, mental health centers and departments of social services have counselors, psychologists, and social workers who specialize in family interventions. Other community resources include family counseling services sponsored by United Way Agencies, churches, universities, and other non-profit organizations. Knowing which agencies and institutions offer these kinds of services enables school counselors to pursue appropriate referral avenues.

By collaborating with family services in the community, school counselors recognize the influence of family dynamics in child and adolescent development. Harnessing this influence and using it to establish positive goals and strategies is imperative, and family relationships between schools and family practitioners are an avenue through which to accomplish these objectives.

Several opportunities can be created to form collaborative relationships between the school and family practitioners. For example, family counselors can educate school personnel about family needs and stresses, thereby encouraging involvement and inclusion of parents and children in schools in nonthreatening ways. These community professionals can sensitize the school to family break-ups that have destroyed what were once loving relationships, but which now fuel resentment and bitterness among family members. Consultations between school counselors and family counselors allow the school, especially teachers, to become informed about the stress and difficulty affecting childrens' daily lives.

In some instances, school counselors work with entire families (McComb, 1981; Nicoll, 1984). Models of family counseling for implementation in school counseling programs have been encouraged in the counseling literature. Williams, Robinson, and Smaby (1988) proposed a "group skills model that incorporates techniques associated with problem solving and interpersonal communications" (p. 170). They designed a model for intervening with childhood and adolescent problems that stem from dysfunctional family relationships. Amatea and Fabrick (1981) recommended the family systems approach as an alternative to traditional counseling with students. Adlerian counseling, another approach to family service, is also encouraged in school counseling practice and counselor training (Nicoll, 1984). Invariably, those who advocate for family counseling and other family-oriented services by school counselors suggest that the integration of these approaches requires an adjustment in school counselors' schedules to allow evening and weekend hours when necessary (Palmo, Lowry, Weldon, & Scioscia, 1984). In addition, family interventions should cover a wide range of services including family counseling, parent education activities, and parent support groups in a comprehensive program of services.

Comprehensive counseling programs, in contrast to traditional services, plan activities for parents and attempt to focus on entire families when situations suggest a link between the student's development and family functioning. In most comprehensive school counseling programs, however, family and parent education services are limited. For this reason, school counselors who provide family services continue to rely on community agencies and private practitioners as primary referral resources. In some communities, where public services are insufficient to meet the tremendous needs of student populations, school counselors rely on psychologists, psychiatrists, counselors, and other therapists in private practice to assist students and their families.

Private Practitioners

Physicians, counselors, clinical social workers, and psychologists in private practice offer an array of services to children, adolescents, and families to assist with educational, psychological, and social development. By identifying private practitioners in their communities, school counselors expand the list of resources available to students, parents, and teachers. The longer the list, the more options and alternatives available.

When school counselors suggest community resources to assist students and parents with identified concerns, it is best to have a list from which people can choose. In this way, counselors rely on their clients to make the final selection, thereby demonstrating respect for their ability to make responsible decisions. Parents and students will consider costs, personal preferences, and other factors when selecting agencies and professionals for additional services. It is best for the referring counselor to provide as much information as possible, offer a list of two or more options, and let the individual make the final decision of where to go for further assistance.

In all these collaborative relationships with parents, teachers, and administrators, specialists, community agencies, and private practitioners, school counselors call upon their training in communication and consulting skills to establish successful associations. In many respects these consulting skills are similar to the behaviors counselors use in individual and group counseling relationships (Schmidt & Osborne, 1981). While this is so, the consultative roles assumed by school counselors when working with parents and other professionals have a distinct purpose and make a unique contribution to the development and implementation of comprehensive school counseling programs.

Counselors as Consultants

Consultation is not new to the school counseling profession. According to Aubrey (1978), its place in school counseling was first advanced in a 1966 joint report of the American School Counselor Association (ASCA) and the Association for Counselor Education and Supervision (ACES). In the late 1960s, Faust gave particular emphasis to the consulting role of school counselors in his book, *The Counselor/Consultant in the Elementary School* (1968). Similarly, Fullmer and Bernard (1972) referred to the school counselor-consultant as an "emergent role" in the profession (p. 1). Since that time, numerous articles and books have examined and reviewed various ways that school counselors use consulting skills and processes with students, parents, teachers, and other professionals. Research has shown that school counselors spend a considerable amount of time in consulting relationships (Hett & Davies, 1985; Ibrahim, Helms, & Thompson, 1983). In particular, counselors consult with teachers about students' progress, motivation, and class behaviors. As seen earlier in this chapter, they also serve as referral agents for parents and teachers in locating information and resources with which to help students. And, they instruct students, parents, and teachers in issues, topics, and skills to assist all groups in realizing their educational and career goals. There ar numerous perspectives and approaches to consultation for counselors to consider, depending on the purpose and goal of the relationships they form. Space prevents a thorough treatment of this topic here. For a comprehensive overview of consulting models and processes, I recommend *Psychological Consultation: Introduction to Theory and Practice* by Brown, Pryzwansky, and Schulte (1991).

In Chapter 3, you read about different ways that school counselors consult with students, parents, and teachers to distribute information, give instructions, assist with problem-solving services, encourage curriculum changes, and plan schoolwide events. The skills and processes associated with these different consulting roles are not unlike other helping relationships established by school counselors. Yet, structurally there are differences. In this section, we examine some of the aspects that distinguish consulting relationships from direct counseling services.

Consulting Processes

In his mental health model, Caplan (1970) defined consultation as "a process of interactions between two professional persons—the consultant, who is a specialist, and the consultee, who invokes a consultant's help in regard to a current work problem" (p. 19). Likewise, Bergan (1977) described consulting relationships basically as problem-solving processes. In school counseling programs, consultation is used in a broader context to include educational, informational, as well as problem-solving relationships. For example, in some instances counselors assume consulting roles to help their schools *prevent* problems from occurring (Dinkmeyer & Dinkmeyer, 1984). In other cases, counselors as consultants help teachers, parents, and others plan activities to focus on developmental needs of students. It is a triadic relationship consisting of the counselor-consultant, a consultee, and a situation with another person (the client) or other type of external concern.

As noted in Chapter 3, one way to visualize consulting relationships is to illustrate them as triangular associations that consist of a consultant, a consultee, and a situation. Sometimes in group meetings there may be more than one consultee, but the triangular structure is still applicable. In consultations with a preventive focus, the situation is usually an issue to be addressed through instruction or by sharing information. For example, if middle-school teachers want to hone their communication skills to enhance advisor/advisee relationships, the counselor may serve as an instructional consultant. In this scenario, the teachers would be the consultees, and the situation would be to strengthen teacher-student communications. Figure 6–1 illustrates the triangular nature of most consultations used by school counselors. The arrows in the diagram indicate communications, fact-finding processes, and feedback among the three elements in the consulting relationship.

The triangular view of consultation is different from direct counseling because the ultimate goal in consulting is to address or remedy a situational

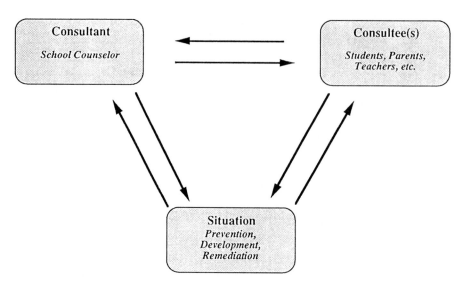

FIGURE 6–1   Triangular Structure for Consulting in School Counseling Program

or other aspect external to the relationship between the consultant and consultee. In this sense, the consultant works with the consultee who in turn makes adjustments or intervenes with the identified situation. By contrast, a counseling relationship is intended to assist another individual in making direct changes in his or her life. Hansen, Himes, and Meier (1990) noted that, unlike counseling relationships, "consultation is not primarily used for private motives of the individual consultee" (p. 5).

Kurpius and Robinson (1978) outlined different modes of consultation that cross instructional, informational, and problem-solving purposes. These modes describe five different roles that counselors can adopt when performing consulting functions. The first role is one of an expert. In this mode counselors provide answers to problems by offering expert information to students, parents, and teachers. In some instances, the "expert" consultant uses direct skills in "fixing" a broken situation. Similar to the "expert mode" is the prescriptive role counselors assume when they gather information, diagnose situations, and recommend solutions. A third consulting role used by counselors is that of an instructor or educator. This is usually the role school counselors take in parent education programs, teacher in-service, and classrooms guidance with students.

Sometimes, when counselors assist consultees who are at odds with each other or with an external situation, the consultation takes on the appearance of negotiation or mediation. In these instances, the counselor-consultant becomes a mediator and negotiator. A mediator attempts to find common ground between conflicting views and negotiates compromises to resolve these conflicts.

Another role consultants assume is that of a collaborator. Kurpius and Robinson (1978) summarized this role as one that establishes an equal relationship among participants to facilitate change. Hansen et al. (1990) disagreed with the use of collaboration as a consulting role because in their opinion: "Collaborators generally carry joint responsibility. The consultee, by contrast, retains responsibility for the management of the case or program" (p. 5). Despite this difference of opinion, the collaborative mode is generally accepted as a viable role for school counselors to assume in consulting relationships with students, parents, and teachers (Brown, Pryzwansky, & Schulte, 1991; Carrington, Cleveland, Ketterman, 1978; Schmidt & Medl, 1983). The collaborative mode is also effective in consulting with school administrators, social workers, and other professionals who seek ways to enhance the educational opportunities and progress of students.

In schools, instructional and informational consultation is clearly different from counseling relationships, but problem-solving consultations resemble counseling processes because the feelings of the consultee are considered in the exploration and selection of viable alternatives and strategies. The use of consulting processes in school counseling programs to convey information, offer instruction, or resolve difficult situations requires different processes. As a result, the roles and processes chosen by school counselors are determined a large part by the goals of the consultation itself. The objective of informational and instructional consultations require preparation, presentation, feedback, and evaluation. Problem-solving consultations on the other hand have a slightly different focus, and therefore require different skills and processes. In situational, problem-solving consultations, counselors gather information, identify the main problem, help consultees explore alternatives, strategies, and options, facilitate decision-making, win agreement, follow up this agreement, and evaluate outcomes. We will now consider these different consulting roles and the processes associated with each of them, beginning with informational and instructional consultation.

Informational and Instructional Consultation The processes and skills used to convey information and present instruction are similar. School counselors plan programs with teachers, lead parent education activities, and facilitate classroom guidance and other instructional programs by using behaviors that are very much alike. In many respects, the skills and processes used by school counselors in these types of activities are similar to the instructional approaches used by classroom teachers. According to Good and Brophy (1987), different instructional approaches can be classified into four categories including information processing, social interaction, individualized education, and behavior modification. In school counseling programs, all four of these approaches are used in various instructional and informational activities with students, parents, and teachers.

Information processing is one type of instruction used by school counselors to disseminate educational and career materials to students and parents. Presenting course information, discussing financial aid opportunities, and reviewing community resources are examples of informational presentations planned and implemented by school counselors.

Social interaction approaches are used in teacher in-service, parent education, and group work with students. In these relationships, participants are encouraged to interact with each other to learn about the topics being addressed by the program. By using social interaction procedures, school counselors rely on the combined expertise of group members to find solutions, offer ideas, and explore alternatives. In this way, counselors avoid becoming sole experts, and instead become facilitators of the learning process.

Individualized consultations provide information and instruction in brief contacts with student, parents, and teachers. The counselor-consultant in these instances acts as a sounding board and resource enabling persons to choose direction, find appropriate material, learn a necessary skill, and reach an identified goal. An example of this type of consultation is when a high-school student seeks a counselors' assistance in deciding to which college to make an application. The counselor would show the student how to review resources, would administer interest inventories about college selection, and would give other assistance to enable the student to narrow down choices.

Behavior modification techniques and strategies are used by school counselors in their individual and group consultations. Behavioral approaches with individual students can be helpful in teaching a skill or learning to cope with particular situations, and can instruct parents and teachers in management skills for home and school. Sometimes, behavioral instruction is a strategy used in problem-solving consultations as well.

Each of these approaches relies on particular processes and skills on the part of the counselor-consultant. In general, these processes and skills include preparation, presentation, evaluation, and feedback.

Preparation Successful instruction and information-sharing require adequate preparation of materials and time. Counselors who present classroom guidance activities, teacher in-service activities, and parent education programs are successful when they choose instructional goals carefully, plan appropriate learning activities, and schedule their presentations within a reasonable time frame. For example, when counselors present classroom guidance, they plan activities that are developmentally appropriate for all students. The content of the lessons and the activities for instruction include vocabulary and concepts that are understood by the elementary-, and middle-, or high-school students for whom they are intended. At the same time, counselors allow an adequate amount of time for the lesson in accordance with the age and development of students. Elementary-, middle-, and high-school students tolerate various types of presentations for different lengths of time. Knowing these differences and planning programs accordingly increases the likelihood that students will attend to the presentation and achieve the intended learning objectives.

When counselors choose developmentally appropriate objectives, use materials and media to which students will be responsive, and schedule beginning and ending times that facilitate optimal learning, their presentations to students, parents, and teachers are more likely to be successful. Adequate preparation begins this process and is followed by effective presentation skills.

Presentation In many respects, successful guidance, in-service, and other presentations by school counselors are dependent on skills similar to those used by effective teachers. Research of effective teacher characteristics has not produced conclusive findings (Ornstein 1985; Wittmer & Myrick, 1980), but consensus among educators highlights teaching skills and behaviors that distinguish effective instruction (Ryan & Cooper, 1988). These behaviors include:

1. Designing lessons and stating goals to let students know what is expected and what they will learn
2. Monitoring students' progress with regular feedback and by task-oriented assignments
3. Using well-paced instruction to maximize the content covered in the lesson
4. Asking high level questions that require students to analyze, synthesize, or evaluate information
5. Communicating high expectations for all students
6. Managing classrooms with appropriate skill, positive reinforcement, and attention to student achievement

The above list is by no means all inclusive. There are other teacher behaviors related to student learning and instructional effectiveness. The above list focuses on those behaviors that are particularly useful in presenting affective lessons such as classroom guidance. Some specific behaviors we would expect counselors and teachers to demonstrate in presenting effective classroom guidance are:

1. Starting the lesson promptly and using time efficiently
2. Stating the purpose of the presentation clearly
3. Giving clear instructions and directions

4. Encouraging participation of all students
5. Demonstrating adequate group management skills
6. Facilitating the session with listening, questioning, reflecting, clarifying, and summarizing skills
7. Respecting the individuality of students
8. Affirming and reinforcing students' willingness to contribute
9. Providing effective feedback to students
10. Using evaluative measures to assess the outcome of the lesson

These behaviors may also be applied to presentations with parents and teachers for instructional or informational purposes. Regardless of the type of presentation, counselors use effective behaviors and evaluate the outcome of their services. In sum, successful presenters are deeply involved in their activity, encourage exchanges between themselves and their audience, facilitate appropriate interaction among group members, use sufficient management techniques to maintain order without inhibiting participation, and pace their presentations to keep a high degree of interest without moving so quickly that some members of the group get lost (Goodlad & Klein, 1974).

Feedback Instructional and informational consultations set goals to distribute information or teach knowledge and skills to certain audiences. To create learning environments in which information is accepted and skills are attained, counselor-consultant seek ongoing feedback from participants. In this way, their presentations become more than didactic discourses, and instead they encourage a free exchange of ideas and opinions about the subject matter being presented. Classroom guidance often has the goal of teaching character education, citizenship qualities, and other traits revered in our society. While it is appropriate and proper to include these objectives in a guidance curriculum, teachers and counselors remain open to views that express different and sometimes conflicting opinions about important issues. Healthy exchanges among students, parents, or other participants in these types of presentations fosters acceptance and instills democratic principles embraced by U.S. society and its schools.

Evaluation Effective presentations are measured by asking two questions:

1. Has the information or content of the activity been acquired by the participants?
2. Have the participants indicated their satisfaction with the presentation?

The first of these two questions is answered by observing the skills acquired by participants, or by assessing whether or not they have obtained the information and knowledge desired. For example, a counselor who presents conflict resolution strategies to middle graders might evaluate the effect of this activity by having the classroom teachers monitor student behavior to measure the acquisition of negotiation and mediation skills. Another type of evaluative process the counselor might try is to have the students complete a questionnaire to measure their understanding of the information presented as well as their satisfaction with the group program. Form 6–1 illustrates a sample questionnaire a counselor might use with a middle-school group on conflict resolution.

By applying evaluative techniques to assess their presentations, school counselors make adjustments in their programs to accurately meet the needs of students, parents, and teachers. There is little reason for counselors to continue activities that do not result in desired outcomes, or are dissatisfying to participants. Because time is limited, counselors must evaluate their activities and services based on how well they meet the needs of intended populations, and then discard those that have minimum effect on program goals and objectives. Later in Chapter 10, we will examine some of the evaluation processes school counselors can use to assess programs and services.

Problem-solving Consultations   In addition to group presentations that focus on developmental learning and facilitate the dissemination of information, school counselors use processes to assist consultees in examining

FORM 6–1   Sample Group Evaluation Form

Your participation in the Conflict Resolution Group has been appreciated. Please help me evaluate our group by answering the following questions. Indicate your answers by marking an "X" over either YES, NO, or UNSURE. Thank you.

1. Did you learn about yourself in this group?	YES	NO	UNSURE
2. Did you learn about other people in this group?	YES	NO	UNSURE
3. Was the group helpful in teaching you about conflict?	YES	NO	UNSURE
4. Did you learn ways to handle conflict?	YES	NO	UNSURE
5. Did the counselor listen to people in the group?	YES	NO	UNSURE
6. Were you allowed to give your opinion?	YES	NO	UNSURE
7. Did other group members help you?	YES	NO	UNSURE
8. Was being in this group helpful to you?	YES	NO	UNSURE
9. Did the counselor's leadership help?	YES	NO	UNSURE
10. Would you recommend this group to other students?	YES	NO	UNSURE

problem situations, exploring solutions, choosing strategies, and evaluating outcomes. Numerous problem-solving models have been developed and presented in the consulting literature for school counselors (Brown, Pryzwansky, & Schulte, 1991; Kurpius, 1978; Kurpius & Brown, 1985; Schmidt & Medl, 1983; Umansky & Holloway, 1984). Generally, these models consist of similar phases or stages. The variations found in these proposed stages or with the language used to describe processes within each stage are usually related to differences in theoretical foundations of the models. For example, behavioral consultations differ from Adlerian approaches, not because of any fundamental difference in their consulting structures, but because of the way each theory views human development and behavior. Behavioral views focus on external forces that influence behavior and development while Adlerian theory emphasizes peoples' perceptual interpretative powers in creating a unique view of the world and their role in it.

The problem-solving and situational consultations performed by school counselors can be illustrated by a generic four-stage model that can be adapted to different, divergent theoretical perspectives. This model consists of an introduction, exploration, implementation, and evaluation phase.

Introduction   In this phase, the counselor-consultant meets the consultee, makes introductions, states the purpose of the meeting, and hears the main concern. The essential goal of this phase is for the consultant to help the consultee clearly identify and express the problem or situation of concern. In this stage, the consultant and consultee establish rapport and begin gathering information which will enable them to agree on what is the main concern and the *actual* problem that needs immediate attention.

An additional aspect of gathering information in the introduction phase is for the consultant and consultee to have data and other material to assist in the exploration of alternatives and possible solutions. Observations, tests, inventories, records, interviews and other processes are used to gather pertinent information. This gathering of vital information is a nonjudgmental process with the consultant accepting input from the consultee as it is given. Later, by evaluating and sorting various pieces of information, the consultant will formulate opinions about various data to give an accurate direction to the consultation, but in this early stage information is simply collected.

Exploration   After the relationship has been established and a clear understanding of the concern or problem has been attained, the roles of the participants must be clarified. This clarification process is essential so that all persons in the relationship know their responsibilities and the other responsibilities assumed by everyone else involved. For example, when a parent consults with a school counselor about a child's behavior at home, both the counselor and parent need to agree that the counselor's role is *not* to go to the home and manage the situation, but rather to offer resources, information, and instructional opportunities from which the parent can select strategies to handle the problem successfully.

When roles are clarified, the consultation is ready to explore the situation and consider strategies for addressing it. In this phase, the information that was gathered earlier is closely examined, strategies and approaches attempted previously are discussed, and additional possibilities are debated. Sometimes consultants encourage brainstorming techniques to expand the possible alternatives. Brainstorming is a process of listing all the ideas available, regardless how outrageous, impractical, or unlikely they might be. Once this list is generated, the consultant and consultee begin to narrow down the alternatives. Whatever process is chosen to explore possibilities, the end result of this phase of the relationship should be to identify and agree on one or more strategies to implement.

Implementation Exploration without action leads nowhere. A successful consulting relationship uses the agreement reached in the exploration phase to design a plan of action, assign responsibilities, and make a commitment regarding these assignments. An action plan lets each participant in the consultation know *what* will be done, by *whom*, and *when* it will be accomplished. Only by designing and implementing an action plan with clear assignments and time lines are counselor-consultants able to perform adequate follow-up and evaluation of their helping relationships.

Evaluation A successful consultation is not complete until follow-up and evaluation are done. In this phase, the school counselor (consultant) assumes responsibility for making contact with all participants in the relationship, receives feedback from each of them, and ascertains whether or not assignments were fulfilled according to the plan. If the counselor discovers that assignments are not completed, the consultation returns to the exploration phase for further clarification of roles and examination of selected strategies. If all assignments are completed, then an assessment of change is needed. Closure in the consulting relationship is possible when the identified problem or concern has been adequately addressed and resolved by implementing the action plan.

The four-phase model for situational consultations presented here provides a structure by which school counselors can process information with students, parents, teachers, and other professionals, and formulate agreements to carry out specific plans of action. In all these phases, there are specific skills consultants incorporate to move the consulting process towards a successful conclusion.

Consulting Skills

Effective consultations, either for situational, informational, or instructional purposes, require a high degree of leadership and communication skill. As noted earlier, the processes and skills of consulting appear similar to those used in counseling and other helping relationships (Kurpius, 1986; Schmidt & Osborne, 1981). In informational and instructional settings, consultants use facilitating skills to convey messages, teach skills, and receive feedback from participants. Generally, these facilitative skills include active listening, reflecting content and feeling, clarifying, questioning, and summarizing (Locke & Ciechalski, 1985; Wittmer & Myrick, 1980). These skills are necessary in delivering successful presentations.

Presentation Skills Through *active listening,* the counselor-consultant communicates to all members of the audience that he or she is interested in what they have to say, and understands the messages these participants send. Active listening skills are illustrated by a variety of behaviors including consistent eye contact, head nodding, squared shoulders, forward - posture, and paraphrasing what is said to indicate reception and understanding. Active listening also takes the form of *minimal encouragers* such as "Yes, tell me more," "I understand," "What you're saying is important."

Reflection of content and feeling extends active listening to let consultees know their messages are received and their feelings are understood. Reflection is a form of paraphrasing that gives back to the speaker what was said in an attempt to convey understanding, or to clarify the meaning of the message. With reflection of content, the consultant restates the message using slightly different words. For example, if a parent says, "The grades my son gets are not going to help him," a counselor-consultant might reply: "You don't think his grades are strong enough to help his career decisions." Reflection of *feeling* moves beyond the immediate content and attempts to address the underlying feeling. In the preceding example, the counselor-consultant might respond, "You worry about your son's future."

When consultants reflect content and feeling, the responses they receive from consultees enable them to assess how accurate their reflections are. It is acceptable to miss the target on some reflections because the consultees will usually indicate whether the consultant is wrong or off target. When this happens, the consultee usually proceeds to correct or alter the reflection, making it more accurate. In this way, even an off-target reflection can be facilitative. As a case in point, the earlier example of reflecting the parent's feeling might result in the parent responding, "No, I'm not worried, but very frustrated with his performance." Through this process, the consultant has encouraged the parent to reveal the true feeling of frustration, and thereby gives a more accurate direction to the consulting relationship.

Clarifying is another skill that assists in directing a consultation. Typically, consultants use a variety of behaviors to establish clarity because clarifying is not an independent skill. For example, the reflecting process described above helped the consultant and consultee clarify the actual feeling the parent was experiencing. The skill used in this clarification process was reflecting content and feeling. Other behaviors used to achieve clarification are paraphrasing, questioning, and summarizing for understanding. Each of these, if used appropriately, can clarify communications so that the information or instruction being conveyed is accurately received.

Counselors and consultants use *questioning* skills in many different types of relationships. In schools, questioning is a skill used frequently by classroom teachers. Volumes have been written about the appropriate use of questioning as an instructional skill and most research indicates that the nature and type of question used determines the success of a relationship (Wittmer & Myrick, 1980). Generally *closed questions* invite only limited responses such as "yes" and "no," and do little to facilitate relationships. By contrast, *open questions* encourage participants to respond in whatever manner and at any length they see fit. In addition, when questions are used too frequently they may hinder the development of productive interactions. By using too many questions, consultants take on the aura of a detective or inquisitor.

By *summarizing* during their presentations, consultants stay on task and check participants for understanding. In addition, summarizing allows consultants to reiterate the goals and objectives of their presentations as information or instruction is being given. Summarizing is also used to bring sessions to a close, and closure is important to successful consultations. A helping relationship that continues on and on without focus or direction is unproductive. By reaching closure on identified issues and concerns, the consultant and consultee are able to identify new concerns if necessary and re-establish a constructive alliance.

All these skills help counselor-consultants present beneficial instructional and informational sessions to students, parents, and teachers in schools. They are also necessary skills in problem- solving and situational consultations when school counselors confer with consultees about specific concerns or problems. Often, these skills are needed in parent and teacher conferences about students' academic progress or school behavior.

Conferring Skills   In addition to active listening, paraphrasing, reflecting, and the other skills mentioned earlier, consulting models include other facilitative and decision-making processes. Mickelson and Davis (1977) presented a problem-solving model that included many of the skills above and more: demonstrating acceptance, giving accurate feedback, testing alternatives, supporting, and developing a plan of action. Moracco (1981) suggested a problem-solving model for teachers to use with students and incorporated these helping skills: empathy, concreteness, respect, genuineness, immediacy, self-disclosure, confrontation, clarifying, brainstorming, summarizing, prompting, questioning, reinforcing, and suggesting strategies.

In this model, these skills span six stages consisting of: (1) an expression of the concern and related underlying feelings; (2) a definition and identification of the concern; (3) a commitment to change; (4) a list of possible alternatives; (5) the selection of one alternative; and (6) an evaluation of the selected alternative.

Figure 6–2 illustrates a problem-solving model using the four phases presented earlier in this section. Consulting skills are listed with each phase, and objectives are stated. The skills, of course, are useful throughout the consulting relationship and may be found in more than one phase. In Figure 6–2, the skills listed are essential for the phase in which they are indicated, but they are also used during other stage of the consultation. As seen in Chapter 4, many of these processes and skills constitute counseling relationships with individuals and groups.

PHASES	*SKILLS*	*OBJECTIVES*

Introduction	Listening & Attending
	Respondent to content &
	  feeling
	Clarifying
	Summarizing for
	  understanding
		Establish rapport
		Identify concerns &
		  problems
		Gather information

Exploration	Questioning Structuring Focusing Clarifying roles Interpreting data Instructing/Informing Brainstorming	Narrow concerns List options Seek agreement on possibilities Move toward action
Implementation	Mediating/Negotiating Confronting Prioritizing Planning	Choose strategies Assign responsibilities Set goals & time lines
Evaluation	Observing Documenting Assessing Summarizing	Evaluate results Follow up agreements Reach closure

FIGURE 6-2 Consulting Phases, Skills, and Objectives

With all the skills recommended in the different types of consulting, a few cautions are necessary. First, the counselor-consultant must be knowledgeable and skilled in the use of these facilitative behaviors (Brown, 1985). Skills used without proficiency are potentially damaging to relationships. Second, the amount a particular skill is used can affect the success of a given session or interaction. A consultant might be very knowledgeable and proficient in the use of paraphrasing, but if it is used repeatedly, the consultee will begin to tire of it. Eventually, the relationship will falter, and the consultee's assistance will be rejected.

A third caveat in using consulting skills is related to timing. Even the best of intentions will miss their mark if they are ill-timed. Successful consultants know *what* to do, and equally important, they know *when* to do it. A well-intentioned question, asked at an inappropriate time, will not achieve its goal. Successful consultations, like magic shows, require precise timing of proficient skill.

Research on Consulting

Research on consultation is plentiful, but as Brown, Pryzwansky, and Schulte (1991) noted, methodological problems are prevalent, making it difficult to draw concise and accurate conclusions. For one thing, consultation lacks clear description and definition due to the variety of structures and models proposed in the literature and used by counselors in schools. Also, research studies on consultation have not compared the effectiveness of processes used by different professional helpers in various programs of services. Much of the literature and research in school consultation for example is found in both school counseling and school psychology sources. But these two professional areas have not been compared to determine if differences exist in the effective practice of consultation with parents, teachers, and other professionals. Future research needs to examine how counselors and psychologists use these approaches to establish whether or not professional focus and training make a difference in consulting relationships.

In school counseling, research has focused on a few theoretical approaches, namely Adlerian (Frazier & Matthes, 1975; Jackson & Brown; Williams, Omizo, & Abrams, 1984) and behavioral programs (Giannotti & Doyle, 1982; Henderson, 1987; Weathers & Liberman, 1975) in examining the effective use of consultation. Some research has reported the effects of special training and consultation programs, such as support groups for abusive parents (Post-Krammer, 1988). While a number of studies examining the efficacy and effectiveness of parent consultation programs have been published, research on counselor-teacher consultation is limited. In one study, Cunningham and Hare (1989) reported success in instructing teachers in child bereavement processes. By training teachers in death education and child bereavement, counselors were able to increase teachers' effectiveness in helping children through the grieving process (Hare & Cunningham, 1988; Molnar-Stickels, 1985).

Generally, limited research indicates positive results with many types of consulting services and programs used by school counselors. However, much more and better designed studies are needed. By way of example, a few studies are summarized here.

Henderson (1987) reported positive results in improving children's alternative thinking skills by combining affective education programs with parental involvement. Students received classroom guidance instruction and parents participated in a seminar titled "Helping Our Children with Reading." While the study did not show significant results on all variables, students whose parents participated in the seminar performed significantly better on alternative thinking measures than students whose parents were not involved. Alternative thinking was defined as children's ability to generate alternative solutions to different types of interpersonal problems.

Giannotti and Doyle (1982) used Parent Effectiveness Training (PET) with parents of learning disabled children to investigate parental attitudes, children's perceptions of parental behavior, children's self-concepts, and children's behavior in school. Using a pretest-posttest control group design, the study found significant differences on all four variables. Parents who participated in PET reported more confidence in their parenting skills, a greater awareness of the effect their behavior had on their children, better understanding of their own needs, and more willingness to trust their children than did parents who were not in PET. In addition, children of parents in the PET group scored higher on self-concept measures than those whose parents were in the control group. Teachers' ratings of student behavior also indicated significant differences in some areas. Students whose parents were in PET were seen as being less anxious about school achievement, having more self-reliance, and seeking more positive relationships with their teachers.

Two studies of *Systematic Training for Effective Parenting* (STEP) a program based on Adlerian principles, demonstrated some support for this type of consultation service. A 1984 study measured changes in parent attitudes after participating in a STEP program (Williams, Omizo, & Abrams, 1984). The study also investigated changes in locus of control measures for the children of participating parents. All of the children in the study were identified as learning disabled. Parents were assigned to either the experimental group (STEP) or a control group. The STEP program was presented to the experimental group for nine consecutive weeks in two-hour sessions. Results indicated that the experimental group showed significant differences from the control group of parents. As measured by the *Parent Attitude Survey* (PAS) in a pre- and posttest design, STEP parents were more accepting and trusting after participation in the program, and they perceived their own behavior as more of a contributing factor in their children's behavior.

Another study of STEP placed 25 parents in an experimental group and 20 in a "waiting list" control group and used an eight- session format of one and one-half hours per session (Jackson & Brown, 1986). The study investigated changes in children's self-concept, perceptions of parent behaviors, and parents' attitudes. Unlike the first study reported above, this investigation found only one significant difference in parent attitudes. Parents in the STEP program scored higher on the trust scale than parents in the control group. No other significant results were found on either parent or children's variables. While the authors noted that these results failed to support findings of previous research, they concluded that the modest support found for the STEP program "should be encouraging to...counselors who hope to influence positively the attitudes of parents toward their children" (Jackson & Brown, 1986, p. 103).

Although much needs to be done in researching the value and effectiveness of consulting approaches, consultation remains an emerging and important practice in school counseling (Umansky & Holloway, 1984). Through individual and group consultation, counselors extend their services to a broad audience and collaborate with other professionals to design and implement appropriate and effective services for students, parents, and teachers. An important aspect of these collaborative relationships is the gathering of accurate, reliable information in order to make suitable decisions about programs and services. This process of gathering information brings us to the next essential service of comprehensive school counseling programs, student appraisal.

Selected Readings

Caplan, G. (1970). *The Theory and Practice of Mental Health Consultation* (New York: Basic Books). This classic book is used as the foundation for much of what is called consultation today. This is especially true for consulting models as applied in the helping professions such as counseling and psychology.

Kurpius, D. (Ed.). (1978), "Special Issue: Consultation I," *Personnel and Guidance Journal, 56* (6), 320–373. This issue of the *Personnel and Guidance Journal* is a classic presentation of consultation models, roles and procedures of consultants, and issues related to consultation in various settings, including schools.

Kurpius, D. (Ed.). (1978), "Special Issue: Consultation II," *Personnel and Guidance Journal, 56* (7), 394–448. This is the second issue of the special series on consultation, and it presents a range of topical issues related to the theory and practice of consulting. It includes a section on training issues and approaches.

Brown, D., Pryzwansky, W. B., & Schulte, A. C. (1991). *Psychological Consultation: Introduction to Theory and Practice*, 2nd Ed. (Boston: Allyn and Bacon). A comprehensive and readable overview of consultation; its historical development, theoretical foundations, and models of practice are clearly presented.

References

Amatea, E. S., & Fabrick, F. (1981), "Family Systems Counseling: A Positive Alternative to Traditional Counseling," *Elementary School Guidance and Counseling, 15,* 223–236.

Aubrey, R. F. (1978), "Consultation, School Interventions, and the Elementary Counselor," *Personnel and Guidance Journal, 56,* 351–354.

Bergan, J. R. (1977). *Behavioral Consultation* (Columbus, OH: Merrill).

Brown, D. (1985), "The Preservice Training of Supervision of Consultants," *The Counseling Psychologist, 13,* 410–425.

Brown, D., Pryzwansky, W. B., & Schulte, A. C. (1991). *Psychological Consultation: Introduction to Theory and Practice* (Boston: Allyn and Bacon).

Caplan, G. (1970). *THe Theory and Practice of Mental Health Consultation* (New York: Basic Books).

Carrington, D., Cleveland, A., & Ketterman, C. (1978), "Collaborative Consultation in the Secondary Schools," *Personnel and Guidance Journal, 56,* 355–358.

Cunningham, B., & Hare, J. (1989), "Essential Elements of a Teacher In-Service Program on Child Bereavement," *Elementary School Guidance and Counseling, 23,* 175–182.

Dinkmeyer, D., Jr., & Dinkmeyer, D., Sr. (1984), "School Counselors as Consultants in Primary Prevention Programs," *Personnel and Guidance Journal, 62,* 464–466.

Faust, V. (1968). The Counselor-Consultant in the Elementary School (Boston: Houghton Mifflin).

Frazier, F., & Matthes, W. A. (1975), "Parent Education: A Comparison of Adlerian and Behavioral Approaches," *Elementary School Guidance and Counseling, 19,* 31–38.

Fullmer, D. W., & Bernard, H. W. (1972). *The School Counselor- Consultant* (Boston: Houghton Mifflin).

Giannotti, T. J., & Doyle, R. E. (1982), "The Effectiveness of Parental Training on Learning Disabled Children and their Parents," *Elementary School Guidance and Counseling, 17,* 131–136.

Good, T. L., & Brophy, J. E. (1987). *Looking in Classrooms,* 4th ed. (New York: Harper & Row).

Goodlad, J. L., & Klein, M. F. (1974). *Looking behind the Classroom Door* (Worthington, OH: Charles A. Jones).

Hansen, J. C., Himes, B. S., & Meier, S. (1990). *Consultation: Concepts and Practices* (Englewood Cliffs, NJ: Prentice Hall).

Hare, J., & Cunningham, B. (1988), "Effects of Child Bereavement Training Program for Teachers," *Death Studies, 12,* 345–353.

Henderson, P. A. (1987), "Effects of Planned Parental Involvement in Affective Education," *The School Counselor, 35,* 22–27.

Hett, G. G., & Davies, A. (1985). *The Counselor as Consultant* (ERIC Document Reproduction Services No. ED 262 348).

House, G., & Brown, S. (1980). *Secondary School Counselors as Counselors: Emerging from the Paper Shuffle.* Paper presented at the Annual Convention of the American Personnel and Guidance Association, Atlanta, GA. (ERIC Document Reproduction Service No. ED 194 837).

Ibrahim, F. A., Helms, B., & Thompson, D. (1983), "Counselor Role and Function: An Appraisal by Consumers and Counselors," *Personnel and Guidance Journal, 61,* 597–601.

Jackson, M. D., & Brown, D. (1986), "Use of Systematic Training for Effective Parenting (STEP) with Elementary School Parents," *The School Counselor, 34,* 100–104.

Kirk, S. A., & Gallagher, J. J. (1989). *Education Exceptional Children,* 6th ed. (Boston, Houghton Mifflin).

Kurpius, D. (1978), "Consultation Theory and Process: An Integrated Model," *Personnel and Guidance Journal, 56,* 335– 338.

Kurpius, D. (1986), "Consultation: An Important Human and Organizational Intervention," *Journal of Counseling and Human Service Professions, 1,* 58–66.

Kurpius, D., & Brown, D. (Eds.). (1985), "Consultation" [Special Issue]. *The Counseling Psychologist, 13,* 333–476.

Kurpius, D., & Robinson, S. E. (1978), "An Overview of Consultation," *Personnel and Guidance Journal, 56,* 320–323.

Locke, D. C., & Ciechalski, J. C. (1985). *Psychological Techniques for Teachers* (Muncie, IN: Accelerated Development).

McComb, B. (Ed). (1981), "Special Issue: Family Counseling," *Elementary School Guidance and Counseling, 15,* 180–278.

Mickelson, J., & Davis, J. L. (1977), "A Consultation Model for the School Counselor," *The School Counselor, 25,* 100–102.

Molnar-Stickels, L. (1985), "Effect of a Brief Instructional Unit in Death Education on the Death Attitudes of Prospective Elementary School Teachers," *Journal of School Health, 55,* 234–235.

Moracco, J. (1981), "A Comprehensive Approach to Human Relations Training for Teachers," *Counselor Education and Supervision, 21,* 119–135.

Morrow, G. (1987). *The Compassionate School: A Practical Guide to Educating Abused and Traumatized Children* (Englewood Cliffs, NJ: Prentice Hall).

Nicoll, W. G. (1984), "School Counselors as Family Counselors: A Rational and Training Model," *The School Counselor, 31,* 279- -284.

Ornstein, A. C. (1985), "Considering Teacher Effectiveness," *Clearing House, 58,* (9), 399–402.

Palmo, A. J., Lowry, L. A., Weldon, D. P., Scioscia, T. M. (1984), "Schools and Family: Future Perspectives for School Counselors," *The School Counselor, 31,* 272–278.

Post-Krammer, P. (1988), "Effectiveness of Parents' Anonymous in Reducing Child Abuse," *The School Counselor, 35,* 337–342.

Ryan, K., & Cooper, J. M. (1988). *Those Who Can Teach,* 5th ed (Boston: Houghton Mifflin).

Schmidt, J. J. (1991). *A Survival Guide for the Elementary/Middle School Counselor* (West Nyack, NY: The Center for Applied Research in Education).

Schmidt, J. J., & Medl, W. A. (1983), "Six Magic Steps of Consulting," *The School Counselor, 30,* 212–216.

Schmidt, J. J., & Osborne, W. L. (1981), "Counseling and Consulting: Separate Processes or the Same?" *Personnel and Guidance Journal, 60,* (3), 168–171.

Umansky, D. L., & Holloway, E. L. (1984), "The Counselor as Consultant: From Model to Practice," *The School Counselor, 31,* 329–328.

Weathers, L. R., & Liberman, R. P. (1975), "The Contingency Contracting Exercise," *Journal of Behavior Therapy and Experimental Psychiatry, 6,* 208–214.

Williams, G. T., Robinson, F. F., & Smaby, M. H. (1988), "School Counselors Using Group Counseling with Family-School Problems," *The School Counselor, 35,* 169–178.

Williams, R. E., Omizo, M. M., & Abrams, B. C. (1984), "Effects of STEP on Parental Attitudes and Locus of Control of their Learning Disabled Children," *The School Counselor, 32,* 126–133.

Wittmer, J., & Myrick, R. D. (1980). *Facilitative Teaching: Theory and Practice* (Minneapolis, MN: Educational Media Corporation).

7

Student Appraisal

In Chapter 1, you learned that early in its development school counseling established a strong focus on student assessment, particularly in the use of standardized tests. Since its inception, the profession has argued for and against the use of assessment instruments and processes in counseling relationships (Vacc & Bardon, 1982). Today, the controversy continues, and with the increased emphasis on school accountability and public demand for higher student achievement there appears to be no end in sight to this debate.

In addition to the national attention given to tests and measurements in schools, counselors are also affected by the Education for All Handicapped Children Act of 1975 (Public Law 94–142), the Family Educational Rights and Privacy Act of 1974 (the Buckley Amendment), and other legislation pertaining to assessment of students, student placement, and school records (Kuriloff & Robinson, 1982). School counselors are frequently asked to coordinate schoolwide testing programs, administer educational assessments to individual students, and interpret test data and other information to parents, teachers, and other professionals who provide services to students. As such, student appraisal functions, those procedures used to collect and interpret data about students' abilities, achievement, interests, attitudes, and behaviors, remain an essential part of the school counselor's role.

As an essential service of comprehensive school counseling programs, student appraisal was briefly introduced earlier. Now, we examine this function in greater detail. In particular, we review standardized tests, testing procedures, and nonstandardized methods used by counselors in the schools. This is not a comprehensive treatment of the subject of measurement and appraisal in schools, but instead a brief description of how student appraisal functions fit into comprehensive school counseling programs. For more in-depth information about this function and related processes, the reader is referred to the sources cited throughout the chapter and listed in the references.

Student appraisal consists of a number of activities and related practices. Before reviewing common appraisal instruments and processes used by school counselors, an explanation of the terms used to describe and define measurement in counseling is appropriate here. Several terms describe the scope of assessment and appraisal procedures in counseling (Shertzer & Linden, 1979, 1982). Through an understanding of these terms, school counselors enable themselves to present and implement clearly their role in the process of student appraisal.

Appraisal is a term is synonymous with evaluation, and encompasses processes for measuring a range of student attributes, abilities, and interest and for making professional judgments based on the results of these measurements. Student appraisal (evaluation) involves collecting data from a variety of sources, forming opinions and making comparisons with those data, and arriving at a conclusion with which to guide students and others in educational and career decisions.

Assessment is collectively, the instruments and procedures to gather data for student appraisal. Educational tests, psychological evaluations, interest inventories, interviews, and observations are samples of assessment procedures used by school counselors, psychologists, teachers, and other school personnel.

Individual analysis is a description of a student's behaviors, with emphasis on strengths and weaknesses. It is a process that includes the observation and interpretation of behavior and, according to Shertzer and Linden (1982), "is a special case of appraisal" (p. 10).

Interpretation refers to processes that explain and give meaning to various data, observations, and information gathered in student appraisal. In particular, behaviors are interpreted to give them meaning and purpose within the context in which they are observed. School counselors interpret test results, school policies, and also help students, parents, and teachers understand behaviors that are problematic.

Measurement is a process for determining the degree and boundaries of specific traits and characteristics being assessed. Measurement assigns a numerical value or an evaluative description to the trait or characteristic in question. It is the aspect of appraisal that tells us "how much?" or "how often?" By themselves, measurement data are of limited use. Only when applied statistically or comparatively do they acquire any meaning.

Diagnosis is an aspect of appraisal that refers to specific identification, grouping, and categorization of measurement results to make the *best guesses* or *best judgments* about "cause and effect relationships" (Shertzer & Linden, 1982, p. 10). Diagnosis has not always been a comfortable, acceptable term for school counselors. Perhaps this is due to its "medical" and "analytic" implications. Nevertheless, diagnosis is one aspect of accurate appraisal, and is an important element of the decision-making process used to select appropriate services for students and other clientele.

Standardized Testing

In the controversy surrounding student appraisal, no single issue has raised more concern, fueled more heated debates, and caused more public uproar than the use of standardized tests. On one hand, this controversy has focused on the plight of education in the United States and the failure of our students to compete successfully with students from other developed countries. An outcome of this concern has been for politicians, parents, school board members, and other decision makers to demand more testing in evaluating student achievement. In school systems and states across the country, money and energy have been spent developing, purchasing, administering, and analyzing test results. Thus far, in spite of all this time, effort, and money, few beneficial outcomes have been noted. In counseling, the use of tests, in and of themselves, has had little impact on student development. According to Goldman (1982), "tests seem to have made little difference in the decision-making, problem-solving, and planning activities of pupils and clients. There is very little evidence from research that tests as used by counselors have made much difference in the lives of the people they serve" (1982, p. 70).

One major criticism of using tests in schools and other settings has been their limitation with culturally diverse populations and the possibility of test bias. Oakland (1982) presented 10 major concerns related to the testing and assessment of minority students. These concerns continue to be relevant to the selection and use of assessment instruments in schools. An adaptation of these concerns offers guidelines for assessment to counselors and other school personnel:

1. Assessment is unfairly discriminatory when students are not tested in their native or dominant language. The purpose of tests is to discriminate, but when unfair biases and unappropriate items are used, the reliability of tests and validity of results are questionable.

2. For the same reason, tests are unfairly discriminatory when they are developed with white, middle-class sample populations, and administered to multicultural or minority populations. The student populations to which tests are administered should reflect the normative populations on which tests are developed.

3. When school counselors are poorly trained in assessment and the characteristics of minority students, they contribute to test bias and discriminatory practices.

4. When minority students are overrepresented in certain special education programs (such as programs for the educable mentally retarded) and underrepresented in others (such as gifted and talented), there is evidence of test bias or improper assessment practices.

5. The practice of permitting minority students to remain in ineffective educational programs for years of schooling without demonstrating reasonable progress is indicative of cultural bias and unreliable assessment procedures.

6. Parental involvement is essential to appropriate assessment practices. When parents are excluded from decision-making processes, or uninformed about tests, testing procedures, and their children's results, full and accurate use of data is questionable.

7. Decisions made on limited test data place students at risk of being deprived access to educational and career opportunities. Proper assessment consists of a wide range of appraisal information and data.

8. Tests and testing results used to reinforce prejudices and stereotypes of minorities are a violation of legal rights and clear examples of unethical practice. Schools must use tests to enhance opportunities for learning and create possibilities for student development rather than to discourage, demean, and deny their potential for growth.

9. When tests intentionally or unintentionally limit a student's choices for educational and career development, they contribute to existing prejudices and contradict the mission of our schools.

10. Tests used in isolation, without consideration of other types of information and data, "promote dehumanized decision-making practices" (Oakland, 1982, p. 109). School counselors who wish to humanize the appraisal process by creating equitable procedures for all students need to include a wider spectrum of people in the decision-making processes to ensure proper selection and use of assessment instruments.

Another aspect of the debate on testing involves the misuse and misunderstanding of test results (Anastasi, 1988; Gibson & Mitchell, 1990; Nolte, 1975). The enthusiasm for finding methods of assessing academic progress has, unfortunately, been dampened by hasty decisions, improper procedures, unreliable scores, and inaccurately interpreted results. None of these conditions adds to the acceptance of assessment processes or measurement instruments in schools. As professionals with training in the appropriate use of tests and other standardized assessment instruments, school counselors have responsibility for assisting their schools and school systems in the selection, administration, and utilization of tests and test results. The first step is to understand the meaning of standardization, and to know the different types of standardized tests.

Standardization

A test is a standardized measure when administered and scored according to uniform procedures (Anastasi, 1988). When tests use the same procedures during every administration with every individual or group of students, it is possible to compare student performance over time or to compare an individual's scores with the scores of other students. Test standardization, therefore, requires uniform testing conditions every time a particular test is given.

Responsibility for adequate standardization rests with both the developer and user. The developer formulates specific test directions as part of the standardization procedure, and the user must adhere to these directions without deviation. Standardization includes the oral instructions given, materials used, time constraints, demonstrations, methods of handling students' questions, and other details related to test administration (Anastasi, 1988). In addition, other subtle factors may alter test administration to such a degree that it violates standardization. For example, if a counselor reads the directions at a pace much quicker than when the standardized procedures were developed, the administration may render the test scores unreliable and invalid.

Another aspect of standardization that allows for the comparison of scores across test administrations, or among students who take a particular test, is the use of *norms*. Standardized tests are developed and administered to a large representative sample of subjects, known as the *standardized sample*, for whom the tests are designed. Norms are the average scores of specified groups within the representative sample. For example, if on a spelling test, the average 10-year-old correctly answers 15 out of 30 items, then the *10-year-old norm* would be a raw score of 15 correct. When reporting scores, standardized tests use either *age norms* or *grade norms*. The above example is of an age norm. Standardized test scores are derived from normal curve distribution theory, which says that on a given trait, individual scores will cluster near the center of the range of scores with a gradual tapering off as the extreme low and high scores are approached. The central score of this curve is called either the *mean, median,* or *mode* depending on the type of statistical average used. These three different types of averages are called *measures of central tendency.* The statistical term used to describe the degree to which students vary from the average score is called a *measures of variability,* and two types of variability are the *range* and *standard deviation.* Figure 7–1 illustrates a normal curve with the percentage distribution of cases across the range of scores.

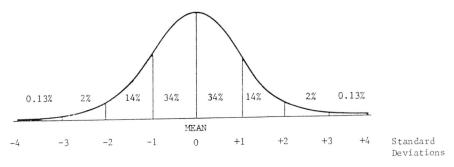

Normal curve showing percentages: 0.13%, 2%, 14%, 34%, 34%, 14%, 2%, 0.13%; MEAN; Standard Deviations −4, −3, −2, −1, 0, +1, +2, +3, +4

FIGURE 7–1 Normal Curve Distribution with Percentage of Cases across a Range of Scores

In addition to age and grade norms, test scores of students are commonly reported by percentiles or standard scores. *Percentile scores* indicate the percentage of students who fall below a particular raw score and show the relative position of students within the representative sample. For example, a percentile score of 45 means that 45 percent of the students in the sample obtained a lower raw score. Although percentiles are relatively easy to understand, they are often misinterpreted and misunderstood. Gibson and Mitchell (1990) warned that when "working with non-test-sophisticated populations, such as parents, students, and most general populations, it is important to emphasize that percentiles do *not* represent percentages" (p. 227). Therefore, the percentile rank of 45, given above, does not mean that the student answered 45 percent of the items correctly. In fact, there is no way from a percentile rank alone to know how many items were on the test or how many correct responses were achieved.

Another type of score, a *standard score* indicates students' performance by the distance above or below the average score for the group. "Basically, standard scores express test performance in terms of standard deviation units from the mean" (Gronlund & Linn, 1990, p. 349). The *mean* is the average score for the sample population and the *standard deviation* is the measure of variability or spread of the scores across the group. As seen in the normal curve distribution illustrated in Figure 7–1, a standard deviation of plus or minus 1 in either direction of the mean includes approximately 68 percent of the sample population. This means that we expect 68 percent of the students' scores to fall within this range.

Unlike percentile bands, standard scores have the advantage of consisting of relatively equal units. Therefore, equal bands of standard scores indicate approximately the same performance difference along the distribution. For example, the difference between the scores of 400 and 500 on a test is the roughly the same as the difference between the scores of 600 and 700. Percentiles do not have this characteristic. The difference in students' performance from the 35th to 45th percentile rank cannot be equated to the difference between the 75th to 85th band. Another advantage of standard scores over percentile ranks is that they can be averaged mathematically.

Examples of tests used by school counselors and reported in standard scores are intelligence tests and college admissions exams. Intelligence tests that use deviation intelligence quotients set a score of 100 as the median (normal IQ = 100), and a standard deviation of 15. As such, the range of +/-1 standard deviation from the norm is 85–115. College admissions exams, such as the Scholastic Aptitude Test (SAT) developed by the College Entrance Examination Board, also use standard scores. For example, the SAT reports a mean score of 500 and a standard deviation of 100. Using the normal curve distribution, therefore, we assume that 68 percent of the students who take the SAT score between 400 and 600.

Stanine scores are a variation of standard scores. A stanine system uses a nine-point scale, where 9 is high and 1 is low, and the mean is 5. Stanines 1 and 9 cover the tails of the normal curve distribution. The remaining stanines, 2 through 8, each include a span of raw scores with a width equal to one half of the standard deviation. Stanines are popular scores, particularly for reporting local norms because they are easy to translate and explain to students and parents, and scores on different tests can be compared (such as between mathematics and language arts). In addition, stanines are easily recorded due to their single digit form, and they are computed like percentiles yet have the arithmetic advantages of standard scores (Gronlund & Linn, 1990).

The above description of standardization and different types of test scores does not do this topic justice in the limited space available. Readers who desire more in-depth explanation and information should consult the references cited in this section. At this point we examine two types of standardized tests used in schools: norm-referenced and criterion-referenced.

Norm-referenced Tests   Tests that compare individual student performance to performance of the group are known as norm-referenced tests. Scores on these tests, such as percentiles ranks and stanines, are used to illustrate a student's relative standing in the normative sample. For example, a stanine of 6 in a language arts subtest indicates the student scored within the first standard deviation above the mean for the group. By the same token, a percentile rank of 34 in mathematics indicates the student scored better than 34 percent of the students in the representative sample (same age or grade level, for example). These tests report scores based on local, state, or national norms, thereby the name "norm-referenced" tests.

While norm-referenced tests are beneficial in comparing students' performance and achievement with other students their age or grade level, the tests are limited in evaluating student knowledge or mastery of subject matter. As an example, if 10 students were evaluated using a norm-referenced mathematics tests, the results would show each student's relative position in comparison to the normative sample on which the test was developed. But these scores alone would not help teachers learn the mathematical strengths and weaknesses of each student. As such, all 10 students could be quite able in math, but their scores would simply rank them against a sample population. One would be ranked highest and one lowest despite their comparable knowledge of mathematics. To evaluate these students' mathematical knowledge, teachers use a second type of assessment called a criterion-referenced test.

Criterion-referenced Tests   These tests are designed to assess student performance in terms of specific standards or learning objectives. Returning to the example above of the 10 math students, a criterion-referenced test would enable students, teachers, and parents to identify which math skills had been mastered by each student and which areas of knowledge and skill needed additional attention. Typically, criterion-referenced test results are reported as the percentage of correct items in a particular knowledge or skill area. In the case above, for example, a student might score 35 percent correct in arithmetic computation for addition and 80 percent correct for subtraction. If the criterion for mastery is 75 percent correct, then this student has mastered subtraction skills, but has not mastered addition.

Both types of tests, norm-referenced and criterion-referenced, have purpose and benefit in student appraisal. On one hand, criterion- referenced tests enable counselors and teachers to describe the performance of students in relation to some set of learning goals and objectives. This type of information is helpful in designing and restructuring instructional programs to meet the needs of all students. This is of particular benefit to curriculum development. By contrast, norm-referenced results allow schools to make comparisons within the school and among schools in a district, state, or region. These comparisons help schools look at student placement, grade assignments, broad instructional issues, and demographic concerns in schools and school systems. Both types of tests have value. The important issue for counselors, principals, and teachers is knowing why a particular test is selected and whether or not it is a reliable and valid measure of the trait being assessed.

Selection of Tests

Because school counselors are professionals trained in tests and measurement, they are often called upon to help with the selection of tests to use in schoolwide testing programs. In addition, counselors select assessment instruments, including tests, to use in individual student appraisal. To give adequate assistance to their schools, and also to select appropriate instruments for individual appraisal, counselors need to be knowledgeable and prepared to give adequate guidance and make the best selections.

Counselors use a variety of sources to learn about new tests and keep abreast of research on testing. One essential source of information is the *Mental Measurements Yearbook* published by the Buros Institute for Mental Measurements. Each yearbook contains descriptions of various tests, test reviews written by testing specialists, selections of test reviews published in other sources, bibliographies for specific tests, and reviews of books on tests and measurement. The Buros Institute also publishes *Tests in Print* a guide for locating information and descriptions about specific tests that are currently published. *Test in Prints* is cross-referenced with past editions of the *Mental Measurement Yearbook* to enable counselors to locate tests and research past reviews. The Institute, located at the University of Nebraska in Lincoln, maintains a database within an on-line computer service offered by Bibliographic Retrieval Services, Inc. (BRS) and accessed through library computer services that belong to BRS.

Other sources for test information include the Educational Testing Service of Princeton, New Jersey, the *Standards for Educational and Psychological Testing* published by the American Psychological Association, the Test Corporation of America, located in Kansas City, Missouri, and a number of professional journals related to tests and measurement. One journal, *Measurement and Evaluation in Counseling and Development,* is published by a division of the American Counseling Association. Another source of information is test publisher's catalogues, which contain brief descriptions of tests, costs, and other facts useful in the selection process. Once counselors have obtained sufficient resources about available tests, they are ready to begin the selection process. They begin by clearly identifying the purpose that underlies the need for gathering test information.

Identifying the Purpose of the Test   Why is a test needed? This is the first question that schools, counselors, administrators, and teachers must answer in selecting appropriate assessment instruments. Oftentimes, tests are selected without a clear purpose and as a result, reports are misused or underused, and the time and cost of administration is wasted. In making an appropriate selection or giving recommendations for particular tests, counselors first need to identify the goals and objectives of the testing process. What are we trying to find out? How will the results be used? And, based on our research of existing tests, which ones appear to offer what we need?

If schools want to assess the reading level of students in third grade, do they want to know reading levels as defined by learning objectives, or as a comparison of students in the third grade? The answer will help narrow the decision between criterion-referenced and norm-referenced tests. In addition, a focus on students' reading level enables counselors and teachers to eliminate full battery achievement tests and limit the selection to reading tests. In sum, the intended use of the test and the type of score reports desired help initiate the screening and selection process.

Considering Administrative Conditions   After identifying the purpose of testing, counselors consider administrative factors that influence the selection of particular tests. Several questions are deliberated. For example, will the test be administered individually or to groups of students? Are there budgetary restrictions and will they preclude the selection of particular tests? How much time will be required to administer the test? Are there other conditions or materials required that will affect the selection of particular tests?

There is little purpose in selecting an appropriate test only to have it administered in a haphazard manner. Therefore, all factors for administering the test correctly are carefully weighed before a decision is made. As learned earlier, standardization requires strict adherence to published testing procedures and directions. Any deviation from these violates standardization and jeopardizes the testing results.

Acquiring Specimen Sets   When a decision is narrowed to a few possible choices, counselors order specimen sets of the tests from publishers. Usually, these sets can be purchased at a nominal cost and include a copy of the manual, a sample test booklet, and information about scoring and score reports. Examination of these materials helps narrow the choices. In particular, counselors and teachers want to examine the test manual to ascertain the uses for which the test is designed, the training and qualifications of test administrators, the knowledge and qualifications needed for interpreting results, evidences of validity and reliability, directions for administering and scoring the test, and information about the normative sample. A thorough examination of the test manual and review of specific test items in the booklet provide valuable information to make appropriate choices. At this stage of the selection process, it is essential to pay particular attention to the validity and reliability data presented by the publisher and to reviewers' critiques if such reviews are available.

Validity and Reliability

Test *validity* pertains to the degree to which an assessment instrument actually measures what it says it does. For example, does a Math Achievement Test actually measure math knowledge and skill, or does it measure a student's ability to *read* and respond to mathematical questions? Another example of the question of validity is whether or not IQ tests actually measure the illusive construct called "intelligence," or do they simply measure knowledge and skill based on experience, background, and education? Anastasi (1988) summarized three major types of test validity—content, criterion-related, and concurrent.

Content validity indicates that the items on a test are a fair representation of the domain of knowledge or tasks the test purports to measure. Content validity is commonly applied in evaluating achievement tests that assess students' performance in particular subject areas.

Criterion-related validity involves the effectiveness of a test in predicting a student's performance in certain situations. Specifically, the student's performance on a test is compared to some *criterion* that is an independent measure of what the test is intended to predict. Such a criterion may be reflected in either concurrent or future situations. For example, a typing test may give results that are compared with the current average speed and performance of secretaries already hired by the firm. By contrast, the Scholastic Aptitude Test (SAT) is presented by the College Entrance Examination Board as a predictor of future success in college based on research of college performance of past examinees.

Construct validity is concerned with abstract, psychological characteristics that a test claims to assess. In schools, counselors and teachers frequently use self-concept questionnaires and scales to assess students' perceptions of themselves. An assumption of these instruments is that a construct, in this case the self-concept, is measurable. In many instances, instruments that rely on construct validity are evaluated by comparing them to other reputable instruments that claim to measure the same construct. Comparable results indicate that the instruments may measure the same quality or characteristic.

Reliability is another important factor to consider in selecting standardized tests. This factor refers to the consistency of test results and outcomes from other assessment processes. If a student is administered a reading achievement test on two successive occasions within a short period of time, we would expect the results to be similar. In this way, reliability refers to the *results* obtained with particular instruments rather than the instruments themselves.

There are many different types of reliability and each uses statistical procedures to quantify the relationship between different sets of test results. This statistical relationship is known as a *correlation coefficient* and is used by counselors, teachers, and other reviewers to examine the reliability of tests. When applied specifically to reliability, this statistic is called a *reliability coefficient.* The reliability coefficient is expressed as a single digit ranging from -1 to +1, where both extremes of the range indicate a perfect correlation and 0 indicates no correlation at all. Therefore a coefficient of .95 indicates that the relationship between two sets of data (such as two separate administrations of the same test) are strongly related in the same (positive) direction. This would be a desirable finding if we were examining the reliability of reading achievement test.

A correlation coefficient of -.95 on the other hand also illustrates a strong relationship between two sets of data, but in the opposite (negative) direction. This finding is desirable when we examine two measurements whose results contradict each other. For example, if we develop an anxiety scale where a low score indicates minimal anxiety, and we want to compare it with a mechanical skills test, we would hope to find that lower anxiety scores correlate with higher mechanical performance. Conversely, if we found these same instruments to be negatively correlated, we would expect higher anxiety scores to relate to lower mechanical performance.

Three types of techniques are commonly used to establish test reliability. One is called the test-retest method where the same test is given after a specified period of time. A second method is called the alternate or equivalent form method. This technique uses different forms of the same test and administers them one after the other, either immediately or with an intervening time interval which allows for stability over time. A third way of determining test reliability is by measuring a test's *internal consistency*. This is done by using either the *split-half* method or a Kuder-Richardson formula. The split-half method compares the scores on two halves of the test items on the same test. Determining how to split the test into the comparable halves is critical. The Kuder-Richardson formulas use statistical techniques to examine subjects' performance on each test item of the same test. This method of measuring a tests *internal consistency* offers an estimate of the degree to which all the items of a selected test measure similar characteristics.

All three methods of determining test reliability have advantages and limitations, and reviewers who select tests need to be familiar with them. According to Gronlund and Linn (1990), three types of consistency are indicated by these three different methods of reliability: consistency of testing procedures, consistency of pupil characteristics, and consistency over different samples of items. The alternate forms method with an intervening time interval is the only method of the three that takes into account all three types of consistency. For this reason it is considered by many to be the most useful estimate of test reliability.

The most important aspect of reliability is its relationship to validity. A test that does *not* offer reliable results, cannot be valid, and a test that is valid yields, by definition, reliable results. At the same time, reliability is not a *sufficient* condition for test validity. It is possible to have a highly reliable instrument that produces very consistent scores without it measuring what it intends to measure. For example, an intelligence test that produces consistent scores but is more an assessment of educational and cultural experiences than it is of cognitive functioning cannot be accepted as a valid test.

Usefulness

A third aspect to consider in the test selection process is the usefulness of the instruments being considered. Once the purpose of the test has been determined and the validity and reliability assessed, the school needs to evaluate how useful this instrument will be in the overall educational program. The same is true for counselors who evaluate individual tests and inventories to use in their school counseling programs. In establishing criteria to evaluate test usefulness, counselors and teachers consider the following questions:

1. Will the time devoted to planning, administering, and interpreting the tests be well-spent? In schools where time is at a premium to cover all the curriculum and provide all the special services such as counseling, will time be available for this particular assessment?

2. Will the test produce useable results to develop an appropriate curriculum, alter instruction to meet individual student needs, or enable people to make important educational and career decisions? Tests that are given to merely satisfy local or state policy without generating useable results are a waste of time, resources, and money.

3. Are the test results reported clearly so that all persons who read them will understand them? Depending on the level of test—elementary, middle, or high school—and the population who will use the data, the results should be clear to students, parents, teachers, counselors, and others who will use the information to create beneficial learning programs and services in the school. Testing procedures that simply receive and file results in cumulative folders because no one understands them should not be tolerated. Either the test should be eliminated or changed, or users should receive adequate training to better understand and use the results appropriately.

Using Standardized Tests

Counselors and teachers who select appropriate tests and learn to use the results for the benefit of individual student development and improved instruction for all students want to ensure the proper use of all standardized tests. In many schools, counselors are responsible for coordinating testing services, so the task of delineating testing procedures rests on their shoulders. In this section, we examine some of the steps counselors consider in coordinating the use of standardized tests in their schools. These steps take up where the selection process discussed earlier ends. They begin with test security.

Test Security

All standardized tests should be kept in a secure location. Test information that is disclosed to students intentionally, or learned by students incidentally, jeopardizes the reliability and validity of the results. For this reason, counselors who are charged with test coordination should have access to a secure storage facility and should caution teachers about using information or items from the test in their instruction.

When certain tests are used frequently in schools, particularly group achievement tests, there is risk that some of the items will become so familiar to teachers who administer the test, they may unintentionally incorporate them into classroom lessons. To protect against this potential violation of test security, schools should review tests periodically and select new tests or new forms as the need arises.

Administration

As indicated earlier, any deviation of testing procedures threatens the standardization of norm-referenced and criterion-referenced tests. As such, counselors and other test coordinators should take pains to help teachers and others who are administering these tests to learn proper procedures and adhere to specific published directions. This is also true for counselors who administer individual tests to students for screening purposes in special education or placement in classroom instruction. Counselors must follow test directions explicitly, even during individual assessment sessions. Drummond (1988) noted that proper testing procedures are described in two documents with which school counselors should be familiar: *Standards for Educational and Psychological Testing* (APA, 1985) and *Responsibilities of Users of Standardized Tests* (AACD, 1980).

In addition to following correct procedures and specific directions, test administrators want to create testing environments conducive to producing reliable and valid results. Locating a quiet room for individual testing and stopping all interruptions and extraneous noises (like school bells) during group testing contribute to proper testing environments. Having all the necessary materials at hand, providing accurate timepieces, checking the lighting, and making arrangements for emergencies (such as a student who becomes ill during testing) are other aspects to be considered. The goal of adequate test coordination is to create a setting in which optimal results are achieved so that accurate decisions and appropriate educational plans can be made.

Interpretation

When test scores are received by schools, counselors, teachers, and administrators use the results in a variety of ways. Accurate analysis and interpretation of these results are essential for the testing program to achieve its intended goals. School counselors are involved in the interpretation of test data with students, parents, and teachers, and they attempt to use test results with each of these groups to ultimately provide adequate instruction, proper placement, and assistance in educational and career decisions.

Students can learn about their test performance to identify strengths and weaknesses and use this information in making decisions about study habits, time management, tutoring, or other processes to help themselves learn. Some tests, such as aptitude tests, can disclose abilities to students that they did not know about, and consequently, help them look at career directions to apply these aptitudes in lifelong goals. Other students might benefit from learning that their abilities compare quite favorably with peers their own age, and this knowledge may instill self-confidence to reach for higher goals. At the same time, test data enable students to accept realistic expectations from themselves and from the helping relationships they form with their school counselors (Goldman, 1971). Of course, as Vacc (1982) noted, this is only the first step of a continuous assessment process that is essential in achieving successful helping relationships.

Interpretation of test results with parents is another responsibility of school counselors. When students complete group achievement or aptitude tests, the score reports usually include a report for the parents. Counselors assist the school and parents by explaining and interpreting these reports in group meetings or individual sessions. In group meetings, used to distribute test reports, counselors explain in general terms the meaning of scores and how parents can interpret their children's results. In most instances where test companies include a parent or home report, the results are given in both numerical form and narrative explanation. Figure 7–2 shows an example of a parent report for a "fictional" *School Achievement Test.* In this example, the student's scores are reported in both national percentile ranks and confidence bands. A percentile band illustrates the range of scores in which the expected "true score" lies. Specific explanations of scores for individual students are usually reserved for private sessions with parents who schedule appointments with the school counselor.

In addition to group testing results, scores on individual aptitude tests, achievement batteries, career interest inventories, and other appraisal instruments are typically interpreted to parents and guardians by counselors in individual conferences. Sometimes these conferences are planned jointly with other school specialists such as an exceptional children's teacher or school psychologist. This is particularly true in situations that address exceptionalities and possible placement in special education programs.

Parent Report

School Achievement Test

<u>Student</u>: Melissa Smith   <u>Grade</u>: Three   <u>School</u>: Hope Elementary

On March 25, 1991, your child took the School Achievement Test for third grade students. The results of your child's performance are printed on the chart below. The Total Battery Score shows that your child performed at the 75th percentile. This means that your child scored better than 75 percent of the third graders who took this test when it was standardized. On the chart beside the Total Battery Score you will find a group of X's to illustrate a percentile band. This band indicates that your child's score would fall within this range if she took the test several times.

Following the Total Battery Score you will find percentile scores for the different parts of the School Achievement Test. Your child's scores on these sections are: Reading - 94; Language Arts - 87; Mathematics - 55; Science - 67; Social Studies - 70. As with the Total Battery Score, these scores are also reported as percentile ranks.

These scores only show how your child compares with other students in the third grade across the nation. To determine whether a score is good or not good, other information is needed. Teachers and counselors at the school have additional information they can share to help you better understand and evaluate your child's performance.

Tests	Nat. Perctle.	National Percentile Bands													
		1	2	5	10	20	30	40	50	60	70	80	90	95	98 99
Total Battery	75										XXXXX				
Reading	94													XXXXX	
Language Arts	87												XXXXX		
Mathematics	55								XXXXX						
Science	67										XXXXX				
Social Studies	70										XXXXX				

FIGURE 7–2 Parent Report for "Fictional" *School Acheivement Test* Scores

Helping teachers understand test results and encouraging them to use reports for improving instruction is another essential aspect of test interpretation. Counselors who coordinate testing programs in schools are responsible for assisting school administrators and teachers in using test reports properly. This responsibility means more than interpreting results to parents and preparing reports for the superintendent and local school board. It includes examining students' performance within the context of the school curriculum and the instructional program. In this way, test results not only contribute to student appraisal, they also affect program planning and evaluation.

The process of using test results to examine the instructional program is best fitted to criterion-referenced tests, or to norm-referenced tests where publishers include item analyses categorized by learning objectives. In recent years, there has been a trend by test publishers to develop combined types of standardized tests that provide norm-referenced data as well as criterion-referenced information (Gronlund & Linn, 1990). With criterion-referenced information, counselors are able to assist administrators and teachers in examining specific strengths and weaknesses of students across a variety of learning objectives. Figure 7–3 illustrates a school summary report for third grade reading on the "fictional" *School Achievement Test*. The summary report is complemented by a sample work sheet (Figure 7–4) developed by the school counselor to assist teachers in reviewing test results for their classes and for planning instructional changes. Specifically, teachers want to identify learning objectives on which their students did not perform equal to the average student in the school and determine what instructional methods need redirection or new emphasis.

Appropriate use of test results and adequate interpretation to students, parents, and teachers are essential responsibilities of the testing program

School Summary Report

School Achievement Test

School: Hope Elementary

Grade: Third

Reading	% Below Standard	% At Standard	% Above Standard
Total Score	35	45	20
Word Analysis	30	50	20
Consonants	45	35	20
Vowels	25	55	20
Vocabulary	45	35	20
Reading Comprehen.	25	45	30

FIGURE 7–3 Partial School Summary of "Fictional" *School Achievement Test*, 3rd Grade Reading Results

Classroom Testing Results
Teacher Worksheet

School Achievement Test: Reading Subtest

School: Hope Elementary   Class: Mrs. Bloom   Grade: Third   Test Date: 3/25/91

Learning Objective	School % At or Above Standard	Class % At or Above Standard	% Difference	Priority Rank
Total Reading	65%	57%	- 8%	N/A
Word Analysis	70%	63%	- 7%	N/A
Consonants	55%	45%	- 10%	1
Vowels	75%	69%	- 6%	3
Vocabularly	55%	58%	+ 3%	4
Reading Comprehension	75%	66%	- 9%	2

Note: Figure 7.4 is an example of a teacher worksheet. In practice, a standardized achievement test would report results for many more learning objectives than shown here. This sample is for illustration only.

FIGURE 7–4   Teacher Worksheet for Reviewing and Analyzing Reading Test Results on the "Fictional" *School Achievement Test* Scores

coordinator. Without adequate and proper use of these results the school's testing program is meaningless. This is true for group testing of all students as well as for individual assessment for educational and career decision-making. Schools utilize a variety of standardized tests and if counselors are responsible for coordinating the testing program, they must be thoroughly familiar with different types of tests that contribute to student appraisal.

Types of Tests

Tests available to counselors and teachers cover a wide range of instruments that, as mentioned earlier, are developed as norm-referenced or criterion-referenced tests, and are administered in either group or individual settings. In addition, tests and other assessment instruments differ in characteristics and structure. For example, some tests are timed precisely, such as group achievement and aptitude tests, while others allow subjects a generous period of time to respond, such as with individual intelligence tests. Some tests require responses to objective multiple-choice or matching items, while others call for subjective answers and, subsequently, subjective scoring. Counselors consider all these factors as they help schools select assessment instruments, and as they choose tests and inventories to use in individual student appraisal. The following sections offer brief descriptions of the major types of tests and inventories used by schools and school counselors.

Achievement Tests

Perhaps the most common standardized tests used in schools are achievement tests and batteries. These tests are similar to teacher-made classroom tests in that they attempt to measure what students know about particular subject areas such as reading, mathematics, science, and social studies. Achievement testing most commonly occurs in the elementary through the middle grades. Assessment of student progress and achievement of basic skills is critical in the early years of schooling. Gibson & Mitchell (1990) indicated that the purpose of achievement testing is to measure:

1. The amount of student learning
2. The rate of student learning
3. Comparisons with other students, or one's achievement in other subject areas
4. The level of student learning in subareas
5. Students' strengths and weaknesses in particular areas of learning
6. Predictions of future learning (p. 240)

Achievement batteries, surveys of a range of subject areas and learning objectives, are perhaps the most popular form of testing in schools. They are efficient, cost-effective assessments that provide a broad overview of student performance. One of the disadvantages of these batteries is that, because they cover such a wide range of areas, they are limited in what they assess for any given subject. For this reason, counselors and teachers sometimes use standardized tests that are specific to certain subject areas. As an example, some of the most common tests used at all levels of education are reading tests. These are used to assess the effectiveness of reading instruction, identify students who need special attention in reading, predict student success in other subject areas, and screen for possible learning problems (Gronlund & Linn, 1990).

Individual achievement tests are also used by counselors and teachers in the student appraisal process. Two examples of these types of tests are the Peabody Individual Achievement Test (PIAT) and the Wide Range Achievement Test (WRAT). These types of tests are either survey batteries or separate subject tests administered to one student at a time with questions usually answered orally, or pointed to by the student. Individual achievement testing has increased as a result of special education services to handicapped students and the need to screen all students being considered for placement in these programs. School counselors also use individual achievement tests to gather data on students new to the school and for whom few records are available to help teachers with appropriate classroom placement and instruction.

Aptitude Tests

A second common test administered to students in schools is the aptitude test. According to Gibson & Mitchell (1990), "*Aptitude* may be defined as a trait that characterizes an individual's ability to perform in a given area or to acquire the learning necessary for performance in a given area. It presumes an inherent or native ability that can be developed to its maximum through learning or other experiences" (p. 236). Traditionally, tests designed to measure learning ability were called *intelligence tests.* While some tests of mental ability remain in use today, controversy surrounding intelligence testing and the meaning of *intelligence,* has contributed to the decline of these terms in favor of *ability* and *aptitude* tests.

Aptitude tests are sometimes in the form of multiple batteries of aptitudes, such as the Differential Aptitude Test (DAT) and the Armed Services Vocational Aptitude Battery (ASVAB). Tests such as these provide scores for a range of aptitudes such as verbal reasoning, mechanical ability, clerical speed and accuracy, language ability, numerical ability, and others. Some group aptitude tests used in schools provide two or more scores on subareas as well as a total aptitude score. The Cognitive Abilities Test, which yields scores for verbal, nonverbal, and quantitative test batteries, is one example. Another is the Scholastic Aptitude Test (SAT), which gives verbal and nonverbal scores, and these are totaled or used separately by colleges and universities in admissions processes.

Sometimes, individual ability tests are used by school counselors to obtain a quick estimate of verbal and nonverbal functioning. Two common examples are the Peabody Picture Vocabulary Test (PPVT) and the Slosson Intelligence Test. Some group ability tests, such as the Henmon-Nelson Tests of Mental Ability, can also be administered individually to students.

Interest Inventories

Because student appraisal consists of more than testing, school counselors incorporate into the assessment process other types of standardized instruments. Among them are interest inventories such as career questionnaires. By assessing students' interests and comparing these results with achievement and aptitude, counselors are in a better position to provide adequate assistance in educational and career counseling. With data from interest inventories, counselors and students can verify career and educational choices, identify previously unknown or unrecognized areas of interest, relate interests to educational and career choices, and stimulate exploration of educational and career opportunities.

In some instances, interest inventories are the vehicles that enable counselors and students to establish initial helping relationships. When administered to students in groups, these instruments yield profiles that counselors explain and interpret in groups and with individual students. During these sessions, students use their profiles to raise concerns with counselors, often leading to self-referrals for group or individual counseling.

Examples of interest inventories used in school counseling programs include the Strong-Campbell Interest Inventory (SCII), the Self-Directed Search (SDS), the Ohio Vocational Interest Survey (OVIS), and many others. The SCII is based on Holland's theory of career development (Holland, 1985), and is scored and interpreted according to the similarity found between the student's expressed interests and the interests of people in particular occupations. Holland, himself, developed the Self-Directed Search (SDS) based on his theory of six personality and environmental themes related to career choice. The SDS is self-administered and self-scored, and can be self-interpreted by the student. After scoring, the student derives a code from across the subtests of the SDS, compared the code with a list of more than 450 occupations, and matches the code from SDS with jobs having the same code. When matches are identified between the student's code and job codes, the student proceeds to follow instructions for further career planning.

Another inventory, developed for use with high school students, is the Ohio Vocational Interest Survey (OVIS). Based on the career model used by the *Dictionary of Occupational Titles*, the OVIS reports its results on 24 different scales generated from responses to a student questionnaire, a local information survey, and an interest inventory (Gibson & Mitchell, 1990).

The Kuder General Interest Survey and the Kuder Occupational Interest Survey are two additional instruments used by counselors. There are several forms of these inventories, which are either computer scored or self-scored, offering a student profile on ten areas of occupational interest: mechanical, scientific, persuasiveness, literary, artistic, musical, social service, clerical, computational, and outdoor activities.

Personality Inventories and Tests

A number of instruments are available to assess student characteristics and traits that may be termed "aspects of personalities." Of course, the concept and construct of *personality* are vaguely defined and rarely agreed on factors in the assessment field. Furthermore, if there is such a trait as *personality*, can it be measured? Researchers and developers of personality assessment instruments respond to this question affirmatively as do many practicing counselors and therapists.

Basically there are two types of personality assessment: personality inventories and projective techniques. Personality inventories usually consist of a series of questions to which the student responds *yes, no, not sure,* or a similar range of choices. These inventories compare the student's score on one or more personality variables with scores of a sample population. Types of variables measured by these instruments include self-concept, social adjustment, problem-solving styles, sexual adjustment, and other traits.

While personality assessment is intriguing to both lay people and professionals, many hazards exist, particularly with self-reporting processes. First, clients may deliberately fake their responses to put themselves in a "better light." Some inventories contain items that attempt to control for this likelihood, but it is impossible to totally eliminate all false answers. As a result, self-reporting procedures inherently include the possibility of producing an inaccurate picture of the client and an invalid assessment of the personality variables being investigated. Second, some authorities question whether all clients have the personal insight to respond adequately to these instruments. With individuals who have personal problems or poor social functioning skills, this lack of insight may further distort their self-image and responses to survey questionnaires. And finally, the nature of personality inventories and the questions involved allow for multiple interpretations by respondents. Questions that include modifiers such as "mostly" and "frequently" invite a range of interpretations, which affect instrument consistency and reliability.

Two examples of personality inventories used by school counselors are the Mooney Problem Checklist and the Myers-Briggs Type Indicator (MBTI). The Mooney Problem Checklist presents a list of problems to which students respond by underlining ones that are of *some* concern to them, circling items that are of *most* concern, and writing a summary in their own words. The MBTI is based on Carl Jung's theory of personality types and includes forms that can be used with high-school students. Though not designed as a vocational assessment, the MBTI is widely used in career development counseling and planning.

A second type of personality assessment, the projective technique, is rarely, if ever, used by school counselors. Projective techniques and instruments are less structured than inventories and more subjective in their scoring. Examples of projective techniques include the Rorschach Inkblot Test, the Draw-a-Person Test, and the Children's Apperception Test. These assessment instruments require special training and supervision before being used by counselors, psychologists, and other professionals. While these types of instruments are not readily used by school counselors, some counselors use selected items as a method of "breaking the ice" and establishing counseling relationships with students. The Children's Apperception Test, for example, consists of pictures that can be shown to young children for their spontaneous responses as a means of building rapport. Rather than scoring a child's responses, the counselor accepts the replies as a basis on which to begin communicating with the student.

All of the preceding tests and instruments contribute significantly to student appraisal in schools. They are, however, only part of a comprehensive appraisal process. To develop adequate appraisal of students, school counselors and teachers incorporate a variety of other assessment procedures, which we will now review.

Other Assessment Techniques

Student appraisal consists of more than individual and group testing to measure achievement, aptitude, or some aspects of personality. School counselors use a variety of assessment procedures to gather data with which to make effective decisions in their counseling relationships with students, and to help teachers plan and implement appropriate instruction.

Adequate student appraisal occurs at the beginning, during, and after the counseling relationship ends. As Vacc (1982) noted, assessment is an ongoing process "viewed not as a one-time prediction activity but rather as continuous throughout the counseling process, a multidimensional activity that serves to establish direction to the counseling process' (p. 40). Through these varied assessment activities, school counselors gather data and information to establish goals, plan strategies, and evaluate the effectiveness of their helping relationships.

Ongoing student appraisal involves different activities including observations, interviews, child-student conferences, self-reports, and sociometric methods. Sometimes these activities are done formally with structured assessment sessions and instruments such as rating scales. At other times, they occur informally and naturally as events happen. In establishing accurate and useful assessment procedures, counselors attempt to select activities "which are unobtrusive and do not place constraints on the counselor and client relationship or the counselor's and client's time and energy" (Vacc, 1982, p. 42). Two assessment activities that fit easily into school structure and student appraisal are observations and interviews.

Observations

Observation "is the best means we have for evaluating some aspects of learning and development" of students (Gronlund & Linn, 1990, p. 375). At the same time, it is "one of the most abused techniques in human assessment" (Gibson & Mitchell, 1990, p. 264). Because observations fit so naturally into the school setting and can be enhanced by the reports of parents, it is understandable why they are readily used and recommended as an assessment technique. At the same time, however, caution is needed. Observational techniques are limited due to the perceptual biases and resulting inaccuracies of the persons who are observing. Human perception is a mysterious and powerful phenomenon, but it is imperfect as an assessment procedure. Simply ask any police officer who has investigated a traffic accident where more than one "eyewitness" has reported the event, and you will see how limited human observation can be in gathering accurate, consistent information. And, as we have seen, consistency is a hallmark of reliability.

With student appraisal, observations occur in many settings, under different conditions, and for limitless purposes. Teachers, parents, and counselors are constantly observing students' action, interactions, and reactions, both individually and in groups. Parents observe children at home and in other settings and summarize these perceptions in conferences with teachers and counselors. Teachers observe students' behaviors and performances in classrooms and other locations in the school, making mental and written notes, or using rating scales. Counselors also observe students in various settings within the school and as part of their counseling relationships. All of these processes and activities add to a comprehensive assessment of students' needs and performance, and enable counselors to recommend appropriate services and strategies to facilitate and improve student development.

Observations of students in schools can be formal or informal, and occur in different settings, at varied times, and with distinctive structures. Sometimes observations occur naturally in classrooms, on playgrounds, and in other areas of school life. When teachers and counselors observe students doing classwork or relating to peers, they may use formal observation instruments, such as rating scales or anecdotal notes. On other occasions, counselors might structure group activities in the counseling center to observe particular students and record their interactions and reactions. During such observations, counselors may impose specific conditions on the activity to see how students handle peer relationships, conflict resolution, rejection, or other situations. Other methods of observation include surveys to gather data on specific behaviors (Blocher, 1987). For example, parents might complete a survey of their observations about how children interact and get along with siblings and friends at home and in the neighborhood.

Gibson and Mitchell (1990) classified three types of observations according to the level of knowledge and training of the observer:

1. *Casual information observations* are unplanned and unstructured measurements that everyone does as part of their daily impressions of people and situations. No formal processes or instruments are used and no training or expertise is necessary for casual observations. Data from these observations are usually gathered by counselors from parents and teachers in initial conferences about students' behavior and school progress. Later, more formal procedures may be planned to affirm pertinent information conveyed in these meetings.

2. *Guided observations* are planned for a specific purpose. In these situations, recording instruments or processes are used. Checklists and rating scales are two examples of observational instruments. Occasionally, planned observations may be recorded simply by writing down every event that occurs as it happens. For example, a counselor may observe a student in class who has been referred because of inappropriate behavior, and use a recording procedure of simply writing down on a legal pad everything the student does during the class period.

3. *Clinical observations* occur in clinical settings, "often prolonged, and frequently with controlled conditions. Sophisticated techniques and instruments used with training, usually at the doctoral level" are the norm (Gibson & Mitchell, 1990, p. 264). In these instances, trained counselors have the primary goal of diagnosing mental health disorders and they rely on resources, such as the *Diagnostic and Statistical Manual of Mental Disorders* (DSM-III-R), to make clinical judgments based on clients' case histories. While this is an important process for mental health counselors and other practitioners in similar clinical settings, the level of diagnostic observation required is beyond the scope of a typical school counseling program and the training of most school counselors. Even school counselors who are trained in these procedures usually decide that this type of observation is more appropriately and efficiently done by counselors in clinical settings whenever possible.

School counselors rely on parent, teacher, and their own observations to add to the student appraisal process and formulate decisions about services. In using observational techniques, counselors become familiar with different methods, locate recording processes and instruments, and learn about the advantages and limitations of the procedures used. Some of the methods and instruments used by school counselors include anecdotal records, checklists, rating scales, direct measurement of records, frequency counting, and interval recording and time sampling (Gibson & Mitchell, 1990; Gronlund & Linn, 1990; Ysseldyke & Marston, 1982).

Anecdotal Records   Observations that enable teachers, parents, and counselors to record descriptions of particular student behaviors during a given situation of event are methods of anecdotal reporting. Since schools began, teachers have recorded notes about students' behaviors and academic progress. Often, these observations were haphazardly done and the resulting records consisted more of biased perceptions and conclusions than of factual data. Today, largely as a result of the Family Educational Rights and Privacy Act of 1974, students' records contain less of this type of biased information. Proper anecdotal procedures, however, remain useful as observational techniques.

Two primary methods of anecdotal observations are found in schools and school counseling programs. One method asks teachers to record significant events and observations as they happen or as soon after as is reasonably possible. These observations gather data on the overall functioning of students, or they track the occurrence of specifically identified behaviors. In training teachers to gather anecdotal information, counselors encourage objective reporting, free from interpretations and conclusions. The idea behind anecdotal records of this kind is to gather as many observations as possible to give a full picture of the trait or behavior of concern. Once the reports are used in making decisions about instruction or special services, they are destroyed. Their usefulness is limited, and their long-term application is questionable. Figure 7–5 illustrates a sample anecdotal record completed by a teacher.

A second method of anecdotal recording is used by counselors to observe particular students for given periods of time in class or other situations during school. This process is especially useful to counselors who have received referrals from teachers about students' behaviors in classes. School counselors observe students as part of their assessment and diagnostic procedures to determine what services would be most beneficial (Schmidt,

---

Observation Notes

Student: Melissa Smith
Date: April 4, 1991

Melissa was observed assisting a student who was standing alone on the playground. The teacher observed her go up to another child without hints or encouragement, and she asked the student if he wanted to play on the swings. This is the second time this week that Melissa has approached another student in a positive manner.

FIGURE 7–5 Anecdotal record of observation completed by a teacher

1991). In developing observation procedures and techniques, counselors will find the following steps useful:

1. Inform teachers at the beginning of each school year about the policy for accepting referrals and incorporating classroom observations. In order to gather the most accurate data to make the best decisions about services the counselor should observe students where and when teachers believe it will be most informative and helpful.

2. Arrive on time when observing students in classrooms. Sit at a desk in an inconspicuous corner of the room, and leave without fanfare after sufficient observations have been recorded. Generally, a period of 40–50 minutes of class time should allow ample observation.

3. Design an observation form to record the student's behavior or use a note pad with time intervals written in the margin. As with other anecdotal reports, counselors should record only *what* they see during these observations and avoid all interpretations and judgments at this time.

4. Schedule a follow-up meeting with the teacher to share the observations and receive the teacher's reactions to what occurred in class. In this conference, the counselor finds out if the class observed, particularly the behaviors of the identified student, was typical. Often, when observers enter a classroom, students may behave differently than normal. The teacher will verify whether or not the class session was typical during the observation.

Rating Scales   In gathering observational data, counselors frequently find that a structured form, such as a rating scale, helps the observer—teacher, parent, or counselor—remain focused on the behaviors, characteristics, or traits being evaluated. Generally, rating scales consist of lists of characteristics or behaviors to be observed and an evaluative scale to indicate the degree to which they occur. Rating scales designed to gather data on students' attributes and behaviors typically have a numerical or descriptive format. With a numerical scale each number indicates a degree to which the behavior is observed. For example, on a five-point scale, the numbers might be assigned values accordingly: 1 = strongly disagree; 2 = disagree; 3 = somewhat agree; 4 = agree; 5 = strongly agree. Rating instruments that use descriptive formats have each item followed by a separate scale of descriptive terms on a line that is checked by the observer. Figure 7–6 illustrates an example of a descriptive scale.

Some commercially produced rating scales are available for use in schools, but counselors and teachers often find that by designing their own scales, instruments can be tailored to specific situations and easily revised as needed. In designing rating scales, counselors should:

1. determine a clear purpose for the instruments,
2. choose characteristics and behaviors that are directly observable,

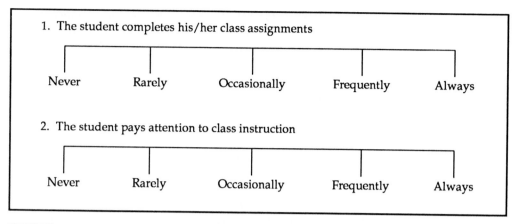

FIGURE 7–6   An example of a descriptive scale for a behavioral rating form

3. write items that clearly and directly relate to the attributes being observed, and
4. determine descriptors for the scale (usually a minimum of three and a maximum of five points).

When designing a new scale, it may be helpful to have a trial run using "practice observers" to check out the clarity of items and directions. In addition, counselors should: (1) determine who will rate the attributes; (2) train raters in the use of the instrument; (3) instruct raters to ignore items they feel unqualified to judge; and (4) use as many raters as reasonably possible. Gathering data from many different raters increases the reliability of the process. For example, in rating a students' responsible behaviors, the counselor may desire ratings from parents and all the teachers who have this student in class.

Checklists   Observers' checklists are similar to rating scales with the difference being the type of judgment required from the observer. As seen above, rating scales ask evaluators to indicate a degree or frequency with which a behavior or attribute exists. Checklists by comparison only ask for the observer to mark *yes* or *no* to indicate whether a trait is observed. While easier to develop and use, these instruments provide a basic, rudimentary assessment and should always be combined with other appraisal procedures.

Both rating scales and checklists can be used in assessing other forms of student performance and information beyond observable behaviors. These methods include direct assessment of products, such as students' homework, frequency counting, and interval recording procedures.

Direct Measurement of Products Students in schools produce many items and products that are useful in the appraisal process. In addition, school records include data that can be screened and incorporated into a comprehensive assessment of student development and needs. Examples of students' products, which can be evaluated either by using a rating scale, a checklist, or simple narrative form, include homework papers, art work, class projects, and journals. School records that can also be evaluated are attendance reports, health cards, test records, and grade reports.

Frequency Counting Sometimes parents and teachers can add to the assessment of particular problematic behaviors by keeping a record of the frequency with which these behaviors occur. Usually there is a specific time frame within which the identified behavior will be monitored (such as between 9 and 10 AM, during a class period, or during recess on the playground). Methods of counting the behavior could include pencil and paper tally sheets, electronic or mechanical counters, and abacuses of some kind (Ysseldyke & Marston, 1982). Frequency counting is particularly useful with behaviors that are clearly defined. That is, they are identified by distinct beginnings and endings.

Interval Recording and Time Sampling When behaviors and attributes are not clearly defined and observable, interval recording and time sampling are appropriate techniques for assessment (Sulzer-Azaroff & Mayer, 1977). There are several different types of interval and time-sampling procedures. With most, the evaluator determines the length of the observation period and divides it into equal segments or intervals. An observer then records when the identified behavior occurs during the time period, counts the number of intervals where the behavior was observed, and computes the percentage of time the behavior occurred (Ysseldyke & Marston, 1982).

In using interval and time-sampling procedures, counselors should be aware of different time-sampling observations (Sulzer-Azaroff & Mayer, 1977). Some observations require that an identified behavior occur for an entire time interval. This is called whole-interval time sampling and is used when it is imperative to know that the behavior is uninterrupted. Other observations use a partial-interval time-sampling technique where only a single occurrence of the behavior in a given time period is required. A third process, momentary time-sampling, observes behaviors which occur at the moment a particular time interval ends (Ysseldyke & Marston, 1982).

Interviews

Another method school counselors and teachers use to gather data and information is interviewing. In a comprehensive assessment of student developmental needs, interviews with students, parents, and teachers are essential. In addition, counselors interview teachers who have had students in former grades, social workers who have assisted students and families, physicians who have examined and treated students, and other professionals who might add to the profiles being developed.

Sociometric Methods

As mentioned in Chapter 3, sociometric methods help teachers and counselors evaluate student relationships, identifying students who are most often chosen by their peers and the ones who are social isolates. While easy to develop and administer, these methods should be used cautiously. Gibson and Mitchell (1990) suggested that the following conditions be considered when using sociometric methods:

1. The length of time the group of students has been together influences the results. The longer a class or group of students have interacted, the more meaningful the outcome of a sociogram.

2. The age of students affects the reliability of students' responses. The older the students the more reliable and valid their responses.

3. Groups that are too small or too large may provide less useful information. There may be too few or too many selections with no distinct patterns emerging.

4. A meaningful group activity provides a logical and natural opportunity for students to select partners and give honest responses. In designing a sociometric method of assessment, counselors and teachers choose an activity familiar to students.

5. The group chosen for the sociogram should be appropriate for the particular appraisal process. If, for example, the assessment is investigating a particular students' comfort in social studies, then that class is where the sociogram should be created.

Figure 7–7 illustrates a sample sociogram for a fifth-grade class. In the activity, the students were asked to select one to five of their classmates with whom they would, or would not, want to work in a group. The students in the center circle of the diagram are those most often selected by their peers. Students in the outer circle are those chosen least often. They are the class loners and isolates. Six students in the class were rejected by classmates and one student (#19) was rejected by two students. By using the same questions over a period of time during the school year and watching for changes in the sociograms that are generated from these students' selections, counselors and teachers are able to assess the effects of strategies and services they plan

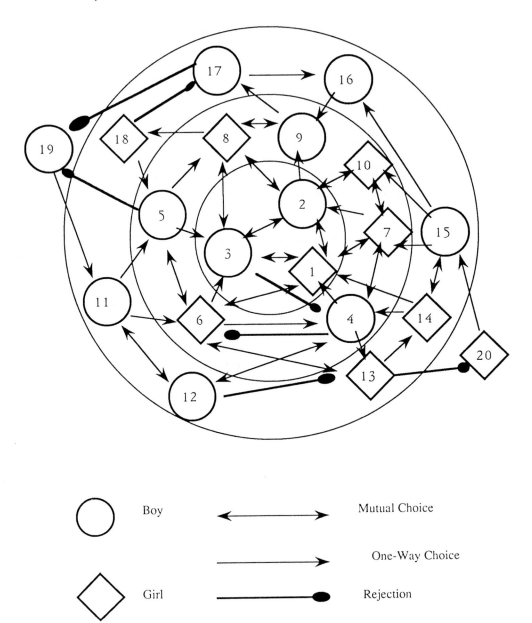

FIGURE 7–7 Sample Sociogram of 5th Grade Students Asked to Select 1 to 5 Classmates they would or *would not,* want to work with in a group

and implement to help individuals and groups of students with peer relationships and social skills.

Child Study Conferences

An additional method used by counselors, particularly at the elementary and middle grades, is a child study conference, sometimes called a staffing. At these meetings, counselors, teachers, psychologists, social workers, nurses, and other professionals pool their knowledge and assessment results to make decisions about services to students and families. In some schools, these meetings are held regularly and, depending on the cases being presented, community practitioners are invited to participate. These practitioners might include mental health counselors, physicians, protective services case workers, and others. The shared information discussed at these meetings enables counselors, administrators, and teachers to plan effective school services and refer to appropriate community services.

All the preceding student appraisal procedures are processes that are typically performed by evaluators *with* or *to* students. In some cases, such as with checklists and rating forms, students may be directly involved as respondents, giving their opinions and observations about themselves. For example, checklists and self-rating scales can be developed to have students assess their attitudes about school, feelings of self-worth, or beliefs about their potential as learners. In addition, counselors use informal methods of having students self-report about themselves and their relationships with others. These informal techniques include the use of essays, journal writing, play, and art work.

Biographical and Self-Expression Techniques

While self-report techniques tend to be suspect in terms of reliability and validity, informal processes can assist counselors in gathering information and establishing rapport in the helping relationship. One process counselors use with students in the intermediate and higher grades is writing exercises such as essays, biographies, and journals.

Writing   Students with at least limited skills in writing can participate in the assessment process through essays about themselves, their families, friendships, and school. These products can be shared with the counselor with the student offering further description and explanation during counseling sessions. Writing experiences such as these are not for the purpose of evaluating literary and language skills, but simply used as vehicles for student expression. For example, one high-school student who was identified as educable handicapped shared several poems she had written with her school counselor. This information was sufficient evidence to encourage re-evaluation of the student's educational program.

Another form of writing students can share with counselors is a journal. This activity allows students to keep an ongoing record of their thoughts and feelings, which gives the counselor a broader, more comprehensive view of the student's perspective than any single assessment does. Students' journals also provide a measure of improvement during their counseling relationships. The ups and downs of a student's life are illustrated in these writings, and students and counselors assess these trends against the overall goals and objectives of their counseling relationships.

Play and Drama   Other informal assessment procedures, used individually and with groups of students, are found in various forms of play and drama. Elementary counselors use play frequently in establishing relationships with students who have limited language development, gathering their views on school, family, and friends. Toys, puppets, games, and other materials take on new meaning as assessment tools in these play activities.

Middle-school and high-school students also can participate in different types of play or drama such as games, role play, experiential exercises, and other activities. These activities allow students to use childlike playfulness and dramatics to simulate real life experiences in safe environments and explore concerns, express feelings, and learn coping skills. Sometimes, these activities take place outdoors with camping, rope climbing, and similar experiences that encourage social risk and cooperation.

Art Work   As with play, drama, and writing, art work is another form by which counselors gather information and establish communication with students (Protinsky, 1978; Roosa, 1981). Using clay, paints, and other media with young students frees them to express themselves in ways not bound by language skills and ability. Older students benefit from art work as well, including photography and cartoons (Gladding, 1992).

All the techniques and activities described in this chapter add to comprehensive student appraisal. In school counseling programs, counselors carefully plan strategies and procedures to contribute to the development of a clear, useable student profile. An important caveat for school counselors is that no single assessment instrument, process, or result should be used when making program decisions or planning intervention strategies. Proper assessment of student development and appraisal of the individual needs of students always include several measurements to adequately design instructional programs or choose appropriate counseling services.

Selected Readings

Vacc, N. A., & Bardon, J. I. (Eds.). (1982), "Assessment and Appraisal: Issues, practices, and programs [Special Issue"], *Measurement and Evaluation in Guidance, 15,* 7–127. This special issue of the measurement and evaluation journal for counseling offers an excellent overview of assessment and appraisal issues. While published a decade ago, the journal addresses topics that remain timely for today's school counselors. The articles include a wealth of bibliographic resources for counselors who wish to research this topic further.

Gronlund, N. E., & Linn, R. L. (1990). *Measurement and Evaluation in Teaching,* 6th ed. (New York: Macmillan). A popular guide to evaluative techniques for teachers, this text is also a readable resource for school counselors. It offers a comprehensive overview of all types of appraisal and assessment procedures.

References

American Association for Counseling and Development. (1980). *Responsibilities of Users of Standardized Tests.* (Falls Church, VA: Author).

American Psychological Association. (1985). *Standard for Educational and Psychological Testing* (Washington, DC: Author).

Anastasi, A. (1988). *Psychological Testing,* 6th Ed (New York, Macmillan).

Blocher, D. H. (1987). *The Professional Counselor* (New York: Macmillan).

Drummond, R. J. (1988). *Appraisal Procedures for Counselors and Helping Professionals* (Columbus, OH: Merrill).

Gibson, R. L., & Mitchell, M. H. (1990). *Introduction to Counseling and Guidance,* 3rd Ed. (New York: Macmillan).

Gladding, S. T. (1992). *Counseling: A Comprehensive Profession,* 2nd Ed. (New York: Macmillan).

Goldman, L. (1971). *Using Tests in Counseling,* 2nd Ed. (New York: Appleton-Century-Crofts).

Goldman, L. (1982), "Assessment in counseling: A Better Way," *Measurement and Evaluation in Guidance, 15,* 70–73.

Gronlund, N. E., & Linn, R. L. (1990). *Measurement and Evaluation in Teaching,* 6th Ed. (New York: Macmillan).

Holland, J. L. (1985). *Making Vocational Choices: A Theory of Careers,* 2nd Ed. (Englewood Cliffs, NJ: Prentice Hall).

Kuriloff, P. J., & Robinson, R. (1982), "The Regulation of Assessment Practices: Challenge and Opportunity for School Counselors," *Measurement and Evaluation in Guidance, 15,* 26- -35.

Nolte, M. (1975), "Use and Misuse of Tests in Education: Legal Implications," *Evaluation Horizons, 54,* 10–16.

Oakland, T. (1982), "Nonbiased Assessment in Counseling: Issues and Guidelines," *Measurement and Evaluation in Guidance, 15,* 107–116.

Protinsky, H. (1978), "Children's Drawings as Emotional Indicators," *Elementary School Guidance and Counseling, 12,* 249–255.

Roosa, L. W. (1981), "The Family Drawing/Story-Telling Technique: An Approach to Assessment of Family Dynamics," *Elementary School Guidance and Counseling, 15,* 269–272.

Schmidt, J. J. (1991). *A Survival Guide for the Elementary/Middle School Counselor* (West Nyack, NY: The Center for Applied Research in Education).

Shertzer, B., & Linden, J. D. (1979). *Fundamentals of Individual Appraisal* (Boston, MA: Houghton Mifflin).

Shertzer, B., & Linden, J. D. (1982), "Persistent Issues in Counselor Assessment and Appraisal," *Measurement and Evaluation in Guidance, 15,* 9–14.

Sulzer-Azaroff, B., & Mayer G. R. (1977). *Applying Behavior- Analysis Procedures with Children and Youth* (New York: Holt, Rinehart & Winston).

Vacc, N. A. (1982), "A Conceptual Framework for Continuous Assessment of Clients," *Measurement and Evaluation in Guidance, 15,* 40–47.

Vacc, N. A., & Bardon, J. I. (Eds.). (1982), "Assessment and Appraisal: Issues, Practices, and Programs [Special Issue]" *Measurement and Evaluation in Guidance, 15,* 7–127.

Ysseldyke, J. E., & Marston, D. (1982), "Gathering Decision Making Information through the use of Non-Test-Based Methods," *Measurement and Evaluation in Guidance, 15,* 58–69.

8

Educational Planning and Career Development

All the essential services provided by school counselors aim at accomplishing two major goals: (1) to assist students with educational planning and success; and (2) to encourage students to explore a wide range of vocational options and make appropriate decisions toward satisfying their career development. In Chapter 2, these two goals were described as part of a comprehensive school counseling program. They were complemented by two additional goals of assisting students with personal and social development. In practice, all four of these objectives are important, and are related to one another in the broad scope of student development.

Students have the opportunity to select from a wide range of career options when they achieve basic skills and acquire sufficient knowledge of language, mathematics, science, social studies, and other academic areas. By the same token, students increase their potential to achieve academically when their personal lives are barrier free and their social lives reflect appropriate, responsible, and accepting behaviors. As seen in the essential services presented in the preceding chapters, counselors offer direct and indirect services to help schools plan appropriate instruction, assist parents in removing obstacles to development and learning, and counsel students about a full range of issues, enabling them to make beneficial decisions. In this way, school counselors assist students with their educational, personal, and social development to achieve academic success and choose appropriate career direction. These are the primary purposes and goals of professional counselors who practice in school settings.

Primary Purpose of School Counseling

All of the services described in this text come together in a comprehensive program of counseling, consulting, coordinating, and appraising activities, enabling all students to develop their fullest potential, achieve educational success, and select appropriate career goals. This has been described by Gysbers and others as the "life career development perspective" (Gysbers & Henderson, 1988, p. 57). This perspective includes four areas of student growth and development: self-knowledge and interpersonal skills; life roles, settings, and events; life career planning; and basic studies and occupational preparation (Gysbers & Moore, 1981).

Self-knowledge and interpersonal skills are achieved through counseling services that increase students' self-awareness and acceptance of others. With individual and small group counseling, in group guidance activities, and through schoolwide events, school counselors and teachers introduce students to concepts and processes that encourage self-exploration and heighten students' awareness of their personal traits and characteristics. At the same time, counselors design programs and activities to help students learn appropriate communication skills and problem-solving strategies. The level of self-awareness achieved by students is vital in helping them make appropriate educational choices and plan future careers. Everything that takes place in a school setting has as its ultimate goal the lifelong purpose of enhancing learning and satisfying individual career interests. School counselors contribute significantly to this goal through comprehensive programs of essential services.

Life roles, settings, and events emphasize the "interrelatedness of various life roles (such as learner, citizen, consumer), settings (such as home, school, work, and community), and events (such as job entry, marriage, retirement) in which students participate over the life span" (Gysbers & Henderson, 1988, p. 59). A challenge for schools has always been to connect the learning objectives of daily instruction to the broader goals faced by students in their overall development. By creating activities and services to help students make this connection, counselors and teachers breathe life into the curriculum and give meaning to the educational process. Unfortunately, students who are unable to accept this relationship between school and their future life goals wander aimlessly through their developmental years, and tragically, leave the educational process prematurely. By contrast, students who understand the interrelationship of school life and aspirations for future career success see their school years as a relatively short-term challenge when compared to their life-long ambitions.

Life career planning is another essential aspect of the overall educational process. A central goal of school counselors is to help students master decision-making skills with which to explore a wide range of career interests, match those interests with their own traits, characteristics, and abilities, and make satisfying decisions accordingly (Gysbers & Henderson, 1988). Again, the array of services and activities initiated by school counselors in comprehensive programs assists with this broad focus. For example, individual contacts with school counselors in counseling and consulting relationships enable students to explore their personal traits and characteristics, receive appropriate up-to-date information, and begin exploring future goals. Figure 8–1 illustrates a sample educational/career planning form to be used by students and counselors in secondary schools. In conferences with school counselors, students would use this form to examine their goals and assess progress in light of their academic and extra-curricular achievements. These conferences might take place during individual contacts with their counselors or in group sessions with other students.

In group experiences, such as small group counseling and classroom guidance, students also have the opportunity to gather information, increase their self-awareness, and learn decision-making skills. Through group processes, students are more able to test the appropriateness of future goals by checking their perceptions with those of their peers. Group work of this kind, as we saw earlier, enables students to do "reality testing" in safe environments with minimal risk of failure. As such, life career planning activities, in groups or individually, help students make responsible choices, gather necessary information to make future decisions, develop adequate interaction skills, and plan their futures.

Basic studies and occupational preparation is the fourth domain of life career development, and it consists of all the learning objectives found in a school's curriculum. The challenge for teachers and counselors in this domain is to design and implement a meaningful curriculum by which students can make the connection between educational development and career satisfaction. Students need to have access to knowledge and skills that enable them to keep abreast of ever-changing career developments. Outdated, outmoded skills and knowledge are of little value to students entering the world of work now and in future years. School counselors have a role in helping teachers, administrators, and curriculum supervisors stay ahead of career trends and developments. The skills and knowledge schools teach today, must be useful not only to current student development and learning, but to students' futures as contributing, productive members of society. This is true at all levels of education and, for this reason, school curricula must be living documents and processes, ever-changing and developing to meet the needs of all students.

The role of school counselors in helping teachers and other educators to create instructional programs with a focus on these four domains is clear. The primary purpose for placing counselors in schools is to provide services and activities that enable all students to achieve academically, reach higher

Alexander High School
Student Planning Form

Student: _____   Date: _____

My Career Interests:
1) _____
2) _____

My Long-term Educational Goal: _____
_____

Course Work Needed to Realize My Goal:

	Courses Taken	Year Completed	Final Grade
Communication Skills:			
Technical Reading:			
Literature:			
Foreign Language:			
Mathematics:			
Statistics & Logic:			
Sciences:			
Social Studies:			
Art/Music/Drama:			
Vocational Courses:			
Other Courses:			

Extra-curricular Experiences: _____
_____
_____

My Planning Conferences with Counselor(s) (or Teacher/Advisors):

Date	Decisions/Plans	Counselor or Teacher

Post-Secondary Tasks I Need to Accomplish (college applications, scholarship applications, entrance exams, job interviews, resume writing, etc.):

Task	Date Completed

****

FIGURE 8–1 Sample Planning Form

levels of functioning in basic skills, assess their strengths and weaknesses, and gather appropriate information about career development.

Sometimes, before counselors can adequately provide these types of services and activities, they need to assist students with personal and social development. This is understandable because optimal learning and career development are less likely to occur if personal and social barriers remain in place. Therefore, while personal adjustment counseling, in and of itself, is not necessarily a primary service of school counseling programs, it frequently is a bridge over which students must travel to realize their educational and career goals.

While career planning and development are widely acclaimed as essential areas of focus for school counseling programs, educational planning has received less attention. Perhaps this is because schools are inherently involved in the education of students, so planning is *assumed* to happen. In practice, however, most educational planning is done by the adults who have responsibility for teaching, guiding, and supervising students. Parents, teachers, counselors, and others share information, assess students' abilities, set instructional goals, and place students in educational programs. Although most of these planning procedures are appropriate, students are frequently left out of the process. Few school counseling texts, if any, have given much attention to the inclusion of students in this important process. Yet, as we have seen, educational planning is a key ingredient in school success and career development. For this reason, we give special emphasis to the school counselor's role in educational planning with all students.

Educational Planning for All Students

Throughout the span of a person's life, many decisions are made that affect development and learning. In some instances, these decisions are made as part of well-designed plans and other times they are haphazard and accidental. In an earlier book, I noted that people who have respect for learning and educational development make intentional plans regarding their educational and career goals, thereby demonstrating a high level of caring towards themselves. "Intentional people recognize the importance of learning, and invite the challenge of becoming educated. They demonstrate this in their formal years of schooling and throughout their adult lives" (Schmidt, 1990, p. 104).

In schools, teachers and counselors observe a wide range of commitment to education on the part of students and their parents. Some students enter school in the primary years with a keen thirst for knowledge and an enthusiastic curiosity for learning. They have benefited from healthy home environments in which parents communicate frequently with their children, read out loud to children during preschool years, and generally encourage a wide range of educational pursuits. Sadly, not all children experience these types of relationships in their formative years. They come to school undirected and misguided in their educational goals, and they are unfamiliar with what other children have been taught about the relationship between learning and successful living.

Schools are challenged by students at both ends of this spectrum and in between. Students who are enthusiastic, curious, and excited about learning must continue to be invited to the celebration of their own development by appropriate curriculum and instruction. When bright and talented students are allowed the freedom to explore, learn at an accelerated pace, and choose educational plans that stretch their potential, they excel in schools and in life. At the same time, students who arrive at school from unnurtured, disadvantaged environments need special attention in designing plans and activities to incorporate educational aspirations into their life's goals. All these students, from the most advantaged and enthusiastic to the most underprivileged and disinterested, require individual as well as group services to encourage educational planning, learn decision-making skills, and set goals for lifelong learning and achievement.

With academically talented students, schools sometimes overlook the need for appropriate educational planning because they come so prepared to learn. This stance may be an erroneous one. The error a school makes with these types of students is to assume that they do not need special attention because they are bright, and that they will achieve regardless of the plans made to provide appropriate curriculum and instruction. On the contrary, when schools remain rigid in their curricular and instructional processes, these students become bored, unchallenged, and disruptive. Such behaviors negate the positive attributes they bring to school and contribute to antagonistic relationships between home and school.

At the other end of the continuum, schools sometimes spend so much effort designing and offering remedial and basic instruction to students from disadvantaged homes that they neglect to inspire, encourage, and plan for future possibilities. While basic education is important, it alone, without optimistic processes to examine and explore future goals, fails to lift less fortunate students out of their current status towards successful career development. The challenge presented by Shertzer and Stone in 1966 remains as true today as it was nearly thirty years ago. Appropriate planning and placement services must be provided for "disadvantaged youth to remove some of the obstacles to their economic and social betterment...Education will have to be made realistic for them in new and more effective ways. Unless such youth are helped by planning and placement, many will continue to remain alienated from education and society. By engaging in planning, such youth learn to manage their problems, mobilize their resources, and gain the capacity to continue on their own" (Shertzer & Stone, 1966, pp. 327–328).

School counselors have an obligation to assist schools in developing and implementing activities that offer a meaningful educational focus for all students. For all services of a comprehensive school counseling program the essential goal must be to help schools create appropriate learning activities, design individual educational plans, and incorporate adequate career exploration for all students throughout their school years. In essence, the role of the school counselor, whether in elementary, middle, or high schools, is to advocate for appropriate educational planning and programming for all students regardless of their backgrounds and preparedness for school.

Student Advocacy

A major responsibility of all school counselors is to assist school administrators and teachers in designing and implementing policies, programs, and processes that equitably support the educational and career development of *all* students. This has always been a fundamental purpose for having counselors in schools. Accordingly, counselors have been viewed as student advocates. This is not to say that other school professionals do not advocate for the well- being of the pupils. Quite the contrary, student advocacy is essential in all aspects of school life by all personnel employed to serve students. Foremost among this group are classroom teachers charged with the educational, social, and personal welfare of their students.

Nevertheless, unlike teachers who are responsible for grading students' progress, school counselors are typically involved in non-evaluative relationships with students, and therefore, are viewed as more *student-oriented* than *school* or *curriculum-oriented*. In this sense, school counselors have special responsibility for student advocacy and work closely with teachers and administrators to ensure the welfare and protect the rights of students.

School counselors contribute to this endeavor by monitoring the placement of students in instructional programs and special services, consulting with parents, teachers, and administrators about the educational progress of individual students, and helping schools avoid stereotypical and prejudicial procedures and policies that discriminate against individuals and groups of students. The consultant role of school counselors is particularly suited for student advocacy (Kurpius & Brown, 1988). In their contacts with parents, teachers, and other professionals who serve students, counselors attempt to assure that every child and adolescent is given adequate and appropriate attention in his or her educational planning, instructional activities, and other services to reach optimal learning and development. Sometimes, because schools and teachers face so many challenges and have so many responsibilities beyond providing essential instruction, they need assistance from counselors to be sure students are not forgotten by the system.

There is no single service or activity by which counselors demonstrate their advocacy role. Every service provided in the school for students, parents, and teachers has as its goal the achievement of an improved learning environment and academic success on the part of the student. Counselors advocate by consulting on a regular basis with teachers about their instructional programs and the placement of students in classes. They also participate in special education placement processes and, in particular, they advocate for exceptional students through their contacts with parents (Filer, 1983; Knoff & Leder, 1985). For example, policies and procedures should be explained to parents in understandable language so they can make informed decisions about their children's placement in these program.s Counselors have the skills to assist with this process and can help parents in the preparation of the Individualized Education Plan (IEP) for these exceptional students.

School counselors also advocate for students when they assist school administrators in reviewing and revising policies. Some regulations or procedures may simply be outdated and as a result they unintentionally discriminate against particular students. For example, an elementary school changed its tradition of having a "fathers' luncheon" once a year because so many students without fathers were unable to participate. Instead the school sponsored a "visitors for lunch" program which enabled all students to invite any adult to share time and lunch with them at school. By slightly changing the focus of the event, more students were included rather than excluded from a worthwhile activity. There are limitless opportunities for counselors to interact with administrators and teachers to examine school programs, such as athletics, extra- curricular activities, and special services, to ensure that the rights and privileges of students are not abridged. Counselors use their observational and communication skills to assess particular aspects of school life and offer suggestions to administrators and teachers on how to affect student development more positively.

Counselors, teachers, and other school personnel also advocate for students in the community by encouraging town governments, city officials, and business leaders to sponsor programs that will benefit children and adolescents. Recreational opportunities, creative outlets, and educational experiences all contribute to the educational efforts begun by the school. By advocating for these types of programs, schools join their communities in a cooperative effort to improve the educational and social lives of children and adolescents. In this way, educational planning and development become community goals and responsibilities rather than solely the obligation of the school.

One way that school counselors use their positions to advocate for students and also make connections with community professionals is through committees that focus on individual student's needs. Sometimes called child study committees or student assistance teams, these groups include counselors, teachers, nurses, psychologists, and social workers from the school as well as health, social services, law enforcement, and other community professionals. The overriding purpose of these types of committees is to assure that all avenues for helping a child or family are explored, while at the same time they protect the student from negligence by the educational system. Through the group efforts of many concerned professionals, schools are more likely to examine situations, generate appropriate ideas for solving educational concerns, and focus on the needs of students being served.

In addition to their consulting roles, school counselors advocate for students through the counseling services and guidance activities they provide. In individual and group counseling as well as through classroom guidance, counselors help students learn about themselves, acquire behavioral skills, such as study skills and relaxation techniques, to improve their educational performance, and understand their rights in school and society in general. With all these services, counselors attempt to help students achieve a sense of value and self-worth, and develop assertive behaviors to seek appropriate educational programs and beneficial career directions. Part of this process is for counselors to instill in students the notion that educational planning and career development do not end when they graduate from high school or college. Rather, these are life-long processes that depend on the foundations people set during their years of schooling. As such, the goal to be instilled is one of lifelong learning.

Lifelong Learning

Formal education in the United States and other countries emerged as a need to educate the citizenry to govern themselves, become self-sufficient, and contribute to the overall productivity and development of the nation. Through the various historical and economic eras of past years, the need for improved educational systems and programs has been documented. As we enter the twenty-first century, the focus on improving education for all people in all communities continues to be a dominant political and social theme highlighted in newspapers, viewed on television, and debated in a variety of settings, from living rooms to national conventions, across the land.

In spite of the attention given to schooling, the state of education in this and other countries remains questionable at best. Many factors contribute to this condition and sufficient blame for less than desirable educational progress appears to be available. The public accuses the schools of incompetent instruction and haphazard planning, the schools point to social and family conditions that overwhelm teachers and severely affect the educational process, businesses fault government leadership for failing to provide sufficient direction, support, and systems of accountability, and the government responds there is enough blame to share with everyone and every institution.

In all this debate and with all the restructuring and redesigning of education, one element seems to be consistently neglected. Education is not an isolated, individual process, aimed at accomplishing finite goals. Rather, it is a continuous endeavor beginning at birth and ending with death. It is lifelong pursuit with limitless goals and divergent purposes. As we look at educational structures and policies in the United States, it becomes clear that this concept of learning for a lifetime has escaped the consciousness of educational planners, leaders, and decision-makers. One does not have to look far for evidence of this omission. Simply look at the design and schedule of our systems of education.

U.S. education continues to be structured in finite blocks of time (elementary, middle, high school, college, and graduate school for example) with particular benchmarks used to move students from one level of learning to the next. Students achieve grades, earn credits, and receive diplomas without any real notion of mastery learning or an application of learning through the life span. The greatest danger in this type of structure is that people come to believe that once a particular segment of the timetable has been completed, future learning and mastery are unimportant and the individual will be content to function for a lifetime at the present level. For example, thousands of students complete high school each year and the pervasive attitude of students, parents, and schools is "Congratulations! You've *finished!*" By the same token, graduates of professional schools and other higher educational institutions falsely believe that their degrees are testimonial to having learned all there is to know about their field of study.

One critical element missing in U.S. education is the philosophy that learning is an integral part of living. Education is not simply a means to an end; it is a fuel that ignites inspiration, desire, compassion, and a host of other human dimensions and emotions that enable us to live our lives fully. As such, the pervasive attitude that only so much learning is needed by any individual or group is as misguided as the notion that people no longer need food and drink once they are full. No matter how many changes we implement, no matter how much money is allocated to improve our schools, we will continue to struggle in this endeavor unless we reconceptualize the purpose of learning and its role in human development.

School counselors play a key role in this effort through the services of their comprehensive programs. The first step is to encourage schools to focus on the broad picture of school climate, parental involvement, mastery learning, and other conditions noted in the effective schools research. Purkey and Schmidt (1987, 1990) identified these elements as people, places, policies, programs, and processes. When schools pay attention to the elements that contribute to healthy learning environments and foster the desire for lifelong learning, they enhance student development and increase the likelihood of academic and personal success. A wide-angle perspective is needed to achieve this goal and school counselors facilitate this process through all their services. In particular, counselors foster lifelong learning by encouraging their schools to:

1. Infuse affective education into daily instruction. As noted in earlier chapters of this text, "guidance" does not occur in isolation but rather as an integral part of the curriculum. Teachers who incorporate life skills into their daily instruction bring their subject areas to life and demonstrate how all learning contributes to successful living.

2. Examine grading, promotion, and other policies that establish the structure by which students move through the educational process. Do school policies contribute to or detract from the notion of lifelong learning? By achieving academic milestones, such as grade promotion or diplomas, are students reaching out for knowledge or simply going through the motions of academic achievement? Education should be more than "learn it, bank it, and forget it," but to view it otherwise, students have to be included in decisions regarding their participation and movement through school.

3. Invite parent participation. Effective schools' research clearly demonstrates the vital role parents and the home play in student development. "Research on parent involvement consistently shows that parents can make a difference in the quality of their children's education if districts and schools enable them to become involved in education in a variety of ways" (Solomon, 1991, p. 360). School counselors assist in this effort by establishing parent volunteer programs, designing and leading parent education groups, consulting with parents about student development and progress, and training teachers on consulting skills and processes to facilitate relationships with parents. Many of the essential services described in this text contribute to this effort.

4. Recognize the value of learning by demonstrating how adults continue to develop throughout their lives. School counselors plan appropriate in-service programs for staff members throughout the school year, seek scholarship funds to enable teachers and others to return to school, and celebrate learning by announcing staff participation in a variety of educational pursuits. For example, a list of staff development activities being attended by staff members could be posted in the school for students and everyone else to see. These activities would include a host of adventures from graduate school studies to piano lessons. No learning experience is insignificant, so all activities should be valued.

5. Focus on career development and its relationship to lifelong learning. Educational planning and lifelong learning are interconnected with career goals and development. A satisfying life is inescapably tied to the vocational

and avocational choices people make, beginning with their school careers and continuing throughout their lives. In all the services designed and implemented by school counselors, career planning and decision-making skills are critical elements to include.

Career Planning and Decision-Making

Throughout its development the school counseling profession has been closely associated with vocational guidance and career development. The industrialism of the late 1800s altered working conditions and vocational needs of society rapidly and immensely (Zunker, 1990). As noted in Chapter 1 these changes influenced the early vocational guidance movement initiated by Jesse B. Davis, Frank Parsons, and others. In the decades since, the focus of vocational guidance on the selection of an occupation has broadened considerably to include all aspects of career development. In addition, the interaction among educational planning, personal development, career choices, and successful living has become clearer. These relationships are affected by a number of technological, industrial, social, and political changes that are rapidly sweeping the globe (Herr & Cramer, 1988; Hoyt, 1988).

Gibson and Mitchell (1990) highlighted several aspects of the changing nature of the world of work that have meaning for counselors in a variety of professional settings, particularly in school counseling. These aspects include the diversity of vocational opportunities, the dangers of gender and cultural stereotyping, the relationship between education and career development, and the future of occupational opportunities. A comprehensive school counseling program in cooperation with the school's curriculum and instructional programs should address each of these aspects.

Career development is a process of many opportunities and probabilities. The future holds a multitude of vocational possibilities for most people. Gone are the times when people would select a career early in youth and follow that choice for a lifetime. Students who enter schools in the 1990s and beyond will be bombarded with ever-changing and rapidly advancing discoveries that alter the workplace and the range of services required of the workforce. Already today it is common for people to change careers several times; sometimes within the scope of a broad vocational area, but even more drastically from one occupational pursuit to a dissimilar one.

School counselors need to assist students with these future decisions by presenting a wide range of career possibilities and encouraging long-term educational planning. It is difficult to forecast exactly where technological advances will lead us, so educational preparation is essential in increasing vocational flexibility and career options.

Gender and cultural stereotyping in career selection is over. Women and men are equal participants and partners in career development. While there are some bastions of resistance to this movement toward equality, the current trends indicate that the process is irreversible. In recent decades women have moved into careers formerly believed to be for "men only" such as construction workers, truck drivers, airplane pilots, politicians, engineers, and countless others. At the same time, men are entering career tracks once considered exclusively for women. Nursing and secretarial work are two examples.

As the world we know today continues to rapidly shrink in light of expanded communication's systems, cultural integration is inevitable. Stereotypical thinking with regards to minority groups and divergent cultures will continue to be an impediment to career development. School counselors and teachers have major responsibility in helping minorities and people of culture remove these barriers from their own thought processes and belief systems, as well as educating majority groups about prejudicial, stereotypical views and behaviors destructive to the welfare of society as a whole.

Schools make a major contribution to the continued integration of the sexes and cultural groups within society. The textbooks chosen and activities created to illustrate career choices must depict a variety of non-traditional occupational opportunities for women and men, as well as the career integration of people from all cultures. School counselors support this process by consulting with administrators and teachers about the texts and materials selected for the curriculum and by planning career awareness, exploration, and decision-making activities to allow students to experience the full scope of career possibilities.

Higher formal education will not necessarily equate to greater career satisfaction. Gibson and Mitchell (1990) indicated that while college education may be required for many future careers, there is evidence that some technical occupations may require educational studies somewhere between secondary school and a college education. If this is true, it is essential that students plan educational careers to match their vocational interests without closing doors on future possibilities. Technical training at all levels of education may be appropriate for a large percentage of students, but, as noted earlier, this decision should be tied to lifelong educational pursuits that encompass not only career goals but also personal objectives for successful living. Hoyt (1988) predicted a surplus of college graduates in the workforce into the twenty-first century. This forecast does not mean that students who comprise this surplus will find their education to be unfulfilling. On the contrary, it may mean their lives consist of balanced goals, satisfied through a wide range of occupational, avocational, and leisure activities. The object in educating people must encompass goals for personal satisfaction as well as career objectives.

The present will no longer predict the future. It has always been a danger-ous posture for counselors and other helping professionals to predict what the future holds for individuals. Today and in the future, this may not only be dangerous, it may be impossible. As Gibson and Mitchell (1990) cau-tioned, "changing technology plus national resource development and de-pletion have made it increasingly difficult, if not almost impossible, in recent years to adequately predict the future by examining only the present and the past" (p. 312). One aspect of the future we can be sure of, in light of all the technological, scientific, and medical advances being made today, is that it will be different from the present, and this includes occupational needs and opportunities.

Because career forecasting is so difficult, school counselors assist stu-dents best by offering communication and decision-making skills to set career goals based on today's knowledge with an eye toward the future. This means acquiring the ability to know oneself, having access to information about career possibilities, and developing the interaction skills to connect with people in positive ways to increase opportunities for career choices. This reliance on others as well as oneself is a final aspect of career develop-ment.

Career development is an interactive process. In times past, individuals could set their own course and create their own fate. Today, because of the complex interaction of so many variables and forces in the world, the likeli-hood of this happening is remote. Striking out on one's own today, without support from others, is in the purest sense of the term "risky business." For this reason, students must learn about how to seek support, gain access to accurate information, and build a foundation for career development. In this process, students learn human relationship skills and coping mechanisms in overcoming barriers to success. In most instances, the failure of people to reach personal and professional goals is less a result of their formal educa-tion and training than it is their inability to form healthy, caring relation-ships with others. It is through these types of relationships that people learn to cope with life's difficulties and nurture the resolve to overcome career obstacles.

The preceding aspects of career development, adapted here from Gib-son and Mitchell's (1990) symptoms of "the changing nature of the world of work" (p. 310), are addressed in comprehensive school counseling programs and by appropriate school curricula. Through appropriate curricula and comprehensive counseling services, students learn about themselves, career opportunities, and educational requirements that fit their life's goals. School counselors in elementary, middle, and high schools contribute to this learn-ing process by designing services that focus on specific needs of students and which are founded on particular theories of career development. Most texts on career counseling and development highlight and differentiate var-ious theories of career development (Crites, 1981; Herr & Cramer, 1988;

Zunker, 1990). Readers who are unfamiliar with the broad field of career counseling and development will want to locate these and other sources to learn about the different theories associated with career awareness and decision-making. For our purposes, this section focuses on how school counselors incorporate counseling and guidance activities into comprehensive programs to enhance student awareness, invite career exploration, and encourage appropriate decision-making at all levels of education.

Some counselors specialize in vocational or career counseling and use the title "career counselor" or "vocational counselor" to identify their particular role in the school. This specialization is most likely found in large high schools where counseling departments are staffed by several counselors and the luxury (or necessity, depending on one's perceptions) of specialization is possible. In some cases, the role of career counseling is mandated due to funding limitations set by federal and state vocational programs. While such specialization exists, most school counselors are charged with a wide range of responsibilities, including career counseling and developmental activities for all students. Consequently, counselors, in collaboration with their teaching colleagues set priorities, develop learning objectives, plan activities, and deliver services to address the areas of student awareness, career exploration, and decision-making skills.

Student Awareness

Typically, the school counseling literature has used aspects of career development, such as awareness, exploration, and decision-making, to structure career activities and design a career focus for programs at the elementary, middle-grades, and high-school levels. This structure and focus generally emphasize career awareness activities and services in the elementary grades, exploration of occupational choices in middle-school and junior high programs, and job placement and career decision-making during the high-school years. As Zunker (1990) and others have noted, however, these areas of career focus are not limited to any single level of education or development. True, elementary children may need assistance with self-awareness and career awareness, but the need for increased familiarity and understanding of one's personal interests and goals within the context of career opportunities is a continuous process that affects learning objectives and activities at all levels of schooling. By the same token, it is through exploratory experiences that young children in elementary schools become aware of themselves, others, and the world around them, including the world of work. As such, exploratory activities in the curriculum and school counseling program are appropriate at all levels. Likewise, decision-making skills are continuously acquired and perfected throughout life, and therefore, should not be limited to one developmental stage of learning.

One difference regarding various approaches to career development is seen in how counselors and teachers at different educational levels assist students in increasing an awareness of themselves and their career interests. In elementary schools, for example, self-awareness and career awareness goals and objectives are incorporated into the curriculum rather than isolated as separate entities focused on by one specialist, such as a school counselor. This incorporation of guidance objectives is important at all levels: elementary, middle, and senior high school. Illustrating this point, Herr & Cramer (1988) offered sample learning objectives for all three levels covering a wide range of cognitive and affective skills and knowledge that relate to vocational choice and career development. School counselors use these types of objectives to assist classroom teachers in developing curriculum goals and designing instructional strategies to address career awareness for students. Knowledge of school curriculum and student development is essential for counselors to provide adequate guidance for teachers in this endeavor.

In middle schools and high schools, the incorporation of career guidance into the curriculum continues, and is complemented by individual counseling and small group work with students facilitated by the school counselor. As we learned in earlier chapters, counselors use individual and small group counseling sessions to enable students, in private, confidential relationships, to discover their inner selves and acquire a deeper, more personal level of understanding. Through this process of personal self-discovery, students become more able to benefit from classroom and small group guidance that addresses various aspects of career awareness and development.

To facilitate students' self-awareness, school counselors use assessment processes as part of their helping relationships. As indicated in Chapter 7 on student appraisal, these assessment procedures include aptitude testing, career interest inventories, and a host of other measurements to assist students in learning about their academic strengths, personal characteristics, and traits related to career interests and decision-making. A number of computerized career assessment programs are available for school counselors to use, and they can be categorized in two ways: information systems and guidance systems (Gibson & Mitchell, 1990).

Career Information Systems (CIS) provide students with a structure for searching for specific occupations, and offer background information, such as educational requirements, for the occupations selected in a search. With some of these systems, assessment data, such as test scores, are introduced as a starting point for the computer search of appropriate occupations. According to Gibson and Mitchell (1990) the development of computer-assisted career information systems "was greatly stimulated by grants produced by the Department of Labor and the National Occupational Information Coordinating Committee, which enabled a number of states to develop statewide career information systems" (p. 334). These *Career Information Systems* (CIS) offer local and regional data and information. The National Occupational Information Coordinating Committee (NOICC) also has state branches (SOICCs) that assist state and local school systems and school counselors. Other computer information systems used in school counseling programs include the *Guidance Information System* (GIS), published by Time Share Corporation of West Hartford, Connecticut and *C-Elect* by Chronicle Guidance Publications, Inc. As with most areas of computer technology and software development, the availability of career information systems is ever-changing. As a result, counselors need to stay informed through their professional associations, journals, and other media.

The second type of computer assessment programs, career guidance systems, tends to have a broader focus than simply the dissemination of information. These systems take students beyond the search of occupational possibilities and into areas including self-assessment processes, instructional modules, planning activities, and decision-making steps. One widely used computer guidance program is the *System of Interactive Guidance and Information* (SIGI-Plus) by Educational Testing Service in Princeton, New Jersey. The SIGI-Plus consists of five components to assist students and their counselors in: (1) self-assessment, (2) identification of possible occupational choices, (3) comparison of pertinent occupational information, (4) review of educational preparation for occupations, and (5) evaluation of the risks and rewards of particular occupations, including consideration of the consequences of particular career choices (Gibson & Mitchell, 1990; Gladding, 1992; Zunker, 1990).

Another popular computer assessment system is *DISCOVER*, which includes programs for elementary through high school, college students, and adult populations (Gibson & Mitchell, 1990). The *DISCOVER* programs, published by the American College Testing Program (ACT), are interactive computer-assisted systems designed to provide: (1) self-assessment, (2) opportunity to explore the world of work, (3) strategies for identifying occupations of interest, (4) detailed information about hundreds of occupations, and (5) educational requirements to assist in career planning.

Another avenue that school counselors and teachers use to enhance student awareness, particularly about career opportunities, is through special events during the school year. These events might include "career fairs" in middle and high schools, field trips to businesses, industries, colleges, and other locations, guest speakers for classroom guidance presentations, and many other activities. In elementary schools, for example, a simple program is to invite parents into classes to talk about how they spend their days in various occupations.

School counselors help their teaching colleagues focus on student awareness through a variety of instructional, computer-assisted programs, counseling services, and special events during the year. These services, activities, and programs help students learn about themselves, their interests and abilities, and career choices that are available to them, or which may be available in the future. Related to this process of developing self-awareness and awareness of career opportunities is the need for students to explore the world of work and the countless vocational possibilities that exist for each of them.

Exploration

As students become aware of themselves and the educational and vocational opportunities that surround them, they are ready to explore more closely available career options. Career exploration begins in the elementary schools as an expansion of awareness activities planned for classroom guidance or as special events such as field trips to local points of interest. It is also reflected in the careful selection of appropriate books, films, and other media selected for the school's curriculum. Media that are void of sexual and cultural stereotyping, and which encourage all students to seek a wide range of career possibilities, are imperative to student development and learning.

At the middle grades and high schools, career exploration becomes more clearly defined and focused for students. Here, their interests, abilities, strengths, and weaknesses begin to take form, and activities can be designed to enable students to examine more closely those careers that fit their personal and professional interests and abilities. In middle schools, it is common for the curriculum to include career exploration classes to assist with this exploration process. At the high-school level, career exploration most likely occurs as a result of special events or individual and small group counseling. Ideally, high school curricula, as in elementary and middle schools, should include classroom career guidance so teachers incorporate career aspects of their subject areas into daily instruction. In this way, while studying poetry in English classes students might discuss the career of a poet or other types of writers. At the same time, the teacher and students could explore the impact of future technology on these literary professions. How will voice-activated printing or voice-activated video-taping change the artistic and creative worlds of poetry and literature? Likewise, in chemistry and other science classes, future career opportunities might be discussed and offered for consideration. By incorporating career exploration in their lessons, teachers bring subject areas to life with real meaning and purpose for their students.

In individual and small group counseling, as well as classroom presentations, school counselors use the computer-assisted programs mentioned earlier to encourage career exploration. In addition, they use other media and resources to facilitate this learning process. Two examples of such resources include the *Dictionary of Occupation Titles* (DOT) and the *Occupation Outlook Handbook*, published by the U.S. Department of Labor.

Gibson and Mitchell (1990) indicated that research efforts have not identified one single method of career exploration that is significantly better than others. The rapidly changing world of work and technological advances anticipated in the future make the likelihood that any single method or approach will emerge as a dominant theme unrealistic (Gysbers, 1990). For this reason, school counselors at all levels must ensure that the curriculum, their direct services, and special programs allow a variety of opportunities in which students can learn about present and future trends and directions in a broad spectrum of occupations. Only through adequate assessment and a wide range of exploratory activities will students be able to make clear plans and appropriate decisions about their future careers.

Decision-Making

As noted earlier, children and adolescents at all levels of education must be guided in their educational plans and decisions because it is through these processes that students increase the likelihood of making successful career choices. Zunker (1990) explained that "Decision-making is now viewed as a learned skill that should be a part of everyone's educational program. The acquisition of decision-making skills is a very vital objective of career counseling" (p. 281). Numerous decision-making theories and models have been presented and these are important for counselors to understand in choosing or designing their approaches. Simple steps can be designed to instruct students in decision-making skills, but the complexity of the decision-making process is revealed when individuals begin to use the steps learned and "apply their own values, interests, aptitudes, and other unique qualities to each decision" (Zunker, 1990, p. 281).

In assisting students with decision-making skills and processes, school counselors often find that group sessions facilitate learning and skill development. This may be particularly true for career decision-making where students in groups share information, reflect on each member's individual assessment, give helpful feedback, and support individual group members in their decisions. As noted in Chapter 5, when personal attributes and other private information are part of the sharing process, group counseling is the most appropriate setting because it offers a safe, non- threatening, confidential relationship. On the other hand, when students need to acquire career information or learn new skills, instructional activities, such as group guidance sessions, are legitimate helping processes. For example, in situations where a decision-making model is going to be taught to students, group guidance is an appropriate process to use. To assure appropriate procedures and media for teaching decision-making skills, counselors want to be aware of current research and literature on the most promising approaches (Herr & Cramer, 1988; Zunker, 1990).

The approaches chosen by school counselors and teachers to facilitate decision-making and planning for career development should offer a wide range of options to students and at the same time encourage future flexibility in the planning process. Because future career trends cannot be predicted with absolute certainty, all students are best assisted by information and skills that identify many career options and paths to reaching identified goals and attaining satisfying life experiences. Methods and approaches that limit options and restrict career choices are detrimental to student development and raise a question about ethical practice on the part of the school counselor. In sum, the methods and models of teaching decision-making skills should open doors for students, not close them. Throughout the chapters about the essential services and primary purpose of comprehensive school counseling programs, you have learned about a range of theoretical approaches, technical skills, philosophical beliefs, and professional characteristics that counselors bring to their helping relationships. The following case study offers a brief illustration of how these approaches, skills, and beliefs merge in an expanded view of a school counselor's role.

Case Study of Gertrude

> Gertrude was an 18-year-old student in her junior year of high school when she and the new counselor first met. She was standing in the middle of the counselor's office, sullen and unkempt, and when the counselor entered she said, "I'm Gertrude, you're my counselor, and if people don't stop picking on me, someone is going to get it." The counselor had learned about Gertrude from the school principal and the chair of the counseling department, both of whom indicated that "Something has to be done about her this year. We cannot allow the fighting and hostility to continue."
>
> Gertrude's file, examined by the counselor after their first encounter, was extensive. In brief, she was identified as educable mentally retarded, had spent over a year in an adult sheltered workshop prior to coming back to high school, had a history of epileptic seizures for which she was prescribed medication, had repeated two grades in school, and lived with her mother, stepfather, and brother. Her stepfather was employed with the city sanitation department and her mother was unemployed. As a black female with all these challenges, Gertrude's future seemed bleak.
>
> After reviewing the folder and interviewing Gertrude, the counselor made tentative plans to:

1. *Establish a relationship with Gertrude where she would make a commitment to stop fighting and select some attainable goals to achieve during the year*
2. *Check with her neurologist about the medication she was taking*
3. *Evaluate her academic record including the year spent in the sheltered workshop*
4. *Contact her parents to assess their involvement in this relationship*
5. *Collaborate with the principal and teachers to determine an appropriate educational program*
6. *Contact the vocational rehabilitation counselor assigned to her case to ensure appropriate career services*

In the initial stages of their relationship, Gertrude and the school counselor met once or twice a week. Basically, the counselor used a person-centered approach to establish rapport and develop trust. Early in the relationship, Gertrude stated that she wanted to graduate from high school. Since the state requirement for graduation included a competency test, this would be a tremendous accomplishment for Gertrude. Given her exceptionality, the counselor wondered if it was a realistic goal. Together, they decided to work toward completing all requirements, taking the state exam, and achieving either a diploma or certificate of attendance. After several sessions, Gertrude brought the counselor a poem she had written about their counseling sessions. The counselor was intrigued with the idea that an educable handicapped person wrote poetry. He put the poem up on his bulletin board and Gertrude beamed with delight. The next session she brought a large looseleaf notebook, filled with poems she had written over the years. Mind you, these were not great poems, but they were a strong indication that Gertrude had a willingness and a desire to learn and improve her life.

The counselor learned in the individual sessions that Gertrude was unsure how much medication she was taking. Her mother was contacted but added little information. The counselor scheduled a meeting with the neurologist and took Gertrude to the appointment. She had not been evaluated in over two years and had not had a seizure since elementary school. After the evaluation, the physician decided to lower the dosage of medication by half. The counselor agreed to keep in touch to report any changes noticed at school. Within the first few weeks, everyone noticed a change. Gertrude became less sullen, and, although she was still quick tempered, she was much more congenial and affable at school.

The counselor and principal reviewed the course work Gertrude completed at the sheltered workshop to determine if any high school credit could be awarded. After the review, six credits were granted for the work completed and Gertrude was promoted to a senior class homeroom during the semester. This change in status made a world of difference in her attitude because Gertrude could now embrace the dream of finishing high school with reasonable chance of it becoming a reality. But now she wanted a diploma more than anything. To receive a diploma, she would have to pass the state competency tests.

The counselor and classroom teachers met with the competency skills teachers to design a plan of action. Because Gertrude had made noteworthy strides in her behavior at the beginning of the year, the teachers were enthusiastic about helping. The competency skills teachers agreed to take her in one of their remedial groups and the counselor scheduled time to work with all the students in the class on their relationships with people. In this way, the competency skills class was used as a support group for Gertrude and the other students.

The counselor continued individual sessions with Gertrude and made contact with her parents by phone and in meetings at home and in school. In these sessions, the counselor outlined the goals Gertrude had chosen and reported on the progress she had made during the year. No specific requests were made of the family except to support Gertrude in her efforts to finish school. Unexpectedly, when Gertrude returned to school after Christmas break, she was a different woman. She wore fine dresses that her mother had purchased at Goodwill Industries and had given to her as presents. She was clean and looked attractive. So much so, that her appearance drew favorable comments from the same boys with whom she used to fight in school!

An appointment was made with a vocational rehabilitation counselor who began sessions with Gertrude at school to discuss future plans and options. Teachers in her classes also offered her guidance about what to do after high school. At the end of the year Gertrude graduated with a state diploma, having completed all requirements and passed the state competency exams in reading and mathematics.

The above case study demonstrates the wide range of services school counselors deliver in helping students, parents, and teachers address a variety of issues. Individual counseling enabled the student and counselor to establish a trustful relationship in which specific goals were identified and commitments were made. Collaborative relationships with teachers, the principal, parents, the physician, and others moved this case forward. Group processes were established with teachers and students in the competency skills class. And school policies were used to review the educational record and award credit for work completed in the sheltered workshop. In this way, comprehensive services, orchestrated to focus on specific goals, resulted in successful outcomes.

In this and the preceding chapters, we have surveyed the components of a comprehensive school counseling program and described the essential services provided by school counselors. We have noted that educational planning and career development are the ultimate goals of the services and activities that comprise a comprehensive school counseling program. School counselors are trained to design and provide these comprehensive services. In the next chapter, we examine the role of the school counselor in elementary, middle, and senior high schools, and review the training necessary to become a professional school counselor.

Selected Readings

Herr, E. L., & Cramer, S. H. (1988). *Career Guidance and Counseling through the Life Span: Systematic Approaches,* 3rd ed. (Boston: Scott, Foresman).

Zunker, V. G. (1990). *Career Counseling: Applied Concepts of Life Planning,* 3rd ed. (Pacific Grove, CA: Brooks/Cole). Both of these popular texts offer a comprehensive view of career counseling and development for school counselors. They also provide an overview of the important theories that have created this field of counseling and student development. Zunker's text includes a supplemental manual for career assessment.

Lowman, R. L. (1991). *The Clinical Practice of Career Assessment* (Washington, DC: American Psychological Association). A comprehensive guide to career assessment, this text integrates the three domains of interest, personality, and ability. While heavily focused on Holland's six-factor typology of career development, this book allows integration of a variety of assessment procedures.

Kapes, J. T., & Mastie, M. M. (Eds.). (1988). *A Counselor's Guide to Career Assessment Instruments,* 2nd ed. (Alexandria, VA: National Career Development Association). This collection of writings from prominent authors in the field of career development offers reviews of a wide range of career assessment instruments. Introductory sections of the book present topics on the counselor's role, selection of instruments, and competencies and responsibilities of counselors.

References

Crites, J. O. (1981). *Career Counseling: Models, Methods, and Materials* (New York: McGraw-Hill).

Filer, P. S. (1983), "The School Counselor as a Parent Advocate," *School Counselor, 31,* 141–145.

Gibson, R. L., & Mitchell, M. H. (1990). *Introduction to Counseling and Guidance,* 3rd ed. (New York: Macmillan).

Gladding, S. T. (1992). *Counseling: A Comprehensive Profession,* 2nd Ed. (New York: Macmillan).

Gysbers, N. C. (1990), "Major Trends in Career Development Theory and Practice" in E. R. Gerler, Jr., J. C. Ciechalski, and L. D. Parker (Eds.) *Elementary school counseling in a changing world* (Ann Arbor, MI: ERIC/CAPS).

Gysbers, N. C., & Henderson, P. (1988). *Developing and Managing your School Guidance Program* (Alexandria, VA: American Association for Counseling and Development).

Gysbers, N. C., & Moore, E. H. (1981). *Improving Guidance Programs* (Englewood Cliffs, NJ: Prentice-Hall).

Herr, E. L., & Cramer, S. H. (1988). *Career Guidance and Counseling through the Life Span: Systematic Approaches*, 3rd ed. (Boston: Scott, Foresman).

Hoyt, K. B. (1988), "The Changing Workforce: A Review of Projections—1986 to 2000, *The Career Development Quarterly*, 37, (1), 31–38.

Knoff, H. M., & Leder, A. L. (1985), "Independent Assessments for Exceptional Children: Advocacy Information for Parents," *School Counselor*, 32, 281–286.

Kurpius, D. J., & Brown, D. (Eds.). (1988). *Handbook of Consultation: An Intervention for Advocacy and Outreach* (Washington, DC: Association for Counselor Education and Supervision).

Purkey, W. W., & Schmidt, J. J. (1987). *The Inviting Relationship: An Expanded Perspective for Professional Counseling* (Englewood Cliffs, NJ: Prentice Hall).

Purkey, W. W., & Schmidt, J. J. (1990). *Invitational Learning for Counseling and Development* (Ann Arbor, MI: ERIC/CAPS).

Schmidt, J. J. (1990). *Living Intentionally and Making Life Happen* (Cary, NC: Brookcliff Publishers).

Shertzer, B., & Stone, S. C. (1966). *Fundamentals of Guidance* (Boston: Houghton Mifflin).

Solomon Z. (1991, January), "California's Policy on Parent Involvement," *Kappan*, 72 (5), 359–362.

Zunker, V. G. (1990). *Career Counseling: Applied Concepts of Life Planning*, 3rd ed. (Pacific Grove, CA: Brooks/Cole).

9

The School Counselor

The essential services introduced in the preceding chapters are offered by school counselors at all levels of practice, in elementary, middle, and high schools. The premise being that in each of these settings, counselors provide a wide range of services in comprehensive programs designed to address the educational, career, personal, and social development of all students. In this chapter, we focus on the professional school counselor who is charged with the responsibility of designing and delivering these services. More specifically, we examine the various roles, training, and credentials of counselors at all levels of school service. We begin with the differences and similarities found among the various levels of professional practice for school counselors.

Varying Roles of School Counselors

The school counseling profession began at the secondary school level with the vocational guidance movement of the early 1900's. Since that time, counselors have been trained and hired to serve students at all educational levels. Recent years have been marked by increases in the number of counselors employed at the middle and elementary school levels. In most instances, these counselors utilize the same basic helping processes—counseling, consulting, coordinating, and appraising—across all school years. Because children in elementary and middle schools have different developmental needs than students in high school, it follows that specific services will vary, depending on the level and needs of students in a particular school.

The role and functions of school counselors are influenced by both the specific level of practice and the needs of particular school populations being served. As learned earlier, school counselors design comprehensive programs first by assessing the needs of students, parents, and teachers who will be served. The variance of these needs from one school to another plays a significant role in helping counselors determine the services and activities most appropriate for their individual schools. This is an important point to remember as you read this chapter.

Descriptions and illustrations intended to differentiate elementary-middle, and high-school counseling are useful as general guidelines, but to be valid, they must be considered within the context of specific populations being served by schools. For example, a high-school counselor who serves students from affluent families with high expectations and promise of educational success will design a program of services that is quite different from a school with a high percentage of students from impoverished backgrounds, who are at risk of school failure. For this reason, the following descriptions of elementary-, middle-, and high-school counselors are general illustrations rather than prototypes of what should be the role of counselors in various educational settings. Ideally, the actual functions chosen by particular counselors focus on the unique needs and characteristics of students and communities served by the school.

The Elementary School Counselor

Historically, the responsibility for student development and guidance in elementary schools has rested with classroom teachers. While a few guidance specialists were present in elementary schools as early as the 1920's, most of these were found in metropolitan areas (Martinson & Smallenburg, 1958; Myrick, 1987). A national survey, conducted in the early 1950's, indicated that over 700 elementary counselors were employed, with more than 400 providing counseling and guidance services half of the time or more. This movement into elementary counseling began a shift from teachers having sole responsibility for student development to a collaborative effort shared by teachers and counselors.

The 1960s saw an emergence of counseling in elementary schools brought about by events such as the publication of the *Elementary School Guidance and Counseling* journal, inclusion of elementary officers in the American School Counselor Association, enactment of the Elementary and Secondary Education Act of 1965, and the extension of the NDEA Act in 1965, which provided funds for training institutes in elementary guidance and counseling. By 1969, elementary counselors were employed in all 50 United States and, in the early 1970s, the number of elementary counselors had grown to nearly 8,000 (Myrick & Moni, 1976).

The 1970s and 1980s saw increased attention on services to elementary children. To some extent this increase is attributed to the passage of the Education for All Handicapped Children Act of 1975 and the *A Nation at Risk* report of 1983. The report, *A Nation at Risk,* which resulted from the National Commission on Excellence in Education, became the springboard for many educational initiatives in states across the country during the 1980s. Included in these initiatives were recommendations for counselors to be placed in all elementary schools (Humes & Hohenshil, 1987). With increased demand and focus on the value of elementary counseling has come closer attention to the need for defining and describing what an ideal elementary counseling program should include.

Recent studies of the elementary counselor's role indicate that the expected major functions are consistent with the role of counselors at other educational levels (Gibson, 1990; Morse & Russell, 1988). Elementary programs include counseling, consulting, coordinating, and appraisal services for students, parents, and teachers in much the same way as their colleagues at upper levels. At the same time, some studies have suggested that the ranking and importance of specific counselor activities may differ from the other levels of school counseling. For example, Morse and Russell (1988) reported that three of the five highest ranking activities used by elementary counselors relate to consulting relationships with teachers and educational specialists. Counselors in this study emphasized the need to help teachers help students. It is noteworthy that this finding supports the position, held by authors more than twenty years ago, advocating a consulting role for elementary counselors (Eckerson & Smith, 1966; Faust, 1968). Consultation, as noted earlier, remains an essential function of today's elementary counselors.

Interestingly, elementary counselors report that their preference is to do more group work with students to help them learn appropriate social skills, to enhance their self-concept, and to develop problem-solving skills (Morse & Russell, 1988). This accent on group services exemplifies the importance elementary counselors place on developmental services for children. In part, this emphasis gives elementary counseling its unique focus; a focus that includes appropriate processes and approaches to counseling with children, adequate attention to developmental activities and services, and strong parent and teacher involvement in the helping process.

Counseling Children   Since the early years of elementary counseling, experts have debated whether or not children can be helped through counseling. In 1967, the American Personnel and Guidance Association (now the American Counseling Association) stated that individual counseling offered children an opportunity to:

1. Establish relationships to see themselves as adequate persons, learn about themselves, and use this knowledge to set life goals
2. Be heard by others (counselors) and express their thoughts and feelings about themselves, others, and the world in which they live

In addition to group processes, elementary counselors use individual counseling with children. Typically, these relationships are established through a series of brief counseling sessions lasting from 20 to 40 minutes in length, depending on the age and maturity of the child. These individual sessions usually are scheduled once or twice a week as the elementary counselor guides the child through successive stages of a helping relationship. As noted in Chapter 4, these stages can be summarized as: (1) an introductory phase of building rapport; (2) an exploration of concerns the child expresses by words and actions; (3) a plan of ways to cope with and remedy these concerns; and (4) closure for this particular helping relationship, while encouraging the child to move on to other areas of development.

Successful individual counseling with young children is dependent on the accurate assessment of the child's readiness for this type of relationship. In particular, counselors assess a child's language development, behavior, cognitive functioning, and ability to understand the nature and purpose of a helping relationship. As explained in Chapters 3 and 4, most individual counseling requires some degree of verbal interaction. Therefore, children who do not have adequate language development will benefit little from these "talking" relationships. In some cases, where children are essentially nonverbal, progress and success in individual relationships can be achieved if the language of the counselor is understood by the child. This is true, for example, with shy children. Frequently, young children are shy and hesitate to speak up in the beginning of individual counseling sessions. Because they have adequate language development and understanding, however, these children benefit from individual counseling when assisted by a competent therapist, such as an elementary school counselor. Elementary counselors use play, puppetry, and other techniques to establish rapport with children whose language development is not fully ready for verbally interactive helping relationships.

Children's behavioral development is also evaluated by counselors when using individual counseling. Severe disturbance, distraction, or other behavioral dysfunction will detract from the potential success of individual counseling with children. A child who has virtually no capacity for staying on task, centering on the subject at hand, or controlling impulsive behaviors needs to acquire some proficiency in these areas before individual counseling can be successful. Behavioral techniques to help children develop these abilities are appropriate precursors to effective on-on-one counseling relationships.

Children who cannot conceptualize their role and responsibility in forming helpful relationships will benefit little from individual counseling that strictly uses talking and listening modes. Without the necessary cognitive development, young children lack the readiness to understand and accept the perceptions of others, select goals that benefit themselves as well as their social group, and alter their views to incorporate the opinions and values of others. These abilities and characteristics are essential if verbal counseling is to help children assess themselves, make appropriate plans for change, and take action toward desired goals.

Young children, whose perceptions are limited by egocentric views of the world and who conceptually do not grasp the notions of social interest and cooperation, cannot fully appreciate the benefits of individual helping relationships and are especially not ready for individual counseling that relies primarily on interviewing and talking techniques. For this reason, elementary school counselors rely heavily on active techniques, such as play, psychodrama, creative arts, and bibliotherapy, to stimulate ideas, explore values, and encourage children to form helping relationships. Group work with children is an important vehicle that counselors use to facilitate children's interaction with others and an exploration of their perceptions within a social context. Group work in elementary schools is most often structured as group guidance or group counseling (Gladding, 1991). You learned in Chapter 5 that group guidance is primarily instructional and informational, while group counseling encourages active change in cognitive, affective, and behavioral aspects of children's lives.

Group guidance occurs in either large or small group settings. In elementary schools, teachers and counselors use group guidance in classrooms to assist children in developing values, social skills, career awareness, and other areas of learning. Ideally, as noted in earlier chapters, these lessons are integrated into the daily curriculum, so that guidance becomes an integral part of language arts, social studies, and other subject areas.

Group counseling, on the other hand, is a service offered to assist children in focusing on concerns that are either crisis-oriented, problem-centered, or developmentally necessary (Myrick, 1987). Groups are small in size, perhaps with five to eight students in a group. An example of an elementary group that is crisis-oriented is one that helps abused children deal with the trauma they have experienced, recognize their own value and worth as human beings, learn about their rights, and make plans to cope in the future. Problem-centered groups help children focus on immediate, yet less critical concerns, such as getting along with peers, and they encourage children to form plans of action to resolve these conflicts. Developmental group counseling helps children learn about social and personal aspects of their development. These growth-oriented groups address topics similar to those learned in classroom guidance, but the nature of small group counseling allows children the opportunity for more interaction and intimacy in a secure, protected relationship. In many respects, developmental counseling is a primary approach used by elementary school counselors.

Developmental Counseling While many children in elementary schools today suffer from critical problems in their families and society, and as a result need crisis-oriented and problem-solving assistance, an overwhelming number of children benefit from services that have a developmental focus. The assumption made by elementary counselors who emphasize developmental approaches is that children become successful when allowed to achieve sequential goals that lead them towards self-fulfillment. As such, developmental counseling considers the stages of child development, including the important life tasks that all children must learn and accomplish in moving to the next level of functioning.

A comprehensive developmental program emphasizes the importance of a positive self-concept and recognizes the essential role that schools play in helping children believe in their value and worth as human beings (Purkey, 1970; Purkey & Novak, 1984). Developmental counseling assumes that the perceptions and beliefs formed by children about themselves and the world around them are learned through countless positive and negative experiences encountered at home, in school, and through other relationships. Children's feelings, attitudes, and behaviors are closely linked to the conclusions they draw about themselves, and how they are accepted or rejected by people they know. For this reason, a developmental counseling program includes everyone and every aspect of an elementary school because *everything counts* (Purkey & Schmidt, 1987; 1990); there is nothing in a school, or in its policies and programs, that is neutral. Everything planned and implemented, from the color of the paint on the walls to the daily teacher-student relationships in the classroom, has an effect on someone, somehow, in the school.

Counseling programs that adopt a developmental focus include everyone in the school community to help children attain educational, social, and career goals. First, these programs seek to establish a strong guidance curriculum, planned by counselors and teachers and integrated into daily instruction. Counselors assist teachers in this effort by helping them plan the integration, locating appropriate resources, and co-leading special guidance units with teachers. Second, these programs include counseling services, individual and group, for students who require more intense assistance than what classroom guidance offers. These counseling services aim to satisfy children's needs and help them make adequate progress in their academic, personal, and social development. In this way, a secondary goal of a school's guidance curriculum is to help teachers and counselors identify students who need additional assistance in reaching their developmental goals.

In a developmental program, the goals of the guidance curriculum are linked to the therapeutic goals of counseling. For example, if a goal of guidance is to help all children learn about their self-development and appreciate who they are, then individual and group counseling services for students who have low self-esteem has this as its primary goal as well. While the activities and processes used in counseling relationships differ from those found in classroom guidance, the developmental goals are essentially the same. At the same time, individual and group counseling can provide children an opportunity to develop skills, evaluate themselves, and achieve beneficial relationships, which will enable them to profit more readily from large group learning experiences. As a result of counseling, these children may benefit even more from the guidance lessons that are incorporated into daily instruction.

Another aspect of developmental counseling programs is the strong involvement of parents. This is especially true in elementary education where parents play a vital role in their children's development.

Parental Involvement   Elementary counselors rely heavily on parental involvement in helping children plan and achieve developmental goals. Without parents' support for the program and services counselors and teachers offer students, progress is an uphill climb. When parents support the infusion of guidance into the curriculum and the inclusion of their children in individual and group counseling experiences, a working partnership is formed between the home and school. Schools that invite parent participation, keep homes informed about programs affecting their children, and encourage parents to become involved in their children's education are more likely to achieve success with their students (Epstein, 1991).

Elementary counselors value parental involvement early in their counseling relationships with children. To win their cooperation, counselors inform parents about the counseling program through brochures, presentations at parent meetings, and individual contacts. While confidentiality is a condition of counseling with children as it is with other clients, elementary counselors appreciate the important contribution parents make in helping children resolve problems, alter behaviors, and set future goals. For this reason, it is appropriate for elementary counselors to encourage young clients to allow their parents to become involved in the helping process as soon as possible. In rare instances, such as with physical abuse, this involvement may not be possible, but, in most cases, elementary counselors encourage collaborative relationships with parents to help children focus on concerns and make appropriate choices.

Parents, teachers, and counselors are partners in the challenging task of helping children develop in a positive, healthy direction. Parental involvement has always been an essential component of elementary counseling as illustrated years ago by Meeks (1968) when she described the role of parents as: (1) helping the school to understand the child; (2) acquiring greater understanding of their children; (3) learning and appreciating what the school is doing to help children achieve; and (4) using encouragement and positive approaches to bring about constructive behavioral change. These elements of a parent's role are important because they identify the "expert" contribution that parents make in helping schools meet the individual needs of children. This expert input, inherent in the parents' role, combines with the instructional expertise of the teacher and the developmental expertise of the counselor to form an effective collaborative relationship.

Elementary counselors encourage parental involvement in ways that include: participating in parent-teacher conferences; enrolling in parent education programs on topics such as positive discipline, helping with homework, handling sibling rivalry, and communicating effectively with their children; and volunteering to help with school programs. Parental involvement has the two-fold purpose of assisting with children's development and enhancing the school as a vital part of the community. Because both of these purposes are so important, a comprehensive elementary school counseling program always incudes direct services for parents through counseling and consulting processes, as well as creative efforts to include parents in the life of the school. One example of including parents in the daily functions of a school, is a tutoring program staffed by parents and coordinated by an elementary counselor. Student tutoring by parent volunteers also provides an avenue to involve teachers in a collaborative effort to deliver services to students. Of course, teacher involvement is another vital component of elementary school counseling programs.

Teacher Involvement   Elementary counselors are colleagues of classroom teachers and other educational specialists who serve the school. To establish effective services in elementary schools, counselors develop strong working relationships with teachers and other school personnel. By doing so, elementary counselors seek to become an integral member of the school staff and the instructional program. They realize that the success of their program is influenced by the personal and professional relationships established with teachers and other colleagues in their elementary school (Schmidt, 1991). These relationships highlight the common goals of teachers and counselors to ensure that all children make adequate progress in their educational, social, and personal development.

Teacher involvement in elementary counseling begins with input about the nature and design of the counseling program. This input is in the form of teacher surveys, the advisory committee, and annual program evaluations. In addition, elementary teachers are actively involved in the school counseling program through the guidance activities integrated in their daily instruction. These guidance lessons are usually planned in conjunction with schoolwide curricular goals and objectives established for each grade level (Gysbers & Henderson, 1988).

Elementary teachers also have a vital role in referral processes for children who need counseling services. Because elementary teachers have contact with students all day long and teach children all the academic subjects—language arts, mathematics, science, and social studies—they are in an ideal position to observe student development and the obstacles preventing normal progress in school. For this reason, counselors rely on teachers' observational and diagnostic skills in referring children for services. Elementary teachers who establish close relationships with their students become the first-line helpers in the school, and as a result, are able to bring critical cases to a counselor's attention.

Another area of teacher involvement in elementary counseling is in fostering parent-school relationships. Because parents of young school children are concerned about their children's welfare, communication between teachers and parents is essential. Teachers who value the services of school counseling programs keep counselors informed about needs parents have expressed, indications of family dysfunction and turmoil, and other factors affecting children in school. When possible, teachers include the elementary counselor in parent-teacher conferences for the purpose of contributing information, facilitating the meetings, and suggesting avenues to deal with areas of concern.

Finally, teachers who have expertise in areas of child development or instruction are vital resources for staff development. Some elementary teachers have special knowledge and skills that are of value to their teaching colleagues. In such instances, counselors wisely ask these teachers to present in-service workshops because they know their teaching colleagues will accept training more readily from someone who has experience and background in the classroom. This is particularly so for training in instructional techniques and classroom management skills. Counselors who recognize this preference seek out teachers who have expertise, are excellent presenters, and are respected by their fellow teachers, and they invite these teachers to become workshop facilitators and presenters.

The Middle-School Counselor

Middle schools are relatively recent organizations, which in many communities have replaced junior high schools during the past few decades. Typically, the range of students in middle schools includes pre-adolescents between the ages of nine and thirteen, usually grades five through eight. The unique needs of this age group require special attention, particularly as related to their physical and social development. Theorists who promote the middle-school curriculum advocate educational programs which appreciate and understand the energy, confusion, and uncertainty that mark these transitional years (Alexander & George, 1981; Stamm & Nissman, 1979; Thornburg, 1979).

With the emergence of middle schools has come an examination and clarification of the role of the middle school counselor (Dougherty, 1986; Schmidt, 1989). Thornburg (1986) noted that the complex development of middle graders requires helping professionals who are skilled in understanding and communicating with these young people. The complexity of pre-adolescent development includes the onset of physical changes coupled with awareness of and curiosity about one's own sexuality as well as relationships with the opposite sex. In pre-adolescence, intellectual development is illustrated by more sophisticated and higher level thought processes. Abstract thinking is more evident and decision-making processes begin to acquire organization and rationale. Wit, humor, and satire now complement silliness, playfulness, and other childlike behaviors. Socially, the middle grader searches for peer acceptance and approval, struggles for independence and autonomy, yet is hesitant to accept full responsibility for the consequences of one's behavior.

Because these developmental tasks are so complex and the pace at which pre-adolescents move through them is so divergent, meeting the needs of these young people is a challenge for all educators who work in middle schools. As Thornburg (1986) warned:

> *It would be a mistake to underestimate the complexity of such a task and an equal mistake to perceive the task as impossible. Counselors and others who influence decisions regarding education must accept the challenge to develop effective school environments for today's middle graders. (p. 170)*

A first step for counselors who accept the challenge of a middle school program is to define their counseling role with the pre-adolescent student. What information, knowledge, and skills are needed to establish effective helping relationships with these transescent young people?

Counseling Pre-Adolescents   The unique needs and developmental stages of middle grade students require counseling approaches that reflect this divergence. Counselors who use one approach or a single format with all students, regardless of the nature of the concern or the developmental level of the student, may find themselves frustrated, and this is particularly true at the middle-school level. Counseling middle graders requires expanded approaches, which include individual helping relationships, group experiences, peer support systems, and other processes. In addition, effective middle-school counselors acquire a high level of knowledge and understanding about the expected developmental tasks of pre-adolescents and adolescents. Finally, and perhaps most importantly, successful counselors understand the ways in which middle graders perceive their world, and comprehend the conclusions students draw from these perceptions.

Individual counseling with middle-grade students has the potential to be successful when nonthreatening, respectful relationships are formed. Of course, such relationships are formed outside the individual helping relationship as well as within it. Middle-school counselors, who are accepted and respected by students, are visible in their schools, greeting students in the halls, having lunch in the cafeteria, and being available to students who seek assistance. It is through these kinds of interactions that middle graders assess the credibility, dependability, and reliability of their counselors. Based on these evaluative processes, students determine whether or not to seek assistance. Counselors who are viewed as believable and reliable are likely to be sought out when students need help.

Several counseling approaches are useful in working with middle graders. The approaches and models presented in Chapter 4 each have potential with this age group. For example, Adlerian counseling is effective in helping adolescents focus on the critical life tasks of career development, love relationships, and social accomplishments (Dinkmeyer, Dinkmeyer, & Sperry, 1987). Rational self-counseling offers a model for teaching children to learn emotionally healthy ways of thinking to achieve emotional self-control (Maultsby, 1986). Accepting responsibility for one's own actions is a key element of reality therapy (Glasser, 1965; 1984), another popular approach with this age student. These and other approaches are also useful in group counseling with middle graders.

Group processes are of particular value in middle-school counseling programs because of the desire of this age student to be a part of a group; to belong and to be accepted. In middle schools, group processes help students focus on developmental or problem-centered concerns and assist one another in achieving tasks and solving problems. Groups are also used in structured programs, such as small group and classroom guidance, to teach new skills or share information. Middle-school counselors rely heavily on processes that facilitate the sharing of new information and teaching of developmental skills as a response to the transitory needs of typical pre-adolescents.

Group and individual relationships are also useful in establishing effective peer helper programs, which have become a focal point for middle-school counseling services (Bowman, 1986; Bowman & Campbell, 1989). As seen in Chapter 3, peer helpers assist counselors by helping students who are new to the school, being first-line helpers of students in need of counseling, referring them to the school counselor, tutoring students who are having academic difficulty, and befriending students who have been excluded, ridiculed, or otherwise rejected by their peers. A strong peer helper program enables counselors to network with students and observe their development and progress through the eyes and ears of others. These programs provide a vital referral source for the middle-school counselor.

Transitional Services Middle-school counselors provide many services that enable students to make smooth transitions from their childhood years to adolescence. Included in these services are: (1) counseling students who are fearful of new surroundings, such as when moving from an elementary to middle school or from a middle to high school; (2) helping students learn about the physical changes in their bodies through guidance activities and counseling services; (3) teaching communication skills to help students develop friendships and relate more effectively to their peers, parents, and teachers; and (4) presenting decision-making models and skills for students to learn how to make choices and to understand the consequences of those decisions.

In many school systems, middle schools are separated physically from elementary and high schools. As a result, children in these systems change schools at least twice during their school years, usually after the fifth grade and then later after the eighth grade. Added to these transitions are adjustments resulting from family divorces and relocations that also initiate moves to new schools. For some students, these periods of change and transition are quite difficult. Middle-school counselors help make these periods less uncertain and anxious by providing services before students leave their elementary schools and prior to entering high school.

Transitional services include coordinating visits of elementary students to the middle school, orienting students who are entering the middle grades, compiling packets of information to help middle graders and their parents become familiar with the school, scheduling field trips for graduating middle graders to visit the senior high school in the spring semester, and planning career exploration activities with teachers to help students relate educational plans to their career interests. Limitless activities and services are created and delivered by counselors and teachers to help middle graders cross this transitional bridge toward adolescence and adulthood.

Individual counseling, group counseling, and classroom guidance provide students with information about physical development, friendships, study skills, and a multitude of developmental tasks students face. Middle-school counselors rely on teachers' observations, peer helper networks, and parental input to make decisions about which students will benefit most from the various services they offer. All students do not benefit equally from every service of a comprehensive counseling program. For example, some middle graders are comfortable talking about sexual awareness and bodily changes in small or large groups, while others hesitate to discuss these matters even in individual private sessions. The mark of a successful middle-school counselor is one who takes time to listen to students, parents, and teachers, and uses their suggestions in making appropriate decisions about services for individual students and the school as a whole. By doing so, these counselors create optimal relationships with all parties, and implement effective transitional services for students. As with elementary counseling, a key to establishing successful middle-school services is the cooperative involvement of teachers.

Teacher Involvement　A comprehensive middle-school counseling program reflects the ingredients and characteristics of effective middle schools (George, 1986). This means that counselors align their program with the mission of the school, helping teachers create and deliver appropriate instruction for all students, encouraging group processes such as instructional teams and advisory groups, and becoming part of the school's leadership team. Counselors who adopt this philosophy are receptive to teacher involvement in establishing comprehensive programs of services.

Many aspects of teacher involvement in a middle-school counseling program are the same as they are for elementary counseling. Planning a guidance curriculum, referring students for counseling, collaborating with counselors about student placement, and including counselors in parent-teacher conferences are as appropriate for middle-school counseling as they are at other levels. One aspect of counseling programs that are built around teacher involvement is particularly essential to middle-school development. This aspect is advisor-advisee services, which (Myrick, 1987; Myrick & Myrick, 1990) referred to as the "teacher as advisor program" (TAP).

Teacher-advisee programs in middle schools respond to the need for broad-based developmental guidance. This response is similar to the emphasis placed on developmental services at the elementary school level, and at the same time relates to the middle school's role of providing transitional services for students. In middle schools, where students no longer remain with the same teacher all day long as they do in elementary schools, teacher-advisee programs provide all students with consistent contacts and relationships with significant adults. In some middle schools, students are assigned to a homeroom or home-base group, which is supervised by their teacher/advisor. During these regular homeroom meetings, students participate in guidance sessions or individual conferences with their adviser (Alexander & George, 1981; Michael, 1986; Myrick, 1987).

Myrick (1987) suggested that these teacher-advisee home-base periods be held at the beginning of each school day for approximately 30 minutes. At least two days a week should be scheduled for developmental guidance with the other days being used for study activities, silent reading and writing, creative music and art, and other developmental activities. Ideally, when students are involved in study or reading activities, the teacher/advisor can hold individual conferences to develop relationships with advisees, check on students' progress, and learn about students' concerns.

Successful teacher-advisee programs usually have strong counselor involvement. Without counselor leadership, these programs might fail to win the endorsement of vital school populations—students, teachers, and parents. George (1986) noted that teacher-advisee programs can be the most desired and simultaneously the most disliked activities by middle school students, parents, and teachers. Students dislike programs that are poorly designed and presented by teachers who are unprepared and unskilled in guidance-type relationships. Similarly, teachers oppose advising responsibilities when they do not comprehend the purpose and value of these relationships, and when they are fearful of lacking skills to be successful in non-teaching interactions with students. Parent opposition occurs when they do not have a clear understanding of the purpose behind teacher-advisee programs, and are unconvinced that the time given to these programs is well spent. To avoid these rejections, counselors assume a major role in presenting information about the program, training teachers in group facilitation skills, and locating resources and materials for teachers to use in guidance sessions with their home-base advisees. In this way, coordination becomes a major function of school counselors in assuring success of teacher-advisee programs.

Beyond providing essential developmental guidance and supportive relationships for student advisees, the teacher-advisee program creates a vital channel in the school counselor's referral network. A teacher-advisee program is not intended to replace school counseling services, but rather is an ancillary component that allows teachers and counselors to work together on behalf of all children. As such, the teacher/advisor is frequently the person who refers students to the counselor for more thorough assessment, in-depth counseling, placement in a group program, or referral to other school and community services.

A teacher-advisee program also provides the initial step in developing positive parental involvement with the school. Teachers who have responsibility for advising students are the contact persons who are in touch with parents on a regular basis. These advisers also encourage their advisees to keep parents informed of school events.

Parental Involvement Middle graders are entering the phase of their development during which they begin to assert their autonomy and seek independence from parents and family. In this transition phase of adolescent development, middle-school counselors and teachers understand the importance of parental involvement. They know that children are assisted in this passage by parents who understand when and how to let go, and when and how to take control. For many parents, this is as much a learning process for them as it is an instructional, nurturing one for their children. For this reason, middle-school counselors and teachers plan appropriate programs for parents to learn about pre-adolescent development. At the same time, they seek parental involvement and input in creating school programs, developing school policies, and designing appropriate curricula.

Because parents of middle graders themselves struggle with entry into these transitional year, programs to assist them with their feelings and skills are appropriate. Counselors in middle schools assume a role in parent education by presenting programs about pre-adolescent and adolescent issues, teaching communication skills to enhance parent-teen relationships, and sharing information about expected developmental tasks and warning signals to look for in a teen's behavior and development. Sometimes, children progress through their elementary years without significant trauma, but then the sky appears to fall during the pre-adolescent stage. Parents who have enjoyed calmness in childhood become confused, angry, frustrated, and combative when faced with an unknown terror in their midst. Educational programs and support groups, led by school counselors are helpful to these parents. One of the most important benefits of these programs is that parents who attend these groups learn they are not alone. It is comforting to know that other parents are facing similar confusion, frustrations, and struggles with their children.

As in elementary schools, middle-school counselors are sensitive to the feelings and rights of parents regarding counseling services for their children. While permission for such services is not usually required, middle-school counselors make every attempt to involve parents when appropriate to do so. Such parental involvement, requires the trust of students who are receiving counseling and a willingness on their part to talk with parents about concerns they raise with counselors.

Middle graders are capable of exploring more complex concepts and deeper feelings than they were as elementary students, and simultaneously they accept more responsible for their decisions. While these two emerging traits allow these pre-adolescents to participate and benefit more fully in counseling relationships, their progress is enhanced immeasurably by parental participation. As a result, middle-school counselors search for ways to include parents in the helping process when students are comfortable accepting this kind of involvement.

The High-School Counselor

Historically, it has been the high-school counselor who is most often identified when people are asked, "What does a counselor do?" This is because high schools were the first to employ counselors, and most people who attended high school since the 1960's have known a counselor. While the present-day high-school counselor's role is changing, the typical counselor continues to assist students by providing information about course selections, career opportunities, test results, colleges, and scholarships. Generally, the helping processes described for elementary and middle-school counselors earlier are used at the high-school level as well. Again, these processes include counseling, consulting, coordinating, and appraising. The difference in how these essential services are delivered is seen in the specific activities chosen and used by school counselors at different levels of practice. As with elementary and middle-school counselors, high-school counselors select services and choose specific strategies and activities to address the unique needs of adolescents preparing to enter young adulthood.

In a study by Ibrahim, Helms, and Thompson (1983) of parents, counselors, administrators, and the business community, a variety of diverse services were viewed by all these groups as important functions of high-school counselors. While the authors noted statistical differences between groups on a majority of the functions, indicating that perceptions varied on the importance of these services, there was general consensus about the value of all these activities for counselors. In this study, thirty-seven functions were listed under the following major categories: (1) program development, (2) counseling, (3) pupil appraisal, (4) educational and occupational planning, (5) referral, (6) placement, (7) parent help, (8) staff consulting, (9) research, and (10) public relations. These functions are similar to the essential services of a comprehensive school counseling program suggested in this text. In another study, Gibson (1990) found that teachers saw the most important functions of high school counselors as: (1) individual counseling, (2) providing career information, (3) administering and interpreting test results, (4) college advising, and (5) group counseling and guidance. In most studies, counseling continues to be a dominant service provided by high-school counselors.

Counseling and Guiding Adolescents

The goals and processes for counseling adolescents are similar to those used with elementary children and middle graders. Although the goals and processes are alike, many concerns targeted in counseling relationships with adolescents are different from those of children and middle graders. For example, Miller (1988) found that secondary counselors rated career assistance and educational planning services significantly more important than did either elementary or middle-school counselors. Adolescents continue to need services that are developmental in nature, focusing on educational and career planning, academic achievement, social acceptance, self-awareness, sexual development, and other factors. Yet, many of their specific concerns are more problem-centered and crisis-oriented than simply developmental in nature. School dropout, teen suicide, pregnancy, drug use, sexual abuse, and a myriad of other troublesome concerns face adolescents in today's high schools.

In surveys of secondary school counselors, teachers, and students, counseling services remain a priority for high-school programs (Gibson, 1990; Hutchinson, Barrick, & Groves, 1986; Hutchinson & Bottorff, 1986; Tennyson, et al., 1989). There are, however, some differences in perceptions about the nature of these counseling services. According to one study, counselors viewed individual personal counseling, academic counseling, group counseling, and career planning as the four most important functions (Hutchinson, Barrick, & Groves, 1986). In practice, however, these same counselors ranked only individual personal counseling and academic counseling in the top four functions they performed. Career planning and group counseling were ranked 9th and 11th respectively out of the 16 items listed in the survey. In actual functions they performed, these counselors ranked scheduling (second) and testing (fourth) higher than either group or career counseling.

In contrast to counselors' perceptions, students in a study of 21 states and 152 high-school counseling programs ranked career counseling, college information, personal counseling, and scheduling as the most needed services (Hutchinson & Bottorff, 1986). However, students who participated in this study were already in college. Noncollege-bound students were excluded by the nature of the sample. This may explain the high ranking of college information and scheduling activities among this sample of students. What is most noteworthy about the results of this study is that less than half of the students said they actually received career counseling and only slightly more than 20 percent received personal counseling. This finding parallels the conclusion that high-school counselors often spend a large amount of time on administrative, clerical, and other none-counseling functions (Hutchinson, Barrick, & Groves, 1986). If surveys such as this are accurate indications of high-school counseling services, it seems that high-school counselors, by their own admission and the perceptions of others, are providing services that may not be direct services for students, and as a result they are taking time away from essential functions that should be part of their counseling programs. Some examples of these non-direct services include record-keeping, special education coordination, testing, and scheduling.

Group procedures are notably underused in high-school counseling programs for both group counseling and group guidance activities (Tennyson et al., 1989). In part, this lack of group work at the high-school level may be due to the fact that group processes are relatively new in the school counseling profession, emerging in the 1960s and being required in counselor training programs only in recent decades. Many high-school counselors, who tend to be older and more experienced than their colleagues in elementary and middle schools, completed their graduate preparation at a time when group counseling and guidance were not emphasized as strongly as they are today. A second obstacle to developing group programs in high schools is the rigidity of daily schedules and the emphasis on earning high-school credits toward graduation. Secondary teachers hesitate to release students from class to receive special services, unless those services have direct impact on students' academic progress. Hence, high-school counselors who work closely with their teachers to design acceptable schedules for counseling services are able to establish successful group programs.

Career Planning And Decision-Making   The studies of high-school counselors' role and functions indicate that career planning is a vital component of secondary programs. As noted in the previous chapter, this function includes guidance and counseling processes, both individually and in groups, to help students assess their strengths, weaknesses, and interests, and choose educational and career plans that are compatible with these characteristics.

Some high-school counselors use individual or group conferences at each grade level so students have the opportunity to check their progress, evaluate life goals, and set new objectives in their high-school careers. These conferences serve as check points for counselors and students to assess what information or other services are needed in planning for the future. They are preventive services planned to help students stay on track and in school. These services also encourage students to seek higher goals than what they may have planned initially. Sometimes, when students enter high school at fourteen or fifteen years of age, the information they have about themselves, the world of work, future employment patterns, and educational opportunities is limited, outdated, or simply inaccurate. Annual conferences with counselors and teachers are one way to acquire and update current, accurate information.

Information Services   Beyond the major functions of counseling, consulting, and appraising performed by high school counselors, another vital service is coordinating information for students, parents, and teachers. While elementary and middle-school counselors also provide information in their programs, at the high-school level this service takes on critical importance as a response to the significant decisions facing senior high students. At the end of their high-school careers, these students will have completed their formative years of development and will make major decisions about their life plans. Vocational, educational, and marital choices occur at this juncture, and the access students have to accurate information about these and other decisions is one responsibility of high-school counselors.

How counselors choose to disseminate information, the processes used to assure that all students have equal opportunity to receive accurate information, is fundamental to a comprehensive high-school counseling program. In large schools where several counselors provide services, these responsibilities often are divided among the staff. In other settings, counselors rely on student and parent volunteers, paraprofessionals, and teachers to help disseminate information. In all cases, counselors call upon teachers of required subject areas, such as English and social studies, assist counselors by presenting guidance activities related to career and educational opportunities, or allowing counselors class time to disseminate information. As such, teachers at this level also have an integral role in the school counseling program.

Parent/Teacher Involvement   The high-school years typically are signified by increasing independence and responsibility for students. As a result, we might expect less involvement of parents and teachers with counselors and students. In U.S. society, however, the increasing importance of post-secondary education at technical schools, community colleges, professional schools, and four-year colleges and universities has extended the need for parental involvement. Today, parents provide financial support, moral guidance, and developmental assistance throughout adolescence and into early adulthood to enhance the career and educational opportunities of their children. This role is expected to continue in the future.

At the same time, high-school teachers today provide more than the instructional content of academic subjects. Frequently, teachers give first-line assistance for critical concerns facing students. To prepare for this role, teachers receive in-service training in basic helping skills and crisis information. For example, they attend workshops on substance abuse and teen suicide to learn observational and communication skills, and receive training in crisis intervention to assist school counselors, psychologists, and other student services professionals. Some high schools have adapted the teacher as advisor program, and have seen positive effects on important criteria, such as school attendance, related to student success in school (Myrick, 1987).

What these trends tell us is that future high-school counseling programs may need to encourage more parental and teacher involvement than has been expected in past years. If so, comprehensive high-school programs of the future will include more parent education and support groups, increased use of guidance activities by teachers in daily instruction, and a significant role for teachers as advisers to high-school students. By increasing parental and teacher involvement in high-school counseling programs, counselors may find additional avenues with which to help students with their educational and career planning. Consequently, high-school counseling will become a more collaborative program of student, parent, teacher, and counselor functions to provide services for all students.

Future trends in elementary, middle, and high-school counseling will be reflected in revised training standards of the profession and changes in existing counselor education programs. The training of school counselors has changed dramatically in the profession's brief history, and new developments occur every year. Continuous revision of counselor training standards and programs can be anticipated, depending on the expected growth of the profession in schools and other settings.

Training of School Counselors

In the 1980s, professional associations noted a decline in interest and enrollment in school counselor training programs (Cecil & Comas, 1987). Toward the end of the 1980s, however, a survey of all the state departments of education indicated that more than 62 percent of the states anticipated increases in school counseling positions (Paisley & Hubbard, 1989). In the same study, less than 10 percent of the states indicated an anticipated decrease in the number of school counselors. This apparent renewed interest in school counseling in some 32 states was not, however, complemented by an increased attention to certification and training standards in all states. Presently, there are over 450 counselor education programs in the United States (Hollis & Wantz, 1990). Because there are no consistent guidelines mandated for training school counselors, a wide variance in requirements is found across the 50 states.

At the national level in recent years, the counseling profession has promoted standards through the National Board of Certified Counselors (NBCC) and the Council for the Accreditation of Counseling and Related Educational Programs (CACREP). However, Paisley and Hubbard (1989) found that over 90 percent of the states indicated that the standards for national certification (NBCC) made little or no difference in employability of school counselors, and more than 70 percent of the states indicated the same for CACREP standards. Eleven states, nevertheless, indicated some value and use of CACREP standards in employing school counselors or for setting certification guidelines.

As the school counseling profession continues to address issues related to its growth and development, the training standards for educational counselors will continue to be reviewed. While all states require certification of school counselors, the requirements for these certifications vary greatly (Barret & Schmidt, 1986; Paisley & Hubbard, 1989). Regardless of what the requirements in particular states are, the development of national certification and counselor education standards by the American Counseling Association, particularly two of its divisions, the American School Counselor Association and the Association for Counselor Education and Supervision, has encouraged training that focuses on specific areas of study. Reputable counselor education programs typically design programs of study to include course work in counseling theory and skill training, human development theory, group procedures, assessment skills, career development theory and information, research, social and cultural foundations, and professional issues. Most of these areas are described in this book as the essential services of a comprehensive school counseling program. Here, we briefly recap these areas of service to illustrate their importance in counselor education training.

The Helping Relationship

A foundation of the counseling profession, regardless of the setting in which counseling is practiced, is a competent understanding of theoretical models and clinical skills used in establishing, maintaining, and evaluating helping relationships. While these models and skills are particularly directed at individual and group counseling services, they also have application in other professional services, such as consulting and appraising. The role of school counselors is influenced by the theoretical models and clinical techniques adapted and applied by counselors in their individual schools. As such, the training counselors receive in helping relationship processes sets the tone for how well they perform basic skills and how comprehensively they design their program of services when employed in schools.

Counseling Theories and Approaches The theoretical foundations learned by school counselors in their training programs are similar to the training received by other professional counselors. Forming helping relationships with students, parents, and teachers in school settings may use different theoretical perspectives, including psychodynamic, behavioral, rational emotive, reality-based, or other views, depending on the orientation of the counselor and needs of clients. At the same time, a variety of counseling approaches and techniques might be observed, even in the same counseling program. Techniques and strategies, such as bibliotherapy, puppetry, life-style questionnaires, psychodrama, positive reinforcement, and modeling, have roots in particular theories of counseling.

Communication Skills As noted in Chapter 4, optimal use of helping processes requires a command of basic communication skills. School counselor training consists of course work and practice in listening, facilitating, and decision-making skills. Listening skills include appropriate attending behaviors, reflective listening techniques, and paraphrasing skills to let speakers know they are being heard. These skills are of particular importance early in the helping relationship to establish regard and respect between the counselor and counselee. Facilitating skills include questioning, structuring, linking, clarifying, probing, and confronting among others. By facilitating a helping relationship, counselors assist counselees toward appropriate decisions. This final phase of the relationship requires competent use of goal-setting, adequate exploration of alternatives, and the application of other decision-making skills. In most instances, this action-oriented process will be successful if counselors are objective, provide encouragement, and allow counselees responsibility for the decisions they make.

The Process of Helping Counseling, as used here, is not advice giving. Rather, it is the process of helping people examine concerns, gather necessary information, explore possibilities, and formulate a plan of action. Some-times, particularly in elementary schools with young children, it is difficult to hold back one's own opinions and allow counselees to explore, experiment, and occasionally fail. In practice, however, this is usually the best way to establish genuine, respectful helping relationships. Accepting another's viewpoint, even when it opposes yours, is a first step toward setting common goals together. Naturally, with some clients, such as young children, counselors must set parameters and structures that are age and developmentally appropriate. But, structure in a relationship can be established without overtly rejecting the views of another, or injecting one's own views into the helping process.

A key element of counseling is that it is a process. Counseling is a series of events aimed at accomplishing a specific goal or goals. Sometimes, this element of counseling is forgotten by school counselors who see students on a regular basis, but fail to monitor the progress of these relationships. Students visit with the counselor, discuss concerns, explore possibilities, but never commit to make changes that will address and alleviate their problems or optimize their opportunities for development. Counseling is more than having conversations with students who need assistance. Instead, it is movement from the identification of a concern to the implementation of a plan of action to address important life goals. Chapter 4 outlined four phases of a helping process, one model which can be adapted for counseling students to help them face a wide range of developmental, preventive, and remedial concerns.

Human Development

A second area of study for school counselors is human development. This area frequently includes courses in developmental and abnormal psychology, sociology, family relations, and learning theory. In addition, elective areas of study include substance abuse, sexual issues, violence, stress management, and other aspects of human behavior and development.

Knowledge of Behavioral Science   One area of development that is an essential knowledge base for school counselors is human behavior. Understanding different theories of behavioral development complements the various counseling theories and approaches used in forming effective helping relationships. In addition, school counselors frequently consult with parents and teachers in helping them understand and respond to children's behaviors. A strong knowledge base in the behavioral sciences gives counselors the foundation to perform competently in these consulting relationships.

A Life-span Approach   At the same time, counselors who work in schools need an appreciation of the life-span of human development theory. Because school counselors work with audiences from all levels, children through adulthood, they require an understanding of where each person is in his or her development. For example, an elementary counselor with a background in adult development has an advantage when trying to understand parents who are struggling with their children, or when assisting teachers who are dissatisfied with their career choice. Understanding human development across the life-span, sensitizes helping professionals to the unique needs of a broad population.

Group Processes

Because schools are staffed by only a few counselors to meet the needs of many students, group skills is essential in providing counseling, informational, and instructional services. You have learned that most of the communication skills learned in developing individual helping relationships are also used in group processes. Listening, facilitating, and decision-making skills are as important with groups as they are in one-on-one relationships. As seen in the beginning chapters, school counselors use these skills with three types of groups: group counseling, group guidance, and group consultation.

Group Counseling   School counselors use group counseling to help selected students focus on common concerns and developmental issues in regularly scheduled sessions. As with individual counseling, group counseling forms a confidential relationship in which students explore concerns and establish plans of action. Group counseling offers the added dimension of encouraging students to help students. In this way, group counseling replicates a social setting in which students feel secure in exploring their concerns, listening to the suggestions of their peers, and trying out suggestions before attempting them outside the group sessions.

Group Guidance   Some of the group skills learned in counselor education programs are useful in providing instructional and informational services. Group facilitation and interaction skills help school counselors deliver guidance services to a large number of students and parents. As noted earlier, teachers and counselors collaborate to present guidance activities to classes. Sometimes teachers become concerned about the sensitive nature of topics, or are otherwise uncomfortable leading particular guidance lessons. In these situations, counselors assist by co-leading class sessions. For counselors who have no large group experiences, training in instructional skills and group management is essential. These same skills can be transferred to other educational activities such as parent education programs, financial aid workshops, and other large group presentations.

Group Consultation   Another group process counselors use in schools is group consultation. Sometimes students can best be assisted if the counselor consults with all the adults who are relating with these students. Group consultations with teachers and other professionals require special understanding of consulting relationships, roles, and communication skills. These skills also complement large group interaction skills and enable counselors to become effective presenters of in-service programs for teachers and other professionals.

Student Appraisal

Assessing students and environments are two more functions of school counselors that require specific training in testing theory, development, and application. In particular, counselors learn about standardized achievement and aptitude tests, career inventories, and personality assessment instruments. While not all school counselors place heavy emphasis on test administration in their programs, they usually are responsible for interpreting and using test results and other measurement data with students, parents, and teachers. A strong background in tests and measurement assures the appropriate use and interpretation of data gathering instruments and processes.

Formal Assessment   Testing and using other instruments to gather data about students and their environments are types of formal assessment processes. School counselors are trained in the availability of these instruments, their appropriate use and interpretation of results, their selection for use in a comprehensive counseling program, and the ethical and professional standards of testing practices.

Formal use of assessment instruments and procedures includes a schoolwide testing program of achievement and ability testing at selected grade levels. By emphasizing a point made earlier, we reiterate that school counselors sometimes have responsibility for coordinating the testing program, including setting the schedule, training test administrators and monitors, securing the tests, and distributing and collecting materials. School counselors also administer individual tests and inventories to help students, parents, and teachers make appropriate educational decisions.

Informal Assessment   School counselors are trained in informal assessment procedures, which include observation techniques, life-style questionnaires, and the use of art, play, or other activity to help counselors collect data and form diagnoses about situations. Caution in using any type of assessment is warranted, and this is particularly true with untested, informal processes. The conclusions counselors draw from these types of procedures are always in conjunction with other data gathered in assessment processes.

Career Development Theory and Information

As mentioned earlier, a primary purpose of school counseling is to assist students with educational and career planning. To choose appropriate strategies in helping students address these career issues, school counselors are trained in career development theories and information services.

Understanding the different theoretical perspectives of career development gives counselors a foundation on which to build their own theory and choose compatible strategies and approaches for their programs. For example, having a broad view of the importance of career planning enables counselors to encourage teachers to incorporate career guidance into daily instruction across subject areas of the curriculum. As such, English teachers invite their students to explore careers that rely on language and communication skills. Likewise, science teachers incorporate the limitless ways that scientific discovery affects countless career choices.

Knowledge and implementation of information services are important to counselors, especially secondary counselors, in helping students have the most recent and up-to-date information about career trends and educational requirements. A current knowledge of career resources, college requirements, technical training programs, vocational interest inventories, and other materials enables counselors to guide students and parents accurately.

Educational Research

Counseling is an unprecise science. For this reason, it is essential that practicing counselors in all professional settings take time to account for the services they provide. School counselors are responsible for demonstrating that the services provided to students, parents, and teachers make a difference in student development and school life. To accept this responsibility and actively design processes for evaluating services, counselors must have a basic understanding of research techniques. This includes a knowledge of statistics and research applications. There are many ways that school counselors evaluate their services and Chapter 10 reviews a number of accountability procedures.

Social and Cultural Foundations

Schools in the United States today serve divergent populations and every indication is that this trend will continue for years to come. To help students adjust and teachers cope, school counselors must acquire an appreciation and understanding of a multitude of sociological phenomena affecting families, communities, and schools of today and tomorrow. Counselor education programs that provide information about the structural, sociological, and cultural changes in society, and explore expected outcomes and trends related to these developments, place their graduates in a stronger position to help schools deliver needed services to students, parents and teachers.

Changing Society In recent decades, U.S. society has seen tremendous social changes in the family unit, educational expectations, sexual mores, and career patterns. Added to these are countless advances in technology, discoveries of medical science, shifts toward a world economy, and rapid changes from industrial to information services in the world market. Counselors who are familiar with these changes and their impact on human development are better equipped to help students and teachers deal with the present consequences of these events, and to predict future trends.

Multicultural Populations Divergent cultures of U.S. society continue to influence educational development in our schools. Counselors who are sensitive to ethnic and racial differences and willingly celebrate the cultural diversity of their schools' communities are able to form beneficial relationships with a broad spectrum of people. To elevate counselors' understanding and appreciation of cultural differences, and especially the unique needs of people from different cultures, counselor education programs address a range of multicultural issues (Pedersen, 1988). School counselors who serve divergent student populations and are able to broaden their cultural vision beyond their own heritage are advantaged and likely to establish a broad-based comprehensive counseling program in their schools.

Ethical and Legal Issues

Counseling as a profession is guided by ethical standards and, in some cases, restricted by legal precedents. School counselors must know the ethical principles put forth by their profession, and balance that understanding with a clear knowledge of local policies, state statutes, and federal laws relating to the practice of counseling in schools. Counselor education programs include study of professional ethics and legal issues as they pertain to the general practice of counseling and special incidents such as child abuse, student rights, suicide, and other matters. In Chapter 11, we will examine several aspects of legal and ethical issues related to counseling in schools.

The School Setting

In addition to the above areas of study, school counselors also study the nature of educational institutions and, specifically, the practice of counseling in a school setting. This area of study is accomplished in part through courses in education, such as educational foundations, curriculum development, and philosophy of education. Students in school counseling are also expected to have practicum and internship experiences in a school setting. A practicum allows students to use newly learned basic helping skills with actual clients in a school. An internship is an expanded experience that offers graduate students an opportunity to become practicing school counselors under the combined supervision of seasoned counselors and university instructors. Internships allow students to perform all of the functions expected of a professional school counselor.

Credentials of School Counselors

Since the 1970s, credentialing of counselors has become a major issue in the profession. While school counselor certification has existed in all states for many years, certification and licensure of counselors in other work settings, such as mental health centers, prisons, and family services, are more recent developments.

In addition to certification and licensure, the counseling profession has worked to create accreditation processes for institutions that train counselors. National, regional, and sate accrediting bodies review colleges and universities to determine if programs of study meet established criteria. When institutions are found to satisfy these criteria, they are granted "program approval" status and their graduates benefit from having been trained in an accredited program.

The National Council for Accreditation of Teacher Education (NCATE) is the most common accrediting body for teacher education and related training programs in departments and schools of education at colleges and universities. As a result, NCATE is frequently the accrediting council for school counseling training programs, which are located in university schools of education. The Council for Accreditation of Counseling and Related Programs (CACREP), which is affiliated with the American Counseling Association (ACA), is another national accrediting body. CACREP reviews and approves training programs for counselors who are being prepared to work in a variety of settings, including schools.

The Association for Counselor Education and Supervision, a division of ACA has recommended standards and procedures for school counselor training and certification (ACES, 1990). In these recommended standards for training, ACES supports a two-year graduate program of studies for school counselors and endorses the use of CACREP standards as minimum requirements for certification of school counselors in all states.

State Certification

To practice as a school counselor, the first credential one must receive is state certification. According to Gibson and Mitchell (1990), all states require certification and the vast majority require a minimum of a master's degree for initial certification. In addition, many states include teaching experience as a prerequisite for school counselor certification. Paisley and Hubbard (1989) found that 29 states required teaching experience before certification and employment as a school counselor. Five of these states, however, allow alternate experiences, such as a counseling internship, to be substituted for teaching experience. It is noteworthy that several states continue to require teaching experience as a prerequisite to counselor employment despite the absence of research showing that such experience relates to effective school counseling.

A majority of states allow counselors to become certified prior to completing all the necessary requirements (Paisley & Hubbard, 1989). Twenty states have provisional school counselor certification, which usually means a person can be hired by a school system while finishing the final requirements at an approved program of study.

State certification for school counselors is usually a credential that must be renewed periodically, such as every five years. To renew certification, counselors are expected to obtain continuing education units (CEU's) or additional course work in counseling or related fields of study. School counselor certification is typically handled by certification offices in state departments of education, and many states have reciprocal agreements so that candidates certified in one state are eligible for certification in another.

National Certification

In the 1980s the American Association for Counseling and Development (AACD), recently renamed the American Counseling Association (ACA), became active in establishing a national certification process for professional counselors. A National Board of Certified Counselors (NBCC) was established and an application, review, and examination process was created. Eight areas of professional training are tested on the national certification exam:

- The helping relationship
- Human growth and development
- Group dynamics, processing and counseling

- Lifestyle and career development
- Social and cultural foundations
- Appraisal of persons
- Research and evaluation
- Professional orientation

Note the similarity of these knowledge areas with the recommended training components for school counselors, listed earlier in this chapter. The eight areas of study recommended by the NBCC for National Certified Counselors (NCCs) are fundamental to the core knowledge base of all specialties in the counseling profession.

The NBCC has also established specialty exams and certifications in career, gerontological, and school counseling. All these certifications are renewable in five-year cycles upon completion of required continuing education experiences. In some states, NCC is being considered as a requirement for school counselor certification. At this time, Maryland is one state that requires the national certification for school counselors.

All these certification and credentialing processes, at state, regional, and national levels aim at improving the identification and performance of practicing counselors. They elevate the counseling profession in the eyes of the public and in the esteem of those who join the profession. Credentials are one way for a profession, such as counseling, to monitor itself, assure that services being rendered are delivered by highly trained persons, and offer a clear identity for these practitioners. In this way, state, regional, and national certification processes for school counselors help define and describe what it is that counselors do in a school setting, and how they are trained to perform these functions.

In this chapter, we have examined the the role of school counselors in elementary through high-school settings. This description integrates the essential services of a comprehensive counseling program across all levels of school practice. It also notes that school counselors work with a wide audience of clients, and cooperate with other professionals to deliver appropriate services. In addition, this chapter has emphasized the necessary training and appropriate credentials of practicing school counselors. Adequate training and minimal credentialing processes attempt to assure the delivery of effective counseling services in schools. In the next chapter, we will review methods by which school counselors assess their effectiveness and demonstrate accountability for their services and programs.

Selected Readings

Gerler, E. R., Ciechalski, J. C., & Parker, L.D. (Eds.). (1990).
Elementary School Counseling in a Changing World (Alexandria, VA: American Association for Counseling and Development). This is a book of readings that illus-

trate the broad role of counselors in elementary schools. It is a timely and relevant review of the many functions of elementary counselors and the knowledge base required to fulfill their responsibilities.

Gerler, E. R., Hogan, C. C., & O'Rourke, K. (Eds.). (1991). *The Challenge of Counseling in Middle Schools* (Alexandria, VA: American Association for Counseling and Development). A collection of journal articles from the 1980s, this book depicts the expanded role of middle-school counselors. It presents a broad range of issues and concern related to pre-adolescent development and the implementation of counseling services.

Pedersen, P. (1988). *A Handbook for Developing Multicultural Awareness* (Alexandria, Va: American Association for Counseling and Development). This book gives a comprehensive overview of multicultural issues faced by counselors and their clients. It is an excellent resource for counselors wishing to examine their own multicultural perspectives or planning to influence the acceptance of cultural diversity in their institutions.

References

Alexander, W. M., & George, P. S. (1981). *The Exemplary Middle School* (New York: Holt, Rinehart and Winston).

American Personnel and Guidance Association. (1967), "Dimensions of Elementary School Guidance," *Elementary School Guidance and Counseling, 1,* 163–187.

Association for Counselor Education and Supervision. (1990), "Standards and Procedures for School Counselor Training and Certification," *Counselor Education and Supervision, 29,* 213–215.

Barret, R. L., & Schmidt, J. J. (1986), "School Counselor Certification and Supervision: Overlooked Professional Issues," *Counselor Education and Supervision, 26,* 50–55.

Bowman, R. P. (1986), "Peer Facilitator Programs for Middle Grades: Students Helping Each Other Grow Up," *The School Counselor, 33,* 221–229.

Bowman, R. P., & Campbell, C. A. (1989), "Positive Peer Influence: A Powerful Tool for Middle School Counselors," *American Middle School Education, 12* (3), 5–16.

Cecil, J. H., & Comas, R. E. (1987). *Development of Strategies for the Preservation of School Counselor Preparation Programs*, Monograph. (Alexandria, VA: American Association for Counseling and Development), ERIC No. ED 288 111.

Dinkmeyer, D. C., Dinkmeyer, D. C., Jr., & Sperry, L. (1987). *Adlerian Counseling and Psychotherapy*, 2nd Ed. (Columbus, OH: Merrill).

Dougherty, A. M. (Ed.). (1986), "Special Issue: Counseling Middle Grade Students," *The School Counselor, 33* (3).

Eckerson, L., & Smith, H. (1966). *Scope of Pupil Personnel Services* (Washington, D.C.: Office of Education, U. S. Department of Health, Education, and Welfare).

Epstein, J. L. (1991), "Pathways to Partnership: What we can learn from Federal, State, District, and School Initiatives," *Kappan, 72* (5), 344–349.

Faust, V. (1968). *The Counselor–Consultant in the Elementary School* (Boston: Houghton Mifflin).

George, P. S. (1986), "The Counselor and Modern Middle-Level Schools: New Roles in New Schools," *The School Counselor, 33,* 178–188.

Gibson, R. L. (1990), "Teacher Opinions of High School Counseling and Guidance Programs: Then and Now," *The School Counselor, 37,* 248–255.

Gibson, R. L., & Mitchell, M. H. (1990). *Introduction to Counseling and Guidance*, 3rd Ed. (New York: Macmillan).

Gladding, S. T. (1991). *Group Work: A Counseling Specialty* (New York: Harper & Row).

Glasser, W. (1984), "Reality Therapy," in R. J. Corsini (Ed.), *Current psychotherapies*, 3rd Ed., (Itasca, IL: F. E. Peacock), pp. 320–353.

Gysbers, N. C., & Henderson, P. (1988). *Developing and Managing your School Guidance Program* (Alexandria, VA: American Association for Counseling and Development).

Hollis, J., & Wantz, R. A. (1990). *Counselor Preparation 1990– 92: Programs, Personnel, Trends*, 7th Ed. (Muncie, In: Accelerated Development).

Humes, C. W., & Hohenshil, T. H. (1987), "Elementary Counselors, School Psychologists, School Social Workers: Who Does What?" *Elementary School Guidance and Counseling, 22*, 37–45.

Hutchinson, R. L., Barrick, A. L., & Groves, M. (1986), "Functions of Secondary School Counselors in the Public Schools: Ideal and Actual," *The School Counselor, 34*, 87–91.

Hutchinson, R. L., & Bottorff, R. L. (1986), "Selected High School Counseling Services: Student Assessment," *The School Counselor, 33*, 350–354.

Ibrahim, F., Helms, B., & Thompson, D. (1983), "Counselor Role and Function: An Appraisal by Consumers and Counselors," *The Personnel and Guidance Journal, 61*, 597–601.

Martinson, R. A., & Smallenburg, H. (1958). *Guidance in the Elementary Schools* (Englewood Cliffs, NJ: Prentice-Hall).

Maultsby, M. C. (1986), "Teaching Rational Self-Counseling to Middle Graders," *The School Counselor, 33*, 207–219.

Meeks, A. R. (1968). *Guidance in Elementary Education* (New York: Ronald Press Co).

Michael, J. (1986). *Adviser-Advisee Programs* (Columbus, OH: National Middle School Association).

Miller, G. (1988), "Counselor Functions in Excellent Schools: Elementary through Secondary," *The School Counselor, 36*, 88– 93.

Morse, C. L., & Russell, T. (1988), "How Elementary Counselors See Their Role," *Elementary School Guidance and Counseling, 23*, 54–62.

Myrick, R. D. (1987). *Developmental Guidance and Counseling: A Practical Approach* (Minneapolis, MN: Educational Media Corporation).

Myrick, R. D., Moni, L. (1976), "A Status Report of Elementary School Counseling," *Elementary School Guidance and Counseling, 10*, 156–164.

Myrick, R. D., Myrick, L. S., (1990). *The Teacher-Advisor Program: An Innovative Approach to School Guidance* (Ann Arbor, MI: ERIC/CAPS).

Paisley, P. O., & Hubbard. G. T. (1989), "School Counseling: State Officials' Perceptions of Certification and Employment Trends," *Counselor Education and Supervision, 29*, 60–70.

Pederson, P. (1988). *A Handbook for Developing Multicultural Awareness* (Alexandria, VA: American Association for Counseling and Development).

Purkey, W. W. (1970). *Self-Concept and School Achievement* (Englewood Cliffs, NJ: Prentice Hall).

Purkey, W. W., & Novak, J. (1984). *Inviting School Success*, 2nd Ed. (Belmont, CA: Wadsworth).

Purkey, W. W., & Schmidt, J. J. (1987). *The Inviting Relationship: An Expanded Perspective for Professional Counseling* (Englewood Cliffs, NJ: Prentice Hall).

Purkey, W. W., & Schmidt, J. J. (1990). *Invitational Learning for Counseling and Development* (Ann Arbor, MI: ERIC/CAPS).

Schmidt, J. J. (Ed.) (1989), "Counseling in the Middle School," *American Middle School Education, 12* (3).

Schmidt, J. J. (1991). *A Survival Guide for the Elementary/Middle School Counselor* (West Nyack, NY: The Center for Applied Research in Education).

Stamm, M. L., & Nissman, B. S. (1979). *Improving Middle School Guidance* (Boston: Allyn Bacon).

Tennyson, W. W., Miller, G. D., Skovholt, T. G., Williams, R. D. (1989), "Secondary School Counselors: What Do They Do? What Is Important?" *The School Counselor, 36,* 253–259.

Thornburg, H. D. (1979). *The bubblegum years: Sticking with Kids from 9 to 13* (Tucson, AR: HELP Books).

Thornburg, H. D. (1986). The counselor's impact on middle-grade students. *The School Counselor, 33,* 170–177.

10

Evaluation of a School Counseling Program

During the early years of the school counseling profession, the focus was on the role of the school counselor and helping relationships with students. As the profession moved into the 1950s and 1960s, the literature afforded more attention to the development of counseling theories and models of practice. In addition, group processes in school counseling gained prominence during this period. Beginning in the 1960s and continuing to the present day, the issue of accountability emerged as a requisite to the role and function of school counselors (Aubrey, 1982; Crabbs & Crabbs, 1977; Hohenshil, 1981). Specifically, attempts to clearly define and describe the role of school counselors included the need to identify and demonstrate effective practices.

In some respects, the same historical events that fueled the expansion of school counseling also contributed to calls for program evaluation and counselor accountability. For example, the national alarm resulting from Sputnik I in 1957 and the *Nation at Risk* report of 1983 were two occasions where the profession reaped the benefits of governmental action, while at the same time, school counselors experienced pressure to demonstrate *what* they do and *how well* they do it.

Some authors have noted that counselors as a group are reluctant participants in this movement towards accountability (Aubrey, 1982; Gibson & Mitchell, 1990; Lombana, 1985). A typical response has been that counseling is such a personal relationship and counselors do so many interrelated activities that it is impossible to measure a counselor's effectiveness or evaluate a program of services. Such avoidance of program evaluation and professional accountability continues as a major barrier to public recognition and acceptance of school counselors as essential contributors to student progress and effective educational programs. As this author noted in an earlier book, "Some counselors believe they are valuable to their schools because they are always 'busy.' To survive as a school counselor, you want to move beyond the notion of 'being busy' toward the realization that the services provided *make a difference* in the lives of students, parents, and teachers" (Schmidt, 1991, p. 16). The future credibility and efficacy of the profession depends on counselors taking the lead and demonstrating their value to the school community and to the educational process.

Lombana (1985) listed several explanations why some counselors are reluctant to demonstrate accountability. Among these she included: (1) the lack of time counselors have to plan and assess their programs; (2) resistance to measuring what counselors do in helping relationships; (3) confusion about the difference between research and accountability; and (4) fear of what the outcomes might be should counselors gather data to assess their effectiveness. Each of these excuses has validity. Time is a critical, precious commodity for everyone. Because school counselors have responsibility for so many services, it is understandable, if not acceptable, that they spend all their time delivering services rather than allotting some time to measure their effectiveness. It is indeed difficult, and at best imprecise, to measure the effects of counseling and consulting services. This imprecision, the difficulty of demonstrating cause and effect relationships, understandably contributes to anxiety about what results counselor evaluation might produce. In part, this lack of confidence is an outcome of school counselors not being sufficiently trained in research and evaluation methods. While these perceptions and feelings are understandable, they should not deter school counselors from acquiring the necessary skills to demonstrate their value and worth to the public who use their services, and to the decision-makers who employ them.

Comprehensive program evaluation and counselor accountability consist of a variety of activities beginning with the needs assessments described in Chapter 2 of this text. In addition, "end of activity evaluations; opinion questionnaires from students, parents, and teachers; program evaluations; self-rating scales from counselors; and processes for appraising counselors' performance" are all part of a comprehensive process for evaluating a school counseling program and assessing the counselor's effectiveness in delivering services (Schmidt, 1986, p. 20).

In this chapter, we examine these two aspects of counselor accountability—program evaluation and counselor effectiveness. The purpose behind training counselors in these evaluation processes is three-fold: (1) to help counselors gather data with which to make educational plans for their own professional development; (2) to enable counselors to make a case of their value and worth for the decision-makers who plan school programs and services; and (3) to invite counselors to participate in research efforts that lend credibility and validity to accepted practices and the future development of their profession.

There are several models and methods of accountability that have been presented for counselors (Atkinson, Furlong, & Janoff, 1979; Fairchild, 1986; Krumboltz, 1974). In general, they suggest the following principles and guidelines:

1. The goals of a school counseling program must be defined and agreed upon by all who will participate in the evaluation process. Counselors who seek input from students, parents, and teachers, and who are evaluated by supervisors and school principals, must clearly describe their program goals and these goals must be understood and accepted by those involved in the program. In some instances, counselors are evaluated according to standards and practices applied to classroom teachers. This approach is invalid if in fact the counselor has been employed to provide comprehensive counseling and consulting services to students, parents, and teachers. Goals that differentiate school counseling from classroom instruction should be reflected in these services.

2. All people who participate in, or are served by, the school counseling program should be involved in the evaluation process. Counselors serve students, parents, and teachers. At the same time, teachers assume an active role in the school counseling program through classroom guidance activities and as advisers to students. Assessment of program goals and evaluation of effective services need to include input from these groups as well as from the counselor, supervisor, and principal.

3. The instruments and processes used for gathering evaluation data should be valid measures of services and goals of the school counseling program. For example, survey instruments should reflect the goals and objectives of the program. At the same time, the functions and competencies of school counselors should be assessed by "reliable and valid instruments" that "relate to counselor training and job expectations" (Schmidt, 1990, p. 92).

4. Program evaluation is a continuous process aimed at identifying beneficial services and effective methods of service delivery. In school counseling, strategies for performing ongoing evaluation should be developed and evaluated as an integral part of a comprehensive program. As such, evaluation procedures are not implemented simply to appease decision-makers or placate the public during crucial times. Rather, they are viewed as vital components in the process of designing, developing, and delivering services to students, parents, and teachers in schools.

5. The central purpose of counselor performance appraisal is to assist counselors in helping the school achieve its mission. Evaluation of school counselors must, by definition, enable supervisors and principals to demon-

strate that the services provided in a comprehensive counseling program contribute to the school's ability to educate all students.

> *Evaluation is the process of determining the degree to which an employee's or a program's objectives have been achieved in order to improve continually the educational institution's ability to accomplish its mission. (Strong & Helm, 1991, p. 22)*

6. Equally important to helping the school reach its goals is the related purpose of enhancing the counselor's professional development and encouraging skillful improvement. Evaluation processes that enlighten and educate counselors about their strengths and weaknesses, and involve these counselors in making decisions about their future professional development, far surpass methods that simply identify weaknesses and call for personnel action to remove or reassign counselors. The purpose of personnel evaluation places emphasis "on improving performance . . . linked to professional development for individual educators and for the collective body of educators in a given school or institution" (Stronge & Helm, 1991, p. 23).

7. Both program evaluation and counselors' performance appraisal imply that action will be taken as a result of the findings gathered in the assessment process. When school counselors assess their programs of services by asking for input from students, parents, and teachers, they commit to review the results of this study and make changes in the program that, based on their findings, are professionally sound and ethically appropriate. By the same token, when supervisors and principals use reliable and valid methods of assessment to evaluate counselors, there is follow-through on the recommendations of these evaluations. To accomplish these goals, school systems offer professional and financial support to counselors to help them further their education, attend workshops, and pursue other avenues of developing and strengthening their knowledge and skills.

8. Evaluation processes are most helpful and effective when they emphasize the positive (Gibson & Mitchell, 1990). As such, program evaluation focuses on the benefits as well as deficiencies of services provided by school counselors and teachers. Likewise, counselor performance appraisal, at times, identifies weaknesses for which counselors may need assistance, but it also highlights strengths for which counselors should be recognized. As one example of recognition, a counselor could be invited to share particular knowledge and skills with colleagues through in-service activities. By focusing on positive as well as negative aspects, evaluation methods offer a balanced perspective, encouraging both program and personnel development and improvement.

Types of Program Evaluation

Program evaluation consists of a variety of procedures to focus on different aspects of a comprehensive school counseling programs. Baruth and Robinson (1987) offered that, "Evaluation of the counseling program is generally of two kinds. These are process evaluation and outcome evaluation" (p. 345). Accordingly, *process evaluation* indicates whether the services and strategies planned for the program were carried out, and answers questions such as: How many people were served? How much time was spent on service delivery? How many sessions were held? *Outcome evaluation* is, as the name implies, an assessment of the outcomes of the services provided by school counselors in comprehensive programs. As we have seen throughout this text, a comprehensive school counseling program consists of a variety of interrelated services. The overall purpose of these services is to assist students in their educational, social, personal, and career development. Outcome evaluation investigates the degree to which specific services assist students in reaching these intended goals. Accordingly, outcome evaluations are performed during the intervention process to assess progress towards the intended goals, as well as at the end of the service, to determine whether or not the goal was reached.

In the following sections we review four methods of program evaluation. These methods cover the scope of process and outcome procedures used by school counselors to evaluate their programs. The first of these, goals attainment, focuses on the implementation of strategies and services to meet stated program goals.

Goal Attainment

In Chapter 2, you learned that a comprehensive school counseling program consists of planning, organizing, implementing, and evaluating processes. Inherent in each of these processes is the belief that school counseling services have a meaningful purpose that ultimately contributes to the broader educational mission of the school. An illustration of this ultimate purpose is found in the goals and objectives chosen for the school counseling program. Usually these goals and objectives, as noted earlier, are chosen as a result of needs' assessments performed by the counselor with students, parents, and teachers. Figure 10–1 illustrates a sample planning sheet used by a middle school counselor to identify students' needs and recommend program goals to classroom teachers.

In Figure 10–1, some of the statements show a high percentage of responses indicating that many students expressed these concerns, thereby justifying them as program goals. As one example, item 2, "Concerned

---

Middle School Counseling Program

Students' Needs based on the 7th grade survey	Recommended Program Goals
1. Want more information about abilities and interests (42%)	1. All 7th grade students will have the opportunity to participate in small groups to explore their educational and career interests and compare these interests with their performance in school.
2. Concerned about friendships (68%)	2. Friendship units will be developed and integrated with social studies lessons in the fall semester.
3. How to deal with feelings about family separation and divorce (37%)	3. Small group counseling will be available and offered to students whose families are experiencing change.
4. Need to develop better study skills (35%)	4. A study skills unit will be developed for teachers to use in language arts block.
5. Have strong feelings of loneliness and am very sad (8%)	5. The counselor will observe and identify students who are isolates or appear depressed, and offer individual counseling or referral services.

FIGURE 10–1 Counselor's planning sheet for aligning needs' assessment with program goals

about friendships," shows 68 percent of the students shared this concern. At the same time, other items with much lower percentages are also identified as needs, and program goals are recommended. An example is item 5, "Have strong feelings of loneliness and am very sad," to which 8 percent of the students responded affirmatively. While this percentage is low in comparison to other items, the serious nature of this question justifies its focus as a student need. If 8 percent of the student population feels sad, lonely, and depressed, this should be a critical concern for teachers and counselors to address.

Some goals are set as a result of local and state mandates and standards that aim at providing equal services to all students. In some states, departments of education set specific learning goals and objectives as part of a guidance curriculum. School counselors and teachers cooperatively decide how and when these goals and objectives will be met in each school's instructional program. All these goals, those set as a result of student needs' assessments and those mandated by the state, become part of a school plan to meet the developmental needs of students. Related to this school plan is the counselor's annual plan of goals, objectives, and services to be provided during the year. In evaluating their programs, counselors measure goal attainment in two ways—through learning-related goals and service-related goals.

Learning-related Goals School counselors select goals for their annual plans with input from administrators and their advisory committees. They review the data gathered from needs' assessments with students, parents, and teachers, and relate these findings to their observations as well as to the observations of administrators and members of the advisor committee. In some cases, the goals selected relate directly to an identified need. For example, if a high-school survey finds that students need to associate their educational success with future career satisfaction, a related goal might be: To increase student awareness of the significant correlation between educational achievement and career development. Such a goal would be student-related and could be addressed directly through the school's curriculum and career guidance activities.

Evaluating this type of goal requires the development of assessment instruments and processes to measure particular learning that is expected of the population being served. With students who participate in career awareness activities, for example, a counselor may create a survey questionnaire to assess students' knowledge before and after participation in the program. In some instances, the trait being measured might be assessed through commercially produced tests or other types of instruments. Figure 10–2 shows a sample survey questionnaire for students who have participated in a career awareness program.

Service-related Goals Sometimes goals indirectly address the expressed needs of students, parents, and teachers. In the above example of increasing students' career awareness, a counselor might choose a broad program goal to demonstrate that specific services are being rendered. This goal might be: To increase the number of career guidance sessions with eighth-grade students. By choosing this type of service-related goal, the counselor addresses the relationship between educational achievement and career success by assessing how often this information is taught. Service-related goals, such as this one, illustrate ways that counselors assess particular standards by defining and describing comprehensive programs of services. There are three ways of evaluating these types of service-related goals. The first is by simply reporting the number of occasions on which a service is provided. A second is by counting the number of people who participate in a given service. And a third method is by surveying people to receive observations about a particular service. This last method is a measure of consumer satisfaction.

Figure 10–3 shows a sample report about group counseling in an elementary school using the combined method of counting sessions and

Students: Please complete the following questions to indicate your feelings and thoughts about the Career Awareness Group in which you have participated. *Circle one response for each question.* Thank you.

1. This group helped me learn things about myself that I did not know before. YES NO UNSURE
2. This group helped me learn about different careers. YES NO UNSURE
3. I have a better understanding of what educaton I need for the job I want to have. YES NO UNSURE
4. The counselor listened and understood my concerns. YES NO UNSURE
5. I would recommend this group to other students. YES NO UNSURE

Students: Please write down some of the careers that interest you *and* the educational goal you would achieve to pursue the careers on your list. (Educational Goals are: High School, Technical School, Two-year Colllege, Four-year College, Graduate School, Beyond Graduate School).

Careers of Interest: Educational Goals:

_____   _____

_____   _____

_____   _____

FIGURE 10–2   Student Career Awareness Questionnaire

participants. On this form, the counselor has reported the number of groups led and the number of students who participated during the month. Such program evaluations *quantify* how counselors spend their time, and show the amount of services provided and the number of people served. This type of quantitative analysis is important when counselors want to show where their time is going, the case loads they are serving, and the balance of their time across varied services and activities that comprise a comprehensive school counseling program.

Figure 10–4 is an example of a survey of teachers who are asked to report their observations about group counseling services. Results from this survey would indicate how the counselor is spending time and also the level of teacher satisfaction. Both Figures 10–3 and 10–4 address the same counseling service, group counseling, but examine its implementation from a mildly different perspective. The type of evaluation procedures chosen by counselors, therefore, depend on what questions need to be answered.

Measuring the number of participants receiving services or the amount of time devoted to a particular activity ensures that counselors offer a broad

---

Month: April

---

1. Number of small group counseling sessions held during the
   month.   _____

2. Total number of students who participated in group counseling
   this month.   _____

3. Number of group guidance sessions led this month (small
   groups and classroom guidance)   _____

4. Total number of students who participated in group guidance   _____

Group Counseling Issues and Topics:

_____

_____

_____

Group Guidance Topics:

_____

_____

_____

_____

FIGURE 10–3   Sample Report of Counselor's Group Work

spectrum of services to meet the needs of a wide population. If school
counselors provide only one or two services, or meet the needs of narrowly
defined populations, they do not design comprehensive programs to deliver
a wide range of services. By quantifying their services, counselors begin to
make decisions of where to adjust their programs and where to place emphasis to meet the needs of more students, parents, and teachers. An example of how these evaluation processes are used to assess and refocus
program services is seen in the following story.

> *A new director of counseling services was concerned about how counselors
> were spending their time. The counselors and director developed a monthly
> reporting form and found that while the elementary and middle school coun-
> selors used group processes frequently, senior high counselors did virtually
> no group counseling. In summarizing and discussing these results with the*

Teachers: Please complete the following questionnaire to help us evaluate the counseling groups that have been part of the school counseling program this semester. *Indicate your response to each item by circling the appropriate number, 1–5, where 1 means you strongly disagree and 5 means you strongly agree.* Thank you.

	Strongly Disagree			Strongly Agree	
	1	2	3	4	5
1. The students who have participated in group counseling have benefited from the service.	1	2	3	4	5
2. I have observed behavior changes with some students who have participated in groups.	1	2	3	4	5
3. The counselor has given me appropriate feedback about students who have particpated in groups.	1	2	3	4	5
4. I would like more students to have the opportunity to be in group counseling.	1	2	3	4	5
5. The counselor has sufficient number of groups available this semester.	1	2	3	4	5
6. The focus of the group counseling sessions seems to be appropriate, based on information recieved from the counselor.	1	2	3	4	5
7. The feedback from students about their participation in group counseling has been mostly positive.	1	2	3	4	5
8. The group schedule has not interfered with student class work.	1	2	3	4	5
9. Parents have expressed concern about their children participating in these groups.	1	2	3	4	5
10. I need more information about what goes on in these groups.	1	2	3	4	5

FIGURE 10–4 Teacher's evaluation of group counseling

counselors, the director learned that most of the secondary counselors were trained in years past when group process and skills were not required in counselor training programs. Thus, the omission of group services was due in large part to the counselors' lack of knowledge and skill. As a result, a consultant was retained to offer group counseling workshops for all the counselors. Follow-up surveys during the next year showed that some secondary counselors began implementing group counseling in their programs. One counselor with twenty-five years of experience who had never lead groups before enthusiastically reported success in starting groups in his high school.

Reports that enable counselors and supervisors to examine where time is being spent and how many students, parents, and teachers are being served are important to program evaluation. However, these types of reports do not adequately address the effectiveness of services. To do so, counselors must examine the outcomes of the services they provide. Specifically, they must evaluate student outcomes.

Student Outcomes

School counseling services assist students in learning information, developing coping skills, adjusting behaviors, and achieving many other objectives. In all cases, the services counselors provide to reach these goals should produce some measurable or observable result. In other words, if counseling services complement the learning process, we should be able to assess their impact through some type of student outcome. Sometimes, these outcomes are generalized across populations. For example, a school might focus on one outcome that covers the entire student body. Let us say that the goal is: To decrease the student absentee rate by 10 percent. This goal can be measured simply by taking account of the student absentee rate before the service begins and comparing that finding with the student absentee rate after the service is complete.

One problem with this type of outcome evaluation is that it fails to identify how individual students have functioned; it simply looks at the broad goal and whether or not it has been achieved. In the example above, we might find that the school absentee rate has improved because students who had relatively good attendance improved their rate even more. On the other hand, students who had high absentee rates could continue to be absent, and because the overall school rate improved, these students would receive little if any notice.

To address the needs of individual students, outcome data for individual cases and small groups should be reviewed. Say, for example, an elementary counselor is seeing a child who is mildly school phobic. The counselor helps the child in individual play therapy, consults with the teacher about classroom strategies, and confers with the parents about how to handle "getting ready for school" in the mornings. The outcome of all these services is measured by asking parents to report instances of high anxiety at home, receiving feedback from the teacher to assess the student's progress by remaining in class without crying, and observing the child's adjustment to the school schedule and classroom environment.

Program evaluation methods of assessing student outcomes usually take one of four forms (Gysbers & Henderson, 1988). First, evaluation can be based on predetermined or prearranged standards such as: "At least 85 percent of the eighth-grade students will be able to complete the course preregistration card correctly." This type of outcome standard is generally based on some minimally acceptable level that teachers and counselors believe can be attained.

A second type of outcome procedure compares students in a specific program with ones who have not yet participated. This type of research or evaluation design uses a "control group" format to demonstrate that the service was a possible causal factor in bringing about a desired change. The following illustration is an example of this type of evaluation procedure.

> At the beginning of the school year, a counselor plans a study skills group of middle graders who participate for nine weeks and after this period, students show higher grade point averages in comparison to their grade reports for the previous year. A second group of students, called the "waiting group," begins the study skills program after the first nine weeks of school are over and the first report cards are issued. This second group, a matched sample of students, show no significant difference in grades from last year's report to the first nine weeks' report. After the first nine weeks of school, this matched group is placed in the study skills program and the experiment is replicated during the second grading period. In this replication, significant changes in grades for the second group of students occur between the two grading periods similar to findings with the first group of students. Given these results, the counselor can be reasonably certain that the study skills program had a positive effect on helping groups of students improve their grades.

Another type of outcome procedure asks students to respond to their reactions and involvement in a particular service, or asks parents and teachers to observe and record their findings regarding changes in students' behaviors, learning, or other goals. This type of assessment might examine student attitudes, knowledge, and behavioral changes as measured through surveys, behavioral checklists, rating scales, or case study reports (Gysbers & Henderson, 1988). As noted in Chapter 7, the reliability and validity of these assessment instruments are vital to the appropriate development of evaluation procedures and the subsequent interpretation of findings.

A fourth type of outcome assessment uses a pretest and a posttest comparison. In this procedure, the counselor gathers data to show where the student is at present and proceeds to include the student in a specific service, such as group counseling. After a period of time, the same instrument or process used in the pretest is repeated and results are compared with the earlier findings. The elementary counselor who assists a school phobic child might use a pre- and posttest procedure by observing and recording behaviors when the child is referred and then noting the changes after counseling and consulting services are offered. Another example of a pre- and posttest design is a group counseling program with middle graders who have high absentee rates. Students' absences could be monitored for a few weeks prior to beginning the group counseling program, and observed again when the students have concluded the group sessions. Positive differences between these absentee rates could demonstrate that the group experience encouraged students to attend school on a regular basis.

All these methods of evaluating student outcomes are available and valuable to school counselors. While measuring student outcomes is essential, it is equally important to satisfy the clients who seek school counseling services. Consumer satisfaction is another method of demonstrating counselor accountability.

Consumer Satisfaction

There are, as you have seen in this text, a wide range of services in a comprehensive school counseling program. Collecting data to measure individual student outcomes may be an impossible task given all the responsibilities of a school counselor. Some outcome research is essential to demonstrate the efficacy of counseling services, but if this is all counselors did, they would have little time to actually deliver the very services they were attempting to evaluate. Lombana (1985) categorized counseling objectives as either client objectives or program objectives and noted that both types of objectives can be evaluated by either *empirical* measures or *perceptual* measures. It is the latter, the perceptual measures that fall into the realm of consumer satisfaction.

School counselors use different methods of gathering data from students, parents, and teachers to assess the overall level of satisfaction with program services. Informally, counselors may have follow-up conversations with students and teachers, or make phone calls to parents. More formally, counselors design survey questionnaires for students, parents, and teachers to complete, expressing their views and opinions about school counseling services. Myrick (1987) suggested that "when it comes to accountability, it is always advisable to ask the consumers of guidance and counseling services—students, parents, and teachers—what they think" (p. 413). For this reason, school counselors use methods to gather information about how these consumers perceive the services of a school counseling program. Figure 10–5 illustrates an example of a student survey with high school students.

Based on the results shown in Figure 10–5, we would conclude that most students believe the counselor is available, listens to students' concerns, and maintains confidential relationships. The counselor might be concerned that a total of 33 percent of the students did not feel, or were unsure, that the counseling sessions helped them make decisions (Question 3). Nevertheless, a strong percentage said they would recommend the counselor to other students who needed services.

Summary Report

Instructions: Please indicate your satisfaction with the counseling services you received this year by circling your responses to each statement. Thank you for your assistance.

	YES	NO	UNSURE
1. The counselor was available to see me when I needed assistance this year.	77%	15%	8%
2. The counselor listened to my concerns and seemed to understand me.	70%	20%	10%
3. The counseling sessions helped me focus on my concerns and make decisions.	67%	25%	8%
4. The counselor kept information I shared in counseling confidential.	98%	1%	1%
5. I would recommend the counselor to other students who need services.	85%	10%	5%

FIGURE 10–5 High School Students' Survey of Counseling Services

One way that counselors in school systems use consumer feedback to influence decisions about their counseling programs and services is to compile results of all the counselors and summarize these findings for the district administration and school board to review. Input from students, parents, and teachers are important in demonstrating the value of comprehensive counseling services and in illustrating what role and functions are essential for counselors in schools. Sometimes, administrators and board members are unaware of all the services counselors provide for students, parents, and teachers. By distributing an annual summary of their program evaluation, counselors take control of *who* they are and *what* services they should offer in helping students reach their educational, personal, and career goals.

An annual evaluation of school counseling programs also enables supervisors of counseling services, school principals, and counselors to make decisions about what services need to be expanded or strengthened, and which ones need to be de-emphasized. With an adequate assessment of all counseling programs across the school system, administrators and supervisors are in a better position to make decisions about personnel needs, budgets, staff development activities, and program changes. In contrast, without adequate evaluation, such decisions are made arbitrarily or intuitively with little or no basis in research evidence. Program and personnel decisions made in this manner reflect a serendipitous style of management and development, and, likewise, assume that counseling is a fortuitous process without foundation in specific knowledge bases, helping skills, or efficacious models of professional practice. Such a position does disservice to the counseling profession and to the students, parents, and teachers who expect reliable and dependable services.

By gathering data from the consumers of school counseling services, counselors and their supervisors are in a stronger position to make purposeful and meaningful decisions about future program directions. Such a posture of purpose and direction has been referred to as *counselor intentionality* (Purkey & Schmidt, 1987; Schmidt, 1984). When related to the process of evaluation, this counselor characteristic refers to an awareness and willingness to receive feedback from others and use that feedback to alter behaviors, develop plans, and change direction to meet the needs of those being served. While this kind of internal feedback from students, parents, and teachers is valuable to school counselors, sometimes an external review of programs is also beneficial.

Expert Assessment

Input from local supervisors, including school principals, and from students, parents, and teachers offers an opportunity for counselors to broaden their perspectives of what services are effective and what new services may be needed. However, if only these types of internal perspectives are used, counselors and their supervisors will limit annual evaluations to restricted and repetitious views of what should be. In addition, they risk neglecting broader visions that reflect national and international trends and issues in the school counseling profession. To guard against this kind of parochial stance, counselors and supervisors occasionally seek assistance from outside experts in school counseling who offer an external perspective to the evaluation process.

Expert assessment of school counseling services includes a range of evaluation processes from observing a single counselor in an individual activity, such as group counseling, to gathering data about all the services of a comprehensive program across an entire school system. By using outside experts to gather information, counselors and supervisors increase the objectivity of the evaluation process and thereby ensure more reliable results. Because of the expense of hiring outside consultants to perform this type of evaluation, however, it is not a method that is used very often. For this reason, internal evaluations should be used in conjunction with the external reviews for comparison purposes.

In designing an external evaluation of school counseling programs, counselors and supervisors formulate several questions. By asking appropriate questions and giving serious thought to their responses, counselors and supervisors ascertain the potential value of an external review and determine whether the time and cost will produce results to strengthen their program of services. Some questions that counselors and supervisors might entertain are:

1. *What do we want to know?* A proper evaluation begins with asking clear questions about what counselors and counseling supervisors want to find out about the program of services. These questions can be generated in meetings with counselors, administrators, and teachers. In general, the questions asked will focus on specific areas of concern, such as: Are the essential services being provided by counselors an efficient means of addressing the needs of students in our school? Given the personnel available, are school assignments and ratios of counselors to students appropriate at all levels? Are there more effective and efficient methods of providing services than currently being done?

2. *Who should be involved in designing the evaluation?* Because school counseling services are an integral part of the educational program, a wide representation of school populations should be included in planning an external review. School counselors should join with supervisors, principals, teachers, other student service specialists, and parents to assure that all questions are asked and all areas of concern are considered. In secondary schools, student representatives should also be included.

3. *Who are the outside experts to conduct the evaluation?* Depending on the location of the school system and the availability of external resources and internal funds, an evaluation committee will recommend to the superintendent of schools who should be invited on the review team. By using the questions formulated during the planning phase, the committee is able to narrow the field of reviewers needed. Examples of possible external reviewers include counselor educators from local and state colleges and universities, consultants from state departments of education, counselors and counseling supervisors from neighboring school systems, renowned professionals in counseling, and officials in state and national school counselor associations. Credentials of potential reviewers and cost factors are considered in making this recommendation to the superintendent and local school board.

4. *What instruments and processes will be developed as part of this evaluation?* In most instances when an external consultant is hired to perform an evaluation, the design of the study, including the instruments to be used, is part of the contract. The evaluation committee presents the major questions and issues to be reviewed and the consultant designs the instruments and the processes for gathering data. In some instances, the evaluation committee might ask potential consultants to design a study and sample instruments as part of the process of selecting an external reviewer.

5. *Who will receive the results of the study and how will they be used?* As with other types of assessment processes, such as testing and observing students, program evaluation requires careful and appropriate use of data. The evalu-

ation committee is responsible for determining how the results will be reported and for whom the report is intended. These decisions are guided by the overall purpose of the external review and the specific questions included in the design of the study. In most cases, the report of an external review is shared with the local school board through the superintendent's office.

The preceding evaluation processes, from service-related accounting methods to external reviews, aim at helping counselors, supervisors, and school principals assess the direction and benefits of a comprehensive school counseling program. Evaluation methods, such as those suggested in this section, provide an overview of programs and assess the value of specific counseling and consulting services. An equally important aspect of the evaluation process, and one which we now consider, is the actual performance appraisal of school counselors.

School Counselor Evaluation

With increased attention on the performance of our schools, the educational community has placed greater emphasis on evaluation and accountability of professional personnel. In general, this emphasis has been directed at evaluation of classroom teachers with little attention being paid to other professionals and specialists in the schools. Stronge and Helm (1991) commented that the "evaluation literature reveals very little pertaining to the evaluation of professional support personnel—the 'staff administrators' and certified professionals serving students, teachers, and/or other clients" (p. 3). By and large, adequate evaluation of school counselors has been a rare occurrence. When counselor performance appraisal has occurred, little written documentation has justified the evaluation processes used, or worse, the performance of counselors has been rated on instruments and with processes designed for teacher evaluation. In Wisconsin, one study found that only 17 percent of the school counselors evaluated was assessed by written standards and criteria developed especially for school counselor performance appraisal (Gorton & Ohlemacher, 1987).

In recent years, there is some indication that evaluation of school counselors is receiving more serious attention. Some states and local school systems have developed specific criteria and designed processes that are particularly suited for school counseling practice (Breckenridge, 1987; Housley, McDaniel, & Underwood, 1990; Schmidt, 1990). Generally, the standards for assessing school counselors include criteria related to program planning and organization, group and individual counseling skills and processes, consulting skills and processes including group guidance presentations, coordination of services, ethical practice, and professional development. The types of evaluation objectives used in counselor performance appraisal parallel the process and outcome goals used in program assessment described earlier in this chapter. Specific procedures for gathering data related to these standards and goals, however, have not been systematically developed. Furthermore, when processes have been developed, it remains unclear who are the most suitable observers and evaluators to gather data and make judgments about counselor performance. These issues help outline some of the major concerns surrounding the evaluation of school counselors. The first is to determine what needs to be evaluated.

What Will Be Evaluated?

As noted throughout this text, the role and functions of school counselors emerged over a brief history, beginning with the vocational guidance movement of the early 1900s. In spite of an extensive range of literature and research explaining the role of school counselors, developing models of practice, and creating theories of counseling, there still exists uncertainty about the counselor's role and purpose in schools. As Ficklen (1987, p.19) pointed out, "the basic problem for administrators . . . is this: What, exactly, are counselors supposed to be accomplishing?" This question is not only critical for determining the overall role and major functions of school counselors, it is also essential in identifying the practices that illustrate effective functioning (Schmidt, 1990).

The first step in developing appropriate evaluation procedures for school counselors is determining their essential functions and identifying specific activities that define these functions. In this text, the essential functions of a comprehensive school counseling program have been identified as: (1) planning, organizing, and evaluating services; (2) counseling individuals and groups; (3) consulting with students, parents, and teachers, individually and in groups; (4) appraising students' interests, abilities, behaviors, and overall educational progress; and (5) coordinating student services in the school. In addition to these essential functions, counselor evaluation also examines the extent to which these practices are used ethically and legally, and the attention the counselor pays to his or her own professional development.

Once the essential functions and practices of school counselors are described, the next step in the evaluation process is to determine the nature of measurement to be used in assessing performance. Generally, there are three approaches to consider. One, as we saw earlier in program evaluation, is to assess the *outcomes* of particular practices and activities selected by a counselor to address identified concerns. For example, a counselor who uses group guidance activities with middle graders to help them develop friendships might be evaluated in part by the results of a questionnaire on which students indicate what they have learned in the group and how many new friendships they have attempted as a result of being in the group. A second method of assessing counselor success, as with program evaluation, is to examine performance in relation to preagreed standard. An example of this would be when a counselor chooses individual counseling to assist students in decreasing their absentee rates, with the goal being that all students who participate will decrease unexcused absences by at least 50 percent. In this approach, the counselor is evaluated not by the outcome itself, but by the *level* at which the outcome is observed. A third way of measuring counselor performance is by combining the first two procedures. That is, by stating what outcomes should be observed and at what level of performance these outcomes are expected (Stronge & Helm, 1991).

Identifying major functions and essential activities and determining the standards of performance provide the overarching framework for the evaluation process. The next step is to design and create specific methods of gathering data with which judgments and decisions can be made about whether or not services have been rendered, and the level of performance at which they have been delivered.

How Will Evaluation Be Done?

Because school counselors function with a wide range of services and activities as part of their responsibility, it is difficult to narrow down or limit the methods of evaluating their performance. Unlike teacher evaluation, which relies heavily on classroom observations, school counselor appraisal must call on diverse methods of data collection and documentation. Included in these methods are observations, interviews, simulated activities, self-assessments, product development, video and audio tapes, schedules, consumer feedback, records of services, and memos of personnel action (Schmidt, 1990; Stronge & Helm, 1991). The variety of activities expected of a school counselor and the confidential nature of some services in a school counseling program raise questions about methods of gathering data for performance appraisal. For this reason, it is important that counselors and supervisors jointly plan and agree on the methods to be used. Ideally, this planning process would take place at the beginning of the school year with the supervisor and counselor determining which major functions are going to receive attention and how to collect data to assess their performance.

Observations While some counseling services cannot be observed directly due to their confidential nature, other activities used by school counselors can be evaluated through observation. Large and small group guidance, parent education programs, and teacher in-service presentations are examples of activities that could be observed to assess instructional and communication skills. These activities usually have an instructional or informational purpose without the element of personal, confidential relationships. Sometimes observations could occur during helping relationships, such as in parent or teacher consultations, but these must be carefully planned and permission of all participants is recommended.

Stronge and Helm (1991) reviewed two types of observations used in gathering data with specialists such as school counselors. These include *systematic observations,* which are structured, planned observations of a specific activity that usually focus on a particular skill or practice agreed upon by the supervisor and counselor prior to the observation. The second type of observation, *incidental observation,* is less structured and more informal. Incidental observations might include a counselor's interactions with students and staff in the office, conversations in the hallways, participation at faculty meetings, and exchanges with administrators. The focus on these types of observations should be on factual data and information that has some bearing on the counselor's performance of one or more of the major functions. When incidental information has little or no relationship to essential practices, cannot be documented by formal observations, and cannot be altered through additional training or other assistance, it should not be part of a school counselor's evaluation.

Audio and Video Taping   When an observation would be an intrusion to the helping relationship, other evaluation methods are recommended. An alternative method of collecting information is through the use of video or audio taping. In their training, school counselors use video and audio taping to demonstrate command of basic helping skills and these same methods are available to supervisors and counselors in assessing performance on the job. When tapes are used as part of the evaluation process, clients need to grant permission and understand how these tapes will be used. With young children, elementary school counselors should seek parental permission because of the uncertainty, in a legal sense, of the child's ability to give permission (Schmidt, 1990).

Supervisors who listen to or watch tapes to assess performance and assist counselors' with their professional development should be highly trained in the skills they attempt to evaluate. Supervisors who are untrained, such as school principals, are able to offer little assistance and guidance in helping counselors identify specific areas that need further development. Since a major purpose of performance appraisal is to help individuals identify areas for professional growth and development, supervisors who are unable to provide this information offer little assistance. Such as assessment process is, at best, incomplete.

Interviews   Another method of gathering information about a counselor's performance is to interview the counselor about program plans, specific services, and student outcomes. The most effective use of interviews is with a structured format to focus on specific issues, skills, or other aspects of the school counseling program. A general interview without such a specific focus will not generate clear information with which to assess strengths and weaknesses. In addition, a single interview may not be sufficient. Ideally, a series of structured interviews about the same topic may be the most desirable format.

Simulations At times when observations are inappropriate and taping is impractical, counselors and supervisors may find that simulated sessions are adequate for gathering information. An example of using simulations is when counselors want to demonstrate appropriate student appraisal skills in individual testing situations. It would be awkward for an observer to actually sit in on such a testing session, and would jeopardize validity of the results. By asking a student or other person to participate in a "practice" test situation, counselors illustrate proper testing procedures, and the observation does not interfere with actual testing. In this instance, the test session and results do not count for the person who volunteers to be tested. Hence, the observer is less intrusive and does not risk influencing the testing results. Yet, the counselor is able to demonstrate appropriate testing skills and knowledge of published practices.

Self-assessments In some respects, an evaluation may be incomplete without the counselor's perspective. An honest self-assessment can assist the supervisor and counselor in identifying initial areas of focus for annual performance appraisal. The American School Counselor Association (ASCA) has published three self-audit manuals to help counselors with this assessment process: *Profession Development Guidelines for Secondary School Counselors: A Self-Audit* (ASCA, 1986), *Professional Development Guidelines for Middle/Junior High School Counselors: A Self-Audit* (ASCA, 1990), and *Professional Development Guidelines for Elementary School Counselors: A Self-Audit* (ASCA, 1990).

Self-assessment processes enable counselors to identify their own strengths and weaknesses and fully recognize these aspects of their professional practice. By identifying areas for further development, counselors are in a stronger position to seek assistance, both supervisory and financial, and develop plans of action to improve their performance. In addition, self-assessment procedures allow counselors to gather evidences of appropriate and adequate practice to share with supervisors and evaluators during performance appraisal conferences throughout the evaluation cycle.

Products School counselors create many products and reports for their schools and programs. These items can be assessed as part of the overall performance appraisal process. Specific competencies that might be addressed by examining materials and reports produced by school counselors include: writing, program planning, and public relations. Examples of products that counselors and supervisors might review are: the annual plan for the school counseling program, brochures developed to advertise specific services, evaluation forms designed to assess program functions, sample memos to teachers, and letters to parents.

Counselors also develop instructional and information materials to use in classroom guidance, group counseling, and other services with students, parents, and teachers. These materials demonstrate a counselor's knowledge of developmental stages, understanding of how to use various media in different activities, and creativity in designing useful materials for presentations. Such materials should be included in the assessment process.

Consumer Feedback Earlier, you learned about the importance of asking students, parents, and teachers for feedback in evaluating specific functions and activities of the school counseling program. These observations are also valuable in helping counselors assess their performance. Figure 10–5, presented earlier, is an example of how student feedback can be used to assess a specific program function as well as a counselor's performance.

Sometimes, as noted in the section on program evaluation, consumer feedback is received incidentally by counseling supervisors, school principals, and counselors. These informal and often unsolicited comments and suggestions about a school counselor's performance are useful when they provide reliable information, are supported by documented evidence, and can be realistically acted on to bring about appropriate change (Schmidt, 1990). Feedback that is heard infrequently or contradicts other overwhelming evidence to the contrary is less useful. If supervisors and principals cannot validate and support incidental feedback with their own observations or other data, it is unwise to use such information in the performance appraisal process. Finally, if incidental feedback is used in counselor evaluation, the implication is that some action to remedy a negative situation or reward a positive report will be taken. If no action is possible, incidental feedback should not be included in the evaluation process.

Schedules and Records The school counselor's role is described as a planned program consisting of varied activities to assist specific populations in achieving identified goals. If this is true, then part of an evaluation should include the plans counselors write, the goals they set, the schedules they make, and the records they keep. Of all these evidences, records are ones that may be most difficult to include in the performance appraisal process. Because many of the relationships counselors form with clients are confidential in nature, opening up records to a supervisor or principal is inappropriate unless specific constraints are set and guidelines are followed.

There are two types of records counselors can share as part of their performance appraisal process, if they take the necessary precautions. These include records of decisions made regarding the type of services to be provided and records of outcomes of services rendered. In all cases when counselors share these types of records, the client's identification must be deleted and the anonymity of the client maintained. The purpose of sharing these types of data is not to find out *who* has received services, but rather to assess *what* concerns have been addressed by the counselor, *why* the counselor chose certain services and techniques in assisting with these concerns, and *what* were the results of the services provided. By reviewing these kinds of service and outcome records, a supervisor can advise and support the school counselor about clinical and program decisions he or she has made. It is through these evaluation processes that the counselor and supervisor are able to assess diagnostic skills and decision-making processes used to determine services for students, parents, and teachers.

Personnel Memos   Finally, others documents to include in performance appraisal are memoranda used to cite specific instances where a counselor has not met a performance standard (Stronge & Helm, 1991). Memoranda such as these are used when counselors perform in unsatisfactory ways and a plan for improvement must be established and carried out. In cases where a plan for improvement does not ultimately result in satisfactory performance, personnel action to terminate or reassign a counselor may be necessary. Memos of visits, conferences, and plans of action, as well as other documents filed during this phase of the performance appraisal process, are essential in protecting the rights of the individual counselor, assuring the integrity of the school counseling program, and verifying support offered by the supervisor and school system to remedy the situation.

Who Will Evaluate?

The last question to consider in designing a performance appraisal process for school counselors is, who will do the evaluation? In most instances, school counselors report directly to building principals who are ultimately responsible for the counselor's evaluation. This reality is a dilemma for both the counselor and principal who want to create reliable and valid performance appraisal processes. Generally speaking, school principals have little or no training in the practices and competencies that have been identified as essential functions of professional school counselors. The "efficacy of counselor performance appraisals is jeopardized when critical functions cannot be adequately assessed so that strengths can be recognized and weaknesses remediated" (Schmidt, 1990, p. 91). Given this caveat, the challenge is to find ways that counselors can receive appropriate supervision and accurate evaluation for the services they provide in schools (Borders & Leddick, 1987).

Among all the essential services counselors offer in school settings, most can be assessed by competent observers and evaluators who have little or no training in counseling skills. A qualified principal who understands the broad purpose of students services, including counseling services, will be able to assess a counselor's ability to plan a comprehensive program. At the same time, an effective administrator should be able to assess general employee behaviors such as punctuality, staff relationships, and communication skills. Where a school principal or other non-counselor may have difficulty in performing adequate performance appraisal is in those skills and competencies unique to the counseling profession. These skills include student assessment competencies particularly in the area of tests and measurement, understanding of counseling theory and techniques, and consulting processes. Occasionally, principals may have adequate training in some of these areas, but most training programs in educational administration are not oriented towards theories of human development and basic helping skills. For this reason, effective models of counselor performance appraisal should include observations, interviews, and other methods of collecting and analyzing data by trained supervisors of school counseling programs (Schmidt, 1990).

One way to create appropriate performance appraisal procedures is for principals and counseling supervisors to cooperatively participate in the evaluation of school counselors. In such cooperative models, principals and supervisors jointly assess the counselor and combine their talents in offering sufficient program supervision. By designing a collaborative model for counselor evaluation, schools assure that administrative supervision by principals is adequate, while at the same time they encourage appropriate clinical and technical supervision and support from qualified counseling supervisors.

In many school systems, the luxury of having a trained supervisor of counselors is unrealistic due to fiscal restraints. In such cases, other models of supervision should be explored. These models might include peer supervision approaches where "lead counselors" in a school district assume supervisory duties to help their peers assess clinical and technical performance. Other models include the use of counselor educators from neighboring colleges and universities to assist with counselor supervision, or contracts with counselors in private practice who consult with counselors and principals in designing adequate performance appraisal processes. The goal in all these alternative approaches is to design evaluation processes that help counselors improve their services and enhance their professional development.

All methods of gathering data to assess counselor performance have value when used for professional improvement, and when they are collected and analyzed by competent evaluators. In part, the competency of the evaluator is either enhanced or diminished by the validity of the processes and instruments used in the assessment process.

Performance Appraisal Processes and Instruments

School counselors not only assist in the development of appropriate procedures for their performance appraisal, they also participate in designing adequate tools with which to do an accurate assessment. Specifically, the instruments designed to gather data for school counselor performance appraisal should relate to particular areas of counselor training and practice as well as job expectations. For example, an instrument created to evaluate a counselor's skill in group counseling is of little benefit if the school inhibits the scheduling and use of group procedures. By the same token, an instrument normally used to observe teachers in classroom instruction is useless in assessing individual counseling sessions. Instruments designed to evaluate counseling services must be related to specific approaches and behaviors that are generally accepted as indicators of a particular professional practice.

The first step in designing adequate and appropriate instruments is to identify the essential services expected of a school counselor. After this is done, the counselor, supervisor, principal, and other appropriate people can begin to list specific practices that should be observed if these services are to be judged as being performed at a satisfactory level. Earlier in this chapter you learned about survey and other evaluation methods to gather data for program evaluation. Similar instruments can be designed or adapted to gather information about a counselor's performance. Figure 10–6 is a sample of an observation instrument designed to assess a counselor's group presentation skills in classroom guidance, parent education programs, or teacher in-service training. Implicit in this instrument is the understanding that the observer/evaluator who uses the instruments is trained and skilled in these instructional methods and facilitative practices.

Although some counseling practices are more difficult to assess by observation, with client permission it is possible to do so and appropriate instruments can be designed. The interview method described earlier is one way of avoiding the difficulties of observing confidential relationships. A trained supervisor of counseling programs, for example, could plan a structured interview with a counselor about individual counseling services in the program. By using a series of short, structured interviews, the supervisor is able to give constructive feedback about the counselor's use of assessment and diagnostic procedures, knowledge of counseling approaches, and understanding of the helping process. While such interviews will not help in

Large Group Observation Form[1]

Instructions: Use this form to observe the school counselor when presenting group instructional or informational sessions. Record the counselor's behaviors during the presentation by using the observation code below and through any additional comments you may have.

Observation Code: * Appropriate use of practice
+ Strong indication of practice
- Weak or negative use of practice
N/O Not Observed

****

COMPETENCIES & PRACTICES   OBSERVATIONS

1.   USE OF TIME
1.1 Has all materials ready for presentation
1.2 Begins the presentation on time   _____
1.3 Uses presentation time efficiently   _____
1.4 Ends the presentation on schedule   _____
                                                                    _____

Comments: _____

2.   INSTRUCTIONAL PRESENTATION
3.1 States purpose and makes goals clear to group
3.2 Gives clear instructions and directions   _____
3.3 Speaks clearly   _____
3.4 Listens to group members' comments and opinions   _____
3.5 Uses appropriate group skills (e.g. questioning, structuring, linking, etc.)   _____
3.6 Remains open to comments and suggestions from group members   _____
3.7 Uses appropriate media and instructional methods for the presentation   _____
3.8 Summarizes main points of presentation   _____
                                                                    _____

Comments: _____

3.   GROUP BEHAVIOR AND MANAGEMENT
2.1 Encourages participation of all group members
2.2 Maintains participants' attention   _____
2.3 Demonstrates appropriate group management skills   _____
2.4 Respects the individuality of participants   _____
                                                                    _____

Comments: _____

4.   LEADER RESPONSES
4.1 Affirms group members
4.2 Reinforces participants' willingness to share   _____
4.3 Answers questions clearly and concisely   _____
4.4 Gives feedback to all participants when appropriate   _____
                                                                    _____

Comments: _____

5.   GROUP OUTCOMES
5.1 Asks participants for feedback during presentation   _____
5.2 Uses evaluation measures and methods to assess outcomes   _____

Comments: _____

****

[1] Adapted from the *Counselor Group Presentation Observation Instrument* developed by John J. Schmidt, Ed.D. for the North Carolina State Department of Public Instruction, Raleigh, NC, 1988.

FIGURE 10–6   Counselor Observation Form for Group Presentatiions

assessing specific counseling skills and techniques, they do provide information about the counselor's knowledge and use of specific approaches to counseling. From such an assessment, a supervisor may decide whether or not specific counseling skills need to be evaluated more thoroughly by observation or through audio/video taping. Figure 10–7 illustrates a sample questionnaire designed to assess a counselor's use of individual counseling.

When counselors evaluate their programs of services, there are many processes and methods available to them in formulating goals, planning new strategies, and refocusing their programs. No single method of assessment is ever adequate in gathering data to make these critical decisions. In performance appraisal of school counselors, this caution is even more criti-

---

Instructions: This structured interview form may be used to ask the counselor about specific individual counseling relationships. Ideally, the questionnaire should be used in a series of interviews about the same case.

1. Understanding of client's concerns, and appropriate use of diagnostic methods and procedures.

    Question: Tell me about the concerns of the student you are seeing. How does the student perceive the main issues, problems, and areas of concern?

    Question: Describe the assessment procedures you have used and how the results of these methods led you to decide on the intervention(s) you have chosen for this student.

2. Understanding of the helping process and the stages of a counseling relationship.

    Question: Where are you and the student in your relationship at this point? Relate the progress you have made to the phases of a helping relationship.

    Question: Given the nature of the student's concerns, are you satisfied with where the helping relationship is at this point?

3. Knowledge of counseling approaches and techniques.

    Question: Tell me about specific techniques, strategies, and interventions you have used in this counseling relationship.

    Question: What was the rationale for choosing these approaches?

4. Use of evaluation methods to assess progress.

    Question: How much longer do you expect to be seeing this student?

    Question: What are your goals for the remainder of the counseling relationship?

    Question: What methods do you plan to use to evaluate the overall success of this intervention?

FIGURE 10–7   Structured Interview of Counseling Relationship

cal. Because the instruments and processes for evaluating counselor performance are at best primitive, great care should be taken to resist forming firm conclusions without ample evidence. School counselor performance appraisal, ethically and legally, must provide the best reasonable processes and instruments to judge a counselor's effectiveness. The school counselor who is being evaluated shares this responsibility with the building principal, the counseling supervisor, and any other person involved in the process.

By ensuring adequate evaluation of school counseling programs and of the competencies demonstrated by counselors, school counselors and those responsible for their supervision behave in professionally ethical and responsible ways. Ethical behaviors, and legal issues surrounding the practice of counseling in school settings, are the topics addressed in the next chapter of this text.

Selected Readings

Borders, L. D., & Leddick, G. R. (1987). *Handbook of Counseling Supervision.* (Alexandria, VA. Association for Counselor Education and Supervision). This handbook is a handy reference for counselors and supervisors about major issues surrounding counselor supervision and evaluation. It offers a broad overview of theories and models of counselor supervision.

Stronge, J. H., & Helm, V. M. (1991). *Evaluating Professional Support Personnel in Education* (Newbury Park, CA: Sage). This text gives the reader a comprehensive view of the issues and problems involved in performance appraisal of non-teaching personnel, such as school counselors. It provides a conceptual framework for evaluating school counselors and other student services professionals.

References

American School Counselor Association. (1986). *Professional Development Guidelines for Secondary School Counselors: A Self-Audit* (Alexandria, VA: Author).

American School Counselor Association (1990). *Professional development guidelines for middle/junior high school counselors: A self-audit* (Alexandria, VA: Author).

American School Counselor Association. (1990). *Professional Development guidelines for Elementary School Counselors: A Self-Audit* (Alexandria, VA: Author).

Atkinson, D. R., Furlong, M., & Janoff, D. S. (1979), "A Four-Component Model for Proactive Accountability in School Counseling," *The School Counselor, 26,* 222–228.

Aubrey, R. F. (1982), "Program Planning and Evaluation: Road Map of the 80s," *Elementary School Guidance and Counseling, 17,* 52–60.

Baruth, L. G., Robinson, E. H. (1987). *An Introduction to the Counseling Profession* (Englewood Cliffs, NJ: Prentice Hall).

Borders, L. D., & Leddick, G. R. (1987). *Handbook of Counseling Supervision* (Alexandria, VA: Association for Counselor Education and Supervision).

Breckenridge, A. (1987), "Performance Improvement Program Helps Administrators Assess Counselor Performance," *NASSP Bulletin, 71,* 23–26.

Crabbs, S. K., & Crabbs, M. A. (1977), "Accountability: Who Does What to Whom, When, Where, and How?" *The School Counselor, 25,* 104–109.

Fairchild, T. N. (1986), "Time Analysis: Accountability Tool for Counselors," *The School Counselor, 34,* 36–43.

Ficklen, E. (1987), "Why School Counselors are So Tough to Manage and Evaluate," *The Executive Educator, 9,* 19–20.

Gibson, R. L., & Mitchell, M. H. (1990). *Introduction to Guidance and Counseling,* 3rd ed. (New York: Macmillan).

Gorton, R., & Ohlemacher, R. (1987), "Counselor Evaluation: A New Priority for the Principal's Agenda," *NASSP Bulletin, 71,* 120–124.

Gysbers, N. C., & Henderson, P. (1988). *Developing and Managing your School Guidance Program* (Alexandria, VA: American Association for Counseling and Development).

Hohenshil, T. H. (1981), "The Future of the Counseling Profession: Three Issues," *Personnel and Guidance Journal, 60,* 133–134.

Housley, W. F., McDaniel, L. C., & Underwood, J. R. (1990), "Mandated Assessment of Counselors in Mississippi," *The School Counselor, 37,* 294–302.

Krumboltz, J. D. (1974), "An Accountability Model for Counselors," *Personnel and Guidance Journal, 52,* 639–646.

Lombana, J. H. (1985), "Guidance Accountability: A New Look at an Old Problem," *The School Counselor, 32,* 340–346.

Myrick, R. D. (1987). *Developmental Guidance and Counseling: A Practical Approach* (Minneapolis, MN: Educational Media Corporation).

Purkey, W. W., & Schmidt, J. J. (1987). *The Inviting Relationship: An Expanded Perspective for Professional Counseling* (Englewood Cliffs, NJ: Prentice Hall).

Schmidt, J. J. (1984), "Counselor Intentionality: An Emerging View of Process and Performance," *Journal of Counseling Psychology, 31,* 383–386.

Schmidt, J. J. (1986), "Becoming an "Able" Counselor," *Elementary School Guidance and Counseling, 21,* 16–22.

Schmidt, J. J. (1990), "Critical Issues for School Counselor Performance Appraisal and Supervision," *The School Counselor, 38,* 86–94.

Schmidt, J. J. (1991). *A survival Guide for the Elementary/Middle School Counselor* (West Nyack, NY: The Center for Applied Research in Education).

Stronge, J. H., & Helm, V. M. (1991). *Evaluating Professional Support Personnel in Education* (Newbury Park, CA: SAGE Publications).

11

Professional Ethics and Legal Issues

As with other helping professionals, school counselors practice according to standards, regulations, laws, and codes established by professional associations, state and federal governmental bodies, the courts, and other institutions. School counselors make decisions about correct services and proper conduct based on current literature, research findings, training standards, certification criteria, federal and state laws, local school board policies, administrative regulations, and professional ethics. The ethical guidelines followed by most school counselors are the *Ethical Standards for School Counselors* adopted by the American School Counselor Association (1984, 1992) (see Appendix A) and the *Ethical Standards of the American Association for Counseling and Development* (Herlihy & Golden, 1990).

By themselves, ethical standards do not always provide clear choices for counselors to avoid conflict, make the best decisions for all involved, or maintain freedom from legal entanglement. They are, as their name implies, *guides* to professional practice, which counselors must apply to individual situations using their own personal and professional judgment. Ethical standards serve as a broad framework within which counselors interpret situations, understand legal and professional implications, and make reasonably sound judgments in assisting clients. As such, these standards "present only a rationale for ethical behavior that can be difficult to apply to specific situations" (Engels, Wilborn, & Schneider, 1990, p. 115). For this reason, it is essential that school counselors have a clear understanding of their professional standards, acquire knowledge of local, state and federal policies, and stay abreast of legislation that governs schools and counseling practices.

In this chapter, we examine the ethical standards developed by the American School Counselor Association and consider legal issues related to the ethical practice of school counseling. In some respects, the ethical issues school counselors face today are similar to ethical dilemmas of their predecessors twenty years ago (Christiansen, 1972). Confidentiality, testing procedures, use of school records, and appropriate referral processes remain critical issues for school counselors today, just as they were for counselors more than two decades earlier. For example, contemporary school counselors struggle with the challenge of how to maintain helpful, trusting relationships with students who exhibit antisocial behaviors, while at the same time, attempting to serve school and society. They balance the goal of helping individual students with the understandable need for parents to be involved in educational decisions regarding their children. At the same time, counselors in schools are concerned about maintaining professional relationships with community agencies, classroom teachers, and others who have a vested interest in the education of children and adolescents.

Today's ethical issues are complicated by ever-changing social structures and a technologically advancing society. So, while broad topics are similar to those of years past, contemporary school counselors experience increasingly complex issues when dealing with ethical and legal questions. As one illustration, changing family structures make parent's rights difficult to ascertain. In a blended family, for example, where stepparents have custodial responsibilities and natural parents share legal custody, decisions about who has access to school records, who can see a child at school, and what permissions schools need to talk to family members about a child's progress are not easily defined.

The explosion of computer technology has also added a new dimension to ethical practice (Ibrahim, 1985; Sampson, 1990). Increased accessibility to students' records, use of computer-assisted instructional programs, and the need for adequate training of counselors in the use of computer technology are a few areas of concern. Counselors who use computers to maintain records, present computer-assisted instruction, administer computer-scored inventories, and manage data for a comprehensive school counseling program must be knowledgeable of ethical guidelines and aware of legal parameters within which to utilize this expanding technology. There is no end to the computer applications envisioned for the future. As a result, knowledge of ethical standards and legal precedent will continue to be a necessary condition of professional practice.

With all these considerations of present and future situations, the first step for school counselors to take in understanding their ethical responsibilities and in learning about how these obligations influence daily practice is to embrace a particular professional code of conduct. As mentioned earlier school counselors generally are guided by the ethical standards of the American Counseling Association and, specifically, by the standards of the American School Counselor Association (ASCA, 1984). For the purposes of this text, the ASCA standards are presented as the foundation and framework for the ethical practice of school counseling.

Ethical Standards of School Counselors

Ethical standards provide the framework for professional practice and responsible behavior, and at the same time contribute to the identity of the particular profession that is governed by these measures of conduct. The standards themselves are not absolute guides for every decision school counselors must make in their daily practice. Instead, they are general guidelines that enable counselors to establish a foundation of ethical behavior. In serving clients, assessing needs, sharing information, and performing the wide array of services expected of them, counselors must search for additional guidance to complement their knowledge and understanding of ethical guides and legal restraints. Mabe and Rollin (1986) cautioned that "A responsible member of the counseling profession must look to various sources for guidance. We fear that many professions may see a code of ethics as the sole basis for explicating responsibility for its members" (p. 294). While an ethical code of conduct plays a central role in defining a professional's responsibilities, it is not a sufficient guide. As such, part of a school counselor's responsibilities is to understand the limits of the profession's standards of ethical behavior and supplement one's knowledge of sound ethical and legal practices with information from many resources and learning activities. Several sources are available to assist counselors in acquiring this understanding, including workshops, conferences, and publications. Some comprehensive texts and readings of the strengths and limitations of professional codes are: *Ethical and Legal Issues in School Counseling* (Huey & Remley, 1988), *Issues and Ethics in the Helping Professions* (Corey, Corey, & Callanan, 1988), *Ethical Standards Casebook* (Herlihy & Golden, 1990).

In addition to serving the three major populations of students, parents, and teachers, school counselors are responsible for carrying out assignments delegated to them by school principals and counseling supervisors. In performing these functions, school counselors work with other professionals, such as school social workers, nurses, and psychologists, as well as professionals in the community. The responsibilities associated with such a wide range of clients and professionals make it necessary to delineate ethical guidelines according to different areas of accountability and service. For this reason, the ethical standards put forth by ASCA are divided according to the counselor's responsibilities with students, parents, other professionals, the school, the counseling profession, and oneself. By aligning these different responsibilities enumerated in the ASCA code with guidelines from the ethical standards of the American Association for Counseling and Development, school counselors develop a broader understanding of how their profession views ethical behavior and professional practice.

In the following sections, the responsibilities outlined by the ASCA ethical standards are used to define and explain the ethical practice of school counselors. Appendix A at the end of this text may be used as a reference as you read these sections. In addition, you may want to locate other professional codes of ethical conduct, such as those for school social workers and school psychologists, and compare them to the standards for school counselors. The first area of ethical behavior for school counselors addresses their responsibilities to students.

Responsibilities to Students

School counselors have primary responsibility for ensuring that their counseling services and the educational program of the school consider the total development of every student, including students' educational, vocational, personal, and social development. Counselors accept responsibility for informing students about the purposes and procedures involved in counseling relationships, and use appropriate assessment and diagnostic techniques and strategies in determining which services to provide.

The ethical guidelines state that school counselors should avoid imposing their values on counselees, and, as such, should encourage students to explore their own values and beliefs in making decisions about educational plans and life goals. This responsibility is not an easy task. Counselors, too, have strong values and in dealing with young people, particularly minors in a school setting, these "convictions are not readily pushed aside or effectively concealed. Attempting to deny a position or to try to ignore values may undermine the trust necessary for a productive counseling relationship" (Huey, 1986, p. 321). The challenge for school counselors is to balance their views with the goals and purposes of the helping relationship as understood by the student. In this way, counselors may find it appropriate to express their views and allow students to consider these opinions while broadening their available options. Note that we see a distinct difference between the process of expressing one's views and that of imposing one's values. When a counselor's values and views are so strongly opposed to those of the student's that a healthy and helpful relationship is impossible, the counselor is obliged to assist the student in finding another professional with whom a beneficial relationship can be established. Ethically, the counselor must assist with this referral.

The ethical standards stipulate that school counselors will protect the confidentiality of students' records and information received from students in counseling relationships. In practice, the concept of confidentiality and its limitations are explained to students at the beginning of a helping relationship. Due to the age levels of students they serve, school counselors are in a unique position regarding confidentiality. Legally, the courts have not always recognized that minors have the capacity to understand and establish confidential helping relationships (Corey, Corey, & Callanan, 1988). For this reason, school counselors not only need to be aware of their professional code of ethics, they also need to know their legal responsibilities regarding confidentiality. To begin, counselors want to know the difference between confidentiality and privileged communication.

The term *confidentiality* refers to the individual's right to privacy that is inherent in professional counseling relationships. The necessity for and appropriateness of confidentiality are expressed in ethical standards of conduct. By contrast, *privileged communication* is a legal term used to indicate that a person is protected from having confidential information revealed in a public hearing or court of law. As such, confidentiality is established in an agreement between the school counselor and student when they form a helping relationship. Privileged communication on the other hand is granted to students by states that have laws protecting the confidences students share in relationships with their school counselors.

In 1987, only 20 of the United States granted some form of privileged communication rights to students in school counseling relationships (Sheeley & Herlihy, 1987). School counselors need not only follow their ethical codes regarding confidentiality, but also be aware of statutes granting students the right of privileged communication. Where statutes exist, counselors want to know the limitations of these laws and be aware that it is the student, not the counselor, who is protected. For example, in North Carolina and Ohio statues grant privileged communication to students except when a judge in court requires disclosure (Sheeley & Herlihy, 1987). At the same time, students may waive their right to privilege communication in which case a counselor has no basis for withholding information that is requested. Some states provide for parental involvement in decisions of whether or not to waive privileged communication, so school counselors should be aware of what the state laws say regarding parent permissions.

An additional note regarding confidentiality and privileged communication pertains to consulting relationships and group processes. Generally, courts have not recognized privileged communications beyond two people. Therefore, when a counselor shares information with a third party, or students self-disclose in group counseling, these confidences may or may not be protected by state statutes. Often, this will be resolved by a judge's opinion in a court of law.

A final consideration about confidential student counseling relationships relates to situations that indicate a clear and imminent danger to a student or to others. When students share information indicating their intentions to harm themselves or others, or when they, themselves, are being abused, counselors cannot keep this information confidential. Sadly, sometimes children and adolescents are forced into abusive situations that include physical harm, sexual assault, emotional or physical neglect, and psychological harassment. Counselors are obligated to learn about laws and procedures governing the reporting of child abuse and neglect, and to fulfill their responsibilities as outlined by such statutes and regulations (Morrow, 1987). In cases of abuse and neglect and instances of imminent danger to students, school counselors must break confidence and report to appropriate authorities. Protection of the student is imperative, so timely reports are essential, and, in cases of potential suicide, the security of students is paramount (Sheeley & Herlihy, 1989).

Responsibilities to Parents

As indicated in an earlier chapter, counselors sometimes form helping relationships with parents in either counseling or consulting roles. Most if not all of the guidelines in Section A, Responsibilities to Students, of the ASCA ethical standards can be adapted to these helping relationships. Informing parents of the purposes and procedures to be followed and maintaining confidences are practices that apply to helping relationships established with parents as well as with students.

Section B of the ASCA standards pertains specifically to counselors' responsibilities for informing parents about services available to students, and involving parents when appropriate. While the ethical responsibility for maintaining confidentiality between a counselor and student may be understood, the legal responsibility of counselors to involve parents in their helping relationships is not as clear (Huey, 1986). These differences between ethical practice and legal requirements sometimes confuse counselors and place them in precarious positions of deciding whether to protect children's rights or please parents.

Generally, school counselors can avoid some of these entanglements by keeping parents informed of the services provided in their counseling programs, making program brochures available to parents, and using other media to advertise services and develop an open dialogue with parents (Schmidt, 1991). Counselors who open communications with parents and speak freely about the types of services they offer to students in schools are in a stronger position to win the confidence of parents and protect the privacy of students at the same time.

In school counseling practice, particularly at the primary and elementary school grades, parental involvement is essential. For this reason, school counselors encourage students in counseling relationships to give permission to involve their parents or guardians at an appropriate time. In many ways, the success of child and adolescent counseling depends on the degree to which parents become involved, are able to alter their own behaviors, and assist their children in achieving educational, career, personal, and social goals. Typically, very young children do not have sufficient control of their lives to make decisions and take the necessary steps toward changing problematic situations. In these cases, parental support is imperative.

Encouraging parental involvement and seeking a student's permission to release information and facilitate this involvement is a delicate matter. Again, counselors search for a balance between their legal obligations and ethical responsibilities. There is no single guideline to direct counselors toward the correct path on every occasion. Each situation is unique because ethical guides are influenced by counselor judgments, and laws are subject to different interpretations. A key element in making sense of counseling relationships and choosing a course of action that protects the student while facilitating communication between the home and school is for school counselors to weigh all aspects and *make a decision*. The counselor who most often falters is not the one who takes reasonable, responsible action and justifies his or her behavior based on ethical standards and legal precedent. Rather, the counselor who most likely errs is one who chooses to do *nothing* out of fear of making a mistake.

Finally, responsibilities to parents include the practice of providing accurate and objective information. By doing so, counselors share assessment data, school policies, and other information in an equitable and objective manner to strengthen parents' understanding of their children's needs and the services available to help students progress in school. Accordingly, counselors are obliged to share information about services in the school and community accurately and fairly without bias or discrimination.

Responsibilities to Colleagues and Professional Associates

In this text, you have read that comprehensive school counseling programs consist of a wide range of services provided and coordinated by school counselors. Earlier chapters presented information about the counselor's responsibilities in collaborating with other professionals in the school system and community. The ethical code of professional conduct addresses this area of school counseling by promoting the qualities of cooperation, fairness, respect, and objectivity. School counselors who function at a high level of ethical practice demonstrate regard and respect for the education profession and their teaching colleagues. A successful and effective school counseling program does not exist without cooperative relationships between and among teachers, administrators, and counselors.

In addition to the teachers and principals who assist counselors in developing and delivering beneficial services for students and parents, other educational specialists also cooperate with school counselors. As mentioned before, these professionals include school nurses, social workers, psychologists, and special education teachers. The services offered by these specialists are further expanded and complemented by services provided in community agencies and by private practitioners. School counselors function in an ethical fashion when they are aware of the availability of these services, judge the effectiveness of these services accurately, and use appropriate resources for the benefit of students, parents and teachers who need assistance beyond what the counselor is able to offer. By establishing collaborative relationships with a wide range of school and community specialists, school counselors avoid the possibility of overextending themselves and reduce the risk of delivering services beyond their level of competency (Schmidt, 1991).

Implied in this section of the ethical standards is the counselor's responsibility to be informed about the effectiveness of these additional sources of information and assistance. To achieve an informed level of professionals within the school as well as to agencies in the community. Determining the level of success another professional has had with a student, parent or teacher, and assessing the client's degree of satisfaction are essential follow-up processes to determine which professionals and agencies to use in the future. Ethical counselors, therefore, keep lines of communication open and within the limits set by confidentiality and privileged communication guidelines, share and receive information to assess services that have been provided. Through this continuous process of referral and evaluation, counselors are able to locate referral sources, professionals, and agencies that are knowledgeable, competent, and effective with the cases they accept from the school.

Responsibilities to the School and Community

Because school counselors focus primarily on the educational development of all students, they also have the responsibility of protecting the integrity of the curriculum and instructional program. Part of being a spokesperson for the welfare of students is accepting the role as an advocate for the educational mission of the school. When outside forces and special interests take students away from their primary purpose in school, counselors are among those who speak out against such infringement. Partly, this responsibility is fulfilled when counselors assess school climate and keep administrators and teachers informed of potential dangers to students' welfare, the instructional program, or the school environment. For example, a special program designed to offer remedial services to needy students may indirectly or unintentionally isolate these very students from the mainstream of school activity. Differentiating student services to this degree may detract from the broader goal of assisting students with their total development. School counselors who are visible in the school, participate in supervisory duties when appropriate, offer services to all students, and communicate regularly with their principals and supervisors are in a position to make assessments and share pertinent information about the school environment and the impact of special programs.

This section of the school counselor's ethical standards also addresses the importance of counselors defining and describing their role and functions in the school, and performing systematic evaluation of these services. An additional note is that school counselors should notify principals and supervisors when conditions in the school "limit or curtail their effectiveness in providing services" (American School Counselor Association, 1992, p. 15). This standard addresses a problem that many school counselors encounter in developing comprehensive programs of services; being asked to perform functions that prevent them from offering suitable direct services to students, parents, and teachers.

Because schools are inundated with tasks and expectations from the central office, state government, federal regulators, and other outside forces, school principals search for personnel to perform a variety of functions. Often these requests have little to do with the major roles for which these professionals were employed. For example, it is not uncommon to find classroom teachers completing paperwork, collecting money, filing forms, or performing other duties that have nothing to do with their instructional role in the school. Likewise, principals occasionally assign counselors clerical and administrative tasks that take them away from their primary functions of counseling and consulting with students, parents, and teachers. According to the ASCA ethical code, it is the counselor who is responsible for raising these issues with appropriate school officials. Sadly, too many school counselors become comfortable with forms, regulations, and administration, and unintentionally avoid contacts with students, parents, and teachers about issues that are emotional, psychological, and socially challenging. When this occurs, counselors lower their ethical standards and distance themselves from the school counseling profession.

A final word about responsibilities to the school and community pertains to counselor's motives for cooperating with other professionals and agencies on behalf of students. School counselors establish relationships with other professionals and agencies for the benefit of students, parents, and teachers without regard for their own interests. Hence, counselors do not accept reward or payment beyond the contracts negotiated with their school systems for services, direct or indirect, provided to school populations.

Responsibilities to Self

When reviewing ethical standards, we sometimes forget about the person who is expected to behave ethically. The school counselor's ethical guidelines address the need for counselors to behave within the boundary of their professional competencies and accept responsibility for the outcomes of their services. Counselors are obliged to choose approaches and use techniques for which they have adequate knowledge, training, and skill. To ensure this level of ethical practice, counselors keep abreast of issues and trends in counseling, attend conferences and workshops, return to graduate school, read professional journals, and choose other avenues to improve their performance and elevate their effectiveness.

A common dilemma for school counselors, which is related to this section of the standards, is deciding when to stop seeing a student in a counseling relationship and refer the student to another professional or agency. The ethical standards address this issue, but give little guidance about how to refer to another source for assistance. There no simple and clear answers to this question, but in setting their own guidelines counselors might ask themselves these questions (Schmidt, 1991, p. 249–250):

1. Do I have the knowledge and skills to help this student explore concerns, examine alternatives, make appropriate decisions, and act accordingly?

2. Is another professional, who is more able to help than I am, available and accessible to the student or other person needing services?

3. Should I involve the parents (or guardians) in this counseling relationship? What is my responsibility if the student refuses to give me permission to involve the parents?

4. If I continue to see this person (student, parent, or teacher) on a regular basis, will I be denying other students valuable services or neglecting other essential functions of my role in the school?

5. Is progress being made in this helping relationship, and can I demonstrate evidence of this progress?

Some students in schools need regular contact with a person in whom they can confide. In most of these instance, students do not require intensive counseling or therapy, they simply need a reliable relationship with someone who will listen and guide them toward appropriate decisions. School counselors who establish these relationships are careful to monitor students' progress in school and social groups, and evaluate the time they allow for these services in comparison to other functions they perform.

Responsibilities to the Profession

School counselors who belong to the American School Counselor Association and follow the ASCA standards accept responsibility for behaving in an exemplary fashion on behalf of their colleagues and the profession they represent. These exemplary behaviors include the research that counselors perform, their participation in professional associations, their adherence to local, state, and federal regulations, and the distinction they make between privately held views and views they espouse as school counseling representatives.

Counselors are responsible for conducting research and reporting their results in an appropriate manner that conforms with acceptable practice in educational and psychological research. In Chapter 10, you learned about program evaluation. The research counselors perform as part of their program evaluations, or through attempts to publish significant findings in professional journals, must be performed according to sound practices, and the results must be reported accurately.

Another area of professional responsibility is participation in counseling and educational associations. It is difficult for practicing school counselors to keep abreast of issues and trends in the profession without belonging to educational and counseling organizations. By belonging to and participating in these associations, counselors have access to current information through conferences, workshops, and professional publications. Counselors who participate in professional organizations, network with colleagues across the state or country, read current research about counseling practices, and assume leadership roles in counseling associations are in a stronger position to promote their profession and perform at a high level of ethical practice.

As mentioned earlier in this chapter, school counselors are sometimes confronted with legal regulations that make ethical practice more difficult. On the one hand, the ethical standards require adherence to local, state, and federal laws, while on the other hand, counselors are expected to protect the best interests of their clients. This dilemma is most apparent when schools establish policies without the best interests of students in mind. For example, when the convenience of a few faculty members or the importance of school maintenance take priority over student welfare, counselors need to intervene. In these cases, it is the counselor's own values and judgments that become most important as he or she chooses and delivers services. "Although the law and ethics share common elements, they are not synonymous. At times there may be conflicts between the two, and in these cases the values of the counselor come into the picture" (Corey, Corey, & Callanan, 1988, p. 4).

One last aspect of this section of the code addresses how counselors behave publicly, particularly when expressing their own personal and professional views. The standards require that counselors make a clear distinction between their own personal and private opinions and views expressed as representatives of the school counseling profession. Counselors should never make statements that portray their own views as being embraced by the profession of school counselors.

Maintenance of Standards

As members of a profession that adheres to a code of ethical standards, school counselors are responsible for seeing that the standards are followed, not only by themselves but by their professional colleagues, their supervisors, and the institutions which hire them. For this reason, when school counselors find they are forced to work under conditions that clearly violate these standards, they must take the necessary action to educate their superiors about this conflict and make alterations as deemed appropriate. When no changes are forthcoming, school counselors face the difficult decision of whether or not to remain in their present position without violating ethical practice.

In instances when a counselor observes a violation of ethical standards, the guidelines encourage the use of available avenues within the school and school system to bring this problem to the attention of appropriate persons. If attempts to resolve the situation go unheeded or are rejected, the counselor's next step is to refer to an appropriate ethics committee in a school counselor association; first at the local level, then at the state level, and finally, at the national association level. When school counselors receive information from a student, parent, or teacher about apparent unethical activity of a counseling colleague or other professional helper, they need to be clear about the nature of the complaint before determining a course of action (Marchant, 1987). For example, a counselor who receives a criminal complaint about a colleague, such as selling drugs, should contact local law enforcement officials. By contrast, a parent who confides that another school counselor routinely breaks confidentiality by reporting private information to the school principal is encouraged to first, "directly approach the colleague whose behavior is in question to discuss the complaint and seek resolution" (American School Counselor Association, 1992, p. 15). If such a resolution is not found, the counselor should use avenues established by the school and/or school system, and if still unresolved should make a report to the local counselor association. In most cases of reported violations, it is best for the person who has first-hand knowledge to make the report. In this way, school counselors need to support their clients in the reporting process (Marchant, 1987).

While ethical standards are the guidelines for appropriate practice established professional organizations, legal parameters are the policies and regulations set by governing agencies, statutes passed by legislatures, and ruling in courts of law. Ethical standards, as we have seen, "tend to be general and idealistic, seldom answering specific questions for the practitioner" (Remley, 1985, p. 181). Professional codes of conduct are necessary guides for school counselors, but they do not replace knowledge and understanding of local, state, and federal laws and regulations. In the remaining sections of this chapter, we examine some of the legal aspects of school counseling practice.

The Nature of Law

Schools are vital institutions in our society and as such reflect the legal standards demanded by the citizenry. In determining what these legal standards are, which ones apply to schools, and how they relate specifically to particular school programs and services, we first need to understand the nature of law.

In the United States, we have inherited a common-law tradition that evolves beyond the simple declaration of specific codes of conduct. This tradition includes a continuous process of developing legislation at different levels of local, state, and national government, interpreting these statutes through legislative and judicial processes, and compiling legal rulings that are derived from specific court cases. The latter of these, known as judge-made or *case law* and sometimes referred to as *common law*, evolves from the common thoughts and experiences of people in a society (Fischer & Sorenson, 1991). As such, the sources of laws in our society include: federal and state constitutions, statutes, case law, and common law. In addition, local school board policies and regulations, which must conform to state and federal laws, may also apply to the practice of school counseling: "Boards of education must, in devising rules and regulations for the administration of the schools, do so within the limits defined by the legislature and cannot exercise legislative authority" (Alexander & Alexander, 1985, p.3).

The Law and Schools

Many factors relate to the interpretation and application of law as it pertains to education and schools. When considering a particular legal issue involving education, counselors review pertinent court cases, local school board policies, state and federal laws, government regulations, and constitutional questions. All of these are sources of law in our society, and thus, they enable us to locate information and make appropriate decisions guided by current legal thinking. Because laws in U.S. society are created as the result of an evolving process, it is important that counselors consider all sources, not as absolute indications of what *must* be, but as origins of a particular law or guideline. By learning the background of law, counselors are better able to understand what needs to happen for law to change or be repealed.

It is noteworthy that one of most renowned educators, John Dewey, had significant influence on judicial proceedings and the development of law in this country. Fischer and Sorenson (1991) were "particularly persuaded by his description of law as a flexible and adaptable process, neither rigidly adhering to historically derived rules and principles nor ignoring their possible relevance and importance to current problems" (p. 3). As counselors practice in schools, they are continuously affected by past regulations, and when appropriate, they attempt to change these rules and guidelines to meet the needs of students, parents, and teachers. At the same time, school counselors seek a balance between legal requirements of their school boards, state legislatures, and federal government and the ethical standards of their profession. By having a clear understanding of the nature and history of law, counselors are in a stronger position to seek changes in regulations that conflict with ethical practice, or as the case may require, alter ethical guidelines to conform with legal precedent.

An initial source of legal information and understanding is the Constitution of the United States. While no mention of education or counseling is found in this historic document, it is clear that as the "supreme law of the land" this document supersedes all other local and state regulations. As such, all rules, regulations, policies, and laws set by local school boards, school administrators, county commissioners, state legislatures, and other bodies must be congruent with the Constitution. When they are not, they are invalid (Fischer & Sorenson, 1991). Counselors who have basic knowledge of educational law can assist their schools in developing appropriate policies and regulations that are consistent with constitutional requirements. This is particularly important in areas of student services that make use of school records, honor the right to privacy, and protect against discrimination.

Other sources of information to help counselors learn about the law are state statutes, local policy manuals, and legal briefs. School administrators, including principals, often subscribe to professional newsletters and other publications that summarize current legal rulings from court proceedings. In addition, general statutes pertaining to educational practice and schooling are often published by state governments as references for school personnel.

Local school board policy manuals are typically found in every building of a school system. In some cases, counselors may have their own copy.

In any event, school counselors must be fully aware of local policies and regulations, especially those that apply to counseling and other student services in the schools. Counselors want to be aware not only of written policies that may be in conflict with existing state or federal regulations, but also of policies that have been omitted from the school system's current manual, particularly those needed to protect students. An example of a policy that might be unknowingly omitted is a statement about the professional obligation and duty to report suspected child abuse. All states have laws regarding the duty to report suspected child abuse (Sandberg, Crabbs, Crabbs, 1988; Morrow, 1987). School systems support this legislation by developing clear policies and procedures to facilitate accurate and proper reporting in cases where abuse in suspected.

School counselors also obtain legal information and support from professional associations and attorneys who specialize in educational law, including their school board's attorney. In large school systems, counseling supervisors and directors are employed, and they assist in gathering information, planning workshops, and seeking legal guidance for counselors. As one example, school counselors are occasionally called to testify in child custody hearings, and workshops to advise them about appropriate actions to take as court witnesses, including how to handle confidential information when testifying as a school counselor, can be helpful. Actual material and information presented in these workshops may differ from state to state because statutes regarding confidentiality and privileged communication vary, but the important point is that these types of workshops inform counselors about their legal responsibilities.

Having access to pertinent information and receiving training in appropriate aspects of law help counselors practice within legal boundaries and gain knowledge about laws that may be problematic for the school and school system. One area of training and information that strengthens a counselor's knowledge of the law is learning about the court system and how case law affects educational practices.

The Courts

The legal system in the United States consists of both federal and state courts. Both levels of the legal system adjudicate criminal and civil cases, "but the jurisdiction of the federal courts is limited by the Constitution" (Fischer & Sorenson, 1991, p. 6). Federal courts hear only those cases pertaining to constitutional questions, such as equal protection under the law as granted by the Fourteenth Amendment of the Constitution. By contrast, state courts have broader responsibility for trying criminal and civil cases as well as those pertaining to federal and state constitutional issues.

When people raise legal questions regarding educational practice and regulation, these inquiries often involve federal issues. As a result, people may choose either the federal or state court system in which to initiate their cases. The plaintiffs and their counsel determine which court has jurisdiction over the matter to be litigated. Their selection of the appropriate court system is the first step in the judicial process.

State Courts   The fifty state court systems typically consist of four levels or categories of jurisdiction (Alexander & Alexander, 1985). These levels include district (or circuit) courts, courts of special jurisdiction, small claim courts, and appellate courts. Courts of special jurisdiction include domestic relations courts, probate courts, and juvenile courts. District courts generally have jurisdiction over all cases except those reserved for special courts. Small claims courts handle lawsuits involving small amounts of money, and in some states these cases are handled by justice of the peace courts. Appellate courts handle appeals of decisions that are ruled in lower courts of general jurisdiction. These appellate courts are called Courts of Appeals or Supreme Courts, and, in some large states, both Courts of Appeals and state Supreme Courts are found. The names used for the appellate courts are not uniform from state to state. As a result, in one state it may be called a Superior Court and in another the Court of Appeals. Furthermore, states with more than one appellate level are inconsistent in how they name these levels: "In New York State, for example, the lowest trial court of general jurisdiction is called the 'Supreme Court,' while the state's highest court is called the 'Court of Appeals'" (Fischer & Sorenson, 1991, p. 7).

Federal Courts   The federal court system of the United States consists of nearly 100 District Courts, Special Federal Courts, 13 Courts of Appeals, and the Supreme Court. Eleven of the 13 Courts of Appeals rule in the judicial circuits of the United States and its territories. One Court of Appeals deals with Washington, D.C. and another handles special copyright and patent issues. Each state has at least one federal District Court and the cases heard in these courts include: (1) issues between people from different states; and (2) litigation involving federal statutes or the Constitution (Alexander & Alexander, 1985). Special Federal Courts include courts in the District of Columbia, the Tax Court, the Customs Court, and the territorial courts among others.

When cases are appealed, they move from the trial courts that make up the U.S. District Court System to the Court of Appeals in the respective judicial circuit, and then to the Supreme court. In addition, a case in the state judicial system can move from the highest state court to the U.S. Supreme Court in the form of a *writ of certiorari*. When litigants lose their case at the state's highest level of appellate court, they may petition the U.S. Supreme

Court to hear the case. If four of the nine Supreme Court justices vote to review, the Court will issue a *writ of certiorari* to have the case sent forward. This usually happens when the constitutional validity of a state statute or federal law is questioned. "Since most school law cases fall within this category, the *writ of certiorari* is the most common means of getting a case before the Supreme Court" (Alexander & Alexander, 1985, p. 16).

School counselors who read about the case decisions of these various federal and state courts want to know the effect that particular decisions will have on their schools and the practice of counseling. Ultimately, the question is whether a particular decision will be binding on a particular state and school district. Decisions of lower federal courts are binding on only those states and territories within their own circuit. Similarly, decisions handed down by state courts are binding only on those specific states. While they are not legally binding beyond the jurisdiction of the ruling court, however, many state court and lower federal court decisions help set precedent and "are often considered persuasive in other jurisdictions" (Fischer & Sorenson, 1991, p. 8). Generally speaking, the decisions of the U.S. Supreme Court are binding in every state and territory.

School Board Policies

School districts have broad responsibility for developing and implementing regulations affecting schools within the limitations and guidelines set by state statutes. As noted earlier, at no time does an individual school or school system have authority to legislate beyond the limits defined by the state. For example, if a state statute grants privileged communication to students in counseling relationships, a school system cannot deny that privilege through local policy unless such authority is expressly permitted by state law.

Although school counselors want to be aware of state and federal court rulings and legislation regarding schools and the practice of professional counseling, most will be particularly concerned about specific policies and regulations passed by their local school boards and administrators. Practically speaking, these are the day-to-day regulations that guide a counselor's actions and occasionally contribute to ethical and legal dilemmas.

School counselors are responsible for being familiar with their local board policies and understanding how these regulations govern their programs of services for students, parents, and teachers. When policies seem to be in conflict with state laws, counselors are duty-bound to raise these issues. In most instances, the appropriate channels for such discussions would begin with school principals, counseling supervisors, and officers of state counseling associations.

A review of school board policies may reveal several areas of potential conflict, but there are particular areas of concern for most school counselors. These areas include students' rights to privacy, parents' rights, issues of sex equity, the use of school records, child abuse reporting, potential liability, and rights of handicapped students. We will consider each of these issues briefly in the next section.

Legal Issues for School Counselors

Many legal issues that arise in schools relate indirectly to practice of counseling because school counselors, as we have seen in this text, are responsible for a wide range of activities with which they serve all students. In this section, we review a few of the major topics involving legal issues and the practice of counseling in a school setting. Some of these issues are governed by local policies and others are regulated by state and federal laws. Counselors need to have appropriate background information about their school policies and district court rulings to make accurate decisions about these issues. Because court rulings frequently change the current thinking and existing policies regarding these issues, counselors need access to accurate, up-to-date information. Texts on school law, such as Fischer and Sorenson's *School Law for Counselors, Psychologists, and Social workers*, Second Edition (1991) are excellent resources. In addition, legal references such as the *Index to Legal Periodicals, Current Law Index*, the *Journal of Law and Education*, and *West's Education Law Reporter* are helpful resources of current court rulings.

Student's Rights

There are many aspects of students' rights related to schooling, and counselors should keep abreast of the latest rulings involving these issues. Some common issues include freedom of expression, the right to due process, appropriate/compensatory education, and the right to privacy. Of these, the most debated issue in the counseling profession is the student's right to privacy when involved in helping relationships with counselors. Earlier we considered the issue of confidentiality and its relationship to legal rights as granted by privileged communication statutes. School counselors need to know, from both an ethical as well as legal perspective, what rights are granted students in their states and by their schools.

Privacy rights are influenced by the nature of the confidential relationship and the age of the student. For example, current law suggests that students who seek information and guidance about abortion in counseling can expect their request to remain confidential, unless their state has a parental notification law. In which case, if the student is a minor, parental notification may be required. Some states require parental notification. In 1990, the U.S. Supreme Court upheld notification laws in two states, (*Ohio v. Akron*) and Minnesota (*Hodgson v. Minnesota* (Fischer & Sorenson, 1991).

Students' rights to privacy also affect policies regarding educational records and student searches. The *Family Educational Rights and Privacy Act of 1974* (FERPA) clarifies student and parent's rights regarding school records. This law, introduced in an earlier chapter, is explained in great detail later under the section titled *The Buckley Amendment*. In another area related to students' privacy, courts have restricted unreasonable searches of students in schools as further protection of their constitutional rights. Counselors want to be fully aware of the legal ruling regarding this issue so they know what constitutes a justified search of students or their property in schools.

Remley (1985) noted that the legal rights of young children in schools are at best uncertain. This may be particularly true when considering the issue of privacy. While school counselors have an ethical obligation of confidentiality with young students, they "often must involve adults in the problems of their clients who are minors. As a result, the child's expectation of privacy sometimes is outweighed by the need to inform parents, guardians, or other adults" (Remley, 1985, P. 184). In most instances, this is a judgment call by the counselor unless evidence of imminent danger or harm to the client, such as suspicion of abuse or suicidal revelations, exists. When counselors choose to inform and involve parents and guardians in helping relationships with students, it is advisable to inform students beforehand and include them in the process of notifying parents. There is a delicate balance that counselors must maintain between the duty to protect the rights of students and their ethical and legal responsibilities to respect the rights of parents and involve them in the education of their children (Schmidt, 1991).

Another area of students' rights, the right to due process, covers a range of issues from students discipline to minium competency testing (Fischer & Sorenson, 1991). Essentially, the intent of due process, as provided by the Fourteenth Amendment, is to protect students from actions and regulations that are inherently unfair. The Supreme Court case of *Goss v. Lopez* in 1975 set the precedent for defining due process and the types of procedures schools need to include in their disciplinary codes to protect students' rights. Procedural due process has subsequently come to include three basic elements: (1) the student must have proper notice about the regulations that have been violated; (2) the student must be given an opportunity for a hearing; and (3) the hearing must be conducted fairly (Alexander & Alexander, 1985).

A second type of due process, called substantive due process, requires the state to demonstrate a valid objective, and reasonable means for reaching this objective, when imposing restrictions or punishments. As such, substantive due process "requires that state officials not impose punishments that are arbitrary, capricious, or unfair" to students in schools (Fischer & Sorenson, 1991, p. 4). For example, a school that deprives a student access to an educational service for which the student qualifies simply because the parents have not kept scheduled appointments with the school might be demonstrating denial of substantive due process. Students have no control over the behaviors of their parents and should not be unfairly penalized for actions over which they have no control.

Parents' Rights

Schools rely on cooperative relationships with parents to provide the most beneficial and appropriate educational programs for children. For this reason, schools need to respect parents' rights in planning programs and making decisions for individual children and adolescents. Distinguishing the lines between students' rights, parents' rights, and the school's obligation to educate all children is not an easy task. This is particularly true when reviewing issues involving school counseling services (Schmidt, 1987).

Today's school counselors face an array of childhood, juvenile, and adult problems that require special relationships beyond the scope of educational and career guidance decisions. Substance abuse, family violence, sexual activity, and pregnancy are among the difficult issues school counselors confront with students. Knowing when and how to involve parents requires knowledge of current laws and clear understanding of local and state policies. A parent's right to be involved varies from case to case and from situation to situation. For example, if a child is in imminent danger of being harmed by someone, the school and counselor have an obligation to inform the parents. This course of action would change, however, if the parent is the suspected perpetrator who is physically abusing the child. In this and other cases of abuse, the school is obligated to report to the appropriate child protective services.

Generally, state and federal courts have ruled that schools have the authority to design educational curriculum and require students to participate in instructional programs (Alexander & Alexander, 1985). In certain instances, parents may object to their children's participation in particular activities, and based on objections, such as religious grounds, may ask that their children be excluded. To date, no judicial rulings have addressed specifically guidance and counseling activities and parents' rights to determine the appropriateness of these services for their children. As a result, school counselors are guided by state mandates and local board policies that may or may not include counseling services as an integral part of the educational program and school curriculum (Schmidt, 1987). Because the courts have ruled that parents have no constitutional right to derive children of an education (Alexander & Alexander, 1985), and, at the same time, have delegated to schools the responsibility of determining appropriate curriculum and educational services, access to school counseling services may fall within this broad area of students' rights How future courts will perceive this issue remains to be seen, but for now a critical condition would seem to be whether or not school counseling services are considered essential to the educational program and if written documents verify this relationship in the state and local system.

Laws and court rulings have helped to clarify some areas of parents' rights in schools. These include access to students' records when children are under the age of 18, and involvement of parents in planning special education programs for their children. Each of these areas is considered under topics in the next two sections of this chapter.

The Buckley Amendment

In Chapter 3 you were introduced to the Family Educational Rights and Privacy Act (FERPA), known as the Buckley Amendment. This legislation gives parents of minor students (and students eighteen years of age or older) the right to review all official school records related to their children (or themselves in the case of eligible students). Included in these records are school cumulative folders, academic reports, test data, attendance records, health information, family background, discipline records, and other pertinent information. In reviewing these records, parents and eligible students may challenge the accuracy of information. If schools reject the challenge and refuse to alter the questionable information, parents or eligible students may ask for a hearing. Eventually, if the school continues to refuse the request for change, parents (or eligible students) may add a statement of disagreement, which the school is obliged to disclose whenever the record is shared with another person or used by school personnel (Fischer & Sorenson, 1991).

FERPA also sets guidelines for disseminating educational records. In addition, schools are required to notify parents and students of their rights under the local policy regarding the use of educational records. Schools must ensure that procedures for disclosing educational records follow appropriate guidelines and that prior consent of parents or eligible students is obtained in writing before records are disclosed.

Gibson and Mitchell (1990) suggested that counselors become aware of the FERPA regulations, as well as their ethical standards and current court rulings, to guide their conduct in matters dealing with student records. Of particular concern to counselors is how their private notes and files regarding confidential counseling sessions might be controlled by this law. Generally speaking, the implementation of FERPA, subsequent interpretations by legislators, and court rulings seem to indicate that the law and its regulations do not necessarily require disclosure of private counseling notes. Once more, school counselors should be informed of interpretations and rulings regarding their services and activities as they are related to the Buckley Amendment. Services and activities of most concern to school counselors include, but are not limited to:

1. Letters of recommendation written on behalf of students
2. Taped recordings of counseling sessions
3. Correction of inaccurate information in educational records
4. Use of testing results
5. Records of handicapped students
6. Destruction of outdated educational records
7. Development or revision of a school policy regarding educational records.

Staying informed of current thinking and rulings about these and other types of counseling services helps practicing school counselors prevent litigation against themselves and their schools. Again, by participating in professional associations, attending workshops and conferences, and reading current resources such as those cited in this chapter, counselors keep abreast of these critical and timely issues.

Public Law 94–142

In 1975 Congress passed the now famous *Education For All Handicapped Children Act*, commonly called Public Law 94–142. Since then, the original bill has been amended and renamed several times to clarify regulations and responsibilities and expand the populations protected under this law. As of 1990, the most recent amendment is known as the *Individual with Disabilities Act* (Public Law 101–476). In practice, however, most people still mention Public Law 94–142 when referring to regulations regarding handicapped students. Generally, the original law guarantees a free and appropriate education to all students regardless of the nature and degree of their handicapping condition. Subsequent amendments and regulations have assisted states and school systems in developing procedures for assessing, identifying, and placing students in appropriate programs of study.

While the role of counselors in assisting with this law is not spelled out, school counselors offer many vital services to exceptional students of all categories. Counselors confer with teachers and parents, help to develop the Individual Education Plan (IEP) for each student placed in a program, provide counseling services when stipulated in a student's IEP, and consult with parents to help them cope with the exceptionalities of their children

As coordinators of student services within their schools, counselors also have responsibility for knowing how the federal law and guidelines affect the school's financial obligations, student transfer policies, and referrals to outside agencies. By and large, courts have ruled that the ultimate responsibility for costs related to the education of handicapped students rests with the state (Fischer & Sorenson, 1991). This means that counselors, teachers, and other school personnel must be aware of local school board policies that govern how educational recommendations, which sometimes include a financial obligation, are made to parents and guardians of handicapped students.

Child Abuse

All states and the District of Columbia have passed legislation addressing child abuse and the obligation of school personnel to report suspected cases. Child abuse covers a range of behaviors that includes physical abuse, sexual abuse, general neglect, psychological and emotional torment, abandonment, and inadequate supervision. A majority of states stipulate a penalty for the failure to report suspected abuse (Morrow, 1987), and all states require reporting by school personnel (Camblin & Prout, 1983). This includes school counselors. As such, any provision of privileged communication for students is superseded by the state's desire to protect children from abuse.

Responsibility for investigating reported cases of child abuse and neglect rests with children's protective services as defined by specific state statutes. The school's role, and accordingly the school counselor's role, is to report instances of suspected abuse. As such, school personnel should cooperate with protective service investigators who need to substantiate whether or not abuse exists in the cases reported. School systems should have clear policies and procedures that guide personnel in the process of following state laws for child abuse reporting.

Counselor Liability

In serving a wide audience of students, parents, teachers, and others, school counselors occasionally become concerned about malpractice and professional liability. Remley (1985) noted that most school counselors "are either immune from malpractice suits because they are employed by a governmental agency or are covered for malpractice damages by insurance purchased by their schools" (p. 187). Nevertheless, counselors want to know what protection they have. In determining their liability coverage, school counselors should learn about insurance carried by their school systems and whether or not they, as counselors, are exempt from coverage under these policies. If counselors find they are not adequately covered by their school systems, they may want to buy an individual policy through a professional organization such as the group plan offered by the American Counseling Association (ACA).

Malpractice suits against school counselors have been rare, but the changing climate of schools and the seriousness of concerns being raised by children, adolescents, and families today elevate the risks counselors take with the wide range of services they provide. Malpractice suits typically address two types of liability: *civil liability* and *criminal liability*. The first, civil liability, occurs when counselors behave in inappropriate or wrongful ways towards others, or fail to act when situations require a dutiful response. For example, school counselors risk civil liability if they neglect to inform parents of a student's threat to commit suicide, or they disclose confidential information in violation of their ethical standards of conduct. These two examples illustrate harmful and inappropriate professional practice. By contrast, criminal liability occurs when counselors behave in unlawful ways, such as being an accessory to a crime, disobeying civil ordinances, and contributing to the delinquency of a minor, (Hopkins & Anderson, 1985).

While proof of criminal wrongdoing rests with the prosecuting office of the county, state, or federal government, the proof of malpractice in civil liability lies with the plaintiff who brings suit against the counselor. To be successful, the suit must demonstrate that harm was done to someone as a direct result of a counselor's negligence or flagrant omission. Furthermore, the plaintiff must show evidence that other counselors in a similar situation would not have behaved the same way (Remley, 1985).

Reaching a judgment of malpractice is difficult when dealing with professional counseling. In part, this is because most states do not have licensing laws that control the practice of school counseling as they do for other helping professions such as psychiatry and clinical psychology. If states are unclear about what responsibilities counselors have and the level of standards for their professional practice, it is difficult for jurors and judges to find fault. Nevertheless, as noted above and throughout this chapter, the practice of counseling is becoming more visible, and standards of practice are being developed through various accreditation and certifying bodies. In the future school counselors will want to know how to prevent legal action from being taken against them. Some preventive measures might include:

1. A clear description of the school counseling program and a counselor's job description that reflects a true accounting of daily functions. School counselors should provide services that are addressed by program statements, school brochures, and school system manuals. When counselors stray beyond the scope of their program or job description in offering services to students, parents, and teachers, they open themselves up for possible litigation. By the same token, when they fail to offer services described in their job descriptions, they are also vulnerable.

2. Reliance on other professionals for guidance and support in providing comprehensive service. School counselors are highly trained professionals, but they cannot provide all the services that may be needed by the school population. Having appropriate referral sources and professionals with whom to consult is good practice for all helping professionals.

3. Knowledge and understanding of professional standards of ethical practice. Counselors are not protected by ignorance of law or of their own ethical standards. Knowing about sound professional practices, and behaving accordingly are essential conditions for preventing legal entanglements.

4. Knowledge and information about legal rulings and ethical interpretations. Legal and ethical issues evolve and change every day. Counselors who read about current cases, attend workshops about legal and ethical practice, and participate in their professional associations take preventive action to avoid misconduct.

In general, the following behaviors and services present the most risk for school counselors:

1. Administering drugs. An increasing number of students come to school with prescription drugs to be taken during the school hours. In schools without nurses, clearly written policies help administrators delegate responsibility and require written instructions from the prescribing physician and written permission from parents (guardians) for the school to dispense medication. In most instances, school counselors are wise to resist accepting responsibility for administering drugs to students.

2. Student searches. Students are protected under the Fourth Amendment to the Constitution from *unreasonable searches*. In the 1985 case of *New Jersey v. T.L.O.*, the U.S. Supreme Court ruled that "Students' legitimate expectations of privacy . . . must be balanced against that need for the search" (Fischer & Sorenson, 1991, p. 141). Searches of students and their property must be carried out only when there is justification and reason to believe that a search will disclose as violation of school policy or law. Counselors who participate in unreasonable and unjustified searches may be liable.

3. Birth control and abortion counseling. Perhaps no areas of school counseling are more explosive and emotional in the responses they bring from counselors and laypeople alike than the issues of birth control and abortion.

As attitudes continue to change and new judicial appointments are made to state and federal courts, legal views and answers to these topics will again be altered. The pendulum of public opinion is forever moving one way or the other. At this time, minors are permitted to seek abortions, but as noted earlier, the Supreme Court has upheld states laws that require parent notification. Local school boards may pass policies regarding birth control and abortion counseling, and school counselors should be informed of all current legislation, court rulings, and local policies regarding this area of counseling.

4. Use of student records. School counselors must adhere to local, state, and federal regulations regarding the use and dissemination of students' records. This area of practice, as we have seen, is guided by the Family Educational Rights and Privacy Act of 1974 (FERPA). Generally, the major question for schools is who has the legal right to see students' records. Two areas seem most problematic: noncustodial parents' rights to see educational records and "special files" for school personnel only. Fischer and Sorenson (1991) clarified that *both* parents, custodial and noncustodial, in separated or divorced families have the legal right to see a child's records. The only exception would be by a judge's order. Regarding the second issue, the law disallows any special educational files being kept private for school personnel use only. Private notes kept by counselors, as indicated earlier, are not addressed by FERPA, and therefore may be held in confidence if in judgment of the counselor it is best to do so (Fischer & Sorenson, 1991).

Title IX

The primary purpose of Title IX of the Education Amendments of 1972 is to protect students against discrimination on the basis of sex. This law stated that "No person in the United States shall, on the basis of sex, be excluded from participation in, be denied the benefits of, or be subjected to discrimination under any education program or activity receiving Federal financial assistance." If schools violate this law, the penalty is loss of federal financial assistance (Fischer & Sorenson, 1991).

Courts have applied Title IX to the concept of equal access for both girls and boys to join athletic teams and enroll in courses in the school's curriculum. This law has been used to guarantee equity for students' participation in all aspects of school life regardless of gender or marital status. Therefore, pregnant teenagers have the same rights to an education as all other students. In addition, Title IX and the Fourteenth Amendment have been used to help settle disputes over admissions policies that set different standards for girls than boys.

School counselors at all levels of education should be aware of Title IX regulations and pertinent court rulings. As advocates of students, counselors are in an ideal position to monitor school policies and programs and protect against subtle and overt sex discrimination. In part, the counselor's role is to educate staff and administrators and guide them in developing policies and procedures that are free from discrimination.

Another way in which counselors prevent illegal action or stereotypical behavior is by helping schools select appropriate instructional materials and activities. Textbooks, media, and instructional activities that unintentionally or otherwise depict learning, career choices, or other aspects of student development in inequitable or stereotypical fashion must be avoided. Workshops for teachers and other school personnel about Title IX and sex discrimination, in general, are appropriate vehicles for school counselors to become positive forces in helping develop and implement appropriate programs, policies, and instruction for all students.

Title IX also regulates the professional relationships counselors form on behalf of students, parents, and teachers beyond the schoolhouse doors. Counselors cannot cooperate with community organizations or persons who discriminate against people on the basis of sex (Knox, 1977). Title IX includes criteria for exempting certain organizations such as Boy Scouts and Girls Scouts, but unless an organization is exempt, counselors will want to refer boys and girls alike. For example, if an employer is seeking weekend help from teenagers, a high school counselor is obliged to announce this opportunity to all students regardless of the nature of the work or the specific preferences expressed by the employer for either boys or girls to fill the positions.

With this chapter, we have completed the overview of the school counseling profession, including its brief history, a description of essential services, background about the professionals who are trained and certified to be school counselors, and ethical and legal guidelines that assist these counselors in their professional practice. The information presented thus far describes where we have been and where we are in the profession of school counseling. The final chapter of this text explores some futuristic questions about professional directions for school counseling in the years to come.

Selected Readings

Fischer, L., & Sorenson, G.P. (1991). *School Law for Counselors, Psychologists, and Social Workers,* 2nd ed. (New York: Longman). This text is a comprehensive guide to legal issues that confront school counselors and other student services professional on a daily basis. Written in clear understandable language, the book presents each topic through a series of related questions and answers.

Huey, W.C., & Remley, T.P., Jr. (Eds.). (1988). *Ethical and Legal Issues in School Counseling.* (Alexandria, VA: American School Counselor Association). This book of readings offers a range of articles from the major journals of the American Association for Counseling and Development. Ethical and legal issues related to school practice and to counseling in general are addressed.

References

Alexander, K., & Alexander, M.D. (1985). *American public school law*, 2nd Ed. (St. Paul, MN: West Publishing Co).

American Association for Counseling and Development. (1988). *Ethical standards*, rev. ed. (Alexandria, VA: Author).

American School Counselor Association. (1984). *Ethical Standards for School Counselors*. *(Alexandria, VA: Author)*.

American School Counselor Association. (April, 1992). Ehtical Standards for School Counselors, *The ASCA Counselor, 29* (4), 13–16.

Camblin, L.D., Jr., & Prout, H.T. (1983), School Counselors and the Reporting of Child Abuse: A Survey of State Laws and Practices, *The School Counselor, 30*, 358–367.

Christiansen, H.D. (1972). *Ethics in Counseling: Problem Situations*. (tucson, AZ: The University of Arizona Press).

Corey, G., Corey, M.S., & Callanan, P. (1988). *Issues and Ethics in the Helping Professions*, 3rd ed. (Pacific Grove, CA: Brooks/Cole).

Engels, D., Wilborn, B.L., & Schneider, L.J. (1990), Ethics Curricula for Counselor Preparation Programs, in B. Herlihy & L. B Golden (Eds.), *Ethical standards casebook (Alexandria, VA: American Association for Counseling and Development), pp. 111–126.*

Fischer, L., & Sorenson, G.P. (1991). *School law for counselors, psychologists, and social workers*, 2nd ed. (New York: Longman).

Gibson, R.L., & Mitchell, M.H. (1990). *Introduction to Counseling and Guidance*, (New York, Macmillan).

Herlihy, b., & Golden, L.B. (1990). *Ethical Standards Casebook*, 4th ed. (Alexandria, VA: American Association for Counseling and Developement).II

Hopkins, B.R., & Anderson, B.S. (1985). *The Counselor and the Law*. (Alexandria, VA: American Association for Counseling and Development).

Huey, W.C. (1986), Ethical Concerns in School Counseling, *Journal of Counseling and Development, 64*, 321–322.

Huey, W.C., & Remley, T.P., Jr. (Eds.). (1988). *Ethical and Legal Issues in School Counseling*. (Alexnadria, VA: American School Counselor Association).

Ibrahim, F.A. (1985), Human Rights and Ethical I Issues in the Use of Advanced Technlogy, *Journal of Counseling and Development, 64*, 134–135.

Knox, H. (1977). *Cracking the Glass Slipper: Peer's Guide to Ending Sex Bias in Your School*. (Washington, D.C.: The NOW Legal Defense and Education Fund).

Mabe, A.R., & Rollin, S.A. (1986), The Role of Code of Ethical Standards in Counseling, *Journal of Counseling and Development, 64*, 294–297.

Marchant, W. (1987), Reporting Unethical Practices: Revised Guidelines, *Journal of Counseling and Development, 65*, 573–574.

Morrow, G. (1987). *The Compassionate School: A Practical Guide in Educating Abused and Traumatized Children* (Englewood Cliffs, NJ: Prentice Hall).

Remley, T.P., Jr. (1985), The Law and Ethical Practice in Elementary and Middle Schools, *Elementary School Guidance and Counseling, 19*, 181–189.

Sampson, J.P., Jr. (1990), Ethical Use of Computer Applications in Counseling: Past, Present, and Future Perspectives, in B. Herlihy & L.B. Golden (Eds.) *Ethical Standards Casebook*, (pp. 170–176).

Sandberg, D.N., Crabbs, S.K., & Crabbs, M.A. (1988), Legal Issues in Child Abuse: Questions and Answers for Counselors, *Elementary School Guidance and Counseling, 22*, 268–274.

Schmidt, J.J. (1987), Parental Objections to Counseling Services: An Analysis, *The School Counselor, 34*, 387–391.

Schmidt, J.J. (1991). *A Survuval Guide for the Elementary/Middle School Counselor* (West Nyack, NYK: The center for Applied Research in Education).

Sheeley, V.L., & Herlihy, B. (1987), Privileged Communication in School Counseling: Status Update, *The School Counselor, 34*, 268–272.

Sheeley, V.L., & Herligy, B. (1989), Counseling Suicidal Teens: A Duty to Warn and Protect, *The School Counselor, 37, 89–87.*

12

School Counseling Today and Tomorrow

Throughout its development, the school counseling profession has been influenced by educational and social trends, both inside and outside the United States, and has responded to these events by way of federal legislation, state initiatives, and changes within the profession itself. While theories and models of counseling have emerged as a result of conceptual development and action research, the role and practice of school counseling have most often been established as a result of reaction to national and world events. The early history of vocational guidance as a reaction to social ills and labor requirements of industrialization was the beginning. The demand for accurate assessment of military recruits in two world wars eventually led to increased use of testing in schools by counselors. Likewise, public fear of Soviet domination in the late 1950s was reflected in national legislation to improve education, particularly in the areas of mathematics and science, which had historic impact on the training and employment of school counselors. Subsequent events, laws, and national reports from that time to the present day have shaped the directions and identity of the school counseling profession.

The work of Rogers in the 1950s and 1960s on the counseling relationship and process was the first notable influence that stemmed from a conceptual, theoretical perspective. His development of client-centered counseling, later to be called the person-centered approach, alerted counselors in schools and other settings of the need to view the entire person in establishing helping relationships, rather than dividing the individual into compartments such as educational and vocational needs. This fresh approach, while itself a holistic and developmental perspective, began another series of reactions within the school counseling profession. Counselors and other educators began promoting the idea that counseling services were necessary earlier in students' lives. Thus, the profession expanded to the junior high school and later to the elementary level. It was not unusual during this period to hear teachers, counselors, and other people comment that counselors were needed in the "early grades rather than high schools" to help prevent problems before they begin. This conclusion is a limited view of human development because it overlooks the need for counseling at all stages of life. Students at all levels of education face challenges and barriers to development. For this reason, it is appropriate to offer counseling services during all years of schooling and throughout the life span.

Today the counseling profession continues to react to social, economic, and political forces of the times, but it also has begun to establish for itself a direction and focus on the future. National counseling associations under the auspices of the parent organization, the American Counseling Association (ACA), have become strong forces in encouraging state and national legislation on a wide range of social and educational issues, on developing national certification standards for the practice of professional counseling, in creating the Council for Accrediting Counselor and Related Educational Programs to promote adequate training, and by giving counselors a unique identity and clear focus among other helping professions. With leadership from the American School Counselor Association (ASCA), the largest division of ACA, professional school counselors have benefited from these developments as well. This progress has occurred in spite of the fact that only about 30 percent of the counselors in the country belong to ACA and its divisions (Gazda, 1991). Approximately 13,000 school counselors were members of ASCA in 1991. While the efforts of ACA and ASCA have helped to chart a course for the future, much more needs to be done to help school counselors establish themselves as a credible and valuable profession.

In this chapter, we examine some possibilities of what the future holds and how these emerging trends and conditions might affect the practice of school counseling. It is risky business predicting the future, but counselors who are in the business of helping others to prepare for the future must be ready to meet the challenges of a changing world. There are numerous factors to consider in looking at the future of school counseling, some positive and some negative, and each having a role in determining how counselors might practice in schools in the years to come. Futuristic projections for the school counseling profession include a wide spectrum of factors including programmatic issues, technological advances, an emerging global economy, and more (Drury, 1984; Hays, 1978; Hays & Johnson, 1984; Schmidt, 1984; Walz, Gazda, & Shertzer, 1991 Wilson & Rotter, 1982). Here, we highlight a few of these factors. In particular, we consider two primary elements because they incorporate all the others: students and schools of tomorrow.

Students of Tomorrow

Who will be the students of the future and for what reasons will they seek assistance from school counselors? In nearly a century of development, the school counseling profession has moved from a limited focus on vocational training and job placement to a wide vision of delivering a broad range of personal, social, educational, and career services to diverse student populations. Will students in the next century continue to need an array of counseling services to optimize their educational development and assure success in life? If present trends in the U.S. family and culture are any indication, the answer is an unequivocal "yes." Students today are facing difficult conditions in many aspects of their development, and there appears to be no sign of this pressure letting up in the future.

In serving the students of tomorrow, school counselors need to be prepared to offer a range of services that address developmental needs, prevent learning difficulties, and remedy existing conditions that inhibit growth and development (Schmidt, 1984). As with students today, students in the future will require services to develop skills, acquire information, and attain knowledge to make appropriate decisions about relationships, educational goals, and career aspirations. There is no reason to believe that these developmental goals will be any less appropriate for tomorrow's students than they are for today's.

Similarly, since we cannot accurately forecast what the future holds, tomorrow's students will want to be prepared to change their goals, make adjustments, and prevent major problems that potentially block their progress. While both preventive and developmental goals are necessary for assisting students in the future, it is unlikely that these objectives will be sufficient. Most likely, tomorrow's students will not be spared the challenges of human existence and the expected hardship of forgoing successful careers. For this reason, future school counselors should create expanded visions to meet the needs of a wide range of students by balancing the need to remedy existing concerns with opportunities for students to experience optimal learning and realize healthy futures. Viewing counseling relationships as simply a "remedy for conflict, anxiety, or personal misfortune seems an unnecessarily narrow definition" while "defining counseling in terms of self-fulfillment without considering barriers to development seems unrealistic" (Purkey & Schmidt, 1987, p. 100–101). We can expect future students to demand a broader context for services provided by school counselors. This context will include relationships to address problems as well as focus on prevention and development.

Remedial Concerns

The changing American scene includes a continuing redefinition and re-structuring of the family. Divorce, remarriage, cohabitation, dual careers, blended families, and a host of other terms have come to describe the array of family structures and lifestyles in U.S. society. Each family with its own set of values and perspectives contributes in unique ways to the culture, attitudes, and beliefs that students bring to school. Accordingly, each family, regardless of how we define it, lays the foundation for educational success. School counselors in the future probably will experience increased diversity in the types of families and groups from which students come, and they will need knowledge and skill to help schools adapt programs and create services to meet these challenges.

In addition to the changing family structure, students of tomorrow might exhibit a range of personal, social, physical, and educational concerns emanating from serious ills of society. For example, the "war on drugs" in U.S. society continues to be waged with few victories won and major losses incurred (Schmidt, in press). Infants born of drug abusing parents during the 1980s are entering school in the 1990s. Unless a significant change in alcohol and drug abuse occurs soon, this condition will have a debilitating effect on students and schools in the years to come. Schools and counselors face a major challenge in designing programs and services to help young people infected by addictions to realize their human potential and succeed in life.

Violence is another phenomenon that, unless curtailed, will have significant impact on schools and learning in the future. Physical, sexual, and psychological child abuse is a disheartening characteristic of a society that prides itself on freedom, human worth, and dignity. If this society does not succeed in securing the rights of children and protecting them from abuse and neglect, school counselors in the future can expect to serve more of these cases (Griggs & Gale, 1977; Holtgraves, 1986; Morrow, 1987; Westcott, 1980). Added to the brutal violation of children's rights by some parents and adults is the growing number of students who are resorting to violent force as a means of addressing their own personal and social conflicts. Fights, homicides, and suicides are all too common among today's students. Simply passing policies to punish students for possessing weapons and fighting in school is not the answer. Helping students of tomorrow handle hostilities in appropriate ways while maintaining an acceptable level of assertiveness to protect their interests and enhance their welfare will be a necessary aspect of school life and the curriculum. Counselors should take a lead role in this effort.

Suicide is a private form of violence that illustrates a desperate attempt to free oneself from psychological and emotional pain, fear, and distress. Students who remain incapable of finding acceptable avenues to resolve social and personal crises will continue to be at risk of hurting themselves or others. Teachers and counselors in schools are often the first-line helpers for young people in distress, and therefore need to be ready and skilled to assist in times of critical need (McBrien, 1983; Schmidt, 1991; Sheeley & Herlihy, 1989).

Substance abuse, as mentioned above, is another area of human concern that continues to threaten educational development. Despite efforts to attend to this national crisis, students at alarmingly younger ages are becoming involved with drug and alcohol use and abuse (Schmidt, in press). If the future holds no promise of turning this destructive behavior around, students will require additional services from counselors to handle family dysfunction, prevent substance abuse, and cope without drugs and alcohol. These and other areas of student behavior and development will continue to be critical in the foreseeable future.

School counselors who ignore threatening and debilitating situations and focus services on students who only require information or instruction will neglect a significant portion of their schools populations. Future counseling programs must maintain comprehensive services to meet the needs of a wide spectrum of students, including those with serious problems. Either through direct service or referral processes, counselors can help these students alter behaviors, change environments, or enhance their situations in beneficial ways. At the same time, most other students will benefit from services that prevent problems from overwhelming them as they progress through their school years.

Preventive Issues

It is difficult to forecast what personal and social issues will be most prominent for children and adolescents of the twenty-first century. For example, the alarming drug and alcohol problem pervasive in U.S. society during the past few decades may escalate in spite of efforts to educate people and provide treatment. Teenage pregnancy, another problem of devastating proportion, continues despite the availability of birth control information and contraceptives. Helping youth establish healthy relationships and choose responsible behaviors will remain an important role of the school. In all likelihood, substance abuse, sexual activity, and many other issues will continue to concern students, parents, and teachers, and school counselors will be expected to offer preventive services to address these topics.

Students in the immediate future will need the same information and education about how to prevent abuse, disease, pregnancy and other life-threatening and debilitating conditions as the students of today require. In addition, as new social issues develop, new preventive approaches will be needed. As old issues are resolved, new challenges will emerge to take their place. This means that future school counselors, as in the present, must be prepared to assess the needs of students accurately and design services for enabling students to make healthy, sound decisions about the challenges before them.

Preventive services of comprehensive counseling programs of the next century probably will retain many of the elements and characteristics of present day approaches. As such, educational programs and counseling services will include assistance for helping students learn decision-making skills, acquire knowledge about sexual development, establish beneficial peer relationships, and develop coping behaviors to deal with the pressure and stress of growing up in a complex, accelerated world. Adding to these direct services, future counselors will establish collaborative relationships with parents, teachers, and other professionals to assure beneficial home and school environments for optimal learning and development.

One threat to student development in the future might be increased loneliness as society relies on more automation and offers fewer opportunities for social interaction. Other challenges include fears fueled by media information about the risk of a nuclear war, the spread of AIDS, environmental catastrophes, and other natural or man-made disasters. More common, perhaps, will be the uncertainty of career choices and decisions in light of a rapidly advancing technology that will leave no area of vocational development untouched. In the future, students will need to expand career options and learn ways to deal with automation and other elements of our changing world. A first step is to identify the knowledge and skills necessary to be employable in the 21st century and beyond. The next step is to design curricula that enable students to attain this requisite knowledge and skill.

Schools and counselors who maintain a futuristic vision will constantly seek ways and create methods to enable students to alter their goals, acquire new skills, cope with transitions, and adapt to emerging trends. In sum, prevention will continue to entail services to help children and adolescents address potential changes in their home, school, and vocational environments and learn behaviors and skills to handle these transformations, variations, and diversifications smoothly and productively.

Developmental Needs

The future will not ignore the developmental needs of students. Students of the next century will have the same biological, emotional, social, and educational expectations as do students of today. The stages of human development as outlined by various theorists in the past will most likely hold true for future generations of school children and adolescents. There is no reason to believe that physical, social, and other transformations will occur so drastically that student development will be significantly altered. While the general process of human development is expected to remain unchanged, the impact of a changing world will remarkably alter specific aspects and elements of that developmental process.

Automation and technology undoubtedly will have an affect on the developmental concerns of students, particularly in regards to career exploration and decision-making. Other areas of students' lives also will be affected by technology and scientific discovery. Medical science, for example, can be expected to make significant progress in expanding further an already ever-increasing life span. While on one hand, this accomplishment is welcomed, it also raises questions of how to help families and children cope with terminal illnesses that no longer kill because advanced technology will give new meaning to the term "life-support system." Such issues cannot be viewed in isolation because they all relate to developmental aspects of tomorrow's students. Counselors and teachers will need to provide services, design activities, and plan instruction to help children and adolescents work through these added dimensions of their development.

In the early 1900s, Alfred Adler through his theory of individual psychology, posited "that mental health can be measured in terms of one's social interest, the willingness to participate in the give and take of life and to cooperate with others and be concerned about their welfare" (Dinkmeyer, Dinkmeyer, & Sperry, 1987, p. 64). A similar concept, individualization, is a futuristic theme for the 21st century predicted by Naisbitt and Aburdene (1990). The first principle of this movement, which these authors call "the triumph of the individual," is a belief in personal responsibility. Simultaneously, embracement of individual worth and responsibility is complemented by a spirit of togetherness and community, two other qualities that should be nurtured by school environments. Recognition of individual worth and value, combined with responsibility for one's own behaviors, means that individuals must come together and contribute to the betterment of all humankind. This notion of community parallels Adler's belief in social interest, and is a familiar theme to schools and school counselors.

Developmental guidance and counseling activities reflect the belief that students will benefit from lessons and relationships designed to enhance their individual dignity and worth. At the same time,their goal is to teach responsible behaviors. Indeed, the works of Dreikurs, Dinkmeyer, Glasser, and other counseling theorists and practitioners are the forerunners of developmental services and activities we can expect to find in future schools with tomorrow's students.

In addition to the issues already presented, two other phenomena will have a tremendous impact on the students' of tomorrow. The first, poverty, will have a serious, divisive consequence on education if not curtailed by future economic policies and progress. The second, diversity, is an inevitable characteristics that will define students of tomorrow and will challenge schools and school counselors in the future.

Poverty

Social equality and individual responsibility are threatened by the rapid growth of poverty of America. All the initiatives at the local and national levels to move schools and students to the next century may be wasted unless we pay attention to growing economic disparities in this country and the world. If this trend continues, economic inequality and disparity will become a wedge that clearly, more than ever before, divides students of tomorrow into the have's and have nots. Reports indicate that the percentage of children in poverty rose from approximately 14 percent in 1970 to about 17 percent in 1980, and then to 20 percent in 1990. At this rate, we can expect more than a quarter of our students to live in economically disadvantaged homes by the year 2000. As a result of poverty, a high percentage of children will suffer from poor nutrition, lack of health care, and other deficiencies that will inhibit their education and development (Howe, 1991).

If this economic wedge continues to separate and distinguish students in the future, it is clear that the school counselor's role and responsibility must incorporate a posture of social activism to seek assistance for the disadvantaged. Such a role would include collaboration with social workers, nurses, and a host of other service providers in the school and community. If this role is assumed, developmental and preventive services for a majority of students will be given a lower priority because remedial services to meet the needs of impoverished students will be demanded.

Poor students are handicapped in so many ways because of the association of poverty with health, learning, familial, and neighborhood problems. As Howe (1991) explained, "Poverty is the parent of school failure, job failure, emotional imbalance, and social rejection" (p. 201). The future of school counseling services will be significantly influenced by the success or failure of the United States to address this issue and turn around this gloomy economic forecast for students in the future.

Diversity

Current predictions are that the United States will more closely reflect the cultural and racial balance of the globe by the end of the next century (Ibrahim, 1991). Mitigating factors, such as immigration policies, worldwide economic depression, and unexpected changes in birth rates, may alter these forecasts. But if these predictions come true and schools eventually reflect this balance, we can estimate that Asian students will make up the majority of the population, followed by white, Hispanic, and African-American students in that order. What this means for 21st century schools is that cultural diversity will become the norm. How schools and school counselors address the needs of culturally different populations and incorporate the concept of multiculturalism into the curriculum will determine their success in educating children and providing beneficial services to students, parents, and teachers. School counselors are in the vanguard of this movement, acting as advocates for all students, addressing issues of equity, designing appropriate services, and assisting teachers with educational curricula and instructional development.

Students of varied cultural backgrounds will require special attention to meet their individual needs and, at the same time, will benefit from learning about the multicultural community in which they live. School counselors in the future will play a pivotal role in helping teachers become aware of cultural differences and enabling schools to celebrate cultural diversity. Such celebrations will not be limited to one day, week, or month during the school year to recognize the backgrounds and heritage of different students. Rather, they will be embedded in the philosophy and mission of the school, and will encompass all aspects of school life from policy development to curriculum planning.

As with other issues related to tomorrow's students, diversity will influence the role of future school counselors. Included in this role will be one of a sentinel for appropriate assessment and evaluation. As noted in an earlier chapter, counselors must guard against the use of inappropriate testing and appraisal instruments and procedures that are culturally or socioeconomically biased. In addition, future counselors will incorporate multicultural activities and materials into their developmental guidance and counseling services to heighten student and staff awareness. Again, since this progression towards multicultural diversity will parallel the emergence of individual worth in the context of community, the role of the counselor as a consultant and collaborator with teachers and administrators to create beneficial learning environments for all students is imperative. We can expect that group work, both instructional and therapeutic, will increase for school counselors in effecting this change in school culture and environment.

In sum, the future needs of students from diverse cultural and socioeconomic backgrounds will be addressed by a wide range of counseling and educational services enabling individual students to establish an identity and accept a beneficial role within the school community. To accomplish this, counselors will encourage the celebration of diversity and broaden the focus of their services to students. Counseling services should "strike a balance between helping students adopt new behaviors that will facilitate their adjustment to school while allowing them to have pride and respect for their heritage" (Schmidt, 1991, p. 155). In this process, counselors will continually examine their own awareness and acceptance of diversity, encourage cultural opportunities in the school and community, monitor school policies and programs for prejudicial aspects, become actively involved with different cultural groups, and develop counseling skills that accommodate cultural diversity (Locke, 1989; Schmidt, 1991).

Pedersen (1991) presented *multiculturalism* as a "fourth force" in professional counseling, "complementary to the other three forces of psychodynamic, behavioral, and humanistic explanations of human behavior" (p. 6). This view gives a broad definition to cultural diversity inclusive of demographic, socioeconomic, ethnic, religious, and other variables that allow the construct of multiculturalism to be applied in all counseling relationships and processes. As such, school counselors in the future must be cognizant of all these cultural variables, as well as traditional theoretical perspectives, in attempting to explain student behaviors and design appropriate services to enhance learning and development.

Schools of Tomorrow

The diversity of tomorrow's students will create schools of the future. Schools are more than buildings, programs, and policies established by communities, organized by administrators, and implemented by teachers. Today and always, schools will be defined and described by the students who enroll, attend, and in effect "become the school." As such, we can expect tomorrow's schools to reflect the diversity of U.S. society. This diversity will include all the aspects predicted earlier for the students of tomorrow: (1) a need to adapt to technological changes and advances; (2) the reality of an increasing lifespan that will simultaneously lengthen the dying process; (3) multiculturalism as an emerging significant force in education; (4) concern about health care and new diseases such as the AIDS epidemic; (5) poverty as a divisive force in schools and society; (6) continued changes in employment trends and how the work week is defined; and (7) increased violence and loss of security in U.S. communities.

Walz (1991a) outlined nine trends that would affect the future of this country. As with all social and economic forecasts, these trends should be considered with some caution. Nevertheless, they provide a stimulus and an opportunity for dialogue about the future practice of school counseling. While none of his predictions specifically address the schools of tomorrow, each has relevancy for the direction schools will take and how counselors will assist in the educational process. Aspects of these nine trends are presented here to illustrate their potential impact on future schools.

1. The population of the United States will slow and mature at the same time. In kindergarten through high school, we can expect enrollments to

stabilize or decline. While fewer students will be entering these grades, college populations will continue to grow as nontraditional students, older students, will pursue formal education. U.S. businesses will continue to demand a better educated work force. More accurately, the demand will be for a work force educated in the applied sciences with technical knowledge and higher order thinking skills. Demands on education will invite alternative education programs such as year-round schools and pre-school programs. The counseling literature has begun to address this trend and the counselor's role in providing services to pre-school populations (Hohenshill & Brown, 1991).

2. As noted earlier, minority populations, particularly Asians, are expected to expand significantly. As immigrants increase, the work force will reflect a multilingual, multicultural society. Schools will be expected to educate a diverse population of students, enabling them to adjust to a new society, become productive in the work force, and realize self-satisfaction in their lives.

3. Increased demands for services, including education, will put greater strain on already overstretched state and federal budgets. Private resources will be sought to respond to social and educational problems. Businesses and government can be expected to join in cooperative ventures to address many of these issues. Schools will see more involvement from business and industry with the expectation that student outcomes become more clearly stated and measured.

4. The ever-changing information technology will have a continuous effect on communications, and on how people work and live. Schools will require resources to keep up with technological advances as they become more important to instructional programs and student learning. Concerns about individual privacy will need to be addressed as new technology becomes available to gather more data on how people live. The opportunity to work at home will increase for many people as access to home computers grows, and home learning will become a normal part of the educational process for many students.

5. The United States' role as an economic, industrial, and military leader will change as the world moves towards globalization. This process has already begun as a new world economy is emerging and global telecommunications and travel are rapidly expanding. At the same time, however, there are signs of "a backlash against uniformity, a desire to assert the uniqueness of one's culture and language, a repudiation of foreign influence" (Naisbitt & Aburdene, 1990, p. 119). If this backlash is real and continues, schools will feel the conflict first hand. It has the potential to be a most disruptive force in the future progress of our schools.

6. Medical developments and health care issues, on one hand, will improve the quality of life for many people, and on the other will be criteria that separate people according to their ability to pay for services. Personal

health concerns will be connected to responsible behaviors, such as with the spread of AIDS, and conflict between environmental responsibility and personal safety will increase. Communities will struggle over where to locate hazardous waste disposal systems, garbage dumps, and power plans. As schools attempt to teach students about these social issues, it will be difficult to remain neutral amidst emotional conflicts that pit neighbors against each other.

7. Economic, technological, and governmental changes in this and other countries will facilitate a restructuring of business and industry worldwide. Consumer markets will change with an aging, multicultural population consisting of the major buyers. These and other changes will have an impact on career choices for the students of tomorrow. Schools of the future will have to implement learning programs that enable students to be flexible in their career development and vocational choices. But more importantly, schools will need to refocus curricula to teach the content and skills needed by workers in a technologically and scientifically sophisticated world.

8. The family unit will be a stabilizing factor amidst all this change. Yet, the family will itself continue to take on new characteristics. Divorce is expected to decline, but two-income families will continue to grow in number. New technology and hi-tech consumer services will alter traditional family behaviors such as meal times, television viewing, house cleaning, and other family chores and activities. Child care, as noted earlier, will be an increasing concern, and schools can be expected to become involved in preschool programs for younger students. School counselors will need to be prepared to work with younger populations (Gerler & Myrick, 1991).

9. To a degree, social issues will replace concerns about economic growth and development that dominated most recent decades. As the nation becomes more involved in global issues, local communities will paradoxically pay attention to violence, homelessness, poverty, and other debilitating concerns of their communities. Schools will become central units of communication and education, much as they were in many communities at the beginning of the twentieth century, helping citizens to address and solve local issues.

If these predictions come true, schools of the future will change in many ways. They will not be isolated from the concerns and needs of the community and society. Neither will schools remain autonomous organizations that ignore input from parents or discourage the involvement of business and industry in matters of education. The restructuring of tomorrow's schools, as we have begun to witness in the 1990s, includes involvement of many aspects of society, cooperation with a multitude of community agencies and institutions of higher education, alternative programs to meet the needs of diverse populations, and shared governance among administrators, teachers, and parents (Center on Organization and Restructuring of

Schools, 1991). Elements of school restructuring that will have particular importance for school counselors in the future are: technology, parental involvement, teacher collaboration, school-based community services, and youth service.

Technology

Schools of the future will be the technology of education (Mecklenburger, 1990). Expanding and changing electronic and computer technology will be used in the broad context of learning for all students. As such, every aspect of learning, including guidance and counseling services, will be influenced by new and expanded technology. School counselors will be actively involved in planning and utilizing technology to deliver services to a wide range of students, parents, and teachers.

Presently, counselors have not come very far since the inception of personal computers in schools. Despite encouragement by authors in professional literature to use computers and other technology to provide an array of guidance, informational, and counseling services, today's counselors have barely begun to tap this tremendous resource. Childers and Podemski (1984) suggested that counselors must confront the barriers that prevent them from adapting the technology of the future to their role in the school. Among these barriers are traditional views of counselors as people-oriented professionals who search for social interactions to satisfy their own career needs. The use of computers and other technology is viewed as a contradiction of this vocational preference. One factor that may inhibit counselors from embracing technology is its close association with instruction, an aspect of schools that allows counselors to resist involvement or permit teachers to exclude counselors from the process. Another element is the fear some counselors have that computers and other technology may replace them in the schools. New technology does not pose a threat to counselors. Instead it enhances the role counselors can assume in delivering services to a broader audience. Just as schools of tomorrow must adapt technology in restructuring learning environments and processes (Sheingold, 1991), counselors too must integrate new systems and services into their programs. As schools restructure for the future, it is inevitable that the programs within schools, such as counseling services, will need to change as well.

The future use of technology by school counselors depends on how counselors view the potential value of these tools. If viewed as a means of facilitating learning and involvement rather than diminishing human interaction, technology can become an asset. The difference may be as simple as the language counselors choose in adapting various technology. For example, Purkey and Schmidt (1987) commented that the phrases "computer-assisted" and "computerized" each convey different intentions. "A computer-assisted program allows counselors and clients to maintain important human interactions while using technology as a tool to store information, present instruction, score inventories, and perform a number of other supplementary and supportive functions" (Purkey & Schmidt, 1987, p. 148). By contrast, "computerized" services denote a process void of human contact and lacking a clear relationship between counselor and student. Counselors who discover and use a positive language to describe these new services will be able to reconceptualize their role in schools and integrate advanced technology with helping relationships and learning processes to benefit students.

Parental Involvement

As noted in earlier chapters, much of the effective schools' research and literature in recent years emphasizes the importance of parental involvement in education. By and large, this research shows that successful students are blessed with strong support from parents and guardians at home, and this support is complemented by appropriate instructional programs at school. Supportive relationships between the home and school will continue as a requisite for the educational success of students in the future. "Effective family/school partnerships may very well be essential for helping more students to reach the ambitious education goals that the nation has set for the year 2000" (Solomon 1991, p. 359).

In the future, school counselors will play a significant role in establishing communication and strengthening relationships between parents and schools. This role can be expected to include the collaborative, consultative, instructional, and counseling services described in this text as essential components of a comprehensive school counseling program. Consequently, counselors will help schools assess parents' needs, set goals for increasing parental involvement, and design strategies to develop beneficial partnerships by encouraging parental involvement in a wide range of activities. These activities include inviting parents to sit on advisory committees for school governance, recruiting parents as tutors in the instructional program, involving parents in fundraising and school development projects, and enrolling parents in educational programs to strengthen parenting skills and learn about child and adolescent development. In addition, future school counselors will continue to provide direct counseling and consulting services to parents as clients who are facing temporary barriers in their family life.

Some of the predicted changes in family lifestyles, including dual career roles and at-home work schedules for parents will alter relationships between the home and school. In the next century more students may stay at home, at least part of the "school day," learning through interactive media and with their parents also at home working. Such arrangements will require more collaboration and cooperation between teachers in the school and parents as the at-home instructional supervisors. Tomorrow's counselors might have a role in facilitating and nurturing these relationships between the home and school.

Teacher Collaboration

In addition to working more closely with parents, teachers in the future will collaborate with each other to ensure that all students have an opportunity to receive adequate instruction and achieve accordingly in their academic pursuits. Again, advanced technology, alternative school programs, flexible schedules, and home instruction are factors that will influence how teachers work together to create effective programs and design responsive learning environments.

To succeed in this cooperative venture, teachers will need relationship skills and support from the school community. School counselors are in an ideal position and have the background to assist teachers with these needs. Helping teachers focus on their combined efforts with each other to meet the needs of *all* students will be a major challenge for future school counselors. By planning teacher workshops and leading support groups, counselors contribute to this collaborative process. The skills teachers perfect for establishing strong working relationships with each other will also benefit their relationships with parents.

If, as predicted, parental involvement becomes an essential ingredient of future schools, teachers will be frontline collaborators with parents. To be successful in this role, teachers will need communication skills and an empathic understanding of the parent's perspective of the school, the child, and the learning process. No longer will teachers be the sole experts in educating students. Instead, they will become leaders among a group of experts, including parents, who strive to design appropriate learning programs for children and adolescents, enabling students to take charge of their futures. Of all the trends predicted, this partnership has the most potential for improving schools and education in the 21st century.

School-Based Services

One collaborative relationship that could emerge in future years is a closer union between school counselors and other helping professionals in local communities. In past years, school counselors have assumed the role of referral agents, helping students and families locate and receive appropriate services to address an array of challenges. As a result, a multitude of public and private agencies have offered a wide range of services from social welfare to psychiatric care for students and their parents. As noted previously, there is little reason to believe that extensive social, medical, and other services will be needed any less in the years to come. What may change, however, is the way these many services are coordinated and delivered by counselors, physicians, and other professionals.

Presently, most of these services are provided outside the school setting. This arrangement requires considerable coordination and follow-up by the school to be sure that appointments are kept, evaluations are performed, and services are received. With divergent student populations expected in the future and the likelihood that additional and expanded services for these students and their families will be needed, school-based service models may provide an efficient and effective alternative to outside referrals. If such service-delivery models emerge, school counselors will have ready access to medical and social interventions for students and parents. In school-based approaches to comprehensive student services, physicians, nurses, social workers, mental health counselors, and other helping professions will be scheduled at school to provide direct services to identified students and their families. Such models have the potential to greatly improve referral and follow-up processes.

School-based services would allow counselors to retain their counseling, consulting and coordinating roles. Counselors would continue to offer all the developmental, preventive, and remedial services extended in the past, but when additional services were indicated, other professionals would be readily available to students and families.

Youth Service

Another trend in U.S. schools involves programs that combine classroom instruction with social service and activism. Known collectively as youth service programs, many of these are already implemented in schools across the country and cover a range of projects from performing environmental clean-up to operating day-care programs (Nathan & Kielsmeier, 1991).

The concept of combing education with service is not new. Civic education, social studies, and other curricular areas have long proposed that students should actively participate in community service and government projects to learn first hand about social responsibility. Since World War I a number of government initiatives, university reports, and educational books have encouraged the incorporation of youth service into the schooling process (Boyer, 1983; Conrad & Hedin, 1991; Goodlad, 1984). Youth services have been promoted periodically by advocates who maintain "that schools should inculcate the values of social reform and teach the attitudes, knowledge, and skills necessary to accomplish it" (Conrad & Hedin, 1991, p. 744).

In some respects, youth service has been reflected in peer helper programs presented and promoted in the school counseling literature of recent years (Myrick, 1987). As with youth service programs, peer helper services are founded in part on the belief that such experiences raise social consciousness, develop understanding for fellow human beings, and create a learning atmosphere that enhances the overall development of students. As Lewis (1991) noted in her book for children on social activism, students who reach out to others in caring and socially active ways "learn to take charge" (p. 2) of their own personal lives. They gain confidence in what they are able to accomplish regarding critical life tasks that encompass aspects of educational, social, and career development.

If social service has the potential to improve learning and foster student development to the extent that advocates assume, future school counselors will want to propose and create such programs. By establishing peer helper programs, encouraging community service and recognizing students who contribute and participate in such endeavors, counselors participate in and contribute to youth service initiatives. As with guidance activities in general, youth service is most effective when integrated into the curriculum as part of an ongoing educational program for all students.

The preceding description of schools of tomorrow merely scratches the surface of myriad ways that the role of school counselors will be influenced by future trends. Technology, parental involvement, teacher collaboration, school-based services, and youth services are among many ideas that have the potential to expand, and in some ways redefine, the counselor's role in school. Whether or not counselors are prepared to meet these expanded demands or readjust their programs to include broader dimensions will in part determine the future of school counseling.

The Future of School Counseling

As students and schools enter the 21st century and confront the range of changes and challenges predicted for the future, school counselors must be ready to assist. As such, the programs and services established by school counselors in the past need to be evaluated in light of the future. Traditional guidance and counseling services will no longer meet the needs of future students and families. School counselors at all levels—elementary, middle, and high school—can be expected to adjust their goals, create expanded services, develop new skills, and serve broader populations in the years to come. To meet these challenges, future counselors will:

1. Develop a broader knowledge of human development throughout the life span. It is clear that counselors in school will work with a wide audience of parents and teachers in helping students be successful. For this reason, communication skills and knowledge of adult learning and development will be required to establish beneficial working relationships.

2. Adapt to new technology. The counseling profession has not yet been affected as dramatically as other professions by the technology explosion of recent years. This will change. Computer-assisted learning, interactive media, voice to print capability, and other innovations will have a tremendous impact on all types of counseling services from information dissemination to therapeutic interactions. At the same time, counselors will monitor the ethical implications of such advances on their professional role and functions in schools.

3. Increase the use of group processes. Parental involvement, teacher collaboration, and youth services will all require additional group methods and processes by school counselors. Similarly, diverse student populations of future schools will demand services that bring individuals together in groups to increase understanding and facilitate helping relationships.

4. Expand their own professional development. Counselor training programs will reflect the emerging trends and future needs of school populations By ensuring closer collaboration with other professions, counselors will become better informed and more skilled at assessing needs, selecting interventions, and referring clients to other resources when appropriate. As noted above, technology will play an increasingly important role in assisting counselors with these functions.

5. Measure the outcome of their services. The school counseling profession can no longer rely on its legacy for survival. With so many demands placed on public funds and costs straining the fiscal limits of all schools, counselors will be required to demonstrate their value to the overall education, welfare, and development of students. This means that counselors must develop methods to illustrate how they serve students, parents, and teachers, and whether these services make a difference in people's lives. The issue of measuring outcomes not only addresses the effectiveness of particular counseling services, but more importantly, it elevates the efficacy of the profession. As Walz (1991b) indicated, "there is a pressing need for research that establishes the credibility of counseling and the desirability of schools, colleges and agencies continuing to offer it" (p. 72).

With this chapter we finish our journey through the past, present, and future of the school counseling profession. As a student of counseling who plans to assume the role of a school counselors, you will join the ranks of thousands before you who helped establish this profession, as well as contemporary colleagues who with you are beginning to create the future. It is a noble challenge. I commend you on your choice of careers and welcome you in this venture of providing beneficial school counseling services for students, parents, and teachers in the future. You have my best wishes for success as a professional counselor.

Selected Readings

Walz, G. R., Gazda. G. M., & Shertzer, B. (1991). *Counseling Futures* (Ann Arbor, MI: ERIC/CAPS). This book offers some thought-provoking ideas about the future of counseling. While directed at counselors in general, many of the topics are relevant to the practice of counseling in school settings.

Sheingold, K. (Guest Editor). (1991), "Restructuring for Learning with Technology: The Potential for Synergy," *Kappan* [Special Section], 73 (1), 17–40; 57–61. In this special section of *Kappan* the authors approach the notion of restructuring schools in the context of incorporating new technology. The roles of telecommunications, computers and other advances are considered. The authors present ideas that will be of interest to future school counselors as they too begin the process of restructuring programs and services.

Pedersen, P. B. (Ed.) (1991), "Multiculturalism as a Fourth Force in Counseling, [Special Issue]," *Journal of Counseling and Development*, 70, (1), 4–250. This special issue of the AACD journal offers a broad perspective on issues related to multiculturalism, including a conceptual framework, counselor education and training issues, research development, and direct counseling services. Future school counselors, as well as counselors in many other settings, must have knowledge and skills to address these emerging issues.

References

Boyer, E. L. (1983). *High School: A Report on Secondary Education in America* (New York: Harper & Row).

Center on Organization and Restructuring of Schools (Fall, 1991), "Criteria for School Restructuring," *Issues in restructuring schools*, Issue Report No. 1, 6–7. Madison, WI: Author.

Childers, J. H., Jr., & Podemski, R. S. (1984), "Removing Barriers to the Adoption of Microcomputer Technology by School Counselors," *The School Counselor, 31*, 223–228.

Conrad, D., & Hedin, D. (1991), "School-Based Community Service: What We Know from Research and Theory," *Kappan*, 72 (10), 743–749.

Dinkmeyer, D. C., Dinkmeyer, D. C., Jr., & Sperry, L. (1987). *Adlerian Counseling and Psychotherapy*, 2nd Ed. (Columbus, OH: Merrill).

Drury, S. S. (1984), "Counselor Survival in the 1980s," *The School Counselor, 31*, 234–240.

Gazda, G. M. (1991), "What Recent Survey Research Indicates for the Future of Counseling and Counselor Education," in G. R. Walz, G. M. Gazda, & B. Shertzer, (Eds.) *Counseling Futures* (Ann Arbor, MI: ERIC/CAPS), pp. 11–26.

Gerler, E. R., & Myrick, R. D. (1991), "The Elementary School Counselor's Work with Prekindergarten Children: Implications to Counselor Education Programs," *Elementary School Guidance and Counseling, 26*, 67–75.

Goodlad, J. L. (1984). *A Place Called School* (New York: McGraw-Hill).

Griggs, S. A., & Gale, P. (1977), "The Abused Child: Focus for Counselors," *Elementary School Guidance and Counseling, 2*, 187–196.

Hays, D. G. (1978), "2001: A Counseling Odyssey," *The Personnel and Guidance Journal, 57*, 17–21.

Hays, D. G., & Johnson, C. S. (1984), "21st Century Counseling," *The School Counselor, 31*, 205–214.

Hohenshill, T. H., & Brown, M. B. (1991), "Public School Counseling Services for Prekindergarten Children," *Elementary School Guidance and Counseling, 26*, 4–11.

Holtgraves, M. (1986), "Help the Victims of Sexual Abuse Help Themselves," *Elementary School Guidance and Counseling, 21*, 155–159.

Howe, H., II (1991), "America 222: A Bumpy Ride on Four Trains," *Kappan, 73*, 192–203.

Ibrahim, F. A. (1991), "Contribution of Cultural Worldview to Generic Counseling and Development," *Journal of Counseling and Development, 70*, 13–19.

Lewis, B. (1991). *The Kids' Guide to Social Action* (Minneapolis, MN: Free Spirit Publishing).

Locke, D. C. (1989), "Fostering the Self-Esteem of African-American Children. *Elementary School Guidance and Counseling, 23*, 254–259.

McBrien, R. J. (1983), "Are You Thinking of Killing Yourself? Confronting Students' Suicidal Thoughts," *The School Counselor, 31*, 75–82.

Mecklenburger, J. A. (1990), "Educational Technology is Not Enough," *Kappan, 72*, 105–108.

Morrow, G. (1987). *The Compassionate School: A Practical Guide to Educating Abused and Traumatized Children* (Englewood Cliffs, NJ: Prentice Hall).

Myrick, R. D. (1987). *Developmental Guidance and Counseling: A Practical Approach* (Minneapolis, MN: Educational Media Corporation).

Naisbitt, J., & Aburdene, P. (1990). *Megatrends 2000: Ten New Directions for the 1990's* (New York: William Morrow).

Nathan, J., & Kielsmeier, J. (1991), "The Sleeping Giant of School Reform," *Kappan, 72*, (10), 739–742.

Pedersen, P. B. (1991), "Multiculturalism as a Generic Approach to Counseling," *Journal of Counseling and Development, 70*, 6–12.

Purkey, W. W., & Schmidt, J. J. (1987). *The Inviting Relationship: An Expanded Perspective for Professional Counseling* (Englewood Cliffs, NJ: Prentice Hall).

Schmidt, J. J. (1984), "School Counseling: Professional Directions for the Future," *The School Counselor, 31*, 385–392.

Schmidt, J. J. (1991). *A Survival Guide for the Elementary/Middle School Counselor* (West Nyack, NY: The Center for Applied Research in Education).

Schmidt, J. J. (in press), " Substance Abuse Prevention: An Expanded Role for Counselors," *Journal of Counseling and Development.*

Sheeley, V. L., & Herlihy, B. (1989), " Counseling Suicidal Teens: A Duty to Warn and Protect," *The School Counselor, 37*, 89–97.

Sheingold, K. (1991), "Restructuring for Learning with Technology: The Potential for Synergy," *Kappan, 73*, 17–27.

Solomon, Z. P. (1991), "California's Policy on Parent Involvement," *Kappan, 75* (5), 359–362.

Walz, G. R. (1991a), "Nine Trends which Will Affect the Future of the United States," in G. R. Gazda, & B. Shertzer (Eds.) *Counseling Futures* (pp. 61–69). Ann Arbor, MI: ERIC/CAPS.

Walz, G. R. (1991b), "Future Focused Generalizations on Counseling," in G. R. Walz, G. M. Gazda, & B Shertzer (Eds.). *Counseling Futures* (Ann Arbor, MI: ERIC/CAPS), pp. 71–78.

Walz, G. R., Gazda, G. M., & Shertzer, B., Eds. (1991). *Counseling Futures* (Ann Arbor, MI: ERIC/CAPS).

Westcott, N. A. (1980), "Sexually Abused Children: A Special Clientele for School Counselors," *The School Counselor, 27,* 198–202.

Wilson, H. H., & Rotter, J. C. (1982), "School Counseling: A Look into the Future," *The Personnel and Guidance Journal, 60,* 353–357.

Appendix A

Ethical Standards for School Counselors

American School Counselor Association

Preamble

The American School Counselor Association (ASCA) is a professional organization whose members have a unique and distinctive preparation, grounded in the behavioral sciences, with training in clinical skills adapted to the school setting. The school counselor assists in the growth and development of each individual and uses his/her specialized skills to ensure that the rights of the counselee are properly protected within the structure of the school program. School counselors subscribe to the following basic tenets of the counseling process from which professional responsibilities are derived.

    1. Each person has the right to respect and dignity as a unique human being and to counseling services without prejudice as to person, character, belief or practice.

    2. Each person has the right to self-direction and self-development.

    3. Each person has the right of choice and the responsibility for decisions reached.

    4. Each person has the right to privacy and thereby the right to expect the counselor-client relationship to comply with all laws, policies, and ethical standards pertaining to confidentiality.

    In this document, the American School Counselor Association has specified the principles of ethical behavior necessary to maintain and regulate high standards of integrity and leadership among its members. The Association recognizes the basic commitment of its members to the *Ethical Standards* of its parent organization, the American Association for Counseling and Development [Author's note: The name of this association was changed to the American Counseling Association (ACA) in July of 1992 after publication of these standards.], and nothing in this document shall be construed to supplant the code. The *Ethical Standards for School Counselors* was developed to complement the AACD standards by clarifying the nature of ethical responsibilities for present and future counselors in the school setting. The purposes of this document are to:

    1. Serve as a guide for the ethical practices of all professional school counselors regardless of level, area, population served, or membership in this Association.

    2. Provide benchmarks for both self-appraisal and peer evaluations regarding counselor responsibilities to students, parents, colleagues and professional associates, school and community, self, and the counseling profession.

    3. Inform those served by the school counselor of acceptable counselor practices and expected professional deportment.

A. Responsibilities to Students

The school counselor:

1. Has a primary obligation and loyalty to the student, who is to be treated with respect as a unique individual, whether assisted individually or in a group setting.

2. Is concerned with the total needs of the student (educational, vocational, personal and social) and encourages the maximum growth and development of each counselee.

3. Informs the counselee of the purposes, goals, techniques, and rules of procedure under which she/he may receive counseling assistance at or before the time when the counseling relationship is entered. Prior notice includes confidentiality issues such as the possible necessity for consulting with other professionals, privileged communication, and legal or authoritative restraints. The meaning and limits of confidentiality are clearly defined to counselees.

4. Refrains from consciously encouraging the counselee's acceptance of values, lifestyles, plans, decisions, and beliefs that represent only the counselor's personal orientation.

5. Is responsible for keeping abreast of laws relating to students and strives to ensure that the rights of students are adequately provided for and protected.

6. Avoids dual relationships which might impair his/her objectivity and/or increase the risk of harm to the client (e.g., counseling one's family members, close friends or associates). If a dual relationship is unavoidable, the counselor is responsible for taking action to eliminate or reduce the potential for harm. Such safeguards might include informed consent, consultation, supervision and documentation.

7. Makes appropriate referrals when professional assistance can no longer be adequately provided to the counselee. Appropriate referral requires knowledge about available resources.

8. Protects the confidentiality of student records and releases personal data only according to prescribed laws and school policies. Student information maintained through electronic data storage methods is treated with the same care as traditional student records.

9. Protects the confidentiality of information received in the counseling relationship as specified by law and ethical standards. Such information is only to be revealed to others with the informed consent of the counselee and consistent with the obligations of the counselor as a professional person.

In a group setting the counselor sets a norm of confidentiality and stresses its importance, yet clearly states that confidentiality in group counseling cannot be guaranteed.

10. Informs the appropriate authorities when the counselee's condition indicates a clear and imminent danger to the counselee or others. This is to be done after careful deliberation and, where possible, after consultation with other professionals. The counselor informs the counselee of actions to be taken so as to minimize confusion and clarify expectations.

11. Screens prospective group members and maintains an awareness of participants' compatibility throughout the life of the group, especially when the group emphasis is on self disclosure and self-understanding. The counselor takes reasonable precautions to protect members from physical and/or psychological harm resulting from interaction within the group.

12. Provides explanations of the nature, purposes, and results of tests in language that is understandable to the client(s).

13. Adheres to relevant standards regarding selection, administration, and interpretation of assessment techniques. The counselor recognizes that computer-based testing programs require specific training in administration, scoring and interpretation which may differ from that required in more traditional assessments.

14. Promotes the benefits of appropriate computer applications and clarifies the limitations of computer technology. The counselor ensures that (1) computer applications are appropriate for the individual needs of the counselee, (2) the counselee understands how to use the applications, and (3) follow-up counseling assistance is provided. Members of underrepresented groups are assured of equal access to computer technologies and the absence of discriminatory information and values within computer applications.

15. Has unique ethical responsibilities in working with peer programs. In general, the school counselor is responsible for the welfare of the students participating in peer programs under his/her direction. School counselors who function in training and supervisory capacities are referred to the preparation and supervision standards of professional counselor associations.

B. Responsibilities to Parents

The school counselor:

1. Respects the inherent rights and responsibilities of parents for their children and endeavors to establish a cooperative relationships with parents to facilitate the maximum development of the counselee.

2. Informs parents of the counselor's role, with emphasis on the confidential nature of the counseling relationship between the counselor and counselee.

3. Provides parents with accurate, comprehensive and relevant information in an objective and caring manner, as appropriate and consistent with ethical responsibilities to the counselee.

4. Treats information received from parents in a confidential and appropriate manner.

5. Shares information about a counselee only with those persons properly authorized to receive such information.

6. Adheres to laws and local guidelines when assisting parents experiencing family difficulties which interfere with the counselee's effectiveness and welfare.

7. Is sensitive to changes in the family and recognizes that all parents, custodial and noncustodial, are vested with certain rights and responsibilities for the welfare of their children by virtue of their position and according to law.

C. Responsibilities to Colleagues and Professional Associates

The school counselor:

1. Establishes and maintains a cooperative relationship with faculty, staff, and administration to facilitate the provision of optimal guidance and counseling programs and services.

2. Promotes awareness and adherence to appropriate guidelines regarding confidentiality, the distinction between public and private information, and staff consultation.

3. Treats colleagues with respect, courtesy, fairness, and good faith. The qualifications, views, and findings of colleagues are represented accurately and fairly to enhance the image of competent professionals.

4. Provides professional personnel with accurate, objective, concise and meaningful data necessary to adequately evaluate, counsel, and assist the counselee.

5. Is aware of and fully utilizes related professions and organizations to whom the counselee may be referred.

D. Responsibilities to the School and Community

The school counselor:

1. Supports and protects the educational program against any infringement not in the best interests of students.

2. Informs appropriate officials of conditions that may be potentially disruptive or damaging to the school's mission, personnel and property.

3. Delineates and promotes the counselor's role and function in meeting the needs of those served. The counselor will notify appropriate school officials of conditions which may limit or curtail their effectiveness in providing programs and services.

4. Assists in the development of (1) curricular and environmental conditions appropriate for the school and community, (2) educational procedures and programs to meet student needs, and (3) a systematic evaluation process for guidance and counseling programs, services and personnel. The counselor is guided by findings of the evaluation data in planning programs and services.

5. Actively cooperates and collaborates with agencies, organizations, and individuals in the school and community in the best interest of counselees and without regard to personal reward or remuneration.

E. Responsibilities to Self

The school counselor:

1. Functions within the boundaries of individual professional competence and accepts responsibility for the consequences of his/her actions.

2. Is aware of the potential effects of her/his own personal characteristics on services to clients.

3. Monitors personal functioning and effectiveness and refrains from any activity likely to lead to inadequate professional services or harm to a client.

4. Recognizes that differences in clients relating to age, gender, race, religion, sexual orientation, socioeconomic and ethnic backgrounds may require specific training to ensure competent services.

5. Strives through personal initiative to maintain professional competence and keeps abreast of innovations and trends in the profession. Professional and personal growth is continuous and ongoing throughout the counselor's career.

F. Responsibilities to the Profession

The school counselor:

    1. Conducts herself/himself in such a manner as to bring credit to self and the profession.

    2. Conducts appropriate research and reports findings in a manner consistent with acceptable educational and psychological research practices. When using client data for research, statistical or program planning purposes, the counselor ensures protections of the identity of the individual client(s).

    3. Actively participates in local, state, and national associations which foster the development and improvement of school counseling.

    4. Adheres to ethical standards of the profession, other official policy statements pertaining to counseling, and relevant statutes established by federal, state, and local governments.

    5. Clearly distinguishes between statements and actions made as a private individual and as a representative of the school counseling profession.

    6. Contributes to the development of the profession through the sharing of skills, ideas and expertise with colleagues.

G. Maintenance of Standards

Ethical behavior among professional school counselors, association members and nonmembers, is expected at all times. When there exists serious doubt as to the ethical behavior of colleagues, of if counselors are forced to work in situations or abide by policies which do not reflect the standards as outlined in these *Ethical Standards for School Counselors* or the AACD *Ethical Standards*, the counselor is obligated to take appropriate action to rectify the condition. The following procedures may serve as a guide:

    1. If feasible, the counselor should consult with a professional colleague to confidentially discuss the nature of the complaint to see if she/he views the situation as an ethical violation.

    2. Whenever possible, the counselor should directly approach the colleague whose behavior is in question to discuss the complaint and seek resolution.

    3. If resolution is not forthcoming at the personal level, the counselor shall utilize the channels established within the school and/or school district. This may include both informal and formal procedures.

    4. If the matter still remains unresolved, referral for review and appropriate action should be made to the Ethics Committees in the following sequence:

- local counselor association
- state counselor association
- national counselor association

    5. The ASCA Ethics Committee functions in an educative and consultative capacity and does not adjucate complaints of ethical misconduct. Therefore, at the national level, complaints should be submitted in writing to the ACA Ethics Committee for review and appropriate action. The procedure for submitting complaints may be obtained by writing the ACA Ethics Committee, c/o The Executive Director, American Counseling Association 5999 Stevenson Avenue, Alexandria, VA 22304.

H. Resources

School counselors are responsible for being aware of, and acting in accord with, the standards and positions of the counseling profession as represented in such official documents as those listed below.

Code of Ethics (1989). National Board for Certified Counselors. Alexandria, VA.

Code of Ethics for Peer Helping Professionals (1989). National Peer Helpers Association. Glendale, CA.

Ethical Guidelines for Group Counselors (1989). Association for Specialists in Group Work. Alexandria, VA.

Ethical Standards (1988). American Association for Counseling and Development, Alexandria, VA.

Position Statement: The School Counselor and Confidentiality (1986).American School Counselor Association. Alexandria, VA.

Position Statement: The School Counselor and Peer Facilitation (1984). American School Counselor Association. Alexandria, VA.

Position Statement: The School Counselor and Student Rights (1982). American School Counselor Association. Alexandria, VA.

Ethical Standards for School Counselors is was adopted by the ASCA Delegate Assembly March 19, 1984. This revision was approved by the ASCA Delegate Assembly, March 27, 1992.

AUTHOR INDEX

SUBJECT INDEX